Guide to
Namibia and Botswana

Guide to Namibia and Botswana

by Chris McIntyre and Simon Atkins

BRADT PUBLICATIONS, UK
HUNTER PUBLISHING, USA

First published in 1991 by Bradt Publications, 41 Nortoft Rd, Chalfont St Peter, Bucks SL9 0LA, England.
Distributed in the USA by Hunter Publishing Inc., 300 Raritan Center Parkway, CN94, Edison, NJ 08810.
Distributed in Southern Africa by Media House Publications, PO Box 782395, Sandton 2146, South Africa.

British Library Cataloguing in Publication data
Mcintyre, Chris
Guide to Namibia and Botswana
1. Travel. Botswana. Namibia
I Title II Atkins, Simon
916.8804329

ISBN 0-946983-64-X

Photos by the Chris McIntyre and Ben Mountfield (rhino and puff adder)
Cover photos: Sossusvlei (Namibia) and Okavango Delta (Botswana)
Back cover photo: Hilary Bradt
Maps by Caroline Crump
Typeset from the authors' disc by Patti Taylor, London NW8 ORJ
Printed by the Guernsey Press, Channel Islands

The Authors

Simon Atkins and Chris McIntyre decided independently to write a travel guide on the region whilst they were both VSO science teachers in schools in rural Zimbabwe. Joining forces, they spent many months travelling throughout Namibia and Botswana by 4WD and thumb, both during the school holidays and following completion of their teaching posts.

Back in Britain, when they aren't slaves to a word-processor, Chris now works as a shipbroker in London and is planning his next trip abroad; Simon makes documentary films on social and environmental issues, and tries to find the time to go walking and climbing.

Major Contributors

Phil Deutschle (information on the people and history of Botswana and general travel information).

A writer and teacher, Phil has recently finished three years teaching in Mapoka (a small village near Ramokgwebane, Botswana). He now intends to stay a while longer, writing a weekly column on village life and a child's book on Botswana activities, with the aim of informing people in Britain and the United States about Botswana.

Robin and Jannice Heath (information on the Caprivi Strip).
The Heaths have travelled extensively throughout southern Africa, and on their latest trip provided us with specific information on areas we were unable to research originally.

Damien Lewis (Articles on the Okavango and Veterinary Cordon Fences).
An environmental research journalist, Damien specialises in detailed and original articles concerning conservation, development and the rights of indigenous peoples throughout the developing world.

Fritz Tallantire (Botswana information and general update).
A veteran 4WD traveller in Namibia and Botswana, Fritz provided much help and was able to update our manuscripts with information from his most recent expedition across the Kalahari. In his spare time he works in London.

Gill Thomas (Drawings and illustrations).
An artist and teacher, Gill has recently returned from three years teaching with VSO, at Mposi, a rural Zimbabwean school. She presently divides her time between drawing, walking and climbing, and trying to earn a living as a TESL and TEFL teacher.

Duncan White (Namibia information, especially Swakopmund).
Duncan had lived in Africa for several years before he delayed a canoeing expedition down the Congo in order to help Chris with some final research in Namibia. His assistance, and his penchant for cold beers, were immeasurable.

Acknowledgements

In the course of our travels in Namibia and Botswana, we have received a great deal of help from various people, both in the form of hospitality and in the form of local or specialist information. We would particularly like to thank the following: the Blackie family; Chris Blomstrand; Shirley Cormack; Alan Elliot; Anne and Lenox Gibson; Alison Martin, for *that* hitch; Irene Johnstone; Brian Jones (DNC in Windhoek); Paula Morris; Benjamin Mountfield, especially for the snake; Louw Schoemann, for an invaluable insight into the Skeleton Coast environment; the Sculpher family; Penny Tavares Da Silva; Surveyor General, Windhoek; Tim and Jo; John Townsend; Dr Nigel Wilson, for original biological data; and finally the many people in Namibia and Botswana whose names we never knew (or have forgotten), for their help and generosity.

Back at home, the following cannot go without mention and thanks: Jabbar Al-Sadoon, for encouragement; Trevor Atkins, Simon's father; Pete Bagley and Gaenor Jenkins, who put Simon up at the start; Veronique Bovington; Maggie Boys, for the letters; Kathryn Bowden; Hilary Bradt, our publisher, for endless patience as we struggled to write everything up; Kylie Brown, Simon's mother; Michelle Chen, for welcome distractions; Ginny Devonshire; Mr and Mrs Fritz; Jane Harley, our copy editor, who also provided us with extra travel information on Botswana; Anne-Marie McDermott, for putting up with Simon's constantly changing deadlines; Peter and Elizabeth McIntyre, Chris' parents, for all the organisation which made these trips possible, and for much else besides; Jonnie Mogford; Alison North; Stuart Raeburn, for information and help at the very beginning; Kevin Savage; Iain Young, for his perspective; and last but not least Purba, Jeremy and Ocky, for their endless mugs of coffee, food, good company and unfaltering support.

Chris McIntyre and Simon Atkins, June 1991, Oxford.

Contents

Part 3 : Botswana

Introduction

Namibia and Botswana epitomise the magic of Africa, conjured up by views of vast game-covered plains under inky-blue skies, or harsh desert landscapes dotted with strange contorted plants — uncharted wilderness where you seem to be the first to tread.

People are few and far between since the region has one of the world's lowest population densities. This makes the scattered towns and villages all the more vibrant. Here is life at its most basic, a raw untapped energy in the land and its people. Theirs is an existence that the West seems to have tragically lost, indeed perhaps never discovered.

Travelling in both countries is remarkably trouble-free, allowing the visitor a freedom, rarely found elsewhere in Africa, to explore at will. Communications are efficient, the towns modern, and both countries offer value-for-money. Neither however is 'cheap'. Botswana, in particular, can be expensive, but offers in return the chance to experience some of the world's top game parks, still little visited.

Your own vehicle will give you the greatest flexibility, allowing you to explore remote areas which would otherwise be impossible to reach. However, some spectacular destinations — such as the Okavango — are accessible using public transport or, of course, by hitching.

For the thrill of safari and perhaps your first sight of lion, Chobe and Moremi are unbeatable, whilst Etosha boasts vast herds of game amidst some of the region's most spectacular scenery. Visiting the Okavango Delta, you can leave your vehicle behind to relax in a dug-out canoe, gliding through lagoons and reeds, past islands teeming with birdlife.

Away from the parks and reserves, the naturalist will be fascinated by the unique flora and fauna which has evolved in the Namib, one of the world's oldest deserts. Here periodic fogs are the only source of moisture, sustaining the white beetles unique to this area and the prehistoric *Welwitschia* plants which can live for over a thousand years.

Intrepid anthropologists may also head for the deserts, seeking the mystical, isolated hills — Gcwihaba, Tsodilo, Brandberg and Aha — which have sheltered bushmen, and their paintings, for millennia.

The hiker has a chance to walk remote seldom-used trails through forbidding yet stunning scenery. These range from trekking along the Fish River Canyon — second in size only to the Grand Canyon — to stalking white rhino on the Waterberg Plateau.

Newly independent Namibia — the youngest member of the United Nations — is fascinating for its diversity of peoples, and burgeoning political life. Its constitution has been hailed as one of the world's most democratic. Botswana has the strongest economy in sub-Saharan Africa, based primarily on its enormous diamond wealth, but is facing growing environmental and social problems. Both countries maintain a strong anti-apartheid stance, but both economies are heavily reliant on their powerful southern neighbour. This conflict continues to preoccupy the region, though shows signs of improving with the current changes in South Africa.

How to use this guide

There are five main types of information contained in this guide.

Background Information to explain something of the history, people, language and environment of Namibia and Botswana (*Part 1,* Chapters 1, 2 and 3).

General Travel Information to help plan your trip, safeguard your health, and make the most of your trips into the bush (*Part 1,* Chapters 4, 5 and 6).

Specific Country Information with details of the individual countries to organise your time in the region. This is dealt with in Chapter 7, *In Namibia*, and Chapter 16, *In Botswana*.

Comprehensive Regional Travel Information to give up-to-date advice on all the main towns, national parks, and other places of interest. This specific information is arranged by region.

Special Interest Boxes which cover a range of topics from the details of Namibia's flora and fauna to the controversial issues surrounding conservation of the Okavango Delta and the Kalahari Desert.

Part 1
General
Information

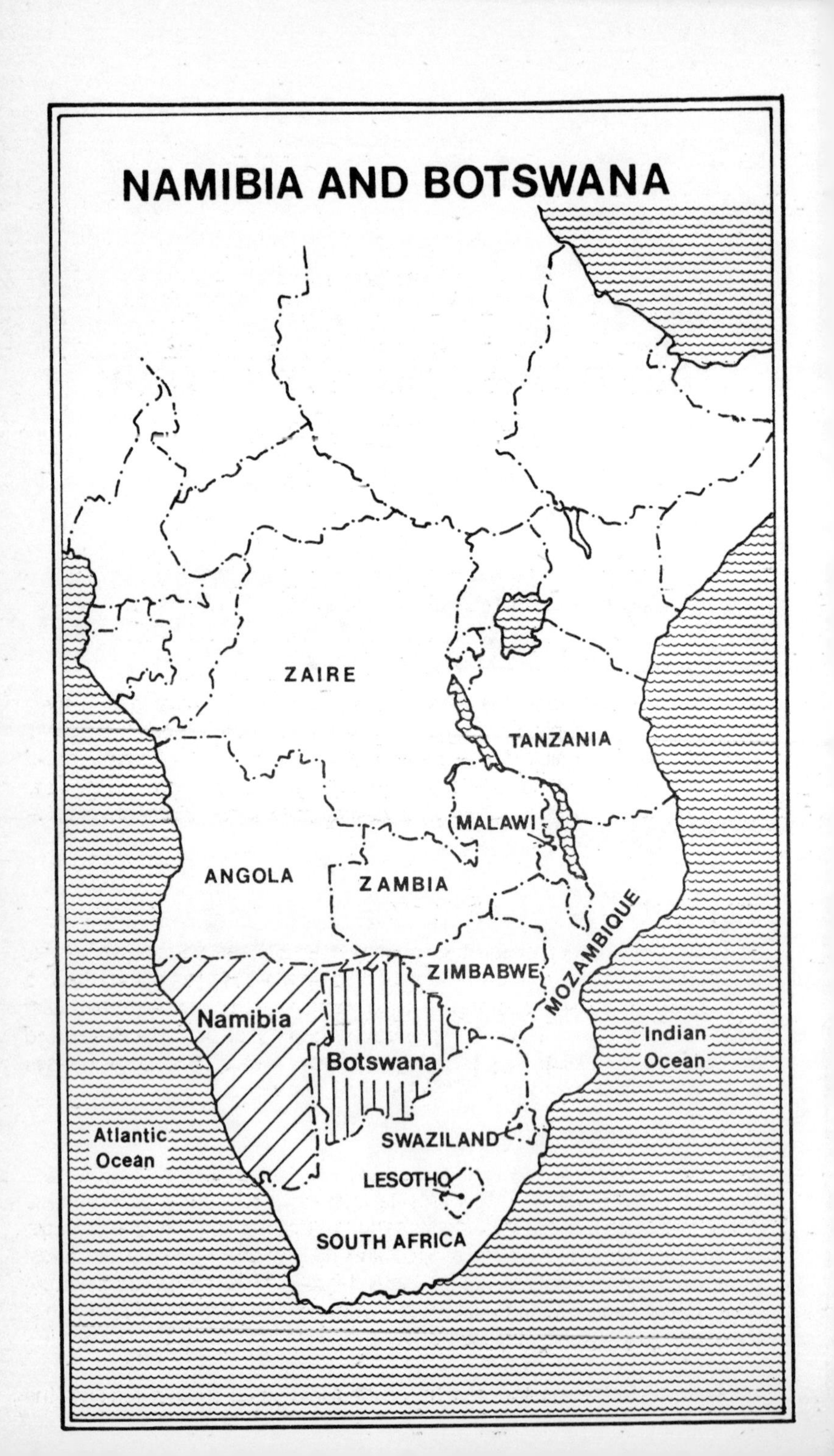
NAMIBIA AND BOTSWANA
ZAIRE
TANZANIA
MALAWI
ANGOLA
ZAMBIA
MOZAMBIQUE
ZIMBABWE
Namibia
Botswana
Indian
Ocean
Atlantic
Ocean
SWAZILAND
LESOTHO
SOUTH AFRICA

Chapter 1

Namibia and Botswana: an overview

FACTS AND FIGURES

Location

Namibia and Botswana are extensive and sparsely-populated countries, situated on the Tropic of Capricorn in the sub-tropical desert region of southern Africa. Namibia extends east into the sub-continent from the south Atlantic Ocean, abutting landlocked Botswana in central southern Africa. Between them they share the Kalahari Desert which dominates the east of Namibia, and most of Botswana.

Size

Namibia is the larger of the two countries at 824,290 square kilometres, compared to Botswana's 581,730 square kilometres. Together they have a land area almost six times that of Great Britain, yet only a tiny combined population of three million. The population density of both Botswana and Namibia is two inhabitants per square kilometre — roughly a hundred times smaller than Britain and one of the lowest in the world.

Topography

Namibia Namibia can be conveniently split into three topographical areas: the Namib Desert in the west stretches for 1,600km along the Atlantic coast in a narrow strip of gravel flats and sand dunes, and is one of the driest places on earth; inland, a deeply incised escarpment climbs up from the coast to the central plateau at 2,000m; from here the interior plateau gently descends to the Kalahari Desert at about 1,000m, merging with Botswana.

Botswana Botswana too can be divided into three distinct regions: the

Kalahari Desert lies in the centre and south-west, covering two-thirds of the land area; the Okavango river basin in the northwest contains the Okavango Delta, an extensive area of swamp and marshland with a tropical climate; by contrast, the developed eastern strip of the country, bordering South Africa, is away from the Kalahari Desert and contains the railway and 80% of the population, with sufficient rainfall for crops.

Climate

Both Namibia and Botswana have a sub-tropical desert climate. Rainfall occurs in the hottest season — generally from December to March — and can be very heavy in northern Botswana, and north-eastern Namibia. The further south or west you go, the drier it gets, with many southern regions of the Kalahari and the whole of the coastal Namib Desert receiving no rainfall at all some years. 'Summer' temperatures can reach an unpleasantly hot (and humid in the north-east) 40°C. In the 'winter' (May to September), it's generally cool, pleasant and clear with day temperatures averaging around 25°C, and nighttime temperatures much colder. Frost is possible in the higher areas and the deserts.

History

Namibia Namibia was a German colony until 1915 when it was invaded by South African and British forces during the First World War. At the end of the war, South Africa received a League of Nations mandate to administer the territory, which it called South West Africa. Despite a UN vote to revoke the mandate in 1978 (Resolution 435), and increasing military pressure by the South West African People's Organisation (SWAPO) led by Sam Nujoma against the occupying South African troops, South Africa held onto the territory for another 10 years. Following extensive talks in 1988, UN Resolution 435 was implemented, and Namibia became independent on March 21 1990.

Botswana From the 18th Century, the original Bushmen inhabitants of the whole region were gradually pushed into the central Kalahari and marginalised by the progressive expansions of Tswana, Ndebele and finally Boer peoples. The British made Botswana a protectorate in 1885 (calling it Bechuanaland), in order to keep it from German expansionism in Namibia and to keep open the north-south trade route. The protectorate was barely developed during the British administration, and remained very poor right up to independence in 1966. A year after independence, diamonds were discovered, and the country has developed rapidly since then.

Government

Namibia The elected president, Sam Nujoma, heads a multi-party government with a SWAPO majority. The main opposition party is the pro-South African Democratic Turnhalle Alliance (DTA), which has 21 of the 72 seats in the Constituent Assembly.

Botswana The Botswana Democratic Party (BDP), founded by Sir Seretse Khama, has held power since independence in 1966, with Khama the first president. Dr Quett Masire succeeded Khama on his death in 1980, and has been president since then. Five of the 32 parliamentary seats are held by minority parties.

Economy

Namibia Diamond mining is the mainstay of the Namibian economy, and there are important reserves of copper, uranium and other minerals. Fishing, cattle rearing and tourism also play an important role. Economically Namibia is very dependent on South Africa, sharing the same currency.

Botswana Immediately after independence, Botswana was ranked in the bottom 20 poorest countries of the world, with cattle ranching the dominant industry and income earner. One year later, the world's second largest diamond pipe was discovered at Orapa and with diamond mining now accounting for up to 70% of export earnings, Botswana has one of the fastest-growing economies in the world. Beef exports to the EEC rank second in importance, though there is growing concern at the damaging extent of over-grazing. The country also mines manganese, copper and nickel, and tourism is of increasing economic value.

Currency

Rates of exchange in July 1991: R4.80 = £1 (Namibia and South Africa); P3.30 = £1 (Botswana).

Namibia's post-independence currency remains the South African Rand, and is likely to remain so for the near future. So long as the Rand and the South African economy remain weak, Namibia is a relatively cheap place to visit compared to Botswana. Both the Botswanan and Namibian currencies and economies are very strong compared to their neighbours in central and east Africa — and therefore more expensive.

Population

Namibia 1,760,000 (1988). There are 11 ethnic groups, of which the largest are the Owambos which make up half the country's population. The Damaras and Hereros make up most of the remaining half. The population is densest in the north (near the Angolan border) and in the central plateau, where rainfall is heaviest.

Botswana 1,285,000 (1990). The Tswana ethnic group accounts for 90% of the population, although there are eight other separate tribes in the country. The Kalahari Desert is the last remaining refuge for the traditional hunter-gatherer existence of the Bushmen.

Language

Namibia Before independence, the official languages were Afrikaans,

English and German. Following independence the official language is now just English. The main ethnic language groups are Bantu and Khoi-San.

Botswana English is the official language of government and business, and is taught at school. It's widely spoken in the main towns and tourist areas. Nearly everybody speaks Setswana — the language of the Batswana people. Other languages include Bakalanga (a Shona dialect) spoken in the north-east, and the Khoi (or 'click') language of the Kalahari Bushmen.

Religion

Namibia and Botswana The main western religion is Christianity, although most people hold traditional African religions and beliefs.

Flora and Fauna

Despite their aridity, both Namibia and Botswana are full of game. The many national parks and game reserves are superb, and far, far away from the tourist hordes of East Africa. In addition, an extra dimension of interest is found in the extraordinary way that the plant, animal, and indeed human populations have adapted to survive in the harsh environment. Bushmen are the only people on earth who have learnt to survive in an environment devoid of any ground water. And strange, contorted plants live in the Namib Desert, with a nightly fog their only source of moisture.

NAMIBIA — A BRIEF HISTORY

Pre-Independence

On March 21 1990, Namibia finally gained its independence, after a bitter liberation struggle and diplomatic activity that stretched back for over 20 years. The legacy of colonialism that it shook off dates back hundreds of years to the European seafarers and explorers who first claimed this land as their own despite the indigenous people.

In the 15th Century, trade between Europe and the East opened up sea routes along the Namibian coast and around the Cape of Good Hope — the first Europeans to step on Namibian soil were the Portuguese in 1485. Diego Cão stopped briefly at Cape Cross on the Skeleton Coast and erected a Limestone cross. On 8th December 1487, Bartholomeu Diaz reached Walvis Bay and then continued south to what is now Lüderitz. However, the coast was so totally barren and uninviting that even though the Portuguese had already settled in Angola, and the Dutch in the Cape, little interest was shown in Namibia.

It was only in the latter half of the 18th Century when British, French and American whalers began to make use of the ports of Lüderitz and Walvis Bay, that the Dutch authorities in the Cape decided in 1793 to take possession of Walvis Bay — the only good deep water port on the coast. A few years later, France invaded Holland, prompting England to seize control of the Cape

Colony and with this Walvis Bay. Very little was known about the interior, and it wasn't until the middle of the 19th Century that explorers, missionaries and traders started to venture inland, with Charles Andersson leading the way.

In 1884, a German merchant called Lüderitz started to buy land on the coast, and established the first permanent settlement in Namibia — the town that grew was named Lüderitz after him. (It was this act that finally prompted Britain to make Bechuanaland a protectorate.) Lüderitz was bought out a few years later by the newly formed German Colonial Company for South West Africa, and shortly after that the administration of the area was transferred directly to Germany's control. The Berlin Conference of 1900 saw Britain and Germany neatly partition their colonial conquests. Amongst many territorial dealings (mostly involving pen and ruler decisions on the map of Africa), a clearly defined border between Britain's new protectorate of Bechuanaland and Germany's South West Africa was established — and Britain ceded a narrow corridor of land to Germany. This was subsequently named after the German Chancellor, Count von Caprivi, as the Caprivi Strip.

During this time, the land was being progressively bought up, or simply taken from, the local inhabitants — leading to many skirmishes and uprisings which were brutally put down by the colonial troops. The last, and perhaps largest of these, was the Herero uprising of 1904, in which many of the Herero people were massacred at Waterberg. The survivors fled east into the Kalahari, some crossing the border into Bechuanaland.

At the onset of the First World War, Britain encouraged South Africa to wrest German South West Africa from the Germans and in July 1915, the German Colonial troops surrendered to South African forces at Khorab — a memorial now marks the spot. At the end of the war, Namibia became a League of Nations 'trust territory', assigned to the Union of South Africa as 'a sacred trust in the name of civilisation' to 'promote to the utmost the material and moral well-being of its inhabitants'. The Caprivi Strip was incorporated back into Bechuanaland (though it was returned 20 years later).

After overcoming their initial differences, South African Boers and the German colonists of Namibia soon discovered a common interest — the unabashed exploitation of the native population whose well-being they were supposed to be protecting. In 1947, after the Second World War, South Africa formally announced to the United Nations its intention to annex the territory. The UN — which had inherited responsibility for the League of Nations trust territories — opposed the plan, arguing that 'the African inhabitants of South West Africa have not yet achieved political autonomy'. Until 1961, the UN insisted on this point year after year and was systematically ignored by South Africa's regime.

Between 1961 and 1968, the UN tried to annul the trusteeship and establish Namibia's independence. Legal pressure, however, was ineffective and some of the Namibian people led by the South West African People's Organisation (SWAPO) chose to fight for their freedom with arms. The first clashes occurred on August 26 1966.

In 1968, the UN finally declared the South African occupation of the country as illegal and changed its name to Namibia. Efforts by the majority of the UN General Assembly to enforce this condemnation with economic sanctions were routinely vetoed by the western powers of the security council — they had vested interests in the multinational companies in Namibia and would stand to lose from the implementation of sanctions.

The independence of Angola in 1975 affected Namibia's struggle for freedom, by providing SWAPO guerillas with a friendly rearguard. As a consequence the guerilla war was stepped up, resulting in increased *political* pressure on South Africa. But strong internal economic factors also played heavily in the political arena. Up to independence, the status quo had preserved internal inequalities and privileges. Black Africans — 90% of the population — consumed only 12.8% of the Gross Domestic Product (GDP). Meanwhile the inhabitants of European origin — 10% of the population — received 81.5% of the GDP. Three-quarters of the agricultural production was in the hands of white farmers. Although average per capita income was (and remains) one of the highest in Africa, whites earn on average over 17 times more than blacks. The white population clearly feared they had a great deal to lose if a majority government committed to addressing these racially-based inequalities came to power.

However, external South African economic factors had perhaps the greatest effect in blocking Namibian independence. South African and multinational companies dominated the Namibian economy and carried massive political influence. Prior to independence, the Consolidated Diamond Mines Company (a subsidiary of Anglo-American) contributed in taxes 40% of South Africa's administrative budget in Namibia. Multinationals benefited from extremely generous facilities granted to them by the South African administration in Namibia. According to one estimate, the independence of Namibia would represent costs for South Africa of $240 million in lost exports, and additional outlays of $144 million to import foreign products.

In South Africa the official government view stressed the danger that a SWAPO government might present to Namibia's minority tribes (since SWAPO membership is drawn almost exclusively from the Owambo ethnic group), whilst taking few serious steps towards a negotiated settlement for Namibian independence. These concerns were not allayed by the timely assassination of an important Herero leader.

On the military side, South Africa stepped up its campaign against SWAPO, even striking at bases in southern Angola. It also supported Jonas Savimbi's UNITA (National Union for the Total Independence of Angola) forces in their struggle against the Soviet/Cuban-backed MPLA (Popular Movement for the Liberation of Angola) government in Luanda. Meanwhile, Cuban troops poured into Angola and aggravated the situation further by threatening the South African forces in Namibia.

On the diplomatic front, a proposal put forward by the UN security council (Resolution 435) called for, amongst other things, the cessation of hostilities, the return of refugees, the repeal of discriminatory legislation and the holding of UN-supervised elections. South Africa blocked this by tying any such agreement to the withdrawal of Cuban troops from Angola, and demanding guarantees that its investments in Namibia would not be affected. SWAPO refused to agree to special benefits for the European population and other minority groups, nor would it accept predetermined limitations to constitutional change following independence.

By 1987, all the states involved in the conflict were showing clear signs of the need to call a halt to hostilities. After 14 years of uninterrupted war, Angola's economy was on the brink of collapse. (The war is calculated to have cost the country $13 billion.) On the other side, South Africa's permanent harassment of Angola, and occupation of Namibia were costing the regime dearly both economically and diplomatically.

In December 1988, after prolonged US-mediated negotiations, an agreement was reached between South Africa, Angola and Cuba for a phased withdrawal of Cuban troops from Angola to be linked to the withdrawal of South African troops from Namibia and the implementation of Resolution 435.

The independence process began on April 1 1989, and was achieved with the help of the United Nations Transition Assistance Group (UNTAG). This consisted of some 7,000 people from 110 countries who worked from nearly 200 locations within the country to ensure free and fair elections and as smooth a transition period to independence as was possible.

In November 1989, 710,000 Namibians (a 97% turn-out) voted in the members of the National Assembly which would draft the country's first constitution. SWAPO won decisively, but without the two-thirds majority it needed to write the nation's constitution single-handedly, thereby allaying the fears of the white and 'international' community. The 72 elected members (68 men and four women) of the Constituent Assembly, representing between them seven different political parties, soon reached agreement on a constitution for the new Namibia, which was subsequently hailed as one of the world's most democratic. Finally, at 12.20am on March 21 1990, watched by Pérez de Cuéllar, the UN Secretary-General, F.W. de Klerk, the South African President and Sam Nujoma, Namibia's first president, the Namibian flag replaced South Africa's over Windhoek.

Politics since Independence

Since independence, there has been every indication that Namibia is standing by its constitution and developing into a peaceful and prosperous state. However, the ownership of Walvis Bay still remains a bone of contention: it is currently under South African rule. South Africa maintains that it has always been a part of the Cape Colony, and thus was never part of the UN mandate, despite being geographically within Namibia. Its immense strategic importance — as the coast's only deep-water harbour — clearly provides a large incentive for South Africa to hold onto this last enclave for as long as it can. In March 1990, South African military installations in Walvis Bay were upgraded. South Africa could easily strangle Namibia's economy by closing the port and the railway that leads to it.

Resources and Economy

Before independence, the South African administration controlled the economy along traditional colonial lines. The country produced what it did not consume and imported everything it needed, especially food. Namibia still exports maize, meat and fish, and imports rice and wheat. It exports minerals and raw materials and, since it has no industries, meets its needs for manufactured goods by importing 90% of its consumer goods from South Africa.

Multinational and South African economic concerns still have a great influence in Namibia, being dominant in the three main sectors of the economy — mining, agriculture and fishing. Mining is the most important industry and the most internationalised. Both livestock and fishing have declined in importance in recent years due to recurrent droughts in the interior, and the overfishing of the coastal waters. Foreign investments in mining have, however, increased — British, North American, German and South African companies control the industry which accounts for three-quarters of Namibia's export revenue.

Following independence, Namibia inherited a well-developed infrastructure, and has considerable remaining mineral wealth. The revenue and foreign exchange from mining is needed to provide the financial muscle for the new government's nation-building programme — in the short-term at least. And realistically, the government is likely to stay intimately involved with the South African economy for the time being — Namibia continues to use the South African Rand as its currency.

Although these are early days, the new government is developing structural changes to make the economy more equitable, to diversify its components and make it less vulnerable to the vagaries of international market prices. Better living conditions for the majority of Namibians might be realised by increasing the productivity of the subsistence areas, particularly in the populated north. By developing the 'informal' part of the economy, future problems of food production, urbanisation and unemployment might be avoided. With hopes for fully-fledged reform in South Africa, there is every reason for considerable optimism for Namibia's future as the world's newest independent state.

BOTSWANA — A BRIEF HISTORY

Pre-Independence

The early history of Botswana is the story of the Bushmen (also called *San*, and in Setswana called *Basarwa*). They had the area to themselves for 30,000 years, leading a sophisticated hunter-gatherer existence. Sometime around the 1400's, the first Bantus arrived. These Bakgalagadi quickly adapted to the desert environment, and lived like the Bushmen, intermarrying with them.

A century later, things began to change when the Batswana expanded into the region with their cattle and highly organised social structure. The chiefs established large communities in the south-east of the country. Disputes were often settled by communities splitting and following their leader-of-choice to another site. If the area was already occupied, a battle might ensue. Later, a chief would die or be assassinated, and the groups would recombine. This system allowed smaller minority groups to be (generally) peacefully subsumed under the larger Batswana umbrella — albeit as the lowest class citizens — and led to the more rapid growth of the Batswana, relative to the other major groups.

Meanwhile, the scramble for Africa was on. The Dutch, British, Portuguese, and Germans were staking out claims on all sides, but they balked at the Kalahari. Who wanted to administer 50 million hectares of sand? However the area did have great strategic importance; the British needed it to connect their valuable colonies to the north with the port of Cape Town, whilst the Portuguese saw advantage in uniting their colonies of Angola and Mozambique. And the Germans, acutely conscious of having largely missed out in the race for 'bagging' colonies in Africa, were increasing their presence to the west in present-day Namibia. Despite this, none of the imperialist powers were willing to take responsibility for Botswana.

In the 1800's, major land pressures arose. The Zulus led by Shaka the Great and then the Ndebeles led by Mzilikazi made repeated forays into the area, having been driven from their own lands in South Africa by the expansion of the Boers. However, the Boers too came at this time, searching for lands free from the expanding British influence around the Cape. They attacked the Batswana, taking control of their pastures and forcing them to work on Boer farms. All this prompted the chiefs to ask the British for protection. The British declined — there was still no profit to be made.

In 1884, after things had settled down, the Germans formally claimed Namibia. The British now terrified of having their trade route to the north cut off, announced to Germany the following year the formation of the Bechuanaland Protectorate. The Batswana received the news themselves after the event. The British quickly imposed a hut tax on the Batswana to pay for their own 'protection' and to try to offset the administrative burden they had found themselves with. Mafikeng became the administrative capital — a town outside the borders of the protectorate!

Then, just 10 years later, Cecil Rhodes asked the British government to incorporate Bechuanaland into his British South Africa Company (BSAC). Britain agreed — Rhodes was building a railway and he would administer and 'protect' the region without the British having to pay anything. Three of the Batswana chiefs (then called kings), who feared a reduction of their own power, travelled to Britain to protest. In London, they were told that the decision was final. Undaunted, the kings took their case to the people, with the backing of the London Missionary Society, and toured Britain spreading word of the evils of Rhodes's BSAC (already infamous in Rhodesia). A flurry of letters was written and the British government, fearing a loss of votes, agreed to keep Bechuanaland as a protectorate.

The British trusteeship prevented political absorption of Bechuanaland by South Africa, through the Anglo-Boer War and two World Wars, but paved the way for Afrikaner economic supremacy. Although Botswana is largely semi-arid, it had come to be one of southern Africa's major exporters of cattle and meat. At the beginning of this century, 97% of the population lived in rural areas, with every family having at least two heads of cattle and the richest even having oxen to plough the land. But, in order to pay the taxes imposed on them by the colonial administration, many Batswana men had to migrate to South Africa to work on the mines, leaving the women to take over all agricultural work. Bechuanaland then began to decline in comparison to its two prosperous neighbours, South Africa and Rhodesia.

By the 1960's, 15% of the population had moved to the cities, and over 40% of the remaining rural population had lost their cattle. This concentration of land ownership enabled Afrikaners to control agricultural production, and to become the suppliers of 60% of all meat products and, therefore, export earnings. When the first nationalist movements arose, their main aim was to put an end both to this inequality and the constant threat of being annexed by South Africa.

In 1966, the British (who had never made any money out of all that sand) willingly granted independence, and the Bechuanaland Protectorate became Botswana. Seretse Khama, leader of the Botswana Democratic Party (BDP), became president, with the BDP polling 80% of the votes. He was knighted a year later by the British. Gaborone became the new capital — this time within the nation's borders.

Politics since Independence

Despite Botswana's economic dependence on South Africa, Seretse Khama managed to keep his distance on the political front by supporting the anti-apartheid movements of the region. Botswana became one of the 'Front Line' nations fighting apartheid (by giving diplomatic support to the Rhodesian and Namibian liberation struggles), and played an important role in the establishment of the Southern African Development Coordination Conference (SADCC) in 1979. The aim of SADCC, is for the member states to become regionally self-sufficient and independent of South Africa's economic domain. However the simultaneous anti-apartheid stance, and economic closeness to South Africa, was and still is an uncomfortable position for Botswana.

Seretse Khama died in mid 1980, and was succeeded by his vice President, Quett Masire, who made few changes to his predecessor's policies. Strong pressures were exerted on Masire by socialist groups to limit the concentration of good arable land in the hands of the whites, and to increase the area allocated to cooperatives, though change has been slow. (Following independence, the BDP pursued a conciliatory approach towards the European descendants who owned 80% of the country's economic resources at the time.) Rural farmers accused the large landowners of raising too much livestock on impoverished lands which would soon become barren if something were not done. A movement also arose demanding the nationalisation of the diamond, iron, copper and nickel mining industries, which are half owned by South African companies. However, Masire's administration openly favours a more capitalist approach and, with the economy in good shape, his party receives little serious opposition. In the 1984 general elections, Masire's BDP kept its huge majority, winning 29 of the 34 elected seats in the National Assembly.

Following Zimbabwe's independence and throughout the 1980's, South Africa used military, economic and diplomatic pressure on Botswana to end its anti-apartheid statements, recognise the 'independent homelands' in South Africa, expel ANC and SWAPO refugees, and sign a 'non-aggression treaty'. The treaty was withdrawn in 1985 following Masire's agreement to stop militant members of the ANC living along the border, or carrying out military activities in exile. But despite this, South Africa launched a surprise attack on Gaborone in June 1985, killing 12 people who had allegedly given refuge to ANC guerillas. This was strenuously refuted by President Masire. Renewed

South African pressure was exerted in the first months of 1987, this time threatening to cut off road communication with Gaborone, Botswana's main connection with the outside world. Botswana did not give in to these pressures but maintained its political support of the ANC.

Resources and the Economy

At Independence, Botswana was one of the world's poorest nations, having inherited virtually no infrastructure or means of self-support from decades of British colonialism. Its prospects were dire indeed. Then remarkably, in 1967, the world's second largest diamond pipe was discovered at Orapa. Within a few years Botswana had become one of the world's major diamond producing countries, in partnership with the South African diamond cartel, De Beers. The world's third largest diamond pipe was discovered at Jwaneng several years later.

The BDP has focused on economic development and, due to financial necessity, stayed on cordial economic terms with South Africa — a difficult balancing act. A large number of Batswana citizens still work in South Africa, and Botswana is a member of the Southern African Customs Union which maintains free trade between South Africa, Namibia, Botswana, Swaziland and Lesotho. Diamonds, along with beef exports to the EEC, have made the country financially secure with one of the fastest growing economies in the world (a record average 12% per annum growth rate between 1978 and 1988). The military budget is kept low, with education and development of the infrastructure given top priority. The government is acutely aware of the precariousness of its reliance on only two main export earners — diamonds and beef — and is committed to the diversification of the economy. The contentious development of the soda-ash plant on Sowa Spit in the Makgadikgadi Pans is one such example. Equally, it's all too aware of its dependency on South Africa for essential imports and as a major export market — almost all imports originate in South Africa or come through Cape Town, whilst 60% of its exports are purchased by South Africa. As a leading member of SADCC, Botswana is striving for regional self-reliance.

Despite the country's calm, problems exist. Immense tracts of land have been destroyed by the overgrazing of cattle, while frequent droughts (almost every seven years) make the small farmer dependent on governmental assistance. The gap between rich and poor widens with increasing rural depopulation and urbanisation — successful businessmen and government officials drive their Mercedes, while the impoverished and jobless put up shanties on the outskirts of town. Although Botswana's population is small, population growth runs at a large 3.4% per annum, threatening to outstrip job creation despite the rapid economic growth. Hard decisions (such as on population control) will have to be made, and the BDP government will need to remain flexible if it's to remain in power, but Botswana does have the resources to do well in the future. No doubt the current political re-orientation in South Africa will prove to have profound ramifications for Botswana (and the whole of the SADCC region) in due course.

Chapter 2

The people and languages of Namibia and Botswana

Namibia — General Impressions

Travelling around Namibia just after independence, you couldn't fail to sense the immense enthusiasm of most people towards the future. Even the Afrikaner whites were optimistic about 'building a new and better country'. They saw it as an opportunity to leave South Africa's racial problems behind and, most importantly, to free themselves of its sanctions. Finally, they had the chance to make a fresh start in a country with rich natural resources. The cultures of the Namibian people have been dominated by South Africa for some 70 years, and by colonial influences for much longer — at present it's very difficult to predict what will emerge as the formative cultural influences of the independent country.

Botswana — General Impressions

Citizens of Botswana are called *Ba*tswana, while a *Mo*tswana is a single individual. However the prefixes *Ba* and *Mo* before *any* of the ethnic group names in Botswana have the more specific meaning of several people, or one person, of that group. This dualism reflects the government's 'we're all Batswana' policy, adopted at independence in an effort to achieve national unity and curb tribal partisanism. School textbooks tell us about the languages that used to be spoken, but now 'we all speak Setswana' (the prefix *Se* implying both the language of the Tswana people, *and* the language of the country). Whilst this has led to the gradual loss of cultural identity of all other ethnic groups, in many ways the policy has been successful — Botswana has avoided the ethnic clashes that have brought disaster elsewhere in Africa. Perhaps Botswana's minority groups have been dominated by Tswana's and Europeans for so long that they've come to accept their lower status.

THE PEOPLES

It has long been a colonial legacy of the west to view the many peoples of Africa in terms of a multitude of culturally and linguistically distinct *tribes* (which were often portrayed as being culturally incompatible and in a state of constant warfare with each other). Whilst of course there are an enormous variety of different ethnic groups, many are closely related to others in language, beliefs, and way of life. Over time there has been (and continues to be) considerable intermixing of peoples and cultures. The Batswana, for example, frequently incorporated other ethnic groups into their society, whilst also splitting into smaller groups themselves as a peaceful way of resolving disagreements.

When the colonial powers carved up their conquests in Africa, national borders bore little relation to traditional areas and frequently cut across land occupied by one ethnic group, splitting it into two or more parts. Many of the ethnic groups described here are split between Botswana, Namibia or South Africa, and are therefore arranged alphabetically rather than under country headings.

Bakgalagadi, Bayei, Hambukushu and Subiya

(mostly in Botswana)

Like all African countries, Botswana has a multitude of minority tribes, each with its own traditions and cultural heritage. Whilst being minorities in a national sense, they may well be the *only* tribe in a given village and so, are far from the minority at home.

The Bakgalagadi were the first Bantu-speakers to move into present-day Botswana. They mixed and lived along with the Bushmen who were already there. Presently, they occupy villages throughout the Kalahari Desert, where they've become servants and herders at large cattle posts.

The Bayei, Hambukushu and Subiya, all live in the north-west of the country, in and around the Okavango Delta. They catch fish, hunt game and grow crops of sorghum, maize, and millet. Their dugout canoes (*mokoros*) are poled or paddled throughout the waterways. If you travel into the Delta, your poler will probably be a Yei.

Bakalanga

(Botswana and Zimbabwe)

The homeland of the Bakalanga is divided by the Botswana-Zimbabwe border, though ties across the boundary remain strong. Their language is an off-shoot of the Shona spoken in Zimbabwe. Most Bakalanga live in and around Francistown, but there are significant numbers in all the large towns.

Traditional Kalangas do not congregate in densely-populated villages, nor do they separate their homes, fields, and cattle into three sites like the Batswana. Instead, they live in sprawling villages, with houses, crops and cattle *kraals* all intermixed. The Kalangas are chiefly farmers, and their few cattle are used for ploughing and for paying the bride-price.

Bakalanga chiefs lead their people and settle disputes, but are not venerated to the degree that Batswana chiefs are. They serve their people, rather than being served. In some areas, due to the absence of missionary influence, oracles still exist who are intermediaries for contacting Mwali (The Almighty) to get advice and to request rain. The Kalanga are the only people in Botswana who continue to hold tribal rain dances.

Names

by Phil Deutschle

Obvious, Knowledge, Beauty, Naughty-Boy, and Precious are all names of people I know. Such exquisite names are often just English translations of common Kalanga names — Shathani means Rejoice, and Musani can be Arousement.

Almost everyone has at least three different names: a Kalanga name (for home), a Setswana name (for school), and an English name (for work). Add to this a plentitude of nicknames and you can be at a loss to know who you're talking about. This weekend, I was being told all about a certain 'Greg'. It was some time before I realised that it was someone who I already knew well, but by the name of 'Ringo'.

Parents are often called according to the names of their first-born children. So the mother of Shathani, who I know as Washule, is Maando at home but is now being called Mmashathani!

Students will give themselves new names as the fancy strikes them. Tom suddenly becomes Cool-Ruler, and Innocent switches to His Master's Voice.

As Botswana develops, new-borns are being given some bizarre names: Roadblock, Extension, or Spar (after a South African chain store). My favourite is the baby boy who was named 'Diploma' by his grandmother.

'His mother went away to school to get an education, to get her diploma,' explains the grandmother, bouncing her grandson. 'But *this* is what she came home with. So that's what I call him — Diploma!'

Baster

(Namibia)

The Basters are the descendants of indigenous Hottentot women and the Dutch settlers who first arrived at the Cape in the early 17th Century. The original 'coloured' or 'bastard' children found themselves rejected by both the white and black communities at the Cape, so keeping together they relocated themselves further north away from the colonialists. Proudly calling themselves 'Basters', they set up farming communities and developed their own distinct social and cultural structures.

During the 1860s, white settlers began to push into these areas so, to avoid confrontation, the Basters crossed the Orange River in 1868 and moved northwards once again. Trying to keep out of the way of the warring Hereros and Namas, they founded Rehoboth in 1871 and set up their own system of government under a *Kaptein* (Headman) and a *Volksraad* (Legislative Council). Their support of the German colonial troops during the tribal uprisings brought them later protection and privileges.

Demands for self-rule and independence were repressed throughout this century until the *Rehoboth Gebiet* was granted the status of an independent state in the 1970s. This move by the South African administration was made with the aim of reinforcing racial divisions amongst the non-whites — rather like in the South African 'independent homelands'. Today, the country's 29,000 Basters have a strong sense of identity and make up about 2.5% of the population. Most still live in the good cattle-grazing land around Rehoboth.

Batswana

(Botswana and South Africa)

Altogether, ethnic Tswanas number some five million, though the majority are citizens of South Africa. Their language, Setswana, is closely related to the Sesotho spoken in Lesotho.

Batswana tend to live in large, closely-packed villages. Some have populations as high as 30,000 while still retaining a village atmosphere. The people often maintain three homes: one in the village, another at the lands (where crops are grown some distance from the village) and the third at the cattle post (where cattle are kept up to several hundred kilometres from their village home).

With this tradition of fragmentation, the Batswana have readily accepted having families scattered in distant towns by the search for jobs. A complete family of mother, father and children is a rarity. Often, the children are left with the grandmother while the mother stays in town and the father is off at the mines. Still, the village is considered home. The richer Batswana build expensive houses at their home villages, even though they might only stay there once a year, at Christmas time.

The Batswana of Botswana are divided into eight major tribes. The well-being of the chief is of paramount importance. A tribe judges its success by the affluence of its chief. The chief presides over traditional court (*kgotla*) meetings, where village matters are freely discussed by all concerned parties.

Ownership of cattle is linked to prestige and some of the largest herds are owned by government officials. Beef is a major export item, but historically the cattle also served as a back-up source of food and income during times of drought.

Bushmen/San

(Botswana, Namibia, Angola and South Africa)

The Bushmen are the oldest inhabitants of southern Africa and undoubtedly one of the most studied and documented ethnic groups in the world. They are, anthropologically, an intriguing group, as a few of them still maintain their traditional lifestyle and are among the world's last hunter-gatherers. Whilst this lifestyle has now almost died out, the Bushmen still exist as a linguistically and ethnically distinct group.

The Bushmen have no collective name for themselves, and all their popular names are in some sense derogatory. *Bushmen* is the most widely used term but has racist and sexist connotations. Many anthropologists and historians have more recently chosen the term *San*, but this refers to the language group, not culture, of the people and isn't used in southern Africa except in academic circles. *Basarwa*, the Setswana word for 'people from the uninhabited country', has negative connotations, and is disliked by the Bushmen themselves, as is the clinical abbreviation *RAD* (Remote Area Dweller) used by the Botswanan government in an effort at neutrality.

The Bushmen are often thought of as desert dwellers, though they used to occupy nearly all of southern Africa. For at least 25,000 years Bushmen have hunted and gathered on the subcontinent, probably spreading throughout much of sub-Saharan Africa. About 2,000 years ago *Bantu*-speaking farmers started migrating south from central west Africa in search of new land, and the Bushmen hunting and gathering areas became increasingly under pressure. The situation was accelerated by the arrival of the Boers at the Cape in the 17th Century. With the Boers taking land for farming in the south and the Bantus expanding to the north, the Bushmen had insufficient land to survive and were forced to take cattle from Bantu and Boer farmers. In retaliation Boer farmers shot the Bushmen as vermin, killing many thousands and resulting in their extinction at the Cape. However, most of the reduction of the Bushmen was not due to slaughter by whites, but caused by their assimilation into black farming communities, where they were often treated as little more than slaves. It was only in the most remote and inhospitable areas, like the central Kalahari, that their traditional way of life survived.

In Botswana, this assimilation has produced direct contradictions. While legally equal, the Bushmen are reviled by many Batswana as the lowest form of humanity — social pariahs. Paradoxically, a Bushmen's yellow skin on a 'real' person is considered beautiful. Bushmen women are especially attractive to Bantu men because of their small stature and pale, yellowish skins. Many Batswana have some obvious Bushmen physical traits — light skin, small size, lack of ear lobes. These people are thought comely, but to imply any hint of Bushman blood is a terrible insult.

Remote bands of Bushmen do still live a traditional lifestyle of hunting and gathering in the central Kalahari desert. Far from being a 'primitive' people who had failed to 'progress' to a sedentary way of life, the Bushmen had evolved a sophisticated and, to us, almost utopian existence with their environment. The sharing of all food and almost all possessions, communal decision making (there were no chiefs) and an all-embracing spiritual life which stressed the one-ness of the world, enabled them to survive where no other people could.

The 'traditional' Bushmen of the central Kalahari know exactly where to go when looking for foodplants, game, or water. Assorted roots, tubers, berries, seeds and nuts form the bulk of their diet — often up to 90%. These are collected by the women and children, while the man's business is to hunt. He sets snares, and hunts using arrows poisoned with beetle larva juice, taking only as much game as is needed. Hunting, and the distribution of meat following a kill, is as important socially as it is nutritionally, emphasising unification and sharing.

Bushmen are amongst the only people in the world who have learned to live with no permanent access to water. While there is no surface water in the Kalahari, there are sufficient amounts of water in other forms. Water is obtained from plants, tubers, melons and other water-storing vegetation, as well as being found underground in *sip wells*, reached by long thin grass straws. Once collected, water is stored underground in hollowed out ostrich eggs.

Of today's 50,000 Bushmen, many have settled into communities where they grow crops and keep livestock. Others work on isolated cattle posts, where they often get no wages, but only food. A few may receive livestock as payment, but they can't sell it without their 'Master's' consent. (Many Bushmen are called, and truly consider themselves to be, their 'Master's' 'subjects', and will regularly vote a 'Master' into elected office.) Poverty, unemployment, powerlessness and above all despair afflict most Bushmen, who are at the bottom of the social ladder in all the countries they inhabit. What most want is the land to combine an agricultural existence with more traditional hunting and gathering, but with the same health and schooling facilities available to their fellow citizens of other ethnic groups. They want to be a part of their country's development, *and* retain their own culture and sense of identity. In the same way that the Bushmen have no common term to call themselves, so also they have little sense of belonging to a common heritage, and very few Bushmen are collectively campaigning for their rights. This is left to individuals like Laurens van der Post and organisations such as Survival International, who have been campaigning on their behalf over the last few decades, if not always from the same perspective.

Damara

(Namibia)

Along with the Nama and the Bushmen, the Damara are presumed to be the original inhabitants of Namibia, speaking a similar 'Khoi' click language. Like the Nama, the Damara were primarily hunting people, who owned few cattle or goats. Traditionally enemies of the Nama and Herero, they supported the German colonial forces at Waterberg against the Herero uprisings and were awarded for their loyalty by an 'enlarged' homeland from the German authorities. Of the 80,000 Damara today, only a quarter manage to survive in this area adjacent to the Skeleton Coast park — the rest work on white-owned farms, in mines or as labourers in the towns. Damara women share the same 'Victorian' style of dress as the Herero and Nama women.

Herero

(Namibia & Botswana)

In 1904, the Herero and the Hottentots staged a massive uprising against the German colonial troops in South West Africa which ended in a bloody massacre of over half the total Herero population at the battle of Waterberg. The few Herero that survived fled into the Kalahari, some crossing into what is now Botswana. Today, the Herero constitute the third largest ethnic group in Namibia, after the Owambo and Kavango — about 8% of the present population. In Botswana, they are a 'minority' group inhabiting Ngamiland, south and west of the Okavango Delta.

Traditionally pastoralists, the Herero prefer raising cattle to growing crops — prestige and influence is dependent on the number of cattle possessed. Today, the majority of Namibian Hereros use their cattle-handling skills on white-owned farms.

The women wear very distinctive long, flowing Victorian gowns and headdresses. Multiple layers of petticoats made from over 12m of material give a voluminous look (two women walking side by side occupy the whole pavement!). This style of dress was introduced in the 1800s by missionaries who were appalled by the Hereros' semi-nakedness. Now the Hereros continue to wear these heavy costumes in their desert environment and it has become their traditional dress.

Himba

(Namibia)

The Himba share a common ethnic origin with the Herero people, having split from the main Herero group on the Namibia/Botswana border and moved west to present-day Kaokoland in search of available land. The land they found, however, is mountainous, sparsely vegetated and very arid. Cattle is central to their way of life, with the size of the herd an indication of wealth and prestige — but overgrazing of the poor lands is a major problem. The Himba are a minority group in Namibia (less than 1% of the population), and live almost entirely in their traditional areas in remote Kaokoland.

Kavango and Caprivian

(Namibia, Angola and Botswana)

The Kavango people share their name with the Okavango River, which forms the northern border of Namibia with Angola. Not surprisingly, they have based their traditional agricultural and fishing existence on the fertile land and good water supply afforded by this environment.

Many of the Kavango who used to live on the northern side of the Okavango River in Angola, fled south of the river into Namibia during the last 10-15 years, away from the civil war between South African-backed UNITA rebels and the Soviet/Cuban-backed MPLA regime — and away from the harassment of the regular incursions by South African troops into the south of Angola. As a consequence, the Kavango population more than doubled in size during the 1970s, and now forms the second largest ethnic group in Namibia, making up almost 10% of the population.

The Caprivi people traditionally live in the fertile, swampy land between the Chobe and Zambezi rivers — at the far end of the Caprivi Strip. Like the Kavango and the Owambo, they farm a variety of crops, raise livestock, and fish — the agricultural potential of the area is one of the highest in Namibia. However, this potential has been largely unrealised — before the war with Angola, and the heavy involvement of South African troops (which brought roads and infrastructure), the whole of the Kavango and Caprivi region was one of the least developed in Namibia.

Nama/Hottentot

(Namibia)

The Nama people are perhaps the closest in origin to the Bushmen, traditionally sharing a similar type of 'click' or Khoi language, the same light-coloured yellowy skin, and a hunter-gatherer way of life. One of the first peoples in Namibia, their tribal areas were traditionally communal property, as indeed was any item unless it was actually made by an individual. Basic differences in the perception of ownership of land and hunting-grounds, led in the past to frequent conflicts with the Herero people. The 50,000 or so Nama today, mostly live in Namaland, north of Keetmanshoop in the south of Namibia — mostly working on white farms. Nama women share the same 'Victorian' traditional dress as the Herero and Damara women.

Owambo

(Namibia and Angola)

The Owambo people (sometimes called Ovambo) are by far the largest group in Namibia and make up just over half the population. The great majority live in their traditional areas — Owamboland — away from the main transport arteries in the remote far north of the country, straddled on the border with Angola. The area receives one of the highest rainfalls in the country, and supports a range of traditional crops as well as allowing good grazing for the extensive cattle herds.

Before independence, the existence of half a million indigenous Namibians on the border with (socialist) Angola, seriously perturbed the South African administration. By investing some money into the region, the administration hoped to establish a protective buffer against Angola to protect the white areas in the interior. The policy back-fired — Owamboland became the heartland of SWAPO during the struggle for independence. With this, harassment by the South African Defence Force, and a rapid population increase (exacerbated by a large influx of refugees from Angola), have left the area over-pressurised and undeveloped. The new SWAPO government has pledged to redress this imbalance.

Whites and Coloureds

(Namibia and Botswana)

The first whites to settle in Namibia were the Germans who set up trading businesses around the port of Lüderitz in 1884. Within a few years, Namibia formally became a German colony, and German settlers began to arrive in ever increasing numbers. Meanwhile, white farmers of Dutch origin (the Boers, who first settled on the African continent at the Cape in 1652,), were moving northwards in search of land free from British interference, following the ceding of the Dutch Cape Colony to the British government. To avoid the Germans in Namibia, and encouraged by Rhodes's British South Africa Company, some Boer *trekkers* headed for Bechuanaland and settled in Ghanzi (in the central Kalahari of Botswana), and in the Tuli Block (land along the Limpopo River, on the border between Botswana and South Africa). Following the transfer of German Namibia to South African control after the First World War, Boers (Afrikaners) moved into Namibia, and soon significantly outnumbered the German settlers. Whites of British origin joined the Afrikaners in British Bechuanaland, and a few moved to Namibia and settled there. The Namibian whites collectively refer to themselves as 'Southwesters' after Namibia's colonial name of South West Africa.

The term 'Coloureds' is generally used in southern Africa to describe people of mixed (black-white) origin. The coloured people maintain a strong sense of identity and separateness from either blacks or whites — though they generally speak either Afrikaans or English (or frequently both) rather than an 'African' language.

NAMIBIAN LANGUAGES

Namibia's variety of languages reflects the country's great diversity of peoples — black and white. Amongst the indigenous languages there are two basic groups which bear no relation to each other — Bantu languages (such as of the Owambo and Herero people), and Khoi-San Languages (such as of the Bushmen and Nama peoples). Unlike Botswana, there is no one African language that is widespread enough to be useful as the *lingua franca*. Most black townspeople speak both Afrikaans and English in addition to their 'mother' language. In the more rural areas, Afrikaans tends to be more widely used than English (which may not be spoken at all) — despite the widespread enthusiasm felt for the latter. In some parts, notably in the farming areas of the central region, German is also commonly found.

Following independence, one of the new government's first actions was to make English Namibia's only official language — removing Afrikaans and German. This step sought to unite Namibia's great diversity of people's and languages under one common tongue ('the language of the liberation struggle'), leaving behind the oppressive and colonial overtones of Afrikaans and German. This choice will also help in international relations and with education — English-language materials are the most easily available.

For the purposes of this guide book, there is little point in giving a language guide to either the many African languages, or to Afrikaans and German. However, in your travels you are likely to come across a number of words — mostly Afrikaans — that have entered the common 'English-speaking' vocabulary of this part of southern Africa. Some of them (self-evidently) have racist connotations, but it is as well to be aware of them.

Southern African terms

baas	'master' (usually white)
bakkie	pick-up truck
beester	cattle
bioscope	cinema
boerwors	sausage
bokki	goat
braiivleis (braii)	barbecue
donga	small ravine
finach	quick
kanatschi	'native' child
klippe	stone
kloof	ravine

koppie	rocky hill
kost	food
kraal	cattle enclosure or African huts (Owambo)
lecker	good, nice
mielie	corn, maize
mieliepap	maize flour porridge (*shadza* in Botswana)
orlag	war
pad	road, track
pontok	'native' hut
rivier	river
robot	traffic lights
rondavel	African hut (round)
suppi	measure of alcohol
tackies	running shoes/sneakers
veld	grassland
werft	'native' settlement (Herero)

BOTSWANA LANGUAGE GUIDE

Compiled by Phil Deutschle

Setswana is the national language of Botswana, while English is the official language. Though many people speak other languages at home, most can converse in Setswana. English will be spoken by all who have been to school, or who have been outside the country. You should not expect to find English-speakers in rural or isolated areas (like the Okavango Delta). Even among the educated, trying to speak some Setswana will show a degree of respect and will open many doors. The largest 'minority' language is *Tjikalanga* (of the Bakalanga ethnic group), spoken in and around Francistown.

Setswana

Learning to speak Setswana is easy. Carry the most important phrases on a slip of paper and practice whenever you can.

Pronunciation

The only difficult sound is the g, pronounced like ch in the Scottish loch or German *Ich*. If you have trouble with that, just say the g like an ordinary h. The r is often rolled. Vowels are pronounced as follows:

a: like a in China
e: like ay in day
i: like ee in see
o: like o in go
u: like oo in too

Greetings

(words in brackets are optional)

English	Setswana
Greetings Sir/Madam. (Informally, 'Hello')	*Dumela Rra/Mma.*
(How) did you rise?	*O tsogile (jang)?*
I have risen (well).	*Ke tsogile (sentle).*
(How) did you spend the day?	*O tlhotse (jang)?*
I spent the day (well).	*Ke tlhotse (sentle).*
How are you? (Informal)	*O kae?*
I'm fine. (Literally, 'I'm here')	*Ke teng.*
It's OK.	*Go siame.*
I am going.	*Ke a tsamaya.*
Stay well. (Said to one staying)	*Sala sentle.*
Go well. (Said to one going)	*Tsamaya sentle.*
Sleep well.	*Robala sentle.*

Basic Phrases

What's your name? (Formal)	*Leina la gago ke mang?*
My name is _____.	*Leina la me ke _____.*
Who are you? (Informal)	*O mang?*
I'm _____.	*Ke _____.*
Where are you from? or Where are you coming from?	*O tswa kae?*
I'm (coming) from _____.	*Ke tswa kwa _____.*
Yes.	*Ee.*
No.	*Nnyaa.*
I don't know (Setswana).	*Ga ke itse (Setswana).*
What is this (in Setswana)?	*Se ke eng (ka Setswana)?*
How goes it?	*Wa reng?*
It goes OK.	*Ga ke bue.*
Thank you.	*Ke itumetse.*
What's the time?	*Nako ke mang?*
Excuse me!	*'Sorry!'*
I'm asking for money/tobacco.	*Ke kopa madi/motsoko.*
I have no money/tobacco.	*Ga ke na madi/motsoko.*

Shopping

English numbers are used.

Where's the shop?	*Shopo e kae?*
What do you want?	*O batla eng?*
I want _____.	*Ke batla/kopa _____.*
There is none.	*Ga go na.*
How much?	*Ke bokae?*
It's expensive/cheap.	*Go a tura/tshipi.*
sugar	*sukiri*

meali meal	*bupi*
tea/coffee	*tee/kofee*
meat	*fnama*
milk	*mashi*
water	*metse*

Travelling Phrases

Where are you going?	*O ya kae?*
I'm going to ____.	*Ke ya ____.*
Where are you coming from?	*O tswa kae?*
I'm coming from ____.	*Ke tswa kwa ____.*
far/near	*kgakala/gaufi*
I'm satisfied. (Regarding food)	*Ke kgotshe.*
It tastes good.	*Go monate.*
Men/Women (On toilets)	*Banna/Basadi*
What do you do? (Your job)	*O dira eng?*

Speaking Setswana

Make sentences with a pronoun and verb – eg *Ke reka borotho* (I buy bread); *O rabala* (You sleep); *Ke ithuta Setswana* (I learn Setswana).

Negatives: *Ga ke reke* (I don't buy); *Ga o robale* (You don't sleep).

Pronouns

I	*ke, nna*	we	*re*
you	*o, wena*	you plural	*lo*
she/he	*o*	they	*ba*

Verbs

apaya	cook	*kwala*	write
bala	read	*duela*	pay
batla	need	*iwala*	be sick
bina	dance	*reka*	buy
bolaya	kill	*rekisa*	sell
bona	see	*robala*	sleep
bua	speak	*sala*	remain, stay
dira/bereka	do/work	*sega*	cut
ithuta	learn	*tsamaya*	depart
itse	know	*tsena*	enter, come in
ja	eat	*utlwa*	hear
kopa	beg, ask for	*ya*	go

Other words

mang?	who?	*eng?*	what?
leng?	when?	*kae?*	where?
jang?	how?	*pula*	rain
moeti	traveller	*tsotsi*	thief/rascal

Mosarwa	Bushman	*jalo*	like that
Tla kwano	Come here	*Tsaya*	Take this
sentle	well, nicely	*voetsak!*	scram!
tsela	path, road	*monate*	nice
fela	only	*gape*	again
dikgomo	cattle	*setulo*	chair
ka moso	tomorrow	*wa utlwa?*	understand?
gompieno	today	*bogobe*	porridge

A Few Phrases of Tjikalanga

Greetings.	*Dumelani.*
(How) did you rise?	*Ma muka (tjini)?*
I rose (well).	*Nda muka.*
It's OK.	*Kwaka lulwama.*
Thanks.	*Nda boka.*

CULTURAL DOs AND DON'Ts

The following piece was written by Phil Deutschle from the point of view of a visitor to Botswana, but the basic ethos is just as relevant to travelling in Namibia — or anywhere in the world for that matter.

'I want to see this. I want to do that. I want to photograph you.' That's essentially what we say when we come travelling. We arrive as uninvited guests and we owe it to our hosts to be as unabrasive as possible, to try to fit in, to show respect for local attitudes.

One of the most important, and easiest, things to do is to learn something of the local language, Setswana. A simple *'Dumela, Mma'*, will bring a great smile to an old woman's face. We English-speakers are exceptionally lax about learning other people's languages, and this can rightfully be considered an insult.

Greetings are indispensable in Tswana society. One must greet everyone when arriving and departing (see page 23). Even in a shop, it is good manners to say *'Dumela, Mma'* to a woman or *'Dumela, Rra'* to a man before doing business. In an office, some sort of greeting (in Setswana or English) is vital to avoid being coldly ignored. The one arriving at a place usually greets first, but if no one greets you, take the initiative. People may not know what to say to you.

Everyone, young and old, shakes hands. Not a firm hand clasp; more of a caress. While shaking with your right hand, use your left hand to hold your own right elbow, as though you were supporting a heavy load. This, at times, can be accompanied by a little bow. Don't be surprised if friends, men or women, after shaking hands, want to continue holding hands while talking.

When giving or receiving anything, such as money or change in a shop, it is polite to use your right hand, and to at least touch your left hand to right elbow. Do this even if you see many Batswana are neglecting to do so. It's proper etiquette that is dying out in the towns. Accepting a gift, including food or a tinned drink, should be done with both hands.

Bidding farewell is as important as greeting. If you're leaving, say *Sala sentle* (Stay well) to the ones remaining. If you're staying, say *Tsamaya sentle* (Go well) to the ones leaving.

Batswana, unlike Europeans, are very casual when asking for things. You may often hear, 'Take me one photo', 'Buy me a drink', or 'Give me money'. This is not because you are a foreigner, so don't be cross. To ask for something is not shameful. In this part of the world, it's just natural to express your wants and needs openly. This giving and receiving forms bonds between people. At the same time, you are not insulting someone when you refuse a request. If you do give things, remember that a 'thank you' is not the cultural necessity that it is in the West, so don't be hurt by its absence.

Begging is another matter. Batswana will often give to an old man or woman who begs, but almost never to a child. What you do must be a personal choice. Kids who beg wearing proper clothes are usually school brats who have learned that a foreigner is an easy mark to get money for buying sweets. Kids in rags are honestly destitute, perhaps having no parents, living in the streets. Since gifts of money might be used for almost anything, giving food is better. Unfortunately, this too gives only temporary relief to a long-term problem.

The clothes worn in Botswana are becoming increasingly westernised. While you will see Batswana men in shorts, and women in trousers, they are viewed as people who don't know better, or youngsters trying to show off the latest fashions. Except in the bush, it is best to dress conservatively in long trousers and skirts — especially in small villages. Hats are not worn indoors or at formal occasions.

Water, perhaps obviously, has special significance to a desert people, and there are strict rules on how and where and in which containers water may be used. At a public water tap, do not let the water run. Do not wash your face, nor your body or clothes at a tap. You may wash your hands, and use your cupped hands to drink from a tap. If you need to wash anything else, fill a container and carry it far afield.

When staying in someone's home, be certain to ask specifically about water use. Don't just assume. Before eating, you will be given water to wash your hands. If the food comes first, wait for the water. Refrain from ever smelling your food, as doing so means that you think the food might be bad. Don't feel compelled to finish a portion of food — this may even imply that you weren't given enough. Two or more people will often share the same plate of food, and pass around a container of water or a calabash of traditional beer. However, a cup of tea or a tinned drink is not shared.

On a bus, people don't usually give their seats to the elderly or to women with babies. After paying, keep your ticket as you may be asked to surrender it when you get off. Do not step over someone's legs in the aisle (or anywhere). This is very rude. If you need someone to move, say 'Sorry, sorry, sorry'. It's the same for getting through a crowd. 'Sorry' is also used when you see someone having a minor accident, like dropping something, even if it has nothing to do with you.

Batswana are very strong supporters of the President's political party, the Botswana Democratic Party (BDP). While freedom of speech legally reigns, no one enjoys hearing criticism from a foreigner. If you want to discuss the apparent contradiction between Botswana's public rhetoric towards South Africa, and its economic policy towards the southern giant, be sure of your audience first. You don't have to be paranoid, but refrain from insulting the President. An expatriate was deported after referring to Botswana's 'Bushman President' in a bar.

Most Batswana enjoy being photographed, but it's polite to ask first.

Specific advice, like 'picking your nose is OK, but farting is frowned upon', can only be carried so far. There are thousands of cultural blunders that a foreigner can make. The best that you can do is to be hyper-aware, and to ask, ask, ask. An example: on my way to a funeral, I met my adopted brother, who looked aghast at my stately clothes of trousers and button-down shirt. 'What's wrong?' I asked. 'Where's your jacket? You have to wear a jacket.' 'My only jacket is bright red.' I had assumed red to be an inappropriate colour for a funeral. My brother looked puzzled. 'But red is all right,' he said. I had assumed wrong. The jacket was essential, and the colour didn't matter, so I returned for my crimson jacket.

Don't assume. Ask.

Building a mud hut

by Phil Deutschle

Even a small child can recognise the type of soil needed for a mud hut — there is something about the colour, containing a specific amount of clay and vegetable matter. When it came time to build a new kitchen in our compound, we were fortunate to have the proper mud-making soil just behind the proposed site. The children were set to work digging, while the women drew the floorplan — a large circle. They checked the size by sitting down with their backs to the soon-to-be-built walls and with their feet stretched out towards the imaginary fireplace. A foundation was dug by scratching a shallow groove in the ground, and next came the mud, called *vu*.

The dirt that the children dug up had to be mixed with the correct proportions of water and sand. The women formed the mixture into bowling-ball sized wads, and kneaded it thoroughly, like bread. I offered to help, but was told, "You don't know how to make *vu*. We will do it."

After kneading, a loaf of mud was rolled into a fat sausage and dropped from hip height onto the ground. This flattened it on one side. Then it was turned over and dropped from a lower height, creating a slab to be used something like a brick. Kopano, the construction forewoman, would take a slab and put it in position on its long edge, pat it into place, and smooth out the back end, forming a parallelogram-shaped brick. The women continued like this, around the circle, completing two layers, totalling a foot and a half high. More than this could not be built in a single day, as any higher layers would squash the lower ones.

Next day, the previous day's now-hard layers were spread inside and out with fresh *vu*, acting as both mortar and plaster. Again, I tried to help, but was rebuked with, "No, you can't do this. Your hands are too big." After the spreading of fresh mud, two more rows of bricks were constructed. The process continued the following day — first spreading mud on the previous day's work and then building two additional rows. After five days it stood at eye level.

While we waited the two weeks needed to get the poles to make the roof, heavy rains knocked down a third of what had been built. No one seemed concerned. Mud huts got washed away all the time. The broken walls just had to be rebuilt.

Roofing poles arrived from the bush, and the construction was done by two hired men. I didn't even suggest that I might help. I'd had enough rejections. They dug nine poles into the ground around the periphery of the kitchen, and on top of that they built a conical framework to hold the grass.

By this point, Kopano had begun conducting rituals to sanctify and protect the new kitchen. Each night she lit a small fire in the centre of the unfinished building and burnt herbs to safeguard the health of her children.

Now came the grass for the roof. It had to be tied into thick mats, each six yards long. These long mats were rolled up and lifted onto the roof supports. Unrolling the mats onto the framework was an easy job, and here I was certain that my great height would be appreciated. Yet again, I was wrong. "Leave it," instructed Kopano, "We will do it." They rolled out the grass in an ever-shrinking spiral and tied it all fast.

Lastly, I watched Kopano struggling to hammer together a wooden door. She gave me a scornful look, but I said nothing. Only much later did I learn the traditions of building — the women work with the mud and grass exclusively, while the men are expected to do all the building using poles and wood. I wish they'd told me!

Chapter 3

The natural environment

THE PHYSICAL ENVIRONMENT

Climate

Most of Namibia and Botswana is classified as an arid to semi-arid region (the line being crossed from semi-arid to arid when evaporation exceeds rainfall). In general, both countries experience a sub-tropical 'desert' climate, characterised by a wide range in temperature (from day to night and from summer to winter), and by low rainfall and humidity. The eastern area of Botswana and the northern strips of both countries (in which the greater part of their population) have much less severe climates.

Temperatures range widely from very hot to very cold, depending on the height of the land above sea level and whether it's 'summer' (October to April) or 'winter' (May to September). In 'mid-summer' (January), the average maximum temperature is around 35°C and the average minimum is around 18°C. In 'mid-winter' (July), the average maximum temperature is around 25°C and the average minimum is around 5°C. These averages, however, conceal peaks of 48°C in summer months, and temperatures as low as minus 10°C in the higher desert regions in winter (this is rare!). Nevertheless night frosts are not uncommon during the months of June, July and August.

Rainfall Most rain falls in the summer months, generally from December to March, and can be heavy and prolonged in northern Botswana and north-eastern Namibia. The further south or west you get, the drier it gets, with many southern regions of the Kalahari receiving no rainfall in some years.

The Namibian coast follows a different pattern. The climate here is largely determined by the interaction between warm dry winds from inland and the cold *Benguela* Current. The sea is too cold for much evaporation to take place and, consequently, rain-bearing clouds don't form over the coast. Most of the coast is classified as desert — rainfall is an extremely low 15mm per annum on average — in some years there may be none at all. However, when hot air from the desert mixes with the cold sea air, it produces a moist fog which 'hangs' over the coastal strip penetrating up to 60km inland. The existence of many species of animals and plants endemic to the Namib is the result of this specialised environment, where the only dependable source of moisture is a periodic morning fog.

Geology and Topography

Geologically, Namibia and Botswana form part of an extremely old region, with *Precambrian* granitic and metamorphic rocks dating back over two billion years. These *shield* or 'basement' rocks are usually covered by more recent sedimentary rocks, mostly deposited during the *Mesozoic* era (65 to 235 million years ago). *Tectonic activity* or movement in the earth's crust over the last 100 million years or so created a number of rifts through which magma was able to reach the surface (see section on diamond pipes below) and resulted in the uplifting of most of the area above sea level.

Kimberlite (diamond) pipes Diamond is a crystalline form of ordinary carbon formed under conditions of extreme pressure and temperature. In nature, such conditions are only found deep below the earth's surface in the lower crust or upper mantle. Under certain circumstances in the past (usually associated with tectonic activity) the rock matrix in which diamonds occurred was subjected to such great pressure that it became 'fluid' and worked its way up to the earth's surface in the form of a volcanic pipe of *fluidised* material. The situation is similar to a conventional volcanic eruption, except that instead of basaltic magma being erupted through fissures in the crust, the volcanic material is a peculiar rock called *kimberlite* which contains a wide assortment of minerals (including diamond) in addition to often large chunks of other rocks which have been caught up in the whole process.

The pipes are correctly termed *kimberlite pipes*, and occur throughout southern Africa from the Cape to Zaire. However, only a small proportion of those discovered have proved to contain diamonds in sufficient abundance to be profitably worked. Botswana mines two kimberlite pipes for diamonds, one at Orapa and one at Jwaneng. Namibia's diamonds derive not from primary kimberlite pipes, but from secondary diamond deposits — areas where diamonds have been washed down and deposited by old rivers which have eroded kimberlite pipes in the interior on their way.

The topography of Namibia and Botswana today can be described in a number of broad regions, each in the past affected in a different way by the tectonic activity of the Mesozoic era. The highest region, at 2,000m, is the central plateau of Namibia which runs roughly north-south. To the west, toward the Atlantic Ocean, the land falls off in a steep escarpment (which is deeply incised by river action), to the narrow coastal strip of the Namib Desert region. To the east of the central plateau the land slopes off much more gradually, merging with the Kalahari Desert region — a plateau at

1,000m, spanning both Namibia and Botswana. North of the central Kalahari, in north-west Botswana, the Okavango river basin region contains the Okavango Delta, an extensive area of swamp and marshland. The great salt pans of Makgadikgadi and Nxai to the north-east of Botswana are an associated region, filling a huge shallow basin that was once a vast inland lake. Finally, the eastern margin of Botswana forms another distinct topographical region with the land dropping slightly to the Limpopo river basin straddling the border between Botswana and South Africa.

Sand dunes

Barchan dunes arise wherever sand-laden wind deposits sand on the windward (up-wind) slopes of a random patch on the ground. The mound grows in height until a 'slip-face' is established by sand avalanching down on the sheltered leeward (down-wind) side. The resulting dune is therefore in a state of constant (if slow) movement — sand is continuously being deposited and blown up the shallow windward slope and then falling down the steep leeward slope. This slow movement, or migration, is more rapid at the edges of the dune than in the centre (there is less wind resistance) which results in the characteristic 'tails' of a mature *barchan* or *crescentric* dune.

Fairly constant winds from the same direction are essential for the growth and stability of *barchan* dunes, which can migrate from anything up to six metres a year for high dunes to 15 metres a year for smaller dunes. Probably the best examples of *barchan* dunes occur in Namibia's Skeleton Coast, where some of the dune crests are highlighted by a purple dusting of garnet sand.

Seif dunes Where the prevailing wind is interrupted by cross-winds driving in sand from the sides, a long *seif* or *longitudinal* dune is formed, instead of a swarm of *barchans*. The shape of *seif* dunes is in the form of a long ridge with high crests, parallel to the direction of the prevailing wind. They commonly occur in long parallel ranges, such as those south of the Kuiseb river which show up so clearly on satellite photographs.

Sand sheets When the land surface is vegetated with grass and scrub, or is covered with rocks and pebbles, the force of the wind is broken and becomes more random. In such situations poorly developed *seif dunes* or irregular *barchans* form, and may often join together to some extent, making an undulating *sand sheet*. From this platform of coarser sand, more erratic dunes often rise.

Sand sheets, in one form or another, are the most common dune formation in southern Africa, since the 'text book' conditions needed to form perfect *barchan* or *seif* dunes are rare. However, the principles remain the same and 'imperfect' dunes of *barchan* or *seif* origin are widespread throughout the Kalahari and Namib deserts.

FLORA AND FAUNA

Regional Flora and Vegetation

The natural vegetation of the region varies from the dry deciduous forests of Chobe, to the vast marsh areas of the Okavango and the barren desert dunes of the Namib. In general it becomes drier toward the south and west and the vegetation cover becomes correspondingly more sparse — although rivers and mountain ranges give much local variation to this trend.

The Caprivi Strip, northern Chobe and northern Owamboland are lush and tropical during and shortly after the rains, but become dry and relatively barren by the middle of the dry season. Where the land isn't used for agriculture, there are deciduous forests of tall *comboretum* and *acacia* trees above thick bush undergrowth.

The Okavango and Linyanti swamps are a patchwork of reedbeds, islands and lagoons linked together by channels. The reedbeds contain dense stands of a number of reed species, while the islands are home to water-loving fig and palm trees. Colourful waterlilies are scattered throughout most of the waterways and in the lagoons.

Northern Kalahari — takes in a broad band across Namibia and Botswana from Etosha pan, through the Tsodilo Hills to Makgadikgadi and Nxai pans — is characterised by a tree and bush savannah, interspersed by patches of open grassland. The soil is a nutrient-poor sand or sand/gravel mix, on which the *mopane* tree grows particularly well. *Mopane* is easily identified by its characteristic paired leaves that have earned it the name 'butterfly tree'. *Mopane's* deep red wood burns well and its bark is home to a large white grub — *mopane worm*, larva of the moth *Gonimbrasia belina* — eaten as a delicacy by the local people. (Try them roasted!)

Namibia's central plateau runs north-south through the centre of the country, dominated by extensive plains of shrub and grass. This is Namibia's agricultural heartland, with the land being used mostly for livestock farming, especially cattle rearing.

The central and southern Kalahari covers the majority of the remaining surface area of Namibia and Botswana. Rolling, mostly stabilised, dunes are interspersed by gravel plains and clay pans. The dunes are often thinly covered with grasses, while the gravel plains sustain a variety of shrubs, grasses and even occasional trees. Perhaps the most remarkable of these, occurring on the Kalahari's edge in southern Namibia, is the very distinctive *Kokerboom (Aloe dichotoma)* which stands aloof on the most inhospitable of rocky hillsides.

The Namib Desert, unlike the Kalahari, appears to the visitor to be a 'proper' desert, consisting of only barren, unvegetated sand dunes. Elsewhere the Namib is a desert of huge gravel plains, often covered with a carpet of fragile and beautiful lichens. On these plains, plants grow slowly and may live for centuries — the strangely contorted *welwitschia mirabilis* can live for over a 1000 years. Winding through even the driest areas are occasional ribbons of green. These linear oases, along the lines of old river valleys, come as a surprise and are sustained by the constant (if small) underground flow of the rivers.

Fauna: Mammals and Birdlife

Namibia and Botswana are both well known for their diverse range of wildlife and birdlife. Most of the major African game species can be found, along with a number of species that are endemic to the region. Compared to the rest of Africa the game has been well protected from the scourge of poaching — both Botswana and Namibia have good wildlife conservation records and, in general, the political will to keep it that way (especially as tourism becomes an increasingly important source of income).

The mammals are typical of savannah areas throughout sub-saharan Africa. Since the climate is drier than the rest of the sub-continent, however, the land can only support a lower density of animals than is the norm elsewhere. But the infrequent permanent sources of water result in game becoming all the more concentrated by the drinking places that do exist during the dry season — a major bonus for the game viewer!

The region's wetlands (Okavango, Linyanti and Caprivi) are a bird-watcher's paradise throughout most of the year. However, the best time of year is undoubtedly from November to April when palaearctic migrants come south, adding to the numerous indigenous species already present. At this time of year many of the pans may partially fill with water and become home to huge flocks of birds overnight.

Whilst here don't overlook the reptiles, insects and smaller animals that abound. Many exhibit fascinating adaptations to their environment, such as the Namib's fog-basking beetles, and are at least as interesting as the larger game. Even the ants here are worth watching — look out for those which forage in columns, if disturbed they'll hiss at you. Descriptions of some of these interesting smaller beasties have been incorporated into the regional guide, many more will fascinate you if you take the time to look for them.

Summary of major game and birdlife areas

Each of the areas described below are dealt with in detail in their respective chapters in parts two and three of the book. However, for ease of seeing at a glance which are the best game or bird-watching areas (and at what time of year), we have included the following summary in alphabetical order:

Chobe Famous for the large herds of elephant that visit the Chobe river during the dry season. Savuti, in the centre of Chobe national park, is excellent for big game, especially lion and buffalo. When the Savuti channel flowed and supplied the Savuti marsh, this was considered to be one of Africa's top game spots.

Etosha In the dry season this is one of Africa's best game areas — don't miss it. As well as huge herds antelope, wildebeest, zebra etc. — and good numbers of cats — the rarities found here include black-faced impala, mountain zebras and red hartebeest. It's also probably your best chance to spot an elusive black rhino.

Bird-watching is also good — Fisher's Pan is the best place for waders, often keeping its water longer than the main pan in the dry season. The large number of raptors include the black, or king, vulture. In the dry season, look out for the snake-eating secretary birds and the startling crimson-breasted shrike.

Kaokoveld Only fairly sparse populations of some of the big game species. Giraffe locally common, as are zebra, gemsbok and springbok but large predators are very scarce. The animals here are often very nervous and should not be approached too closely, even in a vehicle.

Kaudom Good for the quiet game spotter. Kaudom typically has less game than Etosha, but includes the uncommon roan antelope, tsessebe and reedbuck. All the big cats and even wild dog can be found here, but animals tend to be shy.

Khutse The game on the Khutse plains can be scarce and difficult to spot, so come for the experience of the Kalahari landscape more than glimpses of gemsbok! Animals are most plentiful following the rains when there is good grazing, typically from January to March.

Linyanti/Kwando The area is like a smaller version of the Okavango Delta from the point of view of bird-watching. It gets summer migrants, though not in quite the same numbers as the Okavango, and is especially good for cranes and egrets.

Mabuasehube A good reserve for quiet, undisturbed game viewing and probably best at the end of the rainy season, around March to May. Watch out for the Kalahari's 'black-maned' lions, and the entertaining troops of meerkats.

Mahango This is the single best area for bird-watching in Namibia, with over 300 species recorded. Since it's situated at the north-western edge of the Okavango (see below), many species are common to both areas.

Makgadikgadi The presence of the Boteti river ensures game even in the dry season. Numbers are highly variable, however, with wildebeest, zebra and springbok usually in the most common. Look out also for red hartebeest and cheetah.

If the Makgadikgadi pans fill with water then, like Etosha, there's a chance they will be inundated by thousands of breeding flamingos. Don't miss it if you are in the country — although at other times there is much less to see.

Mamili and Mudumu Sitatunga, red lechwe and the very rare puku are the main attractions here, though many species are represented. The bigger game includes elephant, sable, roan and reedbuck and even an occasional leopard or cheetah.

Moremi Gradually building up an excellent reputation (perhaps taking on some of Savuti's mantle), this is the park in which to view the Okavango's big game. Dry season is best, and the copious game includes large numbers of buffalo and lion.

Namib-Naukluft Scattered groups of gemsbok, springbok, mountain zebra and ostrich are often the only visible game here. Many other inhabitants are nocturnal — so come for the scenery and let any animals be a bonus.

Namibian coast For bird-watching the lagoons around Walvis Bay and on the Lüderitz peninsula are frequent haunts for migrant waders, as are the occasional freshwater 'seeps' which occur along the length of the coast. Halifax island, near Lüderitz, has the region's only colony of jackass penguins, while the coast north of Swakopmund is home to the rare and endemic damara tern.

In Sandwich harbour large flocks of flamingos, pelicans and other residents are found, in the company of huge numbers of migrants at the right time of year. It is estimated that over 40,000 birds use these lagoons to overwinter every season.

Nxai Timing is everything — visit at just the right time of year (somewhere between January and April!) and you'll witness the migration of large herds of springbok, wildebeest and zebra, along with attendant lion. In general the open nature of the country favours cheetah and plains species, rather than leopard, elephant or buffalo.

Okavango Delta From a *mokoro* game-viewing is difficult — apart from spotting hippos and crocs! Walking on the islands is sometimes better, but make sure you have a guide who knows what he's doing.

However, for birds, the Okavango Delta is unequalled in the region. Whether you set off in a *mokoro* or aim to drive along the edge of Moremi, you're unlikely to be disappointed. If you're interested in a particular species, good local guides will help you find the best places.

Skeleton Coast Not really a game park, but it does have fascinating populations of desert-adapted elephant and black rhino. The coast and river valleys are home to rare brown hyena, and visited by the odd lion. Further inland zebra, gemsbok, impala and ostrich can be found.

Waterberg Notable as home to nucleus populations of reintroduced species, including roan, sable, tsessebe and white rhino. Existing game includes giraffe, eland, cheetah and leopard — though apparently no lion.

CONSERVATION AND DEVELOPMENT

A great deal has been written about conservation in Africa, much of which is over-simplistic and intentionally emotive. As a visitor, you are in a unique position to experience some of the many issues at first hand and ask the local people for their own perspectives. It's not so much a matter of balancing points of view, but of bringing out and smashing the various preconceptions and prejudices we all sub-consciously harbour — highlighting for once the complexity of the situation in all its detail. In this section we have tried to develop a few of the underlying ideas common to all areas where conservation is seen as being at odds with development. Specific conservation issues in Namibia and Botswana are discussed under their relevant sections in the book.

To start with, *conservation* must be taken in its widest sense — saving the animals, for example, is no use if it is done at the expense of peoples' livelihoods. Most people in 'developing' countries are deeply conscious of their fragile environment, but for many of them the day to day need to feed themselves, and purchase basic commodities, can often result in their environment's degradation. On a larger scale, governments may (understandably) put their nations development at a higher priority than conservation of their environment, seeing conservation as a luxury that only 'developed' countries can afford. There's no point in us sitting comfortably in the West proclaiming the wisdom of conservation, when it's not our livelihood or standard of living being affected.

Whilst there is clearly much that the 'developed' world can and should do to help the situation, any long-term solutions must rest in the approach and work undertaken by the local population and their government. And any such solution can only be in methods which preserve the natural environment as well as allowing continuing economic advance for the local people. In other words, sound ecology also means solving social problems — all too often the worst enemy of nature is simply poverty. In practice this means reconciling, and indeed integrating, the twin objectives of conservation and development — ultimately, anyhow, one cannot exist without the other. For both Namibia and Botswana, development is quite rightly a national priority — in the short as well as long terms. The problems only arise when development is clearly at the expense of conservation.

The *careful and planned* development of tourism is one possible way (of particular relevance to both Namibia and Botswana) in which conservation and development can be integrated. In simplistic terms, an area and its wildlife can be conserved if, by developing tourism, the conserved area can be made to *pay* for itself. If the financial returns from tourism are larger than any other (destructive) use that the area might be put to (for example, mining and cattle grazing), then the area has been safely conserved indefinitely. Any situation where a conserved area could be more profitably used is inevitably in an unstable situation — protective laws can always be changed.

For such a scenario to work, the development of tourism must necessarily be both sustainable and undamaging to the environment. Botswana's approach in its national parks and reserves has, since 1989, been one of high-cost/low-density tourism, together with a limited amount of licensed hunting. This aims to maintain (and even increase) the revenue from the conserved areas, whilst minimising the negative impact that tourists can have upon the environment. In essence it's a damage limitation exercise, but it's questionable if this will prove to be a long term solution. Geologists are presently prospecting for oil in the huge Central Kalahari Game Reserve, whilst the Okavango Delta (most of which is not protected in a conservation area) is under threat of having its valuable water drained for the Orapa diamond mine and agriculture.

Newly independent Namibia is still evolving its own wildlife policy, which often requires the needs of the wildlife to be balanced against those of the local people. All too often throughout the world, indigenous people have been thrown off their land to make way for the establishment of national parks or reserves, which fail to take into account the fact that people are as much part of the environment as flora and fauna.

One positive example is the government designated 'wilderness area' of Namibia's northern coast, where Himba people have lived and hunted animals for centuries. Now, by involving the local people with the controlled *development* of game viewing and tourism in the area, the Himba are able to generate an alternative income (from the safari operators) by becoming the *conservators* of the remaining wildlife. In this instance conservation and development have been successfully united, and the situation appears stable over the long term.

FIELD GUIDES

Many excellent guides to the flora and fauna of Southern Africa are published in South Africa. The following are all available from the Natural History Book Service, 2 Wills Rd. Totnes, Devon TQ9 5XN, England. Their catalogue also contains other natural history books pertaining to southern Africa and not listed here.

General

The Natural History of Southern Africa, D. Bristow and G. Cubitt. New Holland. £14.95. A good overview, illustrated with colour photos.

Nature of Botswana IUCN, Cambridge. £11.95. Of scientific interest only.

Fauna

Birds of Botswana, Kenneth Newman. Southern Books. £12.95. The first fully comprehensive guide to the avifauna of Botswana, describing and illustrating more than 550 species in colour, plus distribution maps.

The Nature Photo-guide to the Birds of Southern Africa, Ian Sinclair. New Holland. £9.95. A new guide showing 250 species most commonly seen in the region.

Ian Sinclair's Field Guide to the Birds of Southern Africa, Ian Sinclair. Collins. £12.95. Illustrated by colour photos; 900 species identified.

Newman's Birds of Southern Africa, Kenneth Newman. Macmillan, £14.95.

Considered by most to be the best of the field guides covering this region. 2000 illustrations.

Robert's Birds of Southern Africa, Gordon Maclean. New Holland, £22.50. The bible of serious birdwatchers; too heavy (848 pages) for most travellers.

Where to Watch Birds in Southern Africa, A.Berruti and J.C. Sinclair. New Holland, £9.95. Contains 64 colour photos

A Field Guide to the Mammals of Southern Africa, C & T Stuart. New Holland, £12.95. Habitat, behaviour and a distribution map for each species. Illustrated with photos.

The Land Mammals of Southern Africa, R. Smithers. Macmillan, £10.95. An informative identification guide to the 200 species most likely to be seen. Illustrated with colour plates.

Predators of Southern Africa, Hans Grobler and others. Southern Books. £8.95. Describes behaviour, tracks, habitat and distribution of 36 species.

Field Guide to the Snakes and other Reptiles of Southern Africa, Bill Branch. New Holland (South Africa). £13.95. Full descriptions, colour photos and maps.

Snakes and Snakebite, John Visser and David Chapman. New Holland. £9.95. Venomous Snakes and management of snakebite in southern Africa. Could be very useful if you are likely to be unusually exposed to snakes.

A Field Guide to the Butterflies of Southern Africa, Ivor Migdoll. New Holland, £9.95. 232 of the more commonly found species, illustrated with photos.

Flora

Flowers of Southern Africa, Auriol Batten. Southern Books. £67. 100 colour reproductions of outstanding paintings of flowers. Too big to be a field guide, but a beautiful souvenir.

Namaqualand wildflower guide, A. Le Roux and T. Schelpe. New Holland. £11.95. Although it only covers a small area of Namibia, this guide will be useful for both countries.

Trees of Southern Africa, E Palmer and N Pitman. A.A. Balkema. Available in South Africa. A detailed reference work — but rather heavy for most purposes.

Chapter 4

Planning and preparations

GETTING THERE

By Air

At present, the options for air travel to Namibia and Botswana are fairly limited. British Airways flies twice a week to Gaborone from London at £625 (a good flexible ticket). At the time of writing, this is also the cheapest ticket to the region from Europe. (British Airways International Reservations (UK) Tel: 081-897 4000.) UTA, the French Airline, also flies to Gaborone from Paris, and Lufthansa has a service from Frankfurt to Windhoek.

If you do decide to fly to Windhoek, then your cheapest option from Europe will probably be via Lusaka on Zambia Airways (as low as £450 from London). Going via Johannesburg is undoubtedly easier, but at present more expensive. The situation is bound to change now that Namibia is independent.

One of cheapest way to get to either Namibia or Botswana is to fly to the 'gateway' countries of either Zimbabwe or South Africa — which you should manage for as little as £550 — and then go overland by rail, bus or hitch. Whilst Botswana is easily accessible from both Zimbabwe and South Africa, Namibia is only readily accessible from South Africa.

Finding cheap tickets is an art in itself — so rather than give specific information here which is bound to be quickly out of date, your best bet is to visit one of the specialist travel agents with specific interest in Africa. These will also often be able to help you with tours, advice, insurance and even vaccinations.

Africa Travel Centre 4 Medway Court, Leigh St, London WC1H 9QX. Tel: 071-387 1211. A small and highly efficient set-up, catering specially for the independent traveller, with the latest cheap flight deals and honest, reliable advice. Strongly recommended.

Trailfinders 42-48 Earls Court Rd, London W8 6EJ. Tel: 071-938 3366. Another specialist outfit, Trailfinders also offers advice on overland trips backed up by an extensive library and a vaccination centre.

STA HQ at 117 Euston Rd, London NW1 2SX. Tel: 071-465 0486. One of the most popular agents for good flight deals, with branches in Britain's main cities, as well as in the USA and Australia. STA has a specific 'Africa Desk', and both the advantages and disadvantages of a large company.

By Land

Botswana has fast and direct road and rail links with Zimbabwe and South Africa. Crossing between Botswana and Namibia is slow and laborious — only for those with their own vehicle, or lots of spare hitching time.

Namibia has fast and direct links with South Africa — good tarred roads and a railway service.

For full details on air, rail and road transport into and out of the region, check the *In Namibia* and *In Botswana* chapters (pages 78 and 202).

Crossing Borders

Namibia-Botswana Between Namibia and Botswana there are three border crossings: Buitepos, on the Gobabis-Ghanzi road (open from 7.30am until 5pm); Ngoma Bridge, between Eastern Caprivi and Kasane (open from 8am until 4pm); and Mohembo, between Popa Falls and Shakawe (should be open from 8am until 6pm but it's not a well-established post and so don't rely too heavily on these times).

Namibia-South Africa Coming into Namibia from South Africa there are two main posts: Nakop, between Upington and Karasburg; and Noordoewer, on the main B1 between Keetmanshoop and Cape Town. These are open from 8am until 6pm.

Botswana-Zimbabwe Ramokwebana on the Francistown-Bulawayo road (open from 6am to 6pm daily); Kazungula Road, on the route from Kasane to Victoria Falls (open 6am to 6pm daily).

Botswana-South Africa There are numerous border crossings between these two countries all the way along the border. The main crossing is Ramatlabama, on the Gaborone-Mafikeng road (open 7am to 8pm).

Botswana-Zambia The Kazungula ferry across the Chobe River (6am to 6pm daily).

VISAS AND ENTRY REQUIREMENTS

Namibia

Citizens of the following countries do not need a visa to enter Namibia:

Angola, Austria, Botswana, Canada, France, Germany, Italy, Japan, Mozambique, Scandinavian countries, Tanzania, UK, USA, Zambia and Zimbabwe. It is best to check, since the situation is likely to change as newly-independent Namibia finds its feet in the international community. Pre-independence Namibia was represented abroad by South Africa — this has now largely changed, and Namibian embassies/high commissions are being established. If there is no Namibian representative near you then Zambian High Commissions are apparently empowered to issue Namibian visas.

The maximum tourist stay is 60 days, but this can be easily extended by application in Windhoek. You may be required to show proof of the 'means to leave' — ie onward air ticket, credit card, sufficient funds, vehicle etc — though so far we have not come across anyone having difficulty at a Namibian border.

Botswana

Citizens of the Commonwealth, EC countries, USA and South Africa do not need a visa (except for Ghana, India, Mauritius, Nigeria and Sri Lanka). Like Namibia, you may be required to show a ticket home and sufficient funds to cover your costs in the country. The maximum allowed stay for a tourist is three months in the year, though only a one month stamp is usually issued at first. You can fairly easily renew your entry stamp at a local Department of Immigration office.

UK Telephone Numbers

Namibia Visas, Tel: 071-589 6655
Namibia General, Tel: 071-408 2333
Botswana High Commission, Tel: 071-499 0031
South African Embassy, Tel: 071-930 4488

WHEN TO GO

There really isn't a bad time to visit Namibia or Botswana, but there are times when some attractions are better than others. You must decide what you are primarily interested in and then, using the specific information in the following relevant chapters, choose accordingly. However, the weather and South African school holidays do provide broad constraints on the best time to go.

Weather

Weather follows a southern hemisphere sub-tropical pattern: mid-May to mid August, 'winter', cool (very cold at night, 0°c-5°c on average) and very dry with clear skies; mid-August to November, 'spring', warming quickly to top temperatures (35°c-40°c on average), no rain but clouds building up; November to mid-March, 'summer', hot and humid, 'rainy' season; mid-March to mid-May, 'autumn', limited rain, temperatures dropping. You are very unlikoly to encounter prolonged heavy rain anywhere except in the extreme north of the region.

The game in specific areas varies with the seasons — in general, the drier parks are best just after the rains (February — April), whilst those with permanent surface water are better toward the end of the dry season (August — October).

South African School Holidays

The South African school holiday periods are times to avoid — Namibia particularly is a popular holiday destination for South Africans. Holiday periods do vary, but lie within the following times: the last two weeks of March and the first two of April; the last week of June and the first two of July; the last week of September and the first of October; the last three weeks of December and the first two weeks of January.

MONEY

Budgeting

Neither of these countries is cheap, but costs can be kept to reasonable levels depending on how you choose to travel. To do even a rough budget, decide on the following main factors (refer to the relevant sections in this chapter and in the '*In Namibia*' and '*In Botswana*' chapters): hiring a vehicle or not; hotels/'camps' or camping; how you visit the Okavango Delta; and how much time you wish to spend in Botswana's game parks.

How to Take your Money

Many travellers take their money mostly as Sterling or US dollars travellers cheques, with just a hundred or so Pula (and/or Rand) for when they first arrive. Banks in the cities will cash any travellers cheques, but American Express and Barclays Visa seem to be particularly well recognised. American Express has a reputation for issuing prompt replacements if they are stolen, and by carrying them you are eligible to use their customer mail-drop facilities in Windhoek and Gaborone — so by choice, these are best. Having said that, the major credit cards (Visa, Mastercard, American Express and Diners Club) are widely accepted — and have the advantage that your bills will take time to filter home through the system. Taking out money at the banks from credit cards is very easy, and you only have to change money as you need it.

WHAT TO BRING

This is an impossible question to answer fully, as it depends upon how you travel and where you go. If you plan to do a lot of hitching or backpacking, then you should plan carefully what you take in an attempt to keep things as light as possible. If you have a vehicle for your whole trip, then weight and bulk will not be such a problem.

Clothing

For most of your time during the day all you will really want is light, loose-fitting cotton clothing. Cotton (or a cotton-rich mix) is cooler and more absorbent than synthetic fibres, making it much more comfortable. For men shorts (long ones) are usually OK, but long trousers are more socially acceptable in towns and especially in rural settlements and villages. For women a knee-length skirt or culottes is the ideal. Botswana and Namibia have a generally conservative dress code — 'revealing' or scruffy clothing isn't respected or appreciated by most Batswana or Namibians, especially outside their capital cities.

For the evenings, or those chilling rides in the back of pick-ups, you will need something warm. Night-time temperatures in the winter months can be very low. If possible, dress in layers — taking along a light sweater and a long sleeved jacket, or a track suit, and a light but waterproof anorak.

Camping Equipment

Tent Mosquito netting and good ventilation is essential, as is a tent that isn't too small. A small tent at home may feel cosy and warm, but is likely to be unbearably hot and claustrophobic in the desert.

Mat A ground mat of some sort is essential for warmth at night, protection of the tent's groundsheet from rough stony ground (put it underneath the tent), and comfort. The ubiquitous closed cell foam mats are good and readily available. Genuine Karrimats and Therm-a-Rest (a combination air-mattress/foam mat) are quite expensive, but much stronger and more durable — worth the investment.

Sleeping Bag A three-season down bag is an ideal choice, being the lightest bag that is still warm enough for the cold winter nights, and yet small and light to carry. Synthetic bag fillings are cheaper, but for the same warmth are heavier and much more bulky. They do have the advantage that they keep their warmth when wet, unlike down, but clearly this is not an important consideration in the Kalahari!

Sheet Sleeping Bag Thin cotton sheet sleeping bags (eg YHA design), are good protection for your main sleeping bag, keeping it cleaner. They can, of course, be used on their own when your main bag is too hot.

Stove 'Trangia'-type stoves which burn methylated spirits are simple to use, light, and cheap to run. They come complete with a set of light aluminium pans and a very useful all-purpose handle. Often you'll be able to cook on a fire with the pans, but it's nice to have the option of making a brew in a few minutes while you set up camp. Canisters for gas stoves are available in the main towns if you prefer to use these, but are expensive and bulky. Petrol- and kerosene-burning stoves are undoubtedly efficient on fuel and powerful — but invariably temperamental, messy, and unreliable in the dusty desert.

Torch (flashlight) Find one that's small and tough — preferably water and sand-proof. Head-mounted torches leave your hands free — very useful when you are cooking over a campfire or mending the car — but some people find them bulky. The new range of small super-strong and super-bright torches (such as Maglites) are good, but have unusual (and expensive) bulbs — bring several spares with you.

Water Containers If you're thinking of hiking, you should bring a strong, collapsible water-bag for times when you will be away from a close source of water. 10 litres is a useful size, and probably the most you'll ever consider carrying on top of your normal kit. (10 litres of water weighs 10kg.) Large plastic containers for the car can be bought when you arrive. For everyday use, a small one-litre water bottle is invaluable.

Other Useful Items

Obviously no list can be comprehensive, or reflect everyone's likes and dislikes. The following items are just intended as ideas and memory joggers: A roll of insulating tape — for taping parcels and general repairs; plenty of 'sunblock' or high factor sun lotion and lipsalve; sunglasses — preferably strong, dark and with high U-V absorption; nylon cord — buy 20m or so, for emergencies and washing lines; a Swiss Army knife — how does anyone survive without one?; a couple of short paperback novels — essential for hitchers; large plastic bags to line your pack and protect your belongings from dust (bin-liners — garbage bags — are good); a light pair of binoculars — essential for game spotting; a plastic bowl, mug and set of cutlery; several disposable lighters; long-life candles; compass and whistle; cheap, waterproof watch; concentrated, biodegradable washing detergent; universal plug; basic sewing kit (with good strong thread suitable for backpacks — dental floss works well); a magnifying glass for a closer look at nature's wonders (eg page 156).

MAPS

A good selection of maps is available in Europe and the USA from specialised outlets. The Michelin map of East and Southern Africa (sheet 995) is probably the best for both Namibia and Botswana; the newly published Freytag & Berndt map of Namibia also looks good.

Imported maps are obtainable in Europe from Stanfords, London (Tel: 071-836 1321) or Geocenter, Stuttgart, Germany (Tel: 711 788 9340). In the USA try Map Link, Santa Barbara, California (Tel: 805 965 4402).

It is cheaper to delay your map buying until you arrive in Namibia or Botswana. If you are venturing into the bush you will need more detailed regional maps, or aerial photographs which may prove a lot more useful for areas where a map can show no more than a massive expanse of sand or bush. Aerial pictures may take a week or more to order.

Namibia The standard visitor's map is published by the DNC and available free at most tourist centres and information offices. It has useful distance tables as well as street maps of Windhoek and Swakopmund on the back.

Regional maps and aerial photos are available from the Surveyor General's office in Windhoek, to the right of the Post Office on Independence Way.

Botswana The deceptively simple Shell Oil map is all that most people need; it has handy maps of the main national parks and reserves on the back. Detailed maps of Moremi, Chobe and Nxai Pan are usually available from book shops or national park offices.

Large scale maps and aerial photos may be bought from the Department of Surveys and Lands in Gaborone, east of the train station, and also (a limited selection) from the Department's offices in Francistown and Selebi-Phikwe. Mail-order catalogues can be obtained from Private Bag 0037, Gaborone. Tel: 53251.

PHOTOGRAPHY

Cameras

35mm SLR cameras with interchangeable lenses offer you the greatest flexibility. For general photography, a mid-range zoom lens (eg 28-70mm) is recommended — it is much more useful than the 'standard' (50mm) lens. For wildlife photography, you will need at least a 200mm lens to allow you to see the animal close in. Alternatively (or in addition), compact cameras take up little space and are excellent to have handy for quick shots of people or scenes — though they are of no use for game.

Film

Film is expensive in both Namibia and Botswana, and the choice is limited. Print films are readily available in main towns, but slide films are only occasionally available and rarely process-paid. Kodachrome used to be unobtainable in Namibia as a result of sanctions, but this is changing.

Bring a range of film speeds depending on what type of photography you are most interested in. For most landscape shots, where you will have plenty of light, a 'slow' film (100ASA or less) will give the best results. For wildlife photography, you will need a 'faster' film (400ASA) to enable you to use your telephoto lens without fear of camera-shake. Films, especially when exposed, can deteriorate very quickly in the heat. Keep all films (and therefore your loaded camera) away from direct sunlight, preferably in a cool box.

Pictures taken at dusk or dawn will have the richest, deepest colours, whilst those taken during the middle of the day often seem pale and washed-out in comparison. Beware of the very deep shadows and high contrast so typical of tropical countries. Film cannot 'see' the huge range from black to white that your eye can. If you want to take pictures of people (or any showing full shadow details) in very bright conditions, then it's worth investing some time learning how to deal with these situations. By restricting your photography to mornings and evenings, you will encounter fewer problems.

Camera equipment should be very carefully protected from dust and sand — use plastic bags if necessary. You should bring some lens tissues and a blower brush to clean the dust from your lenses — and it is a good idea to use the brush to clean any dust from the back pressure-plate of your camera each time you change a film — particles caught here can easily cause long straight scratches along the entire length of your film.

CAR HIRE

Many of Namibia and Botswana's attractions are game reserves and wilderness areas, which are sparsely populated, not well served by public transport, and difficult to get to. To reach them, the visitor must rely on unpredictable lifts, or get together to hire a vehicle.

What kind of vehicle to hire, and where to get it from, should be thought about well before arriving in the country — and if you have arranged a small group to travel with, then it can be worth organising the car hire itself in advance as there are often special deals available outside the country, either through overseas branches of the hire companies or via the airlines. If you are flying into the region, do check these out before you buy your flights.

Avis International Reservations and Information (UK). Tel: 081-848 8733.
Budget International Reservations and Information (UK). Tel: 0800-181181.
Hertz International Reservations and Information (UK). Tel: 081-679 1799.

Choosing the right vehicle to hire will depend largely upon where you intend to visit, and how much money you have. The best for rough roads, and the only ones for some terrain, are high-clearance 4WD vehicles — though they are expensive to hire and run. That said, most of Namibia's sights can be seen using an ordinary 2WD saloon car — the exceptions being Kaudom, the Linyanti Area and the northern parts of the Kaokoveld — so hiring a 2WD for Namibia can work well. Botswana is different — only the roads between the few main towns are accessible by 2WD, in addition to a few parts of northern Chobe and the Makgadikgadi Game Reserve. A trip here really needs a 4WD to get deep into the parks, remote areas and the Kalahari desert. (See also Chapter 6, *Driving and Camping in the Bush*.)

Hiring a Saloon Car

Firstly, where you hire is important, as it can affect the price and the conditions of hire. Because South Africa, Botswana and Namibia belong to the same South African customs union, hired cars can normally move freely across their mutual borders. This allows a regional trip to be planned which takes advantage of the large differences in car-hire rates between various locations. Prices do vary from city to city, with South Africa generally being the cheapest. Botswana and Namibia are more expensive, have rates which differ more widely between the towns, and generally have more restrictions. You seem to get less favourable deals as you go north — but whilst searching for the cheapest rates, beware of excessive drop-off charges on some one-way hires.

The three big hire companies within the region are **Avis**, **Budget rent-a-car**, and **Imperial**. Of these Avis is easily the largest and has the best network of offices (including some in Botswana). Locally, their prices tend to be similar, even if the conditions vary. Imperial is associated with **Hertz** — so any international booking done through Hertz will be with Imperial. Typical on-the-road prices per day from any of these three, based upon unlimited mileage during a three-week rental period are:

	Basic VW Golf	4-door saloon (air conditioned)	Toyota Twin-Cab (4WD)
South Africa	R90 (£18/$30)	R100 (£20/$33)	R200 (£43/$71)
Windhoek (Namibia)	R127(£25/$41)	R142 (£28/$46)	R300 (£63/$104)
Maun (Botswana)	P150(£45/$74)	P180 (£55/$91)	P290 (£88/$145)

Figures in brackets are in pounds sterling/US dollars, based on the current exchange rates (see pages 78 and 202), and should give you a good indication of the relative costs between hiring vehicles in the three countries. Bear in mind that a cheaper deal can often be had from smaller local companies, though you may not find have the same back-up.

If time is not in short supply but money is, consider just hiring for a few days at a time (on a time and mileage basis) to see specific sights. Then, for example, a basic VW Golf in Namibia would cost R65 per day plus 72c per kilometre — which might not be too expensive if you are planning on sitting by waterholes in Etosha all day. Similarly, weekend hire from Avis in Kasane for a few days in Victoria Falls can cost as little as P240 for three days.

Hiring a Four-wheel Drive Vehicle

This requires both money and planning, but having a four-wheel drive (4WD) at your disposal opens up endless possibilities, and gives you the chance to mount an expedition into the wilder parts of the sub-continent. Whilst they are available at some car hire offices, 4WD vehicles are much less numerous and will usually need to be booked in advance and returned by a specified date. The only places where you will find much choice are Maun and Windhoek — or possibly in South Africa.

Of the two, Maun tends to be more expensive, but is arguably more central to the area in which you need such a vehicle. Here Avis — by the airport — will charge around P260 (£78/$130) per day for a basic Toyota Twin-Cab. Perhaps the town's best bargain is Island Safari Lodge's chauffeur-driven 4WD for P190 (£58/$95) per day (100km per day free, then 75 thebe per km), especially for a short trip into Moremi or Chobe's Savuti.

Windhoek is home to the region's only 4WD specialists — **Kessler** car hire (see page 287). Found on the corner of Curt von Francois and Tal St, they have a variety of different types of 4WD — including the twin-cab Toyota Hilux which seats four in comfort — and also a couple of Land Rovers. Costs vary from around the R200 (£42/$69) upwards, depending upon the model, but unlike the larger companies, Kessler aims to hire out vehicles for long trips into the wilds. Equally unusual is a willingness to let vehicles go into Zimbabwe — which most other firms are just beginning to match.

The only drawback if you hire from here is that the car needs to be returned as well, necessitating a circular route — which is not always easy to plan. (A couple of such routes are given under *suggested itineraries* below.)

Note that for circular trips from either Maun and Windhoek you can hire all the camping kit that you will need, and a lot more besides, at Kalahari Kanvas or Gav's Camping Hire respectively.

SUGGESTED ITINERARIES

If you choose to hire a vehicle, your time will probably be limited by money, and you will need to plan carefully to make the most of your trip. These suggested itineraries are intended as a framework only, and the time spent at places is the minimum which is reasonable — if you have less time, then cut places out rather than try to quicken the pace of your trip. When planning your own itinerary, try to intersperse the longer drives between more restful days and avoid spending each night in a new place if you can — shifting camp can become very tedious. When touring Namibia, do book (permits, accommodation etc.) as much in advance as you can through Windhoek's DNC. To allow for this, we've included more detail in the itineraries with sections in Namibia, where advanced booking is sometimes a necessity.

Distances given are necessarily approximate, and are based on the *minimum* distances between two destinations by the shortest reasonable route. The distances do not allow for game driving or general exploration, which you must allow for yourself.

Etosha — Namib Tour, Windhoek round trip

2WD, Namibia, minimum of 2½ weeks, approx. 2,500km

Day 1: Leave Windhoek for Waterberg. 286km.
Day 2: Waterberg Plateau.
Day 3: Buy food at Otavi, eat at Lake Otjikoto, arrive at Namutoni before sunset. 383km.
Day 4: Game viewing around Namutoni.
Day 5: Game viewing around Namutoni.
Day 6: Long lunch at Halali, if open, then to Okaukuejo. 123km.
Day 7: Game viewing around Okaukuejo.
Day 8: Late lunch at Outjo — buy supplies — then to Khorixas. 250km.
Day 9: Visit the burnt mountain, organ pipes, Twyfelfontein and the petrified forest; camp out at Brandberg (no facilities!). 271km.
Day 10: Look around Brandberg; then to Swakopmund via Henties Bay. 232km.
Day 11: Relax and replenish supplies in Swakopmund.
Day 12: Explore the Namib Park; camp at Homeb or Mirabib. 158km.
Day 13: Leisurely drive to Sesriem, via the Gaub Pass and Solitaire. 259km.
Day 14: Pre-dawn drive/walk to Sossusvlei; Sesriem Canyon later. 120km.
Day 15: Short drive to Naukluft, afternoon there. 108km.
Day 16: A longer hike around Naukluft.
Day 17: Return to Windhoek to eat out and relax. 249km.

Okavango — Etosha Tour, Gaborone to Windhoek

2WD/4WD, Namibia and Botswana, minimum of 2½ weeks, approx. 3,200km.

Day 1: Start from Gaborone, buy supplies; sleep at Francistown. 433km.
Day 2: Drive to Makgadikgadi Game Reserve via Nata. Camp in reserve. 360km.
Day 3: Explore Makgadikgadi game Reserve and drive to Maun. 145km
Day 4: Okavango Delta trip. (Must be pre-arranged, or it takes longer).
Day 5: Okavango Delta trip.

Day 6: Okavango Delta trip.
Day 7: Return from Okavango Delta trip.
*Day 8: Leave Maun on long drive to Kasane, via Nata. 616km
Day 9: Early game drive into northern Chobe, stay at Serondela or Kasane.
Day 10: Cross into Namibia via Ngoma Bridge; spend the night and buy food, at Katima Mulilo. 114km
Day 11: A rough day's drive to Popa Falls. 313km.
Day 12: Look around Popa and Mahango; afternoon drive to Rundu. 219km.
Day 13: Long drive to Namutoni, Etosha. 415km.
Day 14: Game viewing around Namutoni.
Day 15: Leisurely lunch at Halali, if open, then onto Okaukuejo. 123km.
Day 16: Game viewing around Okaukuejo.
Day 17: Game viewing around Okaukuejo.
Day 18: Long drive to end tour at Windhoek. 435km.

*4WD alternative: spend day 8 driving to Lake Ngami (95km), days 9 and 10 at the Tsodilo Hills (approx. 320km), and continue to Popa via Shakawe on the Okavango's southern bank (approx. 120km).

Botswana Parks Tour, Maun Round Trip

One self-sufficient 4WD, minimum of 2 weeks, approx. 1,500km.

Day 1: Leave Maun for Nxai Pan National Park. 185km.
Day 2: Explore Nxai Pan National Park.
Day 3: Kudiakam Pan and Baines' Baobabs.
Day 4: Drive to Makgadikgadi Pans Game Reserve. 100km.
Day 5: Explore Makgadikgadi Pans Game Reserve.
Day 6: Drive to Sowa Pan via main Maun-Nata road. 235km.
Day 7: Explore Sowa Pan and Kubu Island; drive to Nata Lodge. 110km.
Day 8: Drive to Serondela via Kasane; relax by Chobe river in evening! 320km.
Day 9: Head into Chobe National Park.
Day 10: Arrive at Savuti by evening. 180km *from Serondela*.
Day 11: Game viewing at Savuti.
Day 12: Drive south into Moremi Wildlife Reserve.
Day 13: Exploring Moremi.
Day 14: Leave Moremi to arrive Maun by evening. 335km including 'grand tour' of Moremi *from Savuti*.

Okavango — Linyanti Tour, Maun Round Trip

One self-sufficient 4WD, Botswana and Namibia, minimum of 2 weeks, approx. 1,500km.

Day 1: Leave Maun for Lake Ngami, camping by the lake. 95km.
Day 2: Early start for the Tsodilo Hills. approx. 320km.
Day 3: Whole day exploring the hills.
Day 4: North into Namibia via Shakawe, staying at Popa. 120km.
Day 5: Day to explore Mahango and Popa.
Day 6: East across the Caprivi Strip, into the Mudumu and Mamili Parks. 310km.

Day 7: Explore Mudumu/Mamili area.
Day 8: Explore Mudumu/Mamili area.
Day 9: Back into Botswana; replenish supplies and stay at Kasane. 114km.
Day 10: Into Chobe, camping at Serondela. 30km.
Day 11: Drive to Savuti; stay at campsite. 180km.
Day 12: Whole day spent exploring the Savuti area.
Day 13: A day game viewing, en route to Moremi Wildlife Reserve.
Day 14: Day in Moremi, returning to Maun by the evening. 245km.

'Grand Tour', Windhoek Round Trip

One self-sufficient 4WD, Namibia and Botswana, minimum of 3 weeks, approx. 3,800km.

Day 1: Leave Windhoek on the C26, go north to Gaga after crossing the Kuiseb, then left and right via Hotsas onto the C28 to Swakopmund. 370km.
Day 2: Day at Sandwich Harbour; stay at Swakopmund. 160km.
Day 3: Via the coast to Brandberg; camp there. 235km.
Day 4: Aim for Palmwag, via Twyfelfontein, the organ pipes and the petrified forest. 287km.
Day 5: Slowly explore the Concession Area near Palmwag.
Day 6: Cross-country to Okaukuejo. 302km.
Day 7: Long lunch at Halali, if open, then to Namutoni. 123km.
Day 8: Game viewing around Namutoni.
Day 9: Leave after lunch to get supplies and stay at Grootfontein. 167km.
Day 10: Full day to reach Popa Falls. 465km.
Day 11: Day trip from Popa to explore Mahango. 80km.
Day 12: Early start south; lunch by the Okavango then to Tsodilo Hills. 120km.
Day 13: Whole day at Tsodilo Hills.
Day 14: Make an early start to reach Maun late afternoon. 355km.
Day 15: Replenish supplies and head out to Moremi Wildlife Reserve in the late afternoon. Approx. 100km.
Day 16: Explore Moremi.
Day 17: Explore Moremi.
Day 18: Leave early for Lake Ngami. 200km.
Day 19: Drive to Ghanzi, leaving time to look around in evening. 215km.
Day 20: Very long drive from Ghanzi to Windhoek via Gobabis. 525km (last 205km on tar!).

Namibian Bush Tour, Windhoek round trip

Two self-sufficient 4WDs, minimum of 3½ weeks, approx. 4,100km.

Day 1: Leave Windhoek for Sesriem, via the C24's Remhoogte Pass. 322km
Day 2: Pre-dawn drive to Sossusvlei; Sesriem Canyon in the afternoon. 140km.
Day 3: Into the Namib Park; camp at Ganab. 221km.

Day 4: More time in the Namib; to Swakopmund in the late afternoon. 140km.
Day 5: Buy supplies and relax in Swakopmund, perhaps see Welwitschia Drive.
Day 6: Whole day trip to Sandwich Harbour. 160km.
Day 7: Leave Swakopmund via the coast road; camp at Brandberg. 235km.
Day 8: Aim for Palmwag, via Twyfelfontein, the organ pipes and the petrified forest. 287km.
Day 9: Slowly explore the Concession Area near Palmwag.
Day 10: Leave for Sesfontein — camp in the bush near there. 115km.
Day 11: Visit Kaoko Otavi and Opuwo, then camp en route to Kamanjab. 160km.
Day 12: Finish off the journey to Okaukuejo. 400km.
Day 13: Game viewing around Okaukuejo — after-dinner drinks at the floodlit waterhole.
Day 14: Long lunch at Halali, if open, then to Namutoni. 123km.
Day 15: Game viewing around Namutoni.
Day 16: Short drive to Grootfontein; replenish supplies. 167km.
Day 17: Full day to reach Popa Falls. 465km.
Day 18: Day trip from Popa to explore Mahango. 80km.
Day 19: Northern Kaudom via Katere; explore Kaudom *omuramba* itself. 147km.
Day 21: A slow trip south to Sikereti camp for the night. 75km.
Day 21: Further exploration of Kaudom, based at Sikereti.
Day 22: Early start for Grootfontein, visiting Tsumkwe en route. 350km.
Day 23: Back to Windhoek. 452km.

IN-COUNTRY TOURS AND SAFARIS

If you do intend to book a package within either Namibia or Botswana then there will be no shortage of choice. Often there is a 10% discount if you book within the country, and residents of southern Africa sometimes get more. Similarly, if you are booking off-season, or at short notice, then you should get a bargain — but don't expect miracles! Balanced against these advantages is the risk that you will not get what you want in the peak seasons.

Generally, if you are flexible about time and are coming in the off-season then look around and book in the country — if your time is limited or you are here when it is busy, then book well before you arrive. The centres for booking are Maun and Windhoek — though Gaborone, Swakopmund and Kasane all have agencies for a variety of trips, and of course Victoria Falls in Zimbabwe (just over the border from Kasane) is a major regional centre for travellers.

Details of how to book are given in *Part 2* and *Part 3*, together with specific information on some of the better deals available.

UK-Based Tour Operators

If you only have a few weeks' holiday you may prefer the security of booking a tour in England (or your home country). The following are reputable tour operators who run trips to Namibia and/or Botswana:

Okavango Tours and Safaris (see page 251). London address: 28 Bisham Gardens, London N6 6DD, England. Tel: 081-341 9442.

Okavango Explorations Regency House, 1/4 Warwick St, London W1R 5WB. Tel: 071-287 9672.

Naturetrek — Birding and Botanical tours. 40 The Dean, Alresford, Hants SO24 9AZ. Tel: 0962 733051.

Safariland Holidays 3 Crescent Stables, 139 Upper Richmond Rd, Putney, London SW15 2TN. Tel: 081-780 0030.

Grass Roots, 8 Lindsay Rd, Hampton Hill, Middx TW12 1DR. Tel: 081-941 5753.

Art of Travel 268 Lavender Hill, London SW11 1LJ. Tel: 071-738 2038.

African Explorations 36 Kirtons Farm, Pingewood, Reading, Berks RG3 3UN. Tel: 0734 500146.

Explore Worldwide 1 Frederick St, Aldershot, Hants GU11 1LQ. Tel: 0252 319448.

Cox and Kings St James Court, 45 Buckingham Gate, London SW1E 6AF. Tel: 071-834 7472.

THE NEXT EDITION

Our readers play a vital part in updating books for the next edition. If you have found changes, or new exciting places, or have a story to share, do write.

The most helpful contributions will receive a free book. Write to:

"Namibia & Botswana", Bradt Publications, 41 Nortoft Road, Chalfont St Peter, Bucks SL9 0LA, UK.

White rhino; once seriously endangered, now the commoner of the two rhino species in southern Africa

The highly venemous puff adder

Cape buffalo, the most dangerous large animal of the bush

Welwitschia mirabilis *plants in the fog belt, Skeleton Coast, Namibia*

Before and after: lichens on a rock that has been doused with water. Such fragile plants are often carelessly damaged

A single Kokerboom weighed down by the nests of social weavers

Two Himba women — note the "erembe" headdress signifying marriage and the characteristic copper armlets

Traditional Himba rondavels in western Kaokoland made of saplings and a mixture of mud and cow dung

Chapter 5

Health and safety

Some Initial Comments

There's always a great danger in writing about health and safety for the uninitiated visitor: it's all too easy to become paranoid about the Pandora's box of exotic diseases he/she may catch; and it's all too easy to start distrusting everyone you meet as a potential thief — falling into an unfounded 'us-and-them' attitude toward the people of the country you are visiting.

As a comparison, imagine an equivalent section in a guide book to a western country — there would be a list of possible diseases and, most relevantly, advice on the risk of theft and mugging in many major western cities would have to be given. Many western cities are dangerous — but with time we learn how to deal with them, accepting almost unconsciously what we can and cannot do.

It's very important to strike the right balance — avoid being either too cautious or too over-relaxed about both your health and safety. In time, you will find the balance that best fits you and the country you are visiting.

Namibia and Botswana stand out in Africa as being particularly healthy and safe. With good preparation and common sense, you should stay healthy and unharassed while here. Windhoek and Gaborone are certainly amongst the safest cities I know, and with most of your time spent outdoors, and plenty of healthy sunshine, you will probably find yourself returning home fitter than when you left.

BEFORE YOU GO

Travel Insurance

Full medical insurance is essential — and you should check that it covers repatriation to your home country if this is required for medical reasons. There are a number of relatively cheap specific travel insurance packages available, which will fully cover you for medical expenses, as well as providing useful cover against theft, lost baggage, and even flight cancellations. Most of these are perfectly adequate on the medical side, but check the exclusions and conditions for loss and theft of your possessions carefully. In particular be sure of the maximum amount you can claim, and the limit for 'valuable items', especially cameras. Often, you won't be able to claim more than about £250 maximum for a lost or stolen camera. If you have your possessions insured at home, you may find that the policy covers you abroad for a limited time — usually 30-60 days a year.

ISIS travel insurance (available from Endsleigh Insurance brokers, or the ubiquitous STA Travel Agents), is one of the most popular and cheapest policies around, but you should check the small print for the exclusions — it may not suit you. AMEX does its own very good, year-round policy that's worth investigating if you have an American Express card, while Avon insurance also comes highly recommended as providing a very good policy.

Planning Ahead

Having a full set of **inoculations** takes time, normally at least six weeks, though sometimes 'cocktails' of inoculations are available which reduce this time drastically. See your doctor early on, or one of the travel health centres listed, to establish an inoculation time-table (see also under inoculations). Equally it's worth allowing time to have a **dental check-up** before you go — you could be several painful days from the nearest dentist. If you wear glasses, bring a spare pair, or at the very least your **glasses prescription**. The same goes for **contact-lens** wearers — do bring some spare glasses in case the all-pervasive sand and dust proves too much for the lenses and your eyes. If you take **regular medication** (including contraceptive pills), bring a good supply with you — it may not always be readily available.

Vaccination Centres in London

British Airways Medical Department, 75 Regent Street, London, W1. Tel: 071-439 9584

MASTA, Bureau of Hygiene and Tropical Diseases, Keppel St, London WC1E 7HT.

Thomas Cook Vaccination Centre, 45 Berkeley Square, London W1. Tel: 071-499 4000.

Trailfinders Immunisation Centre, 194 Kensington High Street, London W8 7RG. Tel: 071-938 3999.

Inoculations

Legal requirements No inoculations are required by law for entry into either Namibia or Botswana if you have come straight from the West. However, a yellow fever vaccination certificate may be necessary if you have come from an area where the disease is endemic — eg East Africa or Zambia. The vaccine is very safe, effective and lasts ten years — so it might be a worthwhile investment, even if you don't legally need it.

Recommended precautions You should carefully check that you are protected against polio and tetanus — it's worth being covered for these whether you are at home or travelling abroad. Vaccinations against cholera and typhoid may be recommended by your doctor, though most now regard the cholera vaccination as ineffective, unpleasant, and only worth having if you need the certificate to enter the country you are visiting — you don't for Namibia, Botswana, Zimbabwe or South Africa. Some protection against hepatitis A can be had from a gamma-globulin jab, but you are unlikely to get this disease in Namibia or Botswana unless you live and travel in very rural populated areas.

Malaria Prophylaxis (Prevention)

Malaria is the most dangerous disease in Africa, and much of the tropical world. Although the risk in Namibia and Botswana is small (least risk in desert areas and those over 1500m in altitude), it is still worth taking malaria pills if you will be travelling into areas of much greater risk — the northern areas of the two countries, and around the Okavango Delta.

Currently recommended pills include: proguanil (Paludrine) — two tablets (200mg base each) every day (after food), and chloroquine (Nivaquine) — two tablets (300mg base each) at the same time every week. The two drugs are usually taken in combination. Some people find that the pills make them feel nauseous — this can be lessened by taking the pills last thing at night and sleeping through the worst! Chloroquine tastes disgusting (it defines bitterness) — so get hold of the sugar-coated varieties, or else develop an impressively fast swallowing technique. It's important to remember to start taking the tablets at least a week before you arrive in a malarial zone, and continue taking them for six weeks afterwards.

Prophylaxis doesn't stop you catching malaria — only stopping the mosquitos biting you will do that (see below) — but it drastically reduces your chances of fully developing the disease and, if it does develop, it will certainly lessen its severity. Falciparum (cerebral) malaria is the most common type in Africa, and must be guarded against — when left untreated it is usually fatal. Fortunately chloroquine-resistant strains are not yet a problem in these two countries — so prophylaxis is effective and treatment is not difficult. However, the situation is always changing so get the latest advice from the Malaria Reference Laboratory (London), tel. 071-636 7921 for a tape recording of up to date prophylaxis advice. Despite all these precautions you could still get malaria. See page 59 for advice in this situation.

Americans also have a source of free information at the Center for Disease Control in Atlanta, Georgia. By phoning (404) 332 4559 you can find out the latest recommended malaria prophylaxis, inoculation requirements and outbreaks of dangerous diseases in various parts of the world.

Medical Kit

Pharmacies in Namibia and Botswana are well stocked with over-the-counter medicines and general supplies — so it's not worth taking too much with you. A basic kit should include most of the following: antiseptic cream, sticking plasters (the roll which you cut to size is much more versatile than the pre-shaped band-aids), micropore tape (for closing small cuts and wounds, and preventing blisters), scissors, sterile bandage, lint and safety pins, aspirins, paracetamol, diarrhoea pills, malaria pills (prophylaxis and emergency treatment), vaseline or lanolin cream for cracked skin, 'lip salve' for dry and cracked lips (the best ones include a sunscreen), eye drops.

STAYING HEALTHY — HEALTH TIPS

Prevention is always better than cure — most of the ailments that afflict travellers or visitors are easily preventable. Keep up your resistance to diseases by eating and sleeping well — for many people, travelling quickly becomes a nightmare marathon of sporadic meals and even more sporadic night's sleep. Your hygiene standards shouldn't suffer when you travel either — be sensible about what you eat and drink, and how you prepare food.

Food and Storage

Most health problems encountered by travellers the world over are contracted by eating contaminated food or drinking unclean water. While Botswana and Namibia are no worse than most western countries, it is still worth being careful — avoid undercooked food and remember that the heat can turn foods inedible very quickly. Cool boxes can help, but it is still not a good idea to keep any animal products for more than a day or two. Instead travel with tins, packets, and fresh green vegetables when you can find them, as these are unlikely to cause food poisoning.

Water and Purification

The piped water available in the towns of both countries is usually safe to drink, so water quality only becomes an issue in the wilds. Here, if you are on a short visit, then your rule should be to purify all the water used for drinking or washing food. To purify water, first filter out any suspended solids — passing it through a piece of closely woven cloth will do fine — then either boil it for 10 minutes, or sterilise it chemically (boiling is more effective, and doesn't fill your system up with unwanted toxins).

The tablets sold for purification (puritabs, sterotabs, *et al*) are adequate, and based on either chlorine or iodine — simply follow the manufacturer's instructions. Iodine is the more effective, especially against amoebic cysts, and if you are travelling for a long period then it is cheaper to take a small bottle of medical quality 'Tincture of Iodine' (2% solution), and a small eye-dropper. Use two to four drops of the solution to purify one litre of water (depending on how contaminated it is), leaving it to stand for 15 minutes (more if it is very cold) before use. The solution can also be used as a general external antiseptic. It stains a deep purple if spilt — so seal the container well.

If you are working in Namibia or Botswana, or on a very long trip, then there is a case for gradually allowing your stomach to get used to drinking unpurified (but still clean) water from natural sources. The Okavango and the rivers of the Kaokoveld are good examples. If attempting this, then ensure your source is crystal clear, running, and not downstream of human settlements. Then introduce yourself very slowly to it, gradually allowing your system to acclimatise. This is possible to do here because of the lack of population; it is not something that I would be happy doing in more crowded African countries.

Heat and the Sun

Heat stroke, heat exhaustion and sunburn are sometimes problems for newly-arrived travellers to Africa, despite being easy to prevent. That said, both Botswana and Namibia have dry climates where the heat is rarely the sticky, oppressive kind that causes most of the trouble. To avoid problems, just remember that your body is under stress and so make allowances for it. Firstly, take things gently — you are on holiday after all. Next, keep your fluid and salt levels high: lots of soft drinks and brews of tea, but go easy on the coffee and alcohol. Thirdly, dress to keep cool, with loose fitting, thin garments — preferably of cotton or silk.

Finally, beware of the sun. Hats and long-sleeved shirts are essential kit. If you must expose your skin to the sun then use sun-blocks and high-factor sun-screens (the sun's so strong that you'll still get a tan!).

Avoiding Insects — Repellents and Mosquito Nets

Research has shown that using a mosquito net and covering up exposed skin (by wearing long-sleeved shirts and tucking trousers into socks) in the evening and at night is the most effective way of preventing malaria. However, I have known mosquitos to bite through clothes, including my new light-weight *Rohan* trousers. Mosquito coils and insect repellents work to some extent. DEET is the active ingredient in repellents, so the greater percentage of DEET, the stronger the effect. Some people swear by repellents, particularly for keeping irritating insects off during the day. I find many of the concoctions so clearly toxic and smelly, that I am reluctant to put any on, especially when washing facilities are limited. Using a moderate strength repellent (eg 50% DEET) is a fair compromise. 'Jungle Formula' have introduced a combination repellent and sunscreen gel which works well.

Bringing a mosquito net with you is strongly recommended. It's worth thinking carefully about the design — some hang from a convenient branch or the ceiling of a room and tuck under the mattress, whilst others are built more like a tent and are perhaps more suitable for camping (without a tent). It's essential that your tent has mosquito netting built in — if it doesn't, consider buying some netting and doing the necessary modifications yourself.

Snakes, Spiders and Scorpions...

Encounters with aggressive snakes or vindictive scorpions are really more common in horror movies than in Africa. Most snakes will flee at the mere vibrations of a human step, whilst you will have to seek out scorpions to see one, and spiders are far more interested in flies than people. If you are careful about where you place your hands and feet — especially after dark — then there should be no problems (see Chapter 6).

Snakes do bite occasionally though, and then it's worth knowing the standard first aid treatment. Firstly, and most importantly, *don't panic*. Remember that only a tiny minority of bites — even by highly poisonous species — inject enough venom to be dangerous. Even in the worst of these cases, the victim has hours or days to get to help, and not a matter of minutes. He/she should be kept calm, with no exertions which would pump venom around the blood system, whilst being taken rapidly to the nearest medical help. The bitten limb should be immobilised and Paracetamol used as a painkiller. (*Never* use aspirin to kill the pain of a snakebite as it may cause internal bleeding.) *Do not* use a tourniquet; this may do more harm to the limb than good, and when released produce a surge of venom into the blood. If the bite is both serious and venomous, tightly (but not over-tight) wrap a bandage over the entire length of the limb which has been bitten.

Forget cutting out the wound, sucking and spitting, or any of the commercial anti-snakebite kits — which vary from being a waste of time to being positively dangerous. The only real treatment is for a specific antivenom to be medically administered. Identification of the snake is very helpful, so killing it and taking it along with you is a good idea if at all possible (!). When deep in the bush, heading for the nearest large farm may be quicker than going to a town — it may have a supply of antivenom, or facilities to radio for help by plane.

DISEASES — AND WHEN TO SEE A DOCTOR

Traveller's Diarrhoea

There are almost as many names for this affliction as there are traveller's tales on the subject. The truth is that in Namibia and Botswana you are unlikely to have any problems at all. Firstly, do resist the temptation to reach for the medical kit as soon as your stomach turns a little fluid. Most cases of traveller's diarrhoea will resolve themselves within 24 to 48 hours without any treatment at all. To speed this process of acclimatisation up, eat well but simply — avoiding fats in favour of starches and, most importantly, keeping your fluid intake high. Bananas and papaya fruit are often claimed to be helpful. If you urgently need to stop the symptoms, for a long bus ride for example, then Lomotil, Imodium or another of the commercial anti-diarrhoea preparations will do the trick — but they will not cure the problem.

When severe diarrhoea gets continually worse, or the stools contain blood or pus, or it lasts for more than 10 days, you should seek medical advice. There are almost as many possible treatments as there are probable causes, and a proper diagnosis involves microscopic analysis of a stool sample — so get yourself back to a town and go straight to the nearest hospital. The most important thing, especially in this climate, is to keep your fluid intake up, preferably with the addition of some dissolved salts and sugars — doctors recommend eight level teaspoons of sugar, and a teaspoon of salt, to one litre of water. If you are really unlikely to be able to reach help within a few days, then come equipped with a good health manual and the selection of antibiotics which it recommends. *Traveller's Health* by Dr. Richard Dawood (see end of this section) is excellent for this purpose — though rather detailed for the normal visitor.

Malaria

You can still catch malaria even if you are taking anti-malarial drugs. Classic symptoms include headache, chills and sweating, abdominal pains, aching joints and fever — some or all of which may come in waves, often starting in the evening. It varies tremendously, but often starts like a bad case of flu. If anything like this happens, your first response should be to suspect malaria — and seek medical help immediately.

If (and only if) this is not possible, then treat yourself by taking two quinine tablets (600mg) eight hourly for up to seven days, until the fever abates. Quinine is a strong drug and its side-effects are disorientating (nausea, buzzing in the ears) and unpleasant — so administering this on your own is not advisable. After the quinine, and if you still have a fever, take a single dose of three Fansidar tablets. Alternatively, for areas where the malaria parasite is still chloroquine-sensitive, instead of the quinine treatment, you can take four ordinary chloroquine tablets (600mg) at once, then two tablets six hours later, then two tablets twice daily for two days.

These drugs are very powerful and taking them in high doses, without medical supervision, is dangerous — at the very least you'll find their side-effects highly unpleasant. Do get to a doctor as quickly as possible. Another complication of treating yourself is that once started, it is much more difficult for a doctor to make a correct diagnosis.

Finally, don't worry about those people on other courses of prophylaxis, there are many possible options — but do stick rigidly to whatever is yours. The vast majority of malaria cases occur because people were not keeping to their regular tablet-taking regime.

AIDS

AIDS is spread in exactly the same way in Africa as it is at home — through body secretions, blood and blood products. This means that it can be spread through close physical contact, such as sexual intercourse, through blood transfusions using infected blood, or through unsterilised needles which have been used on an infected person.

In Namibia or Botswana, there is no special AIDS risk from medical treatment or blood products — all blood is screened for the AIDS virus. Your biggest chance of getting AIDS is through unprotected sexual intercourse. The greater the number of sexual partners, the greater the risk — prostitutes are a particularly high risk group. Practice 'safe sex' — abstain or avoid multiple partners, and always use a condom.

Hepatitis

This is group of viral diseases which generally start with coca-cola coloured urine and light coloured stools, before progressing to fevers, weakness, jaundice (yellow skin and eyeballs) and abdominal pains caused by a severe inflammation of the liver. There are several forms, of which the two most common are typical of the rest: type A (formerly infectious hepatitis) and B (formerly viral hepatitis).

Type A is spread by the faecal-oral route, that is by ingesting food or drink contaminated by excrement or urine. It is avoided as you would avoid any stomach problems, by careful preparation of food and by only drinking clean water. In contrast, the more serious but rarer **type B** is spread in the same way as AIDS (blood or body secretions), and is avoided the same way that one avoids AIDS.

There are no cures for hepatitis, but with lots of bed rest and a good low-fat, no-alcohol diet most people recover within six months. If you are unlucky enough to contract any form of hepatitis, consider using your travel insurance to fly straight home!

Rabies

Rabies is normally contracted when the skin is broken and the wound infected by the rabies virus, which is present in the saliva of infected animals. The disease is almost invariably fatal when fully developed, but fortunately there are now very good post-exposure vaccines which can prevent this. It is possible (if expensive) to be immunised against the disease, but not really worthwhile unless you are working with animals — and even then it's standard practice to treat all cases of possible exposure.

Rabies is rarely a problem for visitors, but the small risks are further minimised by steering well clear of dogs in the cities and small carnivores in the bush. If you are bitten or scratched then clean and disinfect the wound thoroughly and seek medical advice immediately. The early stages of the disease are characterised by itching around the bite, followed by headaches, fevers, spasms, personality changes and hydrophobia (fear of water). Thus animals acting strangely — be they strange dogs in the cities, or unusually friendly jackals in the bush, should be given an especially wide berth.

Bilharzia or Schistosomiasis

Bilharzia is an insidious disease, contracted by coming into contact with infected water, caused by an infestation of parasitic worms which damage the bladder or intestine. Often the parasites are present in the local population who have built up an immunity over time, but the visitor who becomes infected may develop a severe fever some weeks afterwards. A common indication of an infection is a localised itchy rash — where the parasites have burrowed through the skin. Bilharzia is readily treated by medication, and only serious if undetected (the symptoms may be confused with malaria) and untreated.

The life-cycle of the parasites starts when they are urinated into a body of water. Here they infect certain species of water-snails, grow and multiply and finally become free-swimming. At this stage they leave the snails to look for a human, or primate, host. After burrowing through the skin of someone coming into contact with the water, they migrate to the person's bladder or intestine where they remain — producing a large number of eggs which are passed every day in the urine, so continuing the cycle.

To only way to completely avoid risk of Bilharzia infection is to stay well clear of any bodies of freshwater — not even allowing splashes on your skin. Obviously this is very restrictive and could stop you enjoying your trip. More pragmatic advice is to avoid slow-moving or sluggish water, and ask local opinion on the Bilharzia risk — not all water is infected. Generally fast-flowing rivers are free from infection (a bad environment for the snails), as is the Okavango (away from settlements), while dams and standing water are usually heavily infected. If you think you may have been infected, get a test done on your return.

Sleeping Sickness or Trypanosomiasis

This is really a disease of cattle, which may be caught by people on rare occasions. It is spread exclusively by bites from the *tsetse fly*, which is about the size of a house fly, but has pointed mouthparts (designed for sucking blood). They are easily spotted as they bite during the day and have distinctive wings which cross into a scissor shape when resting. Prevention is much easier than cure, so avoid being bitten if you can by covering up and listening for the tell-tale buzz around you. Chemical repellents may be helpful also, but they are far from perfect.

Tsetse bites are quite nasty, so expect them to swell up a little and turn red — that is a normal allergic reaction to any bite. The vast majority of tsetse bites will do no more than this. If, however, a boil-like swelling develops after five or more days in the place you were bitten, and a fever two or three weeks later, then you should seek treatment from a good doctor immediately to avert permanent damage to your central nervous system.

Some Africans view the fly positively — referring to it as 'the guardian of wild Africa' — as fear of the disease's effect on cattle has prevented farming, and hence settlement, from encroaching on many areas of wild bush country. Given Botswana's and Namibia's dependence on cattle for export earnings, the tsetse fly and its eradication are emotive issues. In recent years the tsetse fly has been the subject of relentless spaying programmes over much of the sub-continent, removing the last natural barriers to cattle farming. This is currently happening in the Okavango Delta — the main concentration of tsetse fly in the region — which some believe heralds the end of the Okavango as a cattle-free wildlife sanctuary.

WHEN YOU RETURN HOME

Many tropical diseases have a long incubation period, and it is possible to develop symptoms weeks after returning home from abroad. (This is why, for example, it is important to keep taking the anti-malarial pills for six weeks following your return.) If you do get ill after you return home, make sure you tell your doctor where you have been — and alert him/her to any diseases that you have been exposed to. If problems persist, get yourself a check-up at one of the hospitals for tropical diseases. Several people die from malaria each year in the UK as their doctors are just not used to the symptoms. Note that to visit a hospital for tropical diseases in the UK you need a letter of referral from your doctor.

For further advice or help contact the London Hospital for Tropical Diseases, 4 St Pancras Way, London, NW1. Tel: 071-387 441. The staff here are excellent and are frequently world authorities when it comes to research, treatment and advice on tropical diseases — despite the run down and under-funded appearance of the premises and administration.

Useful Books

Traveller's Health by Dr Richard Dawood.
OUP, £6.95. This has become virtually the standard reference for travellers, including just about everything you might possibly catch — depressing (but gripping) reading!

Health Manual — A Self Help Guide by Dr Veronica Moss.
Lion Publishing, £4.95. The emphasis of this book is on basic, practical advice — which is easy to find in a hurry. The book starts rather helpfully with a section 'Where Does it Hurt?'

THEFT

Theft is really not a problem here unless you are careless. Namibia and Botswana are both very safe and the worst that the traveller is likely to encounter is a pickpocket in one of the major cities. Violent robbery is virtually unknown and most thefts occur because travellers become so lax about their property that they leave it lying around.

How to Avoid it

Be sensible. Keep your passport, credit cards and most of your cash in a money belt, neck pouch or secret pocket — and don't flash this around in public more than necessary. For general use, keep a day's supply of cash handy in a more accessible place. If you are driving, remember to lock the car whenever you leave it, and if you are hitching don't forget to get out of the lift without all your belongings.

Reporting to the Police

The police in both countries are at least as reliable and honest as those at home and will often go out of their way to help a foreigner. They are also surprisingly efficient; I know of one traveller who had his wallet stolen, only to have it returned to him in England by the police by post three months later, completely intact except for the cash. If you need a copy of a crime report for insurance purposes then do explain this carefully to the officer when you begin to report the crime, and try not to be too impatient.

SAFETY

Arrest

To get arrested in Namibia or Botswana you need to try quite hard. Taking photographs of 'sensitive areas' (bridges, government buildings, etc) may be one way, smuggling drugs another, and evading park fees is also a possibility. Perhaps the best way is to argue with a policeman or a soldier — and get angry into the bargain — this will almost certainly get you arrested!

If you are careless enough to be arrested, you will often only be asked a few questions. If the police are suspicious of you, then how you handle the situation will determine whether you are kept for a matter of hours or of days. Be patient, helpful, good-humoured, and as truthful as possible. *Never lose your temper* — it will only aggravate the situation — and avoid any hint of arrogance. If things are going badly after half a day or so, then start firmly to insist on seeing someone in higher authority — and as a last resort you do (in theory) have the right to contact your embassy or consulate, though the finer points of your civil liberties may end up being overlooked by an irate local police chief!

Bribery

Neither of the authors has ever encountered a situation in the region when bribery was demanded or even expected. Offering a bribe to a policeman may, however, be another excellent way to get yourself immediately arrested!

Chapter 6

Driving and camping in the bush

DRIVING

Vehicle Equipment and Preparations

Driving in the bush can present many problems to the uninitiated, but once mastered becomes both safe and great fun. You should prepare yourself well before you start to drive — if you are picking up a hired car then check that there's an accessible spare wheel (or two if you are driving on rough ground), a working foot pump and jack, and suitable basic tools (including a spanner and screwdriver set). Don't forget to bring spare oil and brake and clutch fluid. If you are going into rough 4WD country, then you should also take a more extensive tool kit, spare parts and a maintenance manual for the model of vehicle (plus sufficient personal knowledge and experience to be able to use it!).

Good fuel and water containers are a necessity — how large depends upon the type of environment through which you want to travel. As a general guide, two 20-litre water containers, and about 1,000 miles' worth of spare fuel in jerry cans, is about right for four people going into the wilds. You can easily and cheaply pick up large plastic containers to carry the water, but never carry fuel in these, however strong they seem. Plastic stretches, expands and can crack in the heat — and the tops are rarely strong enough, allowing lethal fuel vapour to escape.

Other useful items are: a spade to dig yourself out of sand; a large polythene sheet to lie on when doing vehicle repairs; a tow rope; and a light for working on the vehicle at night — those which can be connected to the vehicle battery are probably the most useful.

4WD Driving

It is beyond the scope of this section to explain the ins-and-outs of using a four-wheel drive (4WD vehicle). Whilst there is nothing particularly difficult about using a 4WD — even though using one well takes years of experience — you should make a concerted effort to familiarise yourself fully with the operation and limitations of your chosen vehicle. There are, in reality, several different basic varieties of 4WDs which differ markedly in their performance, and the use of their transmission and gear box. In particular, check whether your vehicle has switchable fixed/free-wheeling hubs and how they work — not understanding how these are used can cause many problems and seriously damage the transmission. If by now you are feeling apprehensive (and you can't understand the instruction manual), get hold of a copy of one of the many good books on the subject.

General Driving Advice

Road types Gravel roads can be very deceiving — although relatively smooth, flat and fast, they still do not give you much traction, and you will frequently skid. With practice (at slower speeds!) you will learn how to deal with skids and treat them as normal. However, there will always be the unexpected — an animal wanders into the road, or there's suddenly a massive pothole ahead — so it's very unwise to ever drive over 100kph on these roads. In general it's safer to stick to 80kph. Dust roads should be treated with particular caution after rains — the surface can quickly become muddy and as slippery as ice.

Slowing down Slow down if in any doubt about what lies ahead — road surfaces can vary enormously. Concentrate on looking out for potholes, ruts or patches of soft sand which can put you into an unexpected slide. When passing other vehicles travelling in the opposite direction, always slow down to minimise both the chances of chippings damaging the windscreen, and the danger from a lack of visibility as you enter the other vehicle's dustcloud. Using your headlights or horn can help alert other vehicles of your presence.

Animals and driving at night Wild and domestic animals frequently hang around on the side of the road, and may suddenly take fright and dash into the centre — beware. A high-speed collision with even a small animal (such as a goat), will not only kill it, but will also cause surprisingly severe damage to your vehicle, and possibly fatal consequences for you and your passengers. Driving at night is particularly dangerous in this regard and in general should be avoided.

Using your gears It's generally better to slow your vehicle down using a combination of gears and brakes on non-tarred roads than to use the brakes alone. You are much less likely to skid. Equally, use gears and not your brakes to slow down for a corner. A consequence of using low-ratio gears (ie first or second) more than usual is increased fuel consumption. Take this into account when planning fuel requirements. Air-conditioning units also use a significant amount of fuel — turn them off if you feel you are running short.

Driving in sand Lowering your tyre pressures until there is a distinct bulge in the tyre walls — having first made sure that your hand pump is working — greatly helps traction but increases wear. Pump them up before you drive again on hard surfaces (particularly tar), or they will be badly damaged. Don't fight the steering-wheel if there are clear, deep-rutted tracks — relax and let your vehicle largely steer itself. Driving in the cool of the morning is easier than later in the day — when cool, the sand is more compact and firmer. (When hot, the pockets of air between the sand grains expand and loosen the sand up.)

If you do get stuck, despite these precautions, don't panic. Dig a shallow ramp out in front of all the wheels — reinforcing it with pieces of wood or branches to give the wheels better traction. Lighten the vehicle load (passengers out) and push, keeping the engine revs high as you slowly engage your lowest ratio gear — using your clutch to ensure that the wheels don't spin wildly and dig themselves further into the sand.

Rocky terrain Have your tyre pressures higher than normal and move very slowly. If necessary have any passengers guide you along the track to avoid scraping the undercarriage on the ground.

Crossing rivers The first thing to do is to *stop* and check the river. Wade through the water, and assess the depth, substrate and current flow, to determine the best route to drive along. Before you cross, select your lowest ratio gear, and then progress through the water at a slow but steady rate. It's not worth taking risks — a flooded river will often subside to much safer levels by the next morning.

Grass seeds In grasslands (especially Makgadikgadi, Bushmanland and the approaches to Tsodilo Hills) keep a close watch on the water temperature gauge. Grass stems and seeds get caught up in the radiator grill and block the flow of air, causing overheating and the danger of the grass catching fire. You should stop and remove the grass seeds every few kilometres or so, depending on the conditions. If the engine has overheated, the only option is to stop and turn the engine off — don't open the radiator cap to refill until the radiator is no longer hot to touch.

BUSH CAMPING

The opportunity to be able spontaneously to camp where and when you like in the wilds of Botswana or Namibia, is one of these countries' greatest appeals for the visitor. For most travellers with a vehicle, bush camping is the norm rather than the exception, and when preparing for your trip you should take this into account from the point of view of both budget and equipment. When camping, it takes a little time to develop a system that best suits you — and to work out what you wish you had and what you could do without — but you will soon adapt to the lifestyle and slip into the routine. Don't forget that bush camping in Namibia and Botswana is an entirely different proposition from the cold and wet experience of 'northern climes'.

Where you can camp

Botswana The vast majority of the land in Botswana is not privately owned, and you are more or less free to camp anywhere. If you are near to a village or settlement, then it is polite to ask the chief's permission — perhaps asking him to suggest a suitable spot. Remember that even if the land looks wild, it is likely to be used by someone, and invariably you'll have inquisitive visitors to share your fire with. Some large tracts of land, particularly in the Eastern Corridor, are privately owned — mostly by white farmers in the Tuli Block — and you are not free to camp in these areas without express permission.

Namibia In Namibia, the situation is a bit different. Land was divided up in the early colonial days between white farmers (who took half the land), and nine different 'homelands' for the different ethnic groups (who had 40%, with the remainder taken by national parks and mining areas). This apportionment effectively exists today. As in Botswana, in white farming areas you are not free to camp anywhere, whilst in the ex-'homelands' you can generally camp anywhere you like, but should ask permission from the local chief first.

National Parks The national parks of both countries have their own specific rules for camping, and almost all have designated campsites.

Choosing a campsite

Never camp on what looks like a path through the bush, however indistinct. It is may be a well-used game trail.

Beware of camping in dry river beds — flash floods are very dangerous and can arrive with little or no warning.

Camp a respectable distance away from any isolated source of water — or you may block animals from their only source of water, causing both you and them disturbance. This is not applicable to the Okavango area, where there is of course plenty of water everywhere.

In a marshy or damp area (eg the Okavango), camp on higher ground to avoid cold mists at night. In a dry desert area, it is warmer to camp on lower ground, in the less-exposed sites.

Camp-fires

Camp-fires can add a great atmosphere to a campsite and can warm you on a chilly desert night, but they can also be very damaging to the environment and leave unsightly piles of ash and blackened stones. Dead wood for burning is very limited in desert areas — where vegetation grows very slowly — and by burning dead vegetation you are removing it from the local ecosystem, further depleting the area. On the same note, use only dead wood — never use any living vegetation. Don't be tempted to make huge destructive fires — these are, anyhow, impractical for cooking.

Beware of bush fires. Restrict your fire to a small circle, ringed with stones, that you can control. Always have water handy and never leave the fire unattended.

A fire at night can help keep smaller raiding animals away from the campsite, but is certainly not a foolproof guard against most big game. Animals that are used to being around campsites (eg hyenas at Savuti and lions in parts of Moremi) will often disregard unattended fires to an alarming degree. There is little point in trying to keep a raging fire going all night.

Keep one or two bundles of firewood in the back of your vehicle for camping where wood is scarce or non-existent.

Using a tent (or not)

To use a tent or to sleep in the open is a personal choice, dependent upon where you are. In Chobe or Moremi, or at any well-used campsite in a game area, you should *always* sleep completely inside a tent — a protruding leg can look like a tasty snack to a hungry hyena or curious lion. Away from such well-used sites, the same type of animals are not a problem although it is better to err on the side of caution. Most big animals will avoid an unfamiliar campsite.

Outside obvious game areas you will be fine either in just a sleeping bag or preferably under a mosquito net — with the deep, blue-black skies of Africa overhead. Sleeping beneath a tree will help reduce morning dew on your sleeping bag.

If your vehicle has a large flat roof, sleeping on this will provide you with good protection from animals. You will probably see 4WDs with purpose-built tents on their roof-racks.

Animal dangers for campers

Scorpions can be a problem as you set up and clear a camp — they are often found underneath rocks or branches. Always move rocks with caution, and avoid collecting wood in the dark. Shake out your shoes in the morning before you put them on.

Although snakes will invariably attempt to escape from human 'intruders', they may be caught by surprise and pose a threat if you set up camp in areas of long grass (eg Okavango islands). Be noisy, and give them a chance to move away. When sleeping in the open, it is not unknown for snakes to lie next to you for the warmth. Don't panic, and you won't be bitten — just gently move away without any sudden movements. This is one argument for at least using a mosquito net at night!

In a game area carefully store away — either in your tent, or preferably in your vehicle — anything that can be carried off by an animal. Be particularly careful about putting food away — especially citrus fruits, a delicacy that elephants will do anything for! Needless to say, food is better in your vehicle than your tent.

MINIMUM IMPACT

When you visit, drive through, or camp in an area with *minimum impact*, that area is left in the same condition — or better — than when you entered it. Whilst most visitors would view minimum impact as being clearly desirable, it's worth considering the number of ways that we contribute to environmental degradation, and how these can be avoided.

Driving

Use you vehicle responsibly. Don't go off the road or track if the environment will clearly suffer, or better don't go off the tracks at all. In desert areas, the tracks left by one vehicle can remain scarring the landscape for decades. Desert plants — especially the dry-looking lichens on gravel plains — are easy to kill, and very slow to regrow. Don't disregard the country's regulations — there are usually good reasons for permits being required to enter certain areas.

Hygiene

Human excrement should be well buried away from paths or rivers, and the tissue burnt before it is covered up. This is especially important in desert areas where the tissue won't rot, but may be unearthed only to blow about in the wind.

If you use a river to wash, then soap yourself on the bank (do bring biodegradable soap) and take a pan for scooping water — make sure that no soap finds its way back into the water. Sand makes an excellent pan scrub, even if you have no water to spare.

Rubbish

Bring along some plastic bags with which to remove all your rubbish and dump it at the next town. Even 'biodegradable' rubbish will look very unsightly and spoil the place for those who come after you.

Burying rubbish — particularly containers and cans — is *not* a solution. Animals will always find these and dig them up.

Empty tin cans can be 'cleaned' and made easier to carry away, if you burn them in your fire overnight, then squash them flat.

Host communities

Whilst the rules for reducing impact on the environment have been understood and followed by responsible travellers for many years, the effects of tourism on local people have only recently been considered. Many tourists consider it their right, for example, to take intrusive photos of people, and are angry if the person does not co-operate. They refer to higher prices being charged to tourists as "a rip-off" without considering the hand-to-mouth existence of those selling their products or services. They deplore child beggars, then hand out sweets or pens to kids that crowd around their vehicle.

Our behaviour towards "the locals" needs to be looked at in terms of their culture, with the knowledge that we are the uninvited visitors. Read Phil Deutschle's *Cultural Do's and Don'ts* and aim to leave the local people unchanged by your visit - this is the best present you can give them.

ANIMAL ENCOUNTERS

Whether you are on an organised foot-safari, on your own hike, or just walking from the car to your tent in the bush, it is not unlikely that you will come across some of Africa's larger animals at close quarters. Invariably, the actual danger of the situation is much less than imagined, and a few basic guidelines will enable you to know how to deal with these situations and even enjoy them!

Animals are not normally interested in people — you are not their normal food, or their predator, and so provided you take precautions not to annoy or threaten them, you will be largely left alone. Remember that it is their environment not yours — they are designed for it and their senses are far better attuned to it. To be on less unequal terms, always stay alert in the bush and try to spot animals from a distance. This gives you the option of approaching carefully, or staying well clear.

Bush walking

It's assumed here that you are walking with the intention of maximising your chances of seeing animals, whilst still remaining cautious to potential danger.

Do not walk at all if the vegetation is too thick, you should have a bare minimum of 20m visibility all around you.

Don't walk in large groups — four is a good number, certainly not above eight.

Single file and no chatting may seem strict, but it makes sense. Stay as quiet as you can and stop if you want to whisper something.

Wear dark colours, not light ones, earth tones are best.

Do take your time: rush and you will miss the points of interest and walk unknowingly into problems.

Make the most of the small things that you observe; insect life can be at least as interesting as the big cats at times.

Use your ears and nose as well as your eyes — any strange smells or noises should attract your attention immediately.

If there is a wind, consider your scent. Walking into the wind will help to hide this and thus give animals less warning of you — but you are then in danger of frightening them with a surprise discovery.

Beware: No wild animals are completely safe — even a gemsbok's graceful horns can kill — so keep your distance.

Lion Tracks

by Phil Deutschle

All night long we heard the deep-throated *wouu wouu* of distant lions. At first light, my Wei companion, Obi, and I left the safety of our small island. Obi poled the *mokoro* through the reeds of the Okavango Delta and in a half hour we arrived near to where the lions must be. I jumped barefoot into the water and pulled the *mokoro* half-way onto the bank. A quick search revealed the spoor of lion, but we could have easily found the spot by smell alone. The carcass of a Cape buffalo lay under an acacia tree. The tracks showed that the lions had wandered off into a region of tall grass, where it would be foolish to follow them.

Eight days previously we had begun our trip with no more goal than to see what there was to see. For me it had become an intensive course in the art of tracking and stalking African game. Slowly, I was learning to identify the different species from their prints and droppings and, by observing Obi, I was also discovering how to read the age of the track by the sharpness of the imprint, the occurrence of game across the track, or by faint differences in the colour of the soil.

Together, Obi and I had crawled beneath miles of thorn bushes, waded through waist-deep stretches of water, and sheltered behind innumerable termite mounds, always staying downwind, trying to get ever closer to a reedbuck or a jackal. Each type of beast reacted in a different way when they spotted us. Impala and zebra would passively continue to graze, while giraffe would flee at first sight. Warthog would stay concealed in the grass and bolt away when you were nearly on top of them. Cape buffalo also ran at the last moment, but they were more likely to run over *you* than to run away. We shunned buffalo.

Next morning we left the *mokoro* on the bank of yet another island, and found lion tracks that were several days old. Following a game trail through heavy bush, we emerged at the edge of a large lagoon and cautiously skirted it looking for more tracks. After 300 yards we both stopped. Before us were gigantic prints. 'Now, now' whispered Obi, as he examined the spoor. 'Now, now.' Even I could see how fresh the prints were. The lion had planted its feet in the shoreline to drink, and the water was still seeping into the pug marks. Obi had explained what to do when facing a lion. We were to 'stand quiet and look...the lion looks to us and then goes'. This sounded fine, but what if the lion didn't want to just go away?! The lions of the Okavango can and do break down the doors of huts to drag out the screaming victim inside. Our only protection was Obi's axe, my German knife, and mankind's warped sense of dominance.

The tracks led us back into the bush eventually Obi gave up. The tracks were everywhere. We didn't know where the lion was, and we were becoming apprehensive, figuring that the lion knew exactly where *we* were. I had the feeling that the lion was now behind us, along the way that we had first come, so I took the lead. We cut back thought the tangle of low trees and scrub. We couldn't see more than ten yards ahead of us, and I kept gripping the knife in my pocket, wishing it was something more formidable, like a spear.

Suddenly, we came to the original game trail that we had followed into the bush. There were our tracks, made only minutes before, and there *on top of our tracks* were the lion's huge prints. The lion was now stalking *us*! Obi and I looked at each other, and then without discussion, we quickly and silently left the area. We didn't see our lion, but we would at least still be around to try again another day.

Unexpected or unwelcome face to face encounters

Don't panic! The animal is probably as frightened as you are and also as anxious to remove itself from danger — but some animals will attack if they feel overly threatened. In most cases, back off very slowly — facing the animal — and take care not to trip or make sudden (threatening) movements. Don't just turn around and run.

There are a few exceptions to this basic rule, which require you to have a greater understanding of the animal facing you:

Buffalo To hikers this is probably the continent's most dangerous animal. Short-sighted, but with an excellent sense of smell, they can charge without provocation if they fear that something is sneaking up on them. Avoid a charge by quickly climbing the nearest tree, or by sidestepping at the last minute. If adopting the latter technique, stand very still until the last possible moment as the buffalo may well miss you anyhow!

Black Rhino Like buffalo, these are short-sighted, fairly stupid, and frequently bad-tempered. Similar tactics of tree-climbing or dodging are employed.

Elephant A major problem only if you disturb a mother and calf, so keep well away from these. Lone bulls can usually be approached quite closely, and will mock-charge (ears flapping, head up, noisy) as a warning before they do it for real (ears down, head down, full speed ahead!). Testing this out is not for the faint-hearted — so steer well clear.

Lion A major problem as they are so well camouflaged that you can be next to one before you know it. If you had been listening you would probably have heard a warning growl already! Back off slowly, showing as little terror as you can — but if a lion starts to show too much interest in you then, as a last line of defence, make loud, deep confident noises — shout at it!

Hyena Not so much a problem when walking, though often met at popular campsites at night, where they make raids for anything they can pick up. Show aggression and confidence and you should have no problems.

Hippo Surprisingly account for many deaths in Africa, with a bite that can split a boat in half. Treat with respect in and out of the water. Don't go swimming if there are hippos about! If you are in a boat, never cut off a hippo in shallow water from its escape route to deeper water or it will panic. If necessary, stop paddling and tap loudly several times on the boat to warn the hippos of your presence — they will then all head for the safety of the deeper water, leaving a shallower route by the bank for you to use. Likewise on land, never get between a hippo and the water.

Crocodiles Dangerous only in the larger rivers and the Okavango. Check for tell-tale signs of eyes and nostrils just above the water before going for a swim or even washing on the bank. Ask local people which areas are safe — crocodiles are territorial, and generally only hang around one or two deep pools of water in a given stretch of water. Bathe with someone keeping a look out.

Snakes These really are not the great danger that people imagine. Most will flee when they feel the vibrations of your footfalls, though a few — like the puff adder — will stay still, puffing themselves up as a warning, and for this reason you should always watch where you place your feet. Similarly, there are a couple of arboreal (tree) species which may be taken by surprise if you carelessly grab at vegetation as you walk, requiring you to watch where you place your hands.

Eat a Worm

by Phil Deutschle

Anyone who travels will encounter dubious-looking dishes. Be it duck embryos, blood sausage, or fish eggs, one is caught in a dilemma between the desire to be part-of-the-gang and the fear of being sick in public.

I find it best not to know what I am eating until I am finished — in Botswana this is made easier when eating in a dark and smoky kitchen. Unable to see the food, I just grope into it with my fingers and chew. I try to keep in mind that if everyone else is eating it, it must be OK. That's the essential truth — the food is O.K. It's just our individual biases that are sometimes out of line.

Worms, or to be accurate, the larvae of various insects, are eaten all over Africa. In Botswana they are just common fare, eaten like french fries. The local "worm" is the caterpillar of a large moth, the *gonimbrasia belina*. The caterpillar grows to the size of a finger, and lives solely on the mopane tree, thus its common name, the mopane worm. They are collected in the summer and can be dried for long-term storage. Some educated Batswana, trying to emulate Western Whites, scorn mopane worms, though the majority happily munch mopanes while sipping traditional beer.

After coming to Botswana, and slowly sliding into local society, I began wondering how, or if, I could convince myself to take the plunge and bite into a worm. One day some children presented me with a live mopane that they'd picked up by the side of the path. It was glossy black with iridescent markings of blue and green. Taking it home to be photographed, I soon got culinary ideas. I dropped the beast into boiling water, which caused it to swell to ever larger proportions. After a few minutes came the frying in hot oil laced with a pinch of salt. By then it had lost its colour and no longer resembled a worm, but reminded me of a grilled Vienna sausage. My ministrations with pot and pan had added to the impression that this was now something to *eat*. It felt only natural to bite into it. The taste was like crispy scrambled eggs.

Part 2
Namibia

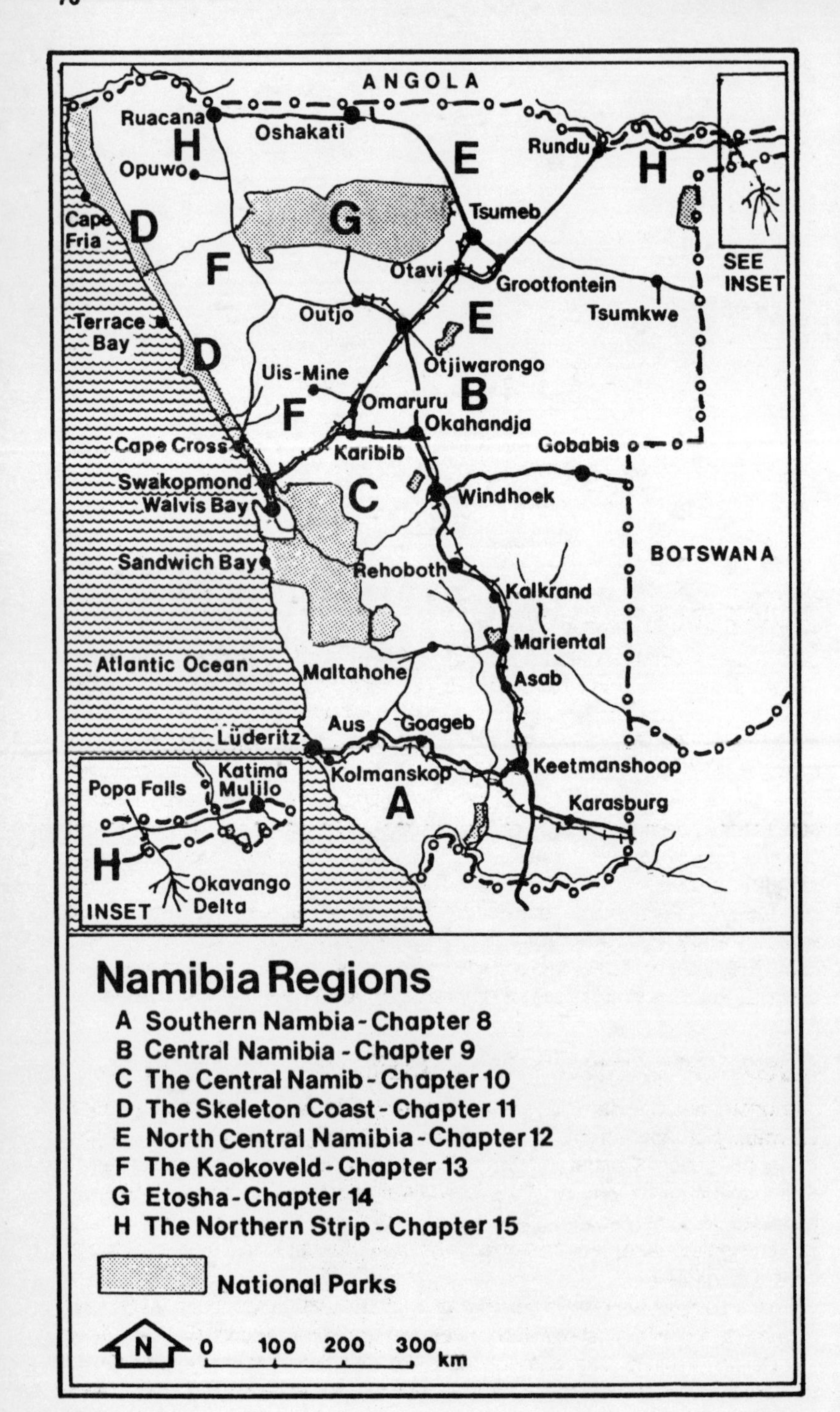
ANGOLA
Ruacana
Oshakati
H
E
Rundu
H
Opuwo
Tsumeb
Cape Fria
D
G
F
Otavi
Grootfontein
SEE INSET
Tsumkwe
Outjo
E
Terrace Bay
D
Otjiwarongo
Uis-Mine
B
Omaruru
F
Okahandja
Cape Cross
Karibib
Gobabis
Swakopmond
Walvis Bay
C
Windhoek
BOTSWANA
Sandwich Bay
Rehoboth
Kalkrand
Mariental
Atlantic Ocean
Maltahohe
Asab
Aus
Goageb
Lüderitz
Kolmanskop
Keetmanshoop
Katima Mulilo
Popa Falls
A
Karasburg
H
Okavango Delta
INSET
Namibia Regions
A Southern Nambia - Chapter 8
B Central Namibia - Chapter 9
C The Central Namib - Chapter 10
D The Skeleton Coast - Chapter 11
E North Central Namibia - Chapter 12
F The Kaokoveld - Chapter 13
G Etosha - Chapter 14
H The Northern Strip - Chapter 15
National Parks
N
0
100
200
300
km

Chapter 7

In Namibia

TOURISM IN NAMIBIA

Until recently most Namibia's tourists were from South Africa. They came, usually in their own vehicles, for the sea fishing and the game parks — both of which have well organised facilities. Now, following independence, there are a greater number of visitors from overseas, though the infrastructure and facilities developed for the South Africans remains. Namibia's attractions are generally well signposted and the national parks and reserves have a centralised booking system — based at the *Department of Nature and Conservation* (DNC) in Windhoek — which can be a great help if you make the effort to use it.

Tourism in Namibia remains on a small scale, although since independence numbers have been growing slowly. You will still find campsites where you are the only people for miles around, while many of the fascinating areas outside the official reserves are still hardly visited at all.

COST OF LIVING/TRAVELLING

I am often asked if Namibia is expensive — the answer depends very much on where you come from, where you go, and how you wish to travel. If you are coming from Central or East Africa, then food and accommodation in Namibia will seem very costly — there is no network of cheap hotels for travellers here. If you arrive direct from Europe, the same things will probably strike you as cheap, with reasonable hotels at half the cost or less of those on the Continent.

Few, if any, of Namibia's attractions are intrinsically expensive — the vast majority being within national parks which charge fairly reasonable fees. Only the DNC's Terrace Bay and the northern section of the Skeleton Coast (private fly-in safaris only) are really expensive places to go, but their prices reflect their isolation and the cost of getting there.

Obviously the style in which you travel will affect your costs greatly. Probably the best way is with your own 4WD vehicle and camping equipment. This is not the cheapest form of travel but it does allow you to camp in most places and cook your own meals — reducing your costs to only food, camping and park fees and the cost of the car. Four people in a vehicle would be ideal — then food, camping and park fees could average about R25 (£5/$9)per person per day — with vehicle costs from R30-R100 each per day, depending upon what you rent, and where you rent it from. (See *Planning and Preparations*, Chapter 4, for more detailed information.)

Without your own vehicle, you'll tend to spend more time in the towns, where money disappears much faster! A good meal will cost about R12 (£2.50/$4) and a cheap hotel room R35 (£7/$12) — you could easily end up spending R60 (£13/$21) per day, excluding transport.

Currency

At present the Namibian unit of currency is the Rand (R), divided into 100 cents — the same as South Africa. This is freely convertible for the visitor so there's no black market and no customs regulations applicable to moving it across borders. Despite some political calls for it to be changed following independence, there is no sign of this at present.

The last few years have seen the rand get progressively weaker against the pound sterling or the US dollar, and thus travel in Namibia for the western visitor has become even better value. In July 1991 the **exchange rates** are £1=R4.80 and US$1=R2.80.

Banks

Changing money at any of the commercial banks is usually easy and often, but not always, quick. Standard banking hours are 0830 to 1530 weekdays and sometimes 0830 to 1100 Saturdays, depending upon the place. These will cash travellers cheques or give cash advances on credit cards. Elsewhere Visa, Mastercard and American Express cards are often accepted, but travellers cheques which are not in Rands can be difficult to use. In the remoter areas cash is essential, and wherever you are, petrol stations always seem to require cash.

TRANSPORT

Air

International flights There are regular flights from J G Strijdom Airport to Maun (single R331) (and connections to Victoria Falls for an extra R181), Lusaka (single R593), Johannesburg (return R568) and Cape Town (return R601). While not a major centre for international flights, Namibia now has direct links with Germany — and ones planned with the UK in the near future. The airlines to watch for the latest developments are British Airways, South African Airways (SAA), Lufthansa and of course Namib Air.

Internal flights Because of its size, Namibia has a good network of internal flights which link Swakopmund (R179), Tsumeb, Oshakati, Rundu, Katima Mulilo, Keetmanshoop, and Lüderitz to the hub of Eros Airport, 3km from Windhoek's town centre. The main carriers are Namib Air and SAA, but there are also several smaller companies and hundreds of other bush airstrips. For the more adventurous, there's a 'Hire and Fly' in Windhoek if you've a private pilot's licence — and the skies are marvellously open and free of hassles.

Rail

There is a good rail network connecting the main towns with South Africa. The trains are pleasant and rarely full, but they do, however, tend to be very slow and stop frequently; travelling by train is not for those in a hurry and most travellers seem to prefer hitchhiking to taking the train.

The carriages are divided into 1st, 2nd and 3rd classes, of which 1st and 2nd have sleeping bunks while 3rd simply has benches. The only advantage of 1st class is that there are only four persons per compartment, rather than six in 2nd class. There is no food or drink available in any class except on the trains between Windhoek and South Africa.

1st and 2nd class must be reserved in advance through the Windhoek booking office (Tel: 2982032), though any station will telegraph for you.

Windhoek-Tsumeb

	Fri/Sun (arrives Sat/Mon)	
Windhoek	2045	
Okahandja	2228	
Karibib	0135	
Omaruru	0426	
Otjiwarongo	0750a	
	0930d	1030d
Otavi	1246	1358
Grootfontein		1645
Tsumeb	1435	

Tsumeb-Windhoek

	Sun		*Fri*	
Tsumeb	0745		0815	
Grootfontein		0940		0815
Otavi	0915	1147	0959	1142
Otjiwarongo	1240a	1435a	1405a	1520a
		1800d		
Omaruru		2121		
Karibib		2400		
Okahandja		0307		
Windhoek		0450		

	Windhoek-Walvis Bay	Walvis Bay-Windhoek
	Tues/Fri/Sun	*Tues/Fri/Sun*
Windhoek	1910	0610
Okahandja	2055	0428
Karibib	2354	0130
Usakos	0111	2352
Swakopmund	0525	1927
Walvis Bay	0655	1815

	Keetmanshoop-Lüderitz	Lüderitz-Keet.
	Fri/Sun	*Fri/Sun*
Keetmanshoop	1830	0554
Seeheim	1942	0435
Goageb	2154	0232
Aus	0123	2237
Kolmanskop	0123	1832
Lüderitz	0605	1800

	Otjiwarongo-Outjo	Outjo-Otjiwarongo
	Mon/Wed/Fri	*Mon/Wed/Fri*
Otjiwarongo	0820	1330
Outjo	1027	1120

Windhoek-De Aar (South Africa)

	Sat	*Wed/Sun*	*Fri*
Windhoek	1200	1845	1845
Rehoboth	1412	2116	2116
Kalkrand	1559	2318	2318
Mariental	1740	0135	0135
Tses	2030	0431	0431
Keetmanshoop	2218a	0635a	0635a
	2254d	0750d	
Grünau	-	1209	
Karasburg	0355	1315	
Upington (RSA)	0910a	1949a	
	0940d	2020d	
De Aar (RSA)	1710	0627	

De Aar (South Africa) - Windhoek

	Sat	*Mon/Thurs*	*Fri/Sun*
De Aar (RSA)	0055	0200	
Upington (RSA)	0831a	1210a	
	0850d	1236d	
Karasburg	1341	1855	
Grünau	-	2031	
Keetmanshoop	1909a	0053a	
	2025d	0135d	1910d
Tses	2215	0326	2119
Mariental	0140	0648	0035
Kalkrand	0318	0832	0219
Rehoboth	0529	1035	0423
Windhoek	0805	1310	0700

Notes

1. De Aar, in South Africa, is the terminus for Namibian trains. From here you can get a South African Railways connection to or from Cape Town or Johannesburg.
2. Where appropriate, arrival times are indicated with **a** and departure times with **d**.
3. These timetables are not comprehensive, the trains stop at far more stops than are named here.

Sample fares in rand (prices are worked out on a per kilometre basis, and can be easily calculated)

	1st	**2nd**	**3rd**
From Windhoek to			
Keetmanshoop	90	64	37
Grootfontein	111	78	45.50
Swakopmund	67	47	27.50
Cape Town	228	105	61
Johannesburg	216	153	89
From Keetmanshoop to			
Lüderitz	65	46	26.50

Bus

Namibia is currently one of the very few African countries with no cheap local buses — or equivalent — that the traveller can use. Occasionally small Volkswagen combis (minibuses) will ferry people from one town to the next, providing a good fast service at about R10 per 100km, but more usually the local people just seem to hitch, often taking several days for a journey.

There is one coach operator, Mainliner, which runs luxury vehicles, complete with food, music, videos and air conditioning, on long distance routes. However, on the Cape Town and Johannesburg routes they often won't let you travel just within Namibia (eg from Windhoek to Mariental). You have to go at least as far as South Africa with them. Note that in South Africa there are many more stops than indicated here:

Mainliner Coach

Timetable	**Windhoek-Walvis Bay**		**Walvis Bay-Windhoek**	
Windhoek	0800	1500	1300	2000
Okahandja	0856	1556	1159	2859
Karibib	1018	1718	1037	1737
Usakos	1043	1743	1012	1712
Swakopmund	1232	1932	0823	1523
Walvis Bay	1300	2000	0800	1500

Fares					
					Windhoek
				Okahandja	24
			Karibib	29	38
		Usakos	20	33	40
	Swakop.	33	36	48	57
Walvis Bay	20	37	39	51	59

	Windhoek-Tsumeb		**Tsumeb-Windhoek**	
	Tues/Thurs	*Sun*	*Mon-Wed*	*Fri*
Windhoek	0700	1400	1300	2000
Okahandja	0755	1455	1200	1900
Otjiwarongo	0954	1654	1001	1701
Otavi	1114	1814	0841	1541
Kombat	1145	1845	0813	1513
Grootfontein	1216	1916	0739	1439
Tsumeb	1300	2000	0700	1400

Fares						
						Windhoek
					Okahan.	24
				Otjiwar.	34	47
			Otavi	28	45	53
		Kombat	20	31	48	57
	Groot.	22	25	36	53	61
Tsumeb	23	26	30	41	59	69

	Windhoek-Cape Town	**Cape Town-Windhoek**
	Mon/Thurs	*Sun/Wed*
	(arrives Tues/Fri)	*(arrives Mon/Thurs)*
Windhoek	1800	0600
Rehoboth	1904	0440
Mariental	2103	0240
Keetmanshoop	2335	0010
Grünau	1310	2210
Cape Town	1200	1200

	Windhoek-Upington	**Upington-Windhoek**
	Mon/Thurs	*Sun/Wed*
	(arrives Tues/Fri)	*(arrives Mon/Thurs)*
Windhoek	1600	0600
Rehoboth	1701	0457
Mariental	1845	0313
Keetmanshoop	2109	0036
Grünau	2305	2253
Karasburg	2337	2221
Upington	0218	1857

Fares	**Wind.**	**Reho.**	**Mari.**	**Keet.**	**Grünau**	**Kara.**	**Uping.**
Upington	147	138	122	98	77	70	
Johannesburg (or Cape Town)	190	184	175	166	156	151	128

Bookings To book Mainliner, you can either phone their reservations office in Windhoek, Tel: (061) 227847 or 227848, or visit one of their agents:

Windhoek: Woker Travel
Okahandja: Okahandja Hotel
Karibib: Ströblhof Hotel
Swakopmund: Trip Travel
Walvis Bay: Woker Travel
Otjiwarongo: Blaauw Travel Bureau
Grootfontein: Tidar Tyre Centre
Tsumeb: Tsumeb Aviation Services
Johannesburg: Computicket. Tel: (011) 331-3233
Cape Town: Rennies Travel or American Express

Taxis

Taxis do operate in Windhoek but tend to be expensive, with the exception of those serving the routes between the townships and the centre which carry a very full load of passengers. See Chapter 9 for details.

Driving

Almost all of Namibia's major highways are tarred. They are usually wide and well signed, and the small amount of traffic makes them very pleasant to travel on. Less important roads are often gravel, but even these tend to be well maintained and easily passable. Most of the sights, with the exception of Sandwich Harbour, are accessible with an ordinary saloon car (referred to as 2WD in this book). Only those going off the beaten track — into Kaudom, Bushmanland or the Kaokoveld — really need a 4WD. (See chapters 4 and 6 for full details.)

Get yourself an **International Driving Permit** before you arrive in Namibia — they are legally required if you wish to drive here. With a British licence they can be obtained at any Automobile Association office (in the UK) for £3, or from Triple A in the USA.

Hitchhiking

Without a vehicle, hitching is probably the best way to travel independently around Namibia, provided that you're patient and don't have a tight schedule to keep. It is certainly one of the best ways to meet people, and can be very speedy and cheap at times. How fast you get lifts is determined by how much traffic goes your way, where you stand, and how you dress. Some of the gravel roads have very little traffic, and people wait days for even a single car to pass — the important part is to set off with enough food and (especially) water to be able to wait for this long. On a busier road, choose your hitching position carefully — junctions can be good places, if they allow you to catch the eye of a driver who's slowed down anyway, but avoid those junctions which require all the driver's concentration as you won't be spotted. Your appearance is important — if you want lifts from the local whites, avoid clothes that identify you as a 'hippy' or 'bum' in their eyes; *look like a visitor*. Dress code is, unfortunately, very conservative in most of southern Africa and tie-dyes fall into the 'hippy' category. So if you want to improve your chances of getting a lift, put on a clean shirt (men) or a skirt (women)!

Finally, for the sake of courtesy and those who come after you, it's important not to abuse people's kindness. Offer to help with the cost of fuel (most people will refuse anyhow) or pay for some cold drinks on the way. Listen patiently to your host's views and if you do choose to differ, then do so courteously — after all, you came to Namibia to learn about a different country.

Maps

See page 52.

ACCOMMODATION

Hotels

The Hotels here are without exception fairly clean and safe, so forget the stories of rats, bats and crawling beasties — just be prepared with your wallet, as few are cheap! We've grouped the hotels into three categories, **A**, **B** and **C**, based both on their price and their merits. Generally you'll get what you pay for, and only in Windhoek and Swakopmund will you find a real choice.

Category A hotels should provide excellent rooms with en suite bath and toilet, as well as a bar and restaurant. You'll normally find the service in these is excellent — equivalent perhaps to a three or four star hotel in England.

Category B hotels are generally comfortable and efficient. Although they lack the plushness or style of category A, they are considerably cheaper.

Category C hotels can vary from incredibly bare, to basic but pleasant. Though you'll probably have to share a bathroom and may have to go out to eat, there are no grounds for dreading them.

Guest Farms

These are private ranches which admit small numbers of guests, usually arranged in advance. They are often very personal and you'll eat all your meals with the hosts and be taken on excursions by them during the day. Some have game animals on their land and conduct their own photographic or hunting safaris, while one or two have interesting rock formations or cave paintings to attract the visitor.

Although the prices are generally high — rarely less than R100 per person and usually nearer R150 — they generally include full board and even day trips. For more specific details consult the current *Accommodation Guide for Tourists* published by the DNC, which has a list of the Guest Farms, their addresses and prices.

Camping

Wherever you are in Namibia, you can almost always find somewhere to camp — either there will be a campsite nearby, or you will be so far from a settlement that you can just camp by the side of the road! The official campsites which are dotted all over the country have *ablution* blocks which vary from a concrete shed with toilets and cold shower, to an immaculately fitted out set of changing rooms with toilets and hot showers. These plusher ablutions will often also have facilities where you can wash clothes and occasionally even have washing machines.

Prices are frequently per site, which theoretically allows for 'a maximum of eight persons, two vehicles and one caravan/tent'. In practice, if you've a couple of small tents you will not usually be charged for two sites — so travelling in a small group can cut costs significantly.

FOOD AND DRINK

Food

Namibia has not developed its own cuisine for visitors and the food served at restaurants tends to be European in style, with a bias towards German dishes and seafood. It is at least as hygienically prepared as in Europe so don't worry about stomach upsets. We've used the cost of the ubiquitous — and often excellent — steaks as a guide to a restaurant's price.

All this shouldn't alarm **vegetarians** unduly. Like Botswana, Namibia is a very meat-orientated society. However, there's usually a vegetarian alternative in most restaurants, and if you eat seafood the choice is widened further. If you're camping then you'll be buying and cooking your own food anyway.

In the supermarkets you'll find pre-wrapped fresh fruit and vegetables (though the more remote you go, the smaller your choice), and plenty of canned foods, pasta, rice, bread, etc. Most of this is imported from South Africa and you'll probably be familiar with many of the brand names.

Alcohol

Because of a strong German brewing tradition the lagers are good, the Hansa draught being a particular favourite. In cans, Windhoek Export is one of a number to provide a welcome change from the Lion and Castle which dominate the rest of the subcontinent.

The wine available is predominantly South African in origin, with very little imported from elsewhere. At their best, the vineyards of the Cape match the best that California or Australia has to offer, and at considerably lower prices. You can get a bottle of something drinkable from a *drankwinkel* (off license) for R4, or a good bottle of vintage estate wine for R8.

Soft drinks

Canned soft drinks, from diet coke to sparkling apple juice, are available ice cold from just about anywhere — which is fortunate, considering the amount that you'll need to drink in this climate. They cost about 50c each and can be kept cold in insulating boxes made to hold six cans, which are invaluable if you have a vehicle. These polystyrene containers only cost R5 and are available from hardware stores.

Water

All water in the towns is generally safe to drink, though may taste a little metallic if it has been piped for miles. Natural sources should usually be purified, though water from underground springs — occasionally found flowing in dry river beds — seldom causes any problems. (See Chapter 5, page 56 for more detailed comments.)

Tipping

Service charges are seldom included on restaurant bills and so a 10% tip usually meets with appreciation. Hotel porters and other attendants should also be tipped — a couple of rand is usually expected. National parks staff, except perhaps the lodge attendants, do not expect tips.

HANDICRAFTS AND WHAT TO BUY

With rich deposits of natural minerals, Namibia can be a good place for the enthusiast to buy **crystals and gems** — but don't expect many bargains as the industry is far too organised! For the amateur, the desert roses — sand naturally compressed into forms like flowers — are very unusual and great value at around R5, while iridescent Tiger's Eye is rare elsewhere and very attractive. For the enthusiast, forget the agates on sale and look for the unusual crystals — in Windhoek the *House of Gems* is a must.

In Kavango and Caprivi you'll find some good local **woodcarvings** of masks, figures and animals, often sold by the side of the road on small stalls.

In the Kalahari regions, **Bushmen crafts** are some of the most original and unusual available on the continent, often using ostrich eggshell beads with very fine workmanship. These can be difficult to find in Namibia, outside a few expensive shops in the major towns — so try Ghanzi in Botswana or possibly hunt around Tsumkwe in Bushmanland.

ORGANISING AND BOOKING

Public holidays

New Year's Day — January 1
Good Friday, Easter Monday
Independence Day — March 21
Worker's Day — May 1
Ascension Day (40 days after Easter Sunday)
Day of Goodwill — October 1
Human Rights Day — December 10
Christmas Day — December 25
Family Day — December 26

National parks

The **Department of Nature and Conservation** (the DNC) — sometimes called the *Directorate of Nature Conservation and Recreation Resorts* — is the government department responsible for all the National Parks and is efficient, if rather pedantic in its bureaucracy. The difficulty with its well organised system is that booking accommodation in advance must be done through the Windhoek office or not at all. There's really no substitute for going along there (on Independence Way, next to the Main Post Office) in person with the dates of your trip, and checking the availability of accommodation as you book it.

You can, theoretically, reserve accommodation by post — though paying for it in advance from overseas could cause problems. Try writing to the Directorate of Nature Conservation and Recreation Resorts, RESERVATIONS, Private Bag 13267, Windhoek. Tel: information section (061) 33875, reservations (061) 36975, or telex NATSWA Windhoek 0908-3180.

Entry permits for most parks are available at the gates, provided you're there before they close and there's space left. There are two main exceptions: permits to stay at Naukluft, Terrace Bay and Torra Bay can only be obtained from Windhoek DNC; permits to drive through the Namib section of the Namib-Naukluft Park are available at most of the regional tourist offices.

COMMUNICATIONS

Post

The post is efficient and reliable. An airmail letter or post card costs 35c and takes about a week to get to Europe. For larger items, sending them by sea is much cheaper (R4.65 to register and post a 1kg packet), but may take up to three months and isn't recommended for more fragile items.

Telephone, fax and telex

The telephone system is currently linked into the South African system, enabling you to dial direct internationally, without going through the operator, from any public phone box — provided you've enough R1 coins. You can then arrange to be called back, which is a lot cheaper than reversing the charges. The larger hotels offer fax facilities, as do many of Windhoek's secretarial companies.

MISCELLANEOUS

Electricity

Sockets supplying power at 220/240V and 50Hz, taking the standard British three pin plug, are available in all the towns — and even at the campsites in Etosha!

Embassies and High Commissions in Windhoek

Angolan Embassy, Ausspannplatz 3, Ausspann Corner House, 4th floor, PO Box 6647. Tel: (061) 32301

Botswanan High Commission, 22 Curt von Francois St, PO Box 20359. Tel: (061) 228451

British High Commission, PO Box 22202. Tel: (061) 223022

Canadian High Commission, 111a Gloudina St, Ludwigsdorf, PO Box 2147. Tel: (061) 222941

Royal Danish Embassy, 29 van Collar St, P.O.Box 20124, Tel: (061) 224923

Egyptian Embassy, 10 Berg St, Klein Windhoek, PO Box 11853. Tel: (061) 221501

Finnish Embassy, 48 Toermalyn St, Eros Park, PO Box 3649. Tel: (061) 224153

French Embassy, 1 Goeth St. Tel: (061) 22 9021

German Embassy, 11 Uhland St, Klein Windhoek, PO Box 231. Tel: (061) 229217

Kenyan High Commission, 35 Promenadewag, Klein Windhoek. Tel: (061) 226836

Malawian High Commission, 56 Bismark St, P.O.Box 23384. Tel: (061) 221391

Nigerian High Commission, 4 Omuramba Rd, Eros, PO Box 23547. Tel: (061) 32103
Norwegian Embassy, 73 Gevers St, Ludwigsdorf. Tel: (061) 31410
Portuguese Mission, 28 Garden St. Tel: (061) 28736
South African Embassy, Corner of Jan Jonker and Klein Windhoek Rds, PO Box 23100. Tel: (061) 229765
Swedish Embassy, 10 Stein St, Klein Windhoek, PO Box 23087. Tel: (061) 222905
Swiss Consul-General, 10 von Eckenbrecher St, Klein Windhoek, PO Box 22287. Tel: (061) 222359
USA Embassy, 14 Lossen St, Ausspannplatz, PO Box 9890. Tel: (061) 221610
Zambian Embassy, 22 Curt von Francois, Corner Republic Rd, PO Box 22882. Tel: (061) 37610
Zimbabwean High Commission, Corner of Independence Way and Grimmy St, PO Box 23056. Tel: (061) 228134

Hospitals, dentists and pharmacies

Should you need one, the main hospitals are of a good standard and will treat you first and ask for money later! The hospital in Windhoek is on Florence Nightingale Rd, off Pasteur St, in the north-west of the city. Dentists are also available in the main towns. When travelling outside the cities you could be many miles from even a basic clinic, let alone a good hospital, so carrying your own comprehensive medical kit is an absolute necessity in case of accident. (See Chapter 5, page 55 for just the basics of a kit.)

Pharmacies in Windhoek stock a full range of medicines, though specific brands are sometimes unavailable. However, do bring with you all that you need, as well as a repeat prescription for anything that you may lose or run out of just in case. A few of the larger towns also have good pharmacies, but don't rely on getting anything out of the ordinary away from the capital.

Imports and exports

Being a member of the Southern African Customs Union (SACU) means that there are few restrictions between Namibia and either Botswana or South Africa. If you wish to export any animal products, including skins or legally culled ivory, make sure you obtain a certificate confirming the origin of every item which you buy. Remember that even with these many countries will not allow skins or particularly ivory to be imported — check the current regulations before you leave.

Newspapers, radio and TV

There are no press restrictions in Namibia, though the government-sponsored Namibia Broadcasting Corporation (NBC) accounts for the radio and TV stations. Out of Windhoek the radio can be difficult to receive, while the TV maintains a restricted service to the major areas. In Windhoek there is a choice of newspapers, but *The Namibian* — with its usually patriotic flavour — is dominant.

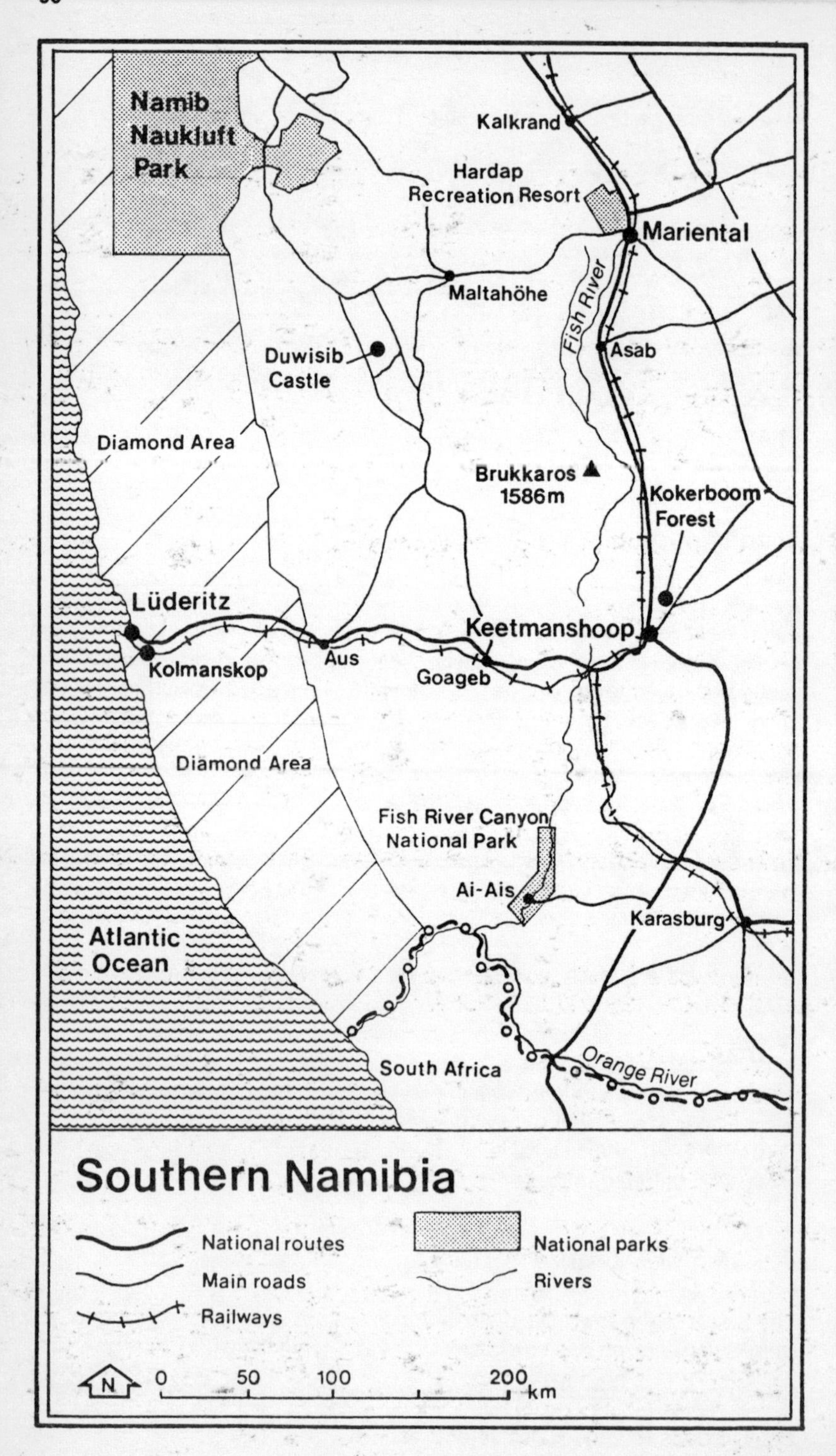
Namib
Naukluft
Park
Kalkrand
Hardap
Recreation Resort
Mariental
Maltahöhe
Fish River
Asab
Duwisib
Castle
Diamond Area
Brukkaros
1586m
Kokerboom
Forest
Lüderitz
Keetmanshoop
Kolmanskop
Aus
Goageb
Diamond Area
Fish River Canyon
National Park
Ai-Ais
Karasburg
Atlantic
Ocean
South Africa
Orange River
Southern Namibia
National routes
Main roads
Railways
National parks
Rivers
N
0
50
100
200
km

Chapter 8

Southern Namibia

If you have journeyed north from South Africa's vast parched plateau, the Karoo, or come out of the Kalahari from the east, the arid landscapes and widely separated towns of Southern Namibia will come as no surprise as you arrive here for the first time. Like the towns, the main attractions of the region are far apart — but special enough to be worth the effort that is needed to reach them.

The Fish River Canyon, perhaps the country's most awe-inspiring sight, is easy to find, hard to forget and invariably empty of the crowds that can spoil the most spectacular places elsewhere in the world. On the coast, Lüderitz is visually less stunning though none the less fascinating for its architecture — while the town's isolated position adds to the almost tangible feeling of history here.

The towns and main attractions are ordered roughly from south to north.

Karasburg

Within easy reach of the South African border, Karasburg is a popular stopover. There are several garages, a good Spar supermarket, and a Sentra hardware shop. Both First National and Bank of Windhoek have branches here open normal hours, 8.30am to 3.30pm and also Saturday mornings.

Where to stay and eat

Category C

The hotels in the town are both well run by the same man and signposted from the centre of this small town. The **Kalkfontain** — PO Box 205. Tel: (06342)172 — is slightly the better as all its rooms are air conditioned and it serves meals. Costs singles R55-R60, doubles R65-R75, triples R100, 4-beds R120, 5-beds R150 — inclusive of breakfast.

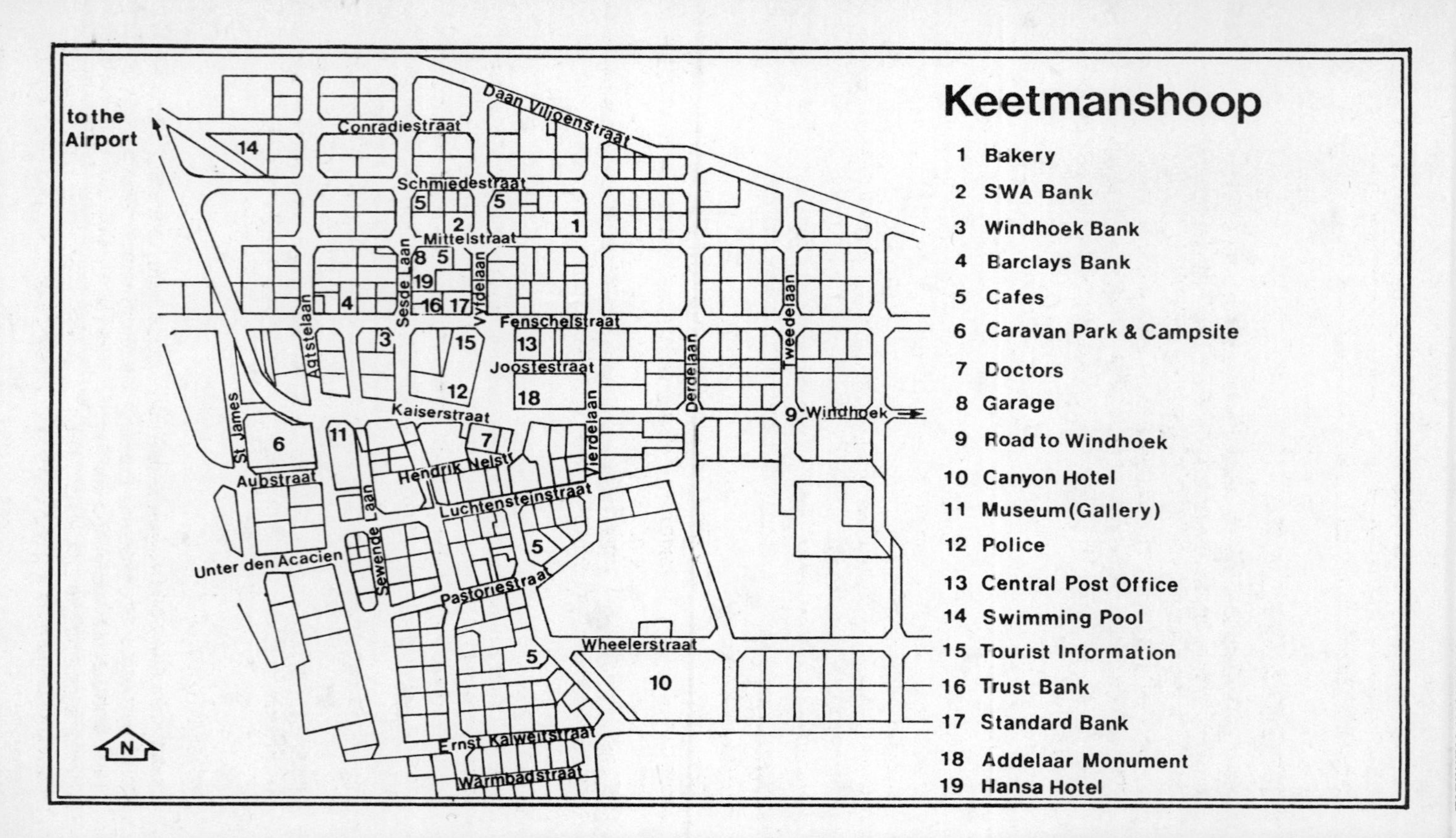
Keetmanshoop
1 Bakery
2 SWA Bank
3 Windhoek Bank
4 Barclays Bank
5 Cafes
6 Caravan Park & Campsite
7 Doctors
8 Garage
9 Road to Windhoek
10 Canyon Hotel
11 Museum(Gallery)
12 Police
13 Central Post Office
14 Swimming Pool
15 Tourist Information
16 Trust Bank
17 Standard Bank
18 Addelaar Monument
19 Hansa Hotel
to the Airport
Daan Viljoenstraat
Conradiestraat
Schmiedestraat
Mittelstraat
Fenschelstraat
Joostestraat
Kaiserstraat
Hendrik Nelstr
Luchtensteinstraat
Pastoriestraat
Wheelerstraat
Ernst Kalweitstraat
Warmbadstraat
Tweedelaan
Derdelaan
Vierdelaan
Vyfdelaan
Sesde Laan
Sewende Laan
Agtstelaan
Windhoek
St James
Aubstraat
Unter den Acacien
N

The rooms at the **Van Reibeck** — PO Box 87. Tel: (06342)23 — are about R5 cheaper, but some are without air-conditioning and there's no food available. Guests are asked to eat at the Kalkfontain!

KEETMANSHOOP

Keetmanshoop, often pronounced 'Keetmansverp', lies about 482km south of Windhoek at an altitude of 1,000m. Originally a Nama settlement on the banks of a seasonal river, the Swartmodder, it is named after the German industrialist Johann Keetman who provided the funds to found a mission there in the 1860s. Now Keetmanshoop is the largest town south of the capital and, being centrally located, makes a good base from which to explore the region.

Getting there

Keetmanshoop is at the hub of the region's road network. The main B1 conveniently skirts the east of the town, which is just north of the turn off to Lüderitz. Hitchers should have few problems. On the railway, the town is the terminus for the Lüderitz trains, and a major stop on the line into South Africa (see chapter 7 for details).

Where to stay

Category A

Canyon Hotel PO Box 950, Keetmanshoop. Tel: (0631)3361. Singles R85, doubles R135; full breakfast R15, continental R12.50. Comfortable — if a bit impersonal, with air-conditioning and all facilities, including a pool. The Canyon is not very central, however, and is found on the southern side of town by following the signs from the B1 (see map).

Category B

Hansa Hotel PO Box 141, Keetmanshoop. Tel: (0631)3344. On Sesdelaan, between streets Mittel and Fenschel. Rooms: single sharing bath R56, single with own bath R76, double R112; all prices include full breakfast. Centrally located with good air-con rooms, and a pleasant, if somewhat seedy, bar.

Municipal camp site. On Agtstelaan and Aub St just off Kaiser St, this costs R5 per site, R2 per person. Camp on the grass around the excellent ablutions, not on the gravel areas. There are washing machines for R1 per load — this must be one of the country's best sites! Tel:(0631)3316.

Where to eat

Both the **Hansa** and **Canyon** hotels serve good food, though the former is definitely overpriced. Probably the best food, and certainly the liveliest bar, are at **Schutzen Haus** — about 400m south of the campsite on Agtstelaan. The restaurant has an intimate atmosphere and steaks for around R19, while the adjacent bar has a good choice of beers and an L-shaped pool table!

What to see and do

If you've a spare half hour, the **museum**, near the campsite on the corner of Sewendelaan and Kaiser St, is worth a visit. Built in 1895, as a church — to replace the original one which was washed away by a flood — it now houses an interesting collection of local memorabilia, including a selection of early cameras. Open weekdays 8.00am to 12.00am, 4.00pm to 6.00pm. Saturdays 8.00am to 12.00am. If you're not going to the Kokerboom forest (see below) then don't miss the few small specimens in the museum garden!

Recently an **art and craft centre** has opened up on the corner of Sesdelaan and Pastorie St. Despite the number of plastic toys and athena prints there, it does have some good locally produced items and is worth a visit.

Getting organised

Keetmanshoop has few obvious attractions, though it's a pleasant town to wander around and a good one in which to visit banks and supermarkets. Entering the town on Kaiser St, from the B1 turn-off, the main shopping area is to be found one block to your right on Fenschel St. In many ways, this is really the main street of town, and here you will find the banks — Barclays, Standard, Trust and the Bank of Windhoek — as well as a couple of supermarkets and shops.

Your next stop should be the useful tourist information centre, opposite the main post office on the central square. This has all the standard maps and tourist guides and is run by a woman who has excellent local knowledge. For those interested in local history, the building itself — which also houses the Namib Air office — was built in 1910 and recently declared a national monument.

Kokerboom Trees

The Kokerboom *(Aloe Dichotoma)* occurs sporadically over a large area of southern Namibia, usually on steep, rocky slopes. Its English name, quiver tree, refers to its use by the Bushmen for making arrow quivers - the inside of a dead branch consists of only a light fibrous heart which is easily gouged out leaving a hollow tube.

The Kokerboom is specially adapted to survive in extremely arid conditions: the fibrous branches and a fibrous trunk are used by the tree for water storage, as are thick succulent leaves, whilst water loss through transpiration is reduced by waxy coatings on the tree's outside surfaces. Additionally, in common with most flora adapted for such harsh conditions, the kokerboom has a very slow growth rate.

Excursions from Keetmanshoop

The Kokerboom Forest

Although it doesn't seem like a forest, this is probably the thickest stand of trees in the region. Here *Kokerbooms*, which sport bright yellow flowers in June and July, cover the hillsides in their hundreds, creating, especially at dusk, a weird and fascinating landscape.

Getting there It's well signposted and about 14km north-west of the city, on the way to Koës. If hitching, walk out on the B1 about 2km from the town to the turning to Koës and try from there — it should be easy to get there and back in a day at most.

Brukkaros

Rising to 650m, the volcanic crater of Brukkaros towers over the expanse of the bare plains which surround it. In the 1930s a solar observation station was built here, on the crater's western side, to take advantage of the clear air in the region — and though the observatory is not used any longer the air seems as clear as ever!

Despite having no water or facilities at all, if you're well equipped, Brukkaros makes an unbeatable place at which to sleep out under the stars — and you will almost never meet another camper. The crater also provides some challenging scrambles around its rim, and the opportunity just to sit and watch dust-devils twist their way for miles around as the sun goes down.

Getting there From Keetmanshoop take the B1 north about 70km, then route 98 west towards Berseba. (Here there are a couple of shops, open in the morning and late afternoon, and one petrol pump.) About 500m before the town is a turn-off north, marked D3904, which eventually rises up to the crater rim, becoming a steep and rocky track. Negotiable all the way with a 4WD, we got to within 1.5km of the top with a 2WD and walked the rest. Don't even think about trying to hitch your way here — you'll have to walk from Berseba, and that is farther than it appears!

Karakul farm

Whilst travelling around this region, people are often surprised to see sheep on the dry pasture of local farms. These are in fact an unusual type of Central Asian sheep known as *karakuls*, which are well adapted to such shrivelled lands, although they do need a daily drink of water!

The original karakul were brought here in the early 1900s by a German fur trader, Paul Thorer, after an unsuccessful attempt to introduce them to the damper climes of Europe. Since then, they have been selectively bred and their pelts marketed under the name of *swakara* (from 'SWA' and 'KARAkul') sometimes known as Persian Lamb.

Prices for pelts depend upon their colour, pattern, and hair quality as well as the fluctuating world market. The most sought after colour is white, which occurs only on this sub-continent, followed by black, grey and brown, all of which are farmed in the USSR and Afghanistan as well as here. The lambs are slaughtered when only 36 hours old (the fur is said to be at its softest) and subsequently the pelts are sold by auction in London.

If you wish to know more, then the head of the government research station, Mr Kotze, will usually be happy to see visitors — though there's no formal guided tour available as yet.

Getting there Take Kaiser St out of town, towards the airport, and then turn left when the airport is in sight. Follow the signs to *Gellap ost karakul* farm.

FISH RIVER CANYON

At 161km long, up to 27km wide and almost 550m deep, it ranks second in size only to Arizona's Grand Canyon, and must be one of Africa's least known natural wonders. This means that you are very unlikely to have a visit here spoiled by coach-loads of tourists, or leave with the feeling that the place is over commercialised. In fact, if you visit outside the holidays, you may not see anyone else here at all.

Formation The canyon probably started to form about 500 million years ago when fractures in the earth's crust created a deep, steep-sided valley, which was then further deepened by glacial erosion during the ice ages. Later faults and more erosion added to the effect, creating canyons within each other, until a mere 50 million years ago when the river started to cut its meandering path along the floor of the valley.

Getting there

Car If you're driving from Keetmanshoop, take the B4 south-west for about 44km before turning off left onto the C12, then continue 77km before taking a right and following the signs to *Vis Rivier* Canyon. This final part of the approach is across undulating ridges and spectacular semi-desert plains, leaving the visitor guessing until the very last moment about the spectacle ahead.

Hitching This can be exceedingly difficult, although getting to the C12 turn-off shouldn't be a problem. If your visit coincides with the start of the South African school holidays, or if you're coming from the south, then it's worth trying an alternative approach starting from the route 316 turn-off on the main B1, about 260km south of Keetmanshoop and 37km north of the South African border.

The Conservation Area

The whole area around the Fish River Canyon has been designated as a conservation area, and a few days spent here — perhaps staying at Hobas — can be very peaceful and pleasant indeed. Keep your eyes open for wildlife, as even on the most barren of plains you will find ostrich and springbok, whilst on the more rocky parts you may see baboon, klipspringer, or even Hartmann's mountain zebra.

After leaving the main observation point, which overlooks the spectacular Hell's Bend, it's worth taking the tracks to the Palm Springs viewpoint, and the opposite one to Hiker's Point, even if they are a bit rough — the views are different, and equally stunning.

Where to stay

The **Hobas Rest Camp** is situated in a slight valley, about 10km from the main viewing point. It has shady campsites with communal facilities, a kiosk for basic supplies, and a pool — and costs R25 per site. It only opens from the second Friday in March to 31 October (the same as Ai-Ais), and though it is best booked at the DNC in Windhoek, you can often find a free site by just turning up. The camp is within the conservation area and whilst we were last there several flocks of ostriches picked their way across the very bare plain around the camp.

Whilst the camp is very pleasant, it is not luxurious and can get very hot, so if you need more comfort — stay at Ai-Ais (see below)!

Hiking

For the physically fit, the Fish River, so called for being Namibia's only river permanent enough to support fish, marks the route for a classic hike. Starting from Hiker's Point, on the north of the main view point, the trail descends to the river itself and follows it 86km to Ai-Ais in the south. It takes four or five days. En route there are hot springs, wind-carved rocks, and glimpses of the shy wildlife, as well as a lot of boulders to clamber over. Fishing is permitted, so you could bring a hook and line with you in addition to your normal kit and a food supply for about six days (neither Ai-Ais or Hobas has good hiking food).

The only way to organise this hike is by booking well in advance at the DNC in Windhoek, and you must have transport to and from the canyon for yourselves. It is best to camp at Hobas on the night before you start, and here you must show a certificate of medical fitness (obtained within the last 40 days) and sign an indemnity form. The hike costs R25 per person, for a group with a minimum size of three. It has been possible for some hikers to join existing groups at fairly short notice, and thus avoid transport problems by sharing costs — talk to the DNC in Windhoek.

Beware: the day temperatures on the floor of the canyon are usually hot, even by Namibian standards, so don't carry any unnecessary weight, or try to rush through the deep sand at the bottom of the canyon — you are on your own, so enjoy it and take your time.

Ai-Ais Hot Springs

2WD. Entrance fees: R5.00 for vehicles, R5.00 per adult, R2.50 for children

Ai-Ais, meaning 'burning water' in the local language, refers to the sulphurous springs which well up from the ground here. It's very much a spar, with an outdoor pool, private hot tubs, shop, filling station, and even a restaurant.

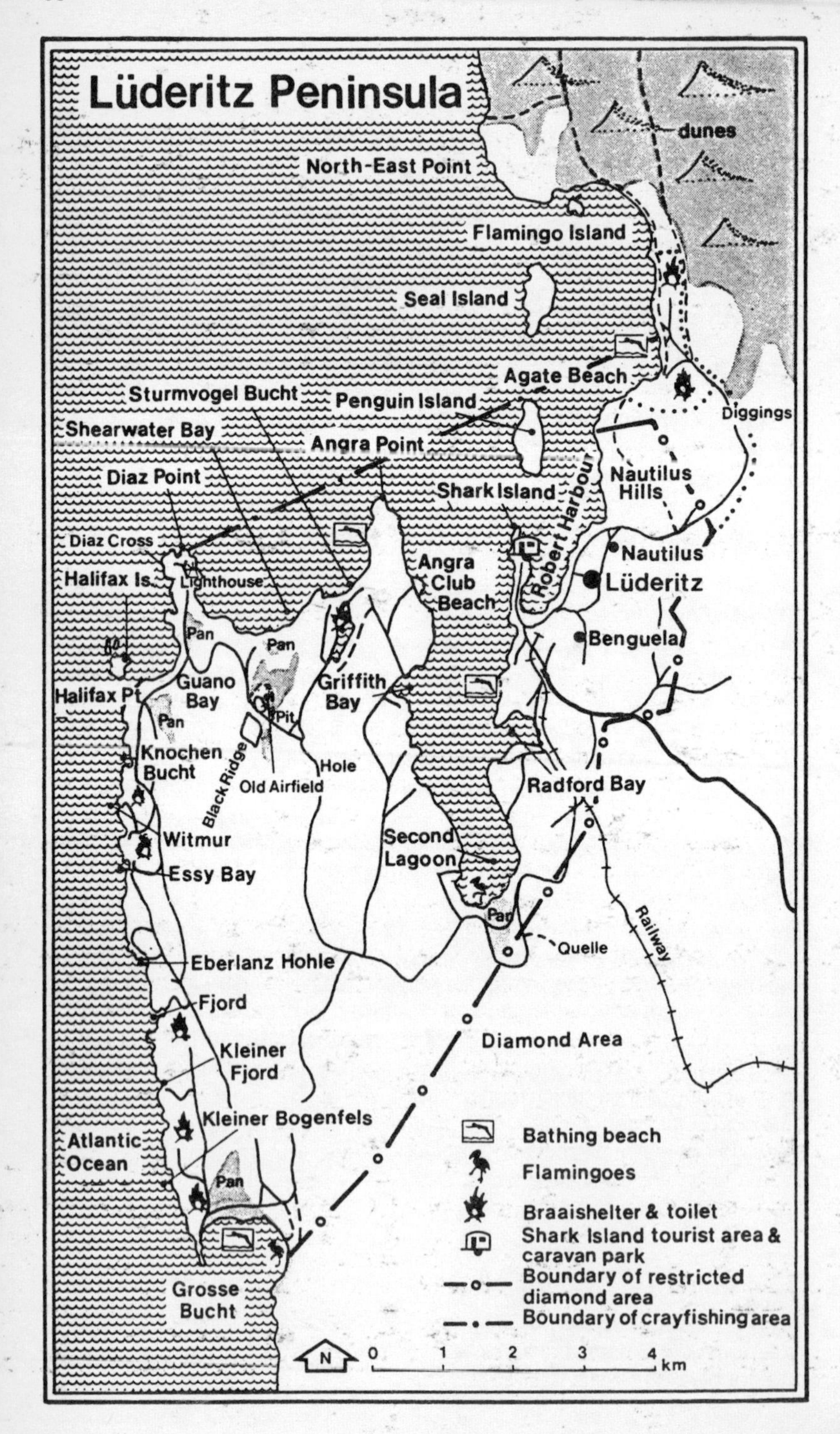
Lüderitz Peninsula
dunes
North-East Point
Flamingo Island
Seal Island
Agate Beach
Sturmvogel Bucht
Penguin Island
Diggings
Shearwater Bay
Angra Point
Diaz Point
Shark Island
Robert Harbour
Nautilus Hills
Diaz Cross
Nautilus
Halifax Is.
Lighthouse
Angra Club Beach
Lüderitz
Pan
Pan
Benguela
Halifax Pt
Guano Bay
Griffith Bay
Pit
Pan
Knochen Bucht
Black Ridge
Hole
Old Airfield
Radford Bay
Witmur
Second Lagoon
Essy Bay
Pan
Quelle
Railway
Eberlanz Hohle
Fjord
Diamond Area
Kleiner Fjord
Kleiner Bogenfels
Atlantic Ocean
Pan
Grosse Bucht
Bathing beach
Flamingoes
Braaishelter & toilet
Shark Island tourist area & caravan park
Boundary of restricted diamond area
Boundary of crayfishing area
N
0
1
2
3
4
km

Getting there

Ai-Ais lies toward the southern end of the Fish River Canyon conservation area and is approached by taking the C10 west from the main B1, south of Grünau. Alternatively, route 324 from just east of Hobas provides some excellent, if distant, views as it meanders southwards parallel to the canyon. This then joins the C10 for the last few km before Ai-Ais which are steep, winding and quite amazing in their own right.

Where to stay

Accommodation is R55 for a four-person hut with communal ablutions, R100 for a four-person flat including bath, shower and toilet. Both include hotplates, fridges and bedding. Camping costs R25 per site. Note that, as for Hobas, Ai-Ais is open only during the winter from the second Friday in March to the 31 October.

The Road to Lüderitz

Travelling from Keetmanshoop to Lüderitz is about 334km, mostly tar, and best done early in the day to avoid a powerful, late afternoon sun from the west. After leaving Keetmanshoop, look out for a mountain on the north known locally as *Kaiserkrone* — the Kaiser's crown — for its unusual conical shape. 106km west of Keetmanshoop you'll pass through **Goageb**, before hitting the gravel section of the road. This lasts for 102km until the **Aus** turn-off, after which the surface is again tar.

To the west of Aus, the road gradually descends onto an increasingly dry gravel plain, circled by distant jagged mountains. Look out around here for the world's only **desert horses** — a herd of around 170 horses which have adapted themselves to the Namib, using a waterhole at Garub as their only drinking point. Once, as we passed them in early March, they were all to be seen grazing photogenically on a thin, green sea of freshly sprouted grass.

Incongruously, half way across this parched plain, someone has created a **picnic site** — complete with tables, chairs, and nine well-watered trees for shade. The opportunity to stop at somewhere so spectacular definitely shouldn't be missed — this could be the continent's most solitary picnic site!

Continuing towards Lüderitz requires care, especially at night — watch for the marching dunes which constantly try to submerge the road in sand, building up into dangerous ramps and mounds as they do so. **Take care**: these do not feel at all soft if you meet them at speed, so slow right down to about 20kph and also keep watch for the bulldozers which fight a constant battle to clear them from the road.

Goageb

This is a is a good place to stop and refuel. There's a simple shop and a small *category C* hotel, the **Konkiep**. Tel: (06362)3321. Here singles are R20 and doubles R35 — it's basic but clean!

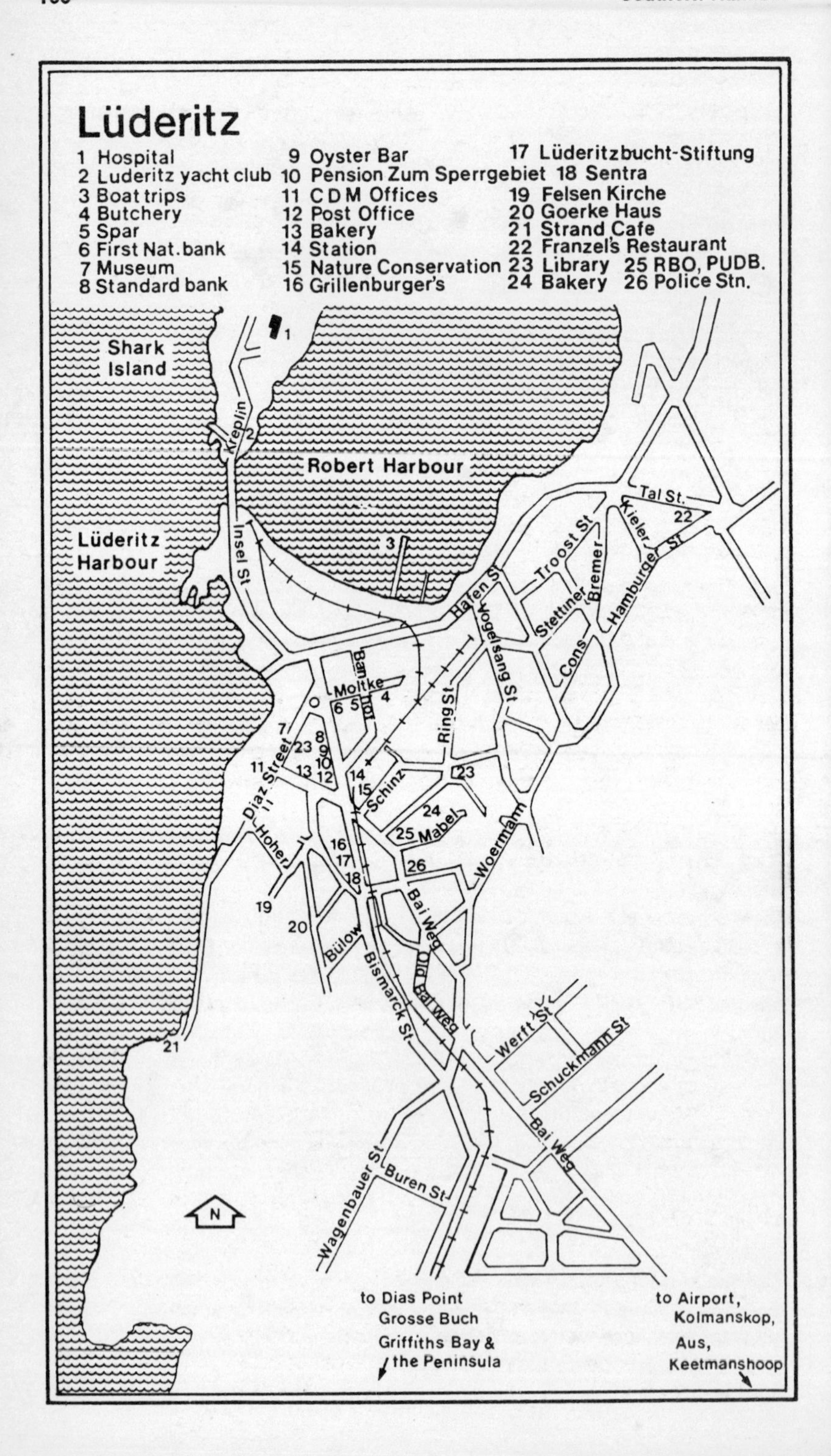
Lüderitz
1 Hospital
2 Luderitz yacht club
3 Boat trips
4 Butchery
5 Spar
6 First Nat. bank
7 Museum
8 Standard bank
9 Oyster Bar
10 Pension Zum Sperrgebiet
11 C D M Offices
12 Post Office
13 Bakery
14 Station
15 Nature Conservation
16 Grillenburger's
17 Lüderitzbucht-Stiftung
18 Sentra
19 Felsen Kirche
20 Goerke Haus
21 Strand Cafe
22 Franzel's Restaurant
23 Library
24 Bakery
25 RBO, PUDB.
26 Police Stn.
Shark Island
Robert Harbour
Lüderitz Harbour
Kreplin
Insel St
Hafen St
Tal St.
Kieler
Troost St
Bremer
Hamburger St
Stettiner
Cons
Vogelsang St
Bahnhof
Moltke
Ring St
Diaz Street
Schinz
Mabel
Hoher
Woermann
Bülow
Bai Weg
Old Bai Weg
Bismarck St
Werft St
Schuckmann St
Wagenbauer St
Buren St
N
to Dias Point
Grosse Buch
Griffiths Bay &
the Peninsula
to Airport,
Kolmanskop,
Aus,
Keetmanshoop

Aus

Aus was the site of a South African prisoner of war camp during the First World War. It's now a fairly quiet town with one small (*category C*) hotel, the **Bahnhof**. Tel: (063332)44. Single rooms are R30-R40 and doubles R40-R60. Breakfast is R8. Two of the ten rooms do have air-conditioning if the heat is really getting to you!

We have heard that the C13, south of Aus, is in navigable condition and can be followed through Rosh Pinah, along the banks of the Orange River, and to Noordoewer on the South African border. This would make a very interesting route indeed if you're going south, though its viability would need to be checked locally!

LÜDERITZ

Trapped between the desiccating sands of the Namib and the freezing waters of the *Benguela* current, Lüderitz struck us as a fascinating old German town, rich in history and full of character. These days its precarious prosperity is based mainly on the seasonal crayfish harvest and, increasingly, on tourists from both home and abroad. Because of its location, Lüderitz is not somewhere to 'drop in on' — you need to make a special journey to reach it — which perhaps gives rise to its sleepy atmosphere.

Unlike much of Namibia, its weather is moderated by the ocean and hence generally mild, though with the occasional morning fogs and strong breezes from August to January. If you do decide to visit, base yourself here for a few days — and don't forget your bathing suit for those bracing afternoon dips!

Getting there

Train There's an overnight train which leaves Keetmanshoop at 1830 on Fridays and Sundays, arriving at 0605. From Lüderitz to Keetmanshoop the trains are also on Fridays and Sundays, but leaving at 1800 and arriving at 0554. Costs: 1st class R65, 2nd class R46, 3rd class R26.50.

Car See *The road to Lüderitz* section above.

Hitching is fairly easy both into and out of the town, but start as early in the morning as you can. It should be fine to accept lifts which only go as far as Goageb or Aus — as unless it is very late in the day you will probably pick up another, and it is not a problem to stay in either town.

Where to stay

Category B

Bay View Hotel. PO Box 100. Tel: (06331)2288. Near the bottom of Bay road (*Bai weg*), this is the town's most expensive hotel. It has a small pool and pleasant, well-kept rooms arranged around a courtyard. Like the Kapps, it's owned by the Lüderitz family! Singles R60, doubles R92, Triples 112, full breakfast R9.

Kapps Hotel. PO Box 387. Tel: (06331)2701. Also found on Bay road, this is the oldest of Lüderitz's hotels — and gives that impression too! Singles R40 without bath, R50 with, doubles R76, full breakfast R10.

Zum Sperrgebiet Hotel. PO Box 373. Tel: (06331)2856. Despite its unimpressive front on Bismark St, Zum's clean and spacious rooms made this our favourite hotel. Shared facilities: singles R45, doubles R60. *En suite* facilities: singles R50, doubles R70, triples R90, four-beds R140. An excellent full breakfast costs R8.80, and you don't even need to be a resident.

Category C
Strand Bungalows. These are small holiday chalets on a hillside behind the Strand Cafe (see map) and right above the town's only real bathing spot. They are individually priced, depending on whether or not they have cookers, fridges, and *en suite* facilities. Singles R15-R50, doubles R20-R75, triples R45-R90, four-beds R50-R100.

Shark Island Campsite. A true island until 1908, this spit of land is now just a picturesque, if windblown, campsite. Costs R10 per site. *Take care*: It's worth pitching your tent firmly, to withstand heavy breezes!

Where to eat

Lüderitz is definitely the place to eat if you're into crayfish in a big way. It won't be cheap (unless you caught it yourself), but at least here it is guaranteed to be fresh and will probably be well prepared.

The **Kapps** and **Bay View** Hotels do have restaurants, although they often won't serve non-residents without prior notice.

Instead try the **Strand Cafe**, open all day for snacks and from 7.30pm to 10pm as a restaurant — it's lively and a good meeting point, though not the place for a romantic meal *à deux*. Crayfish R32 (for a good portion), steaks R19, wine R11.

Franzls restaurant, on Tal St, can be recommended for authentic German food as well as seafood. A quieter atmosphere than the Strand.

What to see and do

The main attraction in the town itself is the large number of magnificent old buildings, built mostly in the German Imperial and Art Nouveau styles. A **walking tour** is an excellent way to spend an afternoon, and you could also visit the small **museum**, open on Tuesdays, Thursdays, and Saturdays from 4pm to 6pm. To this end there are walking guides available containing details of the local history and points of interest — ask at the museum or the DNC offices on Schinz St. Do include a wander up **Nautilus hill**, just above the town, which makes a pleasant detour with some great views.

From the harbour, the yachts *Sagitta* and *Sedina* run trips lasting a few hours to **Diaz Point** and **Halifax Island** (a jackass penguin colony). Costs R25 and can be booked at the agent next to Hotel Zum, or directly with the boats in the harbour. On a hot day these are excellent, and the best (only!) way to get a good look at the penguins.

Visits to the **crayfish processing plants** can be arranged during the season between November and April, as can tours of the **karakul carpet weaving factory**, or the **oyster farm**, all year around. Enquire of the travel agents in town for arrangements and bear in mind that they'll probably be fairly informal affairs.

Finally, no visit would be complete without a dip in the Southern Atlantic, but beware — it's cold!

Excursions from Lüderitz

Agate beach

A beautiful and unusual beach of almost black sand, sprinkled with tiny shining fragments of mica. It may not be white coral sand, but it's pleasant and quiet to lie on or wander along beachcombing — just don't go expecting to find too many agates! There's a good road here — signposted from the corner of Tal and Hamburger St.

Kolmanskop

This boom-town, 9km east of Lüderitz, was abandoned over 30 years ago, and is now preserved to give a fascinating insight into the life of a diamond mining community during the early part of the century. Parts of it, like the old casino, have been specially restored, and there's a fascinating guide on duty who remembers it all as it was at its peak.

With the desert dunes fast encroaching on many buildings, there's a real ghost-town feeling about the place and it's certainly worth visiting on your way out of Lüderitz. To do that, however, you must first obtain a permit from the CDM (Consolidated Diamond Mines of South Africa) offices on Diaz St. These cost R3 and you won't be admitted without one, so stop at the CDM before you leave Lüderitz!

The Lüderitz peninsula

South-west of the town lies the Lüderitz peninsula, surrounded by sea on three sides and yet a desert within. Around its coast are many beaches; some rocky, one or two sandy, all deserted and worth exploring if you've a car. (Whilst driving 2WD cars here, be careful not to follow the tracks across soft sand made by 4WD vehicles — otherwise, like a group we helped, you'll need one to tow you out!). To get there simply take Lüderitz St — the continuation of Bismark St — south, keeping the railway on your left.

Stopping places

Griffith bay gives excellent views of the town on its barren coastline, as well as some crystal clear rock pools to dabble in.

Diaz point, reached by a short wooden bridge, has a marble cross commemorating Bartholomeu Diaz, the first European to enter the bay, who sheltered here in the late 14th Century and called the bay, rather unimaginatively, *Angra Pequena* or 'little bay'.

Going south of Diaz point, into the area where you can legally collect crayfish, there's a reminder of the coast's forbidding nature in the form of a grave marked: 'George Pond of London, died here of hunger and thirst 1906.'

Following the road further south along the peninsula, Halifax Island comes into view with its jackass penguin and cormorant colonies. Further still, *Eberlanz Höhle* is a cave cut deeply into the rock about ten minutes walk from the road. Just keep to the left of the pinnacle before following the path down.

Frequent turn-offs for fishing spots and *braii* sites are passed as you continue until Grosse Bucht is reached, a long sandy bay good for crayfishing. From here you can cut across the neck of the peninsula and back to Lüderitz.

Warning The second lagoon is noted for having stranded motorists on it, as well as flamingos, so don't try to drive across it!

Asab

This small group of buildings 124km north of Keetmanshoop, and 97km south of Mariental is notable mainly for being just to the west of what used to be one of the country's most unusual landmarks — the 'Finger of God.' The pleasant little **Asab Hotel** has singles for R25-R35, doubles for R40-R50 and breakfast at R6.50.

Mukorob, or the **Finger of God** as it was more widely known, was a huge rock pinnacle which had resisted erosion for centuries — balancing some 34m above the surrounding plain, held by only a narrow neck of rock. Unfortunately it collapsed around the 8th December 1988, and now can be seen standing only on local postcards!

The cause of its fall has been the object of intense speculation, especially as local legends linked it with divine approval. At first, it was claimed as evidence that God was displeased with contemporary developments in the Independence process, while later it was suggested that right-wing political extremists might have been to blame — rather than divine intervention!

Subsequent theories have linked it with seismic activity and, in particular, the shock waves from the Armenian earthquake — which occurred on the 7th December at 11.41 local time.

MARIENTAL

Though a pleasant and very central town, there's remarkably little to do here. Most visitors stopping in this region shop here and then head out to Hardap, 20km north-west of the town (see below).

The town itself is just to the east of the main B1, and split into two by a railway running parallel to the road. On the western side is an excellent Central Bottle Stall, a good Spar supermarket, a Standard Bank, a Bank of Windhoek, both of the town's hotels, and most of its garages.

Crayfish or Lobster?

The terms *crayfish* and *lobster* are often incorrectly used by many people — including most restaurant managers! Crayfish and lobsters are different animals both in their appearance and habitat, though they do both belong to the crustacean order *decapod*. While lobsters are marine animals, nearly all crayfish species live in freshwater.

Crayfish are normally found in freshwater streams and lakes. They spend the day concealed under rocks or logs, and come out at night to feed on insect larvae, worms and snails — some even eat vegetation. They are characterised by: a jointed head and thorax and a segmented body; a sharp snout, with eyes on movable stalks; and five pairs of legs, of which the front are a powerful pair of claws. They can live for up to 20 years, and the largest species — from Tasmania — can weigh up to 3.5kg.

Lobsters can be split up into four families: true lobsters; spiny lobsters (or 'sea crayfish' — hence the confusion); slipper or shovel lobsters; and deep-sea lobsters. All are marine and *benthic* (bottom-dwelling), feeding mainly by scavenging for dead animals, but also taking live fish and seaweed. Of these four families, only the true and spiny families are of commercial importance.

True lobsters are distinguished by having claws on their first three pairs of legs, with the first pair being larger and uneven in size. Spiny lobsters do not have such large claws, but have very spiny bodies instead for protection. The rock lobster, *Jacks lanandei*, is a spiny lobster and accounts for most of the 'crayfish' that gets eaten in Namibian restaurants.

Lobster fishing is an important industry in Namibia (especially in Lüderitz) and there are strict legal controls to prevent overfishing. It's illegal to catch animals with a carapace length of below 650mm — ie before they are about 7 years old — and fishing is only permitted within season — from 1st November to 30th April.

The current lobstering fleet is composed of about 20 motherships, which each carrying eight row boats. A further half dozen craft ferry between the shorebound factories and the fishing vessels. The fleet operates along the Namibian coast, from the Orange River to the southern border of the Namib-Naukluft Park (around 100 miles north of Lüderitz) and the industry as a whole employs over 1000 people. Almost all of the catch is processed into frozen lobster products, of which 97% are sold to Japan; the rest — as lobster tails — are sold to the USA.

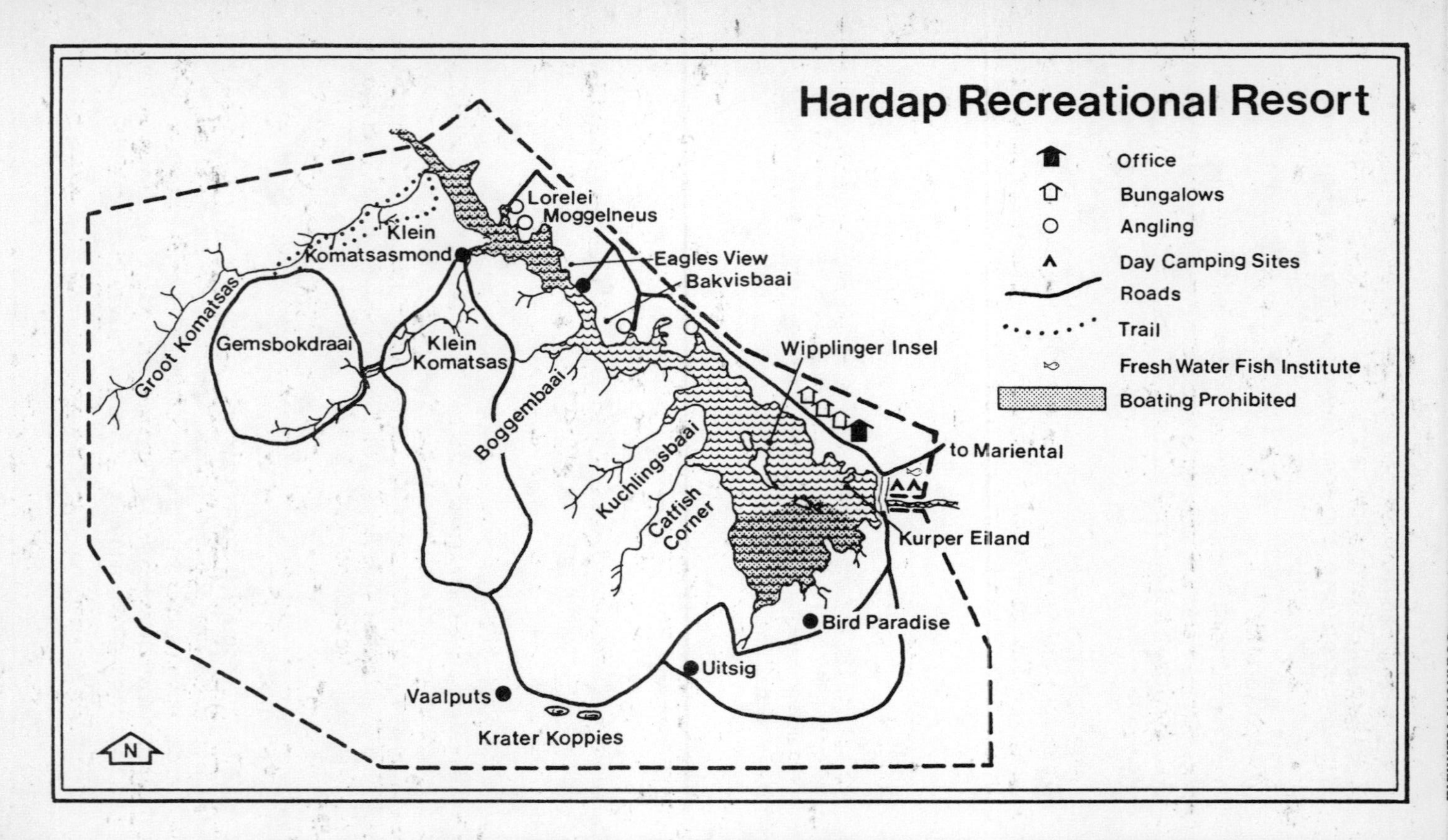
Hardap Recreational Resort
Office
Bungalows
Angling
Day Camping Sites
Roads
Trail
Fresh Water Fish Institute
Boating Prohibited
Lorelei
Moggelneus
Klein
Komatsasmond
Eagles View
Bakvisbaai
Groot Komatsas
Gemsbokdraai
Klein
Komatsas
Wipplinger Insel
Boggembaai
Kuchlingsbaai
to Mariental
Catfish
Corner
Kurper Eiland
Bird Paradise
Uitsig
Vaalputs
Krater Koppies
N

The First National Bank is immediately on the other side, while to reach the Post Office you must cross the railway, take a left along Orieboom St, then bend right onto Ernst Stumpfeweg, and another left at the Top Store.

Where to stay

There's no official campsite — most visitors stay at Hardap. In case of necessity there are two hotels, close together, but very different in character! They are within a few yards of each other, just north of the Spar on the town's main street.

Category B

Mariental Hotel PO Box 671. Tel: (0661)856. Lively bar, quiet TV lounge, spotless rooms, very friendly and helpful staff — though often booked up! Singles R66 (some with facilities, others without), doubles R88, breakfast R8.80.

Category C

Sandberg Hotel PO Box 12. Tel: (0661)2291. A seedy and run down place, with a very unhelpful owner and rooms priced individually. Singles range from R35, doubles from R60. We found the bar to be well worth avoiding and before even ordering a drink we were hassled — generally a great rarity in Namibia!

Hardap Recreational Resort

2WD. Entrance fees: R5 per person and R5 per car (one-off charge).

254km south of Windhoek and 24km from Mariental, lies Namibia's largest man-made lake. It's a popular place for local watersports, and a good place to stop for a night or two.

Where to stay

The self-contained bungalows here are well maintained and good value, while the camping sites can be exposed and windy! 5-bed bungalow R90, 2-bed bungalow R45, 2-bed room R30, camping R25 per site. Accommodation should be booked in advance at the DNC in Windhoek, but out of season you're quite likely to find space available.

Amenities

There is a shop which stocks basic foods, alcohol, gifts and postcards; a marvellously large pool with a small kiosk adjacent for soft drinks; a bar which, though it is small and shuts at 9.30pm, is good when open; and a restaurant which is inexpensive (R12 for a main course) but uninspiring. Fish is your best bet here, and with it check out the extensive range of *Simonsig* estate wines.

What to see and do

A large section on the southern side has been designated as a **game park**, with ostrich, kudu, mountain zebra, gemsbok and even eland as the highlights. There are two walking trails through the area (of 9 and 15km), which are best done early in the morning to escape the heat, and over 80km of game drives.

For ornithologists, **the lake** is an important refuge for many water birds, including ospreys, fish eagles, and several species of heron. On an island amid the lake is one of the country's largest breeding colonies of great white pelicans — binoculars are invaluable!

Near Hardap's entrance is the **Freshwater Fish Institute**, which is at the centre of efforts to preserve Namibia's (understandably!) few indigenous species of fish. Again, there's no 'tourist tour' but if you're interested then call by. We found the staff to be enthusiastic and informative, and their breeding programme fascinating.

For less dedicated fish-watchers, the reception office has an interesting small aquarium, exhibiting various Namibian fish in several large, well-kept tanks, as well as a very useful noticeboard displaying, amongst other things, the **latest road information**. These notices should not be missed, especially if you're heading off the tar during the rainy season!

Maltahöhe

This small town is conveniently placed off the main north-south route, close to Duwisib Castle, the Namib-Naukluft National Park, Sossusvlei and Sesriem (see Chapter 10). There is a fairly comprehensive general store and fuel available.

Where to stay

Category C

Maltahöhe Hotel PO Box 20. Tel: (0661)856. Run by Mr von Fischer, this has singles for R40, doubles for R62, and breakfast at R7.50. In the evening, there is even a restaurant available. Mr von Fischer will take parties out on trips to Sossusvlei in his Land Rover — a possible way of visiting the Namib-Naukluft area for those without vehicles.

Duwisib Castle

A marvellous castle, built of sandstone and containing some fascinating German furnishings and antiques. Originally constructed for Captain von Wolff around 1909, it is currently owned by the DNC and undergoing some changes — so see them before you visit, to check that it's open.

Getting there It's situated about 81km south-west of Maltahöhe. To reach it, take the C14 south for 38km and then turn a right onto the D824. 12km later, turn left onto the D831, then 16km later right onto the D826. After about 15km the entrance gate is on your right. It can be conveniently approached via the D826 direct from Sesriem.

Kalkrand

A small town 75km north of Mariental, on the B1 to Windhoek. There's a First National Bank on Maltahöhe Rd, but it only opens on Tuesday, Thursday, and Saturday from 9.30am until noon. The town has only one hotel, called — surprisingly — the **Kalkrand Hotel** PO Box 5. Tel: (06672)29. (*Category C*) It is reasonably clean and the manager will cook food on request, even if there's no menu! Singles R30-35, doubles R40-45.

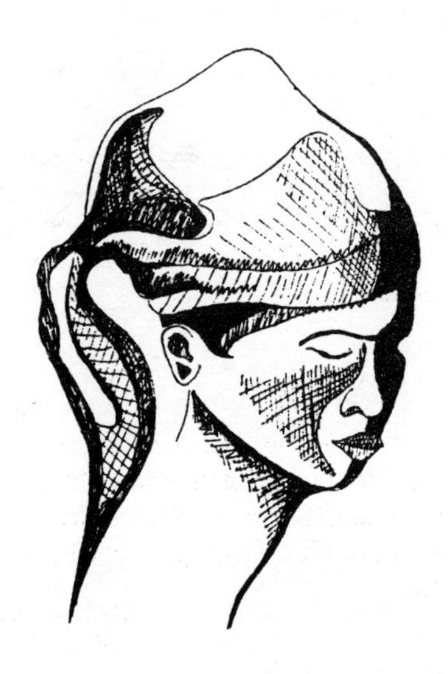

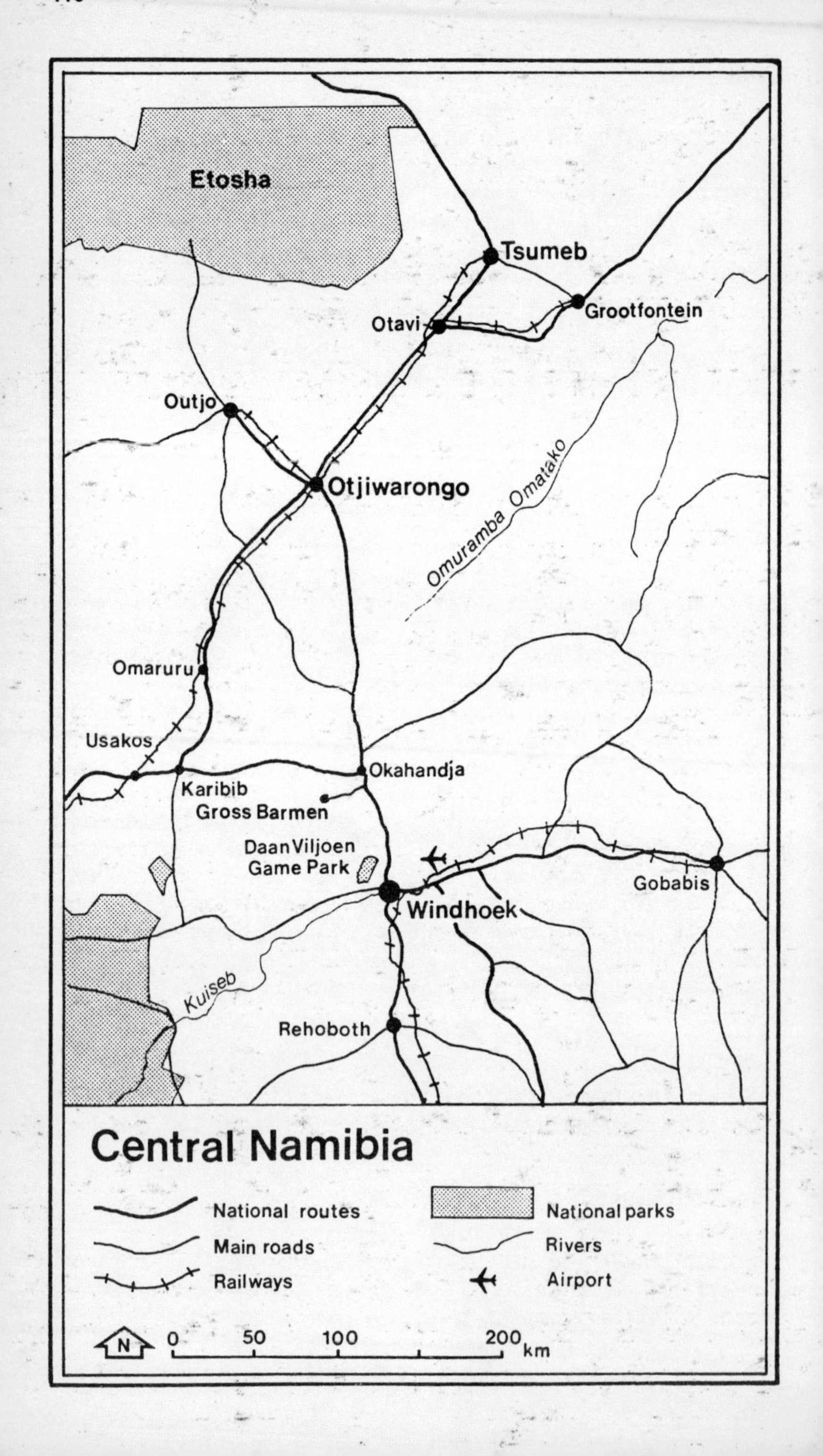
Etosha
Tsumeb
Grootfontein
Otavi
Outjo
Otjiwarongo
Omuramba Omatako
Omaruru
Usakos
Karibib
Okahandja
Gross Barmen
Daan Viljoen
Game Park
Windhoek
Gobabis
Kuiseb
Rehoboth
Central Namibia
National routes
Main roads
Railways
National parks
Rivers
Airport
N
0
50
100
200
km

Chapter 9

Central Namibia

Despite this chapter being dominated by the country's nerve centre, Windhoek, it is worth remembering that the city only occupies a very small fraction of the region's area. It does not sprawl for miles, and a drive of only 10km from the centre will leave you on an open highway — whichever direction you choose. Here lies much of the area's appeal for me, as some of the quieter roads are truly breath-taking.

The C26 route to Swakopmund takes a good six hours to drive — being very steep and winding in places — but the scenery is continually spectacular from the mountain views of the Gamsberg Pass to the deep fissures of the Kuiseb Canyon. The roads leading to Solitaire and the Naukluft mountains are attractions in their own right, while the Bosua Pass on the C28 from Windhoek to Swakopmund is beautiful but very steep. Whichever routes you take — allow plenty of time for safety's sake and to appreciate them all the more.

The towns and places of interest are arranged from south to north.

Rehoboth

Just north of the Tropic of Capricorn and south of Windhoek, Rehoboth is the centre of the country's Baster community (see Chapter 2, page 15).

Where to stay

Category C

The Rio Monte PO Box 3097. Tel: (06272)161. This is the only hotel in the centre of town with singles for R30 and doubles R40. It's above a noisy bar and the rooms are exceedingly bare.

Reho Spa Well signposted on the south-east side of town. There's a memorable jacuzzi of thermal spring water the size of a swimming pool here as well as an outdoor pool and some very good bungalow accommodation. Bungalows cost R30 for 4-beds, R35 for 5-beds and R40 for 6-beds — all have fridges, cookers etc. The place can be marvellously empty if you avoid the weekends and holidays.

What to see and do

Museum Located just behind the post office. It's small, but has an excellent section on bank notes (!) as well as some good local history exhibits.

Oanab Dam

A few kilometres to the west of Rehoboth, this is one of the country's newest dams. There is a display at the lookout point showing 'before' and 'after' photos of the dam's construction, as well as some of the technical drawings used. It's an amazing thought that such a small body of water as this is has a catchment area of about 2700 square kilometres!

WINDHOEK

The Capital of Namibia, Windhoek spreads out in a wide valley between bush-covered hills and appears, at first sight, to be really quite small. Walking through the centre, its pavement and balcony cafes conspire with a warm climate and some picturesque old German buildings to give it a light, airy, European feel. There are lots of tall modern offices around, though none that really class as skyscrapers, and the pace of life here is pleasantly slow.

Though the city and its surroundings have few, if any, major tourist attractions, most travellers will spend at least a few days here at some point in their trip. Those with their own transport will probably want to organise National Park accommodation and permits for the rest of their time in Namibia — the centralised nature of the DNC makes this easy to do — while those without a car can get together with others to hire one, or look for lifts.

Windhoek also has all the embassies, is the country's best destination for money or letters to be sent to, and is generally by far the biggest centre at which to get anything you need. It is also one of the few places where you are guaranteed to meet other travellers. Invariably there will be a few who have just returned from a few weeks in the wilds — with a myriad of helpful hints, and a craving for the city's comforts. This is the most up-to-date source of travel information that you will find — so do not miss the chance to chat.

Despite the end to formal racial segregation with Independence, the city itself in practice is still largely segregated with South African style 'townships' to separate 'black' and 'coloured' people from the 'whites'. Katutura township — for 'blacks' — is furthest from the centre and has shops, a small food market and many houses tightly-packed onto crowded streets. Nearer to the centre is Khomasdal township — for 'coloureds' — similar in all respects to Katutura apart from the skin colour of its inhabitants. Finally, surrounding the centre, are the posh white suburbs with large, security-fenced houses and dogs on guard that set the street barking as you pass. The white suburbs are slowly becoming more mixed, but it will take some time for the colour divisions to disappear.

Getting there

Windhoek is well linked to the other cities in Namibia and to South Africa by air, rail, and coach services (see *In Namibia*, Chapter 7, page 79), though there isn't — as yet — any system of cheap 'African' buses. It's quite likely that this will start to develop with independence, so keep your eyes open!

Air Windhoek has two airports — both are small, modern and very pleasant — at least as airports go. Eros airport, near the Safari Hotel, caters for most of the internal flights and small aircraft, while J.G. Strijdom airport handles the international flights.

Getting back from J.G.Strijdom to the city is no problem at all as the hitching is very easy towards Windhoek, but getting to it can be difficult as it is quite a long way out of town — about 33km along the B6 Gobabis road. To find transport out there, first contact the Namib Air offices, Tel: (061)38220 — there should be a scheduled shuttle service. Alternatively, try at the Kalahari Sands and Safari hotels as these sometimes run courtesy buses for guests. As a last resort take a taxi to the outskirts of town and hitch from there, making it obvious where you are going with a written sign.

Hitchhiking The main problem hitching out of town is finding a suitable hitching spot. If you make it obvious that you're a visitor, then hitching from near the centre sometimes works by getting you a short lift to a better hitching point. Going south towards Rehoboth, aim to hitch on the B1 near the Safari Hotel. You could get there by talking nicely to the driver of the Safari's courtesy minibus, or failing that it's an hour's walk!

To hitch east, walk out on the Gobabis Rd, hitching as you go, until the Klein Windhoek junction. For Swakopmund, Walvis Bay or the north, you need to get to the B1, which is nearly two hours walk away. A quicker way is to get one of the minivans going to Katutura and hop off half way — but check the route with the driver before you set off! For an arranged lift, try ringing the local radio station (start with NBC's number from the phonebook) which has a slot for people offering or needing lifts. They will broadcast your request with a contact phone number — if you have no number then they will take messages for you, but they are rather apt to lose them!

Where to stay

More than any other city in Namibia and Botswana, Windhoek has a real range of different hotels to suit different budgets. None could be regarded as run down, as is often the case in other capitals, so you're unlikely to find yourself in a hole wherever you stay. That said, none is very cheap either!

Category A

Kalahari Sands PO Box 2254. Tel: (061) 36900. Part of the South African hotel group 'Protea Hotels', the Kalahari Sands on Independence Way is

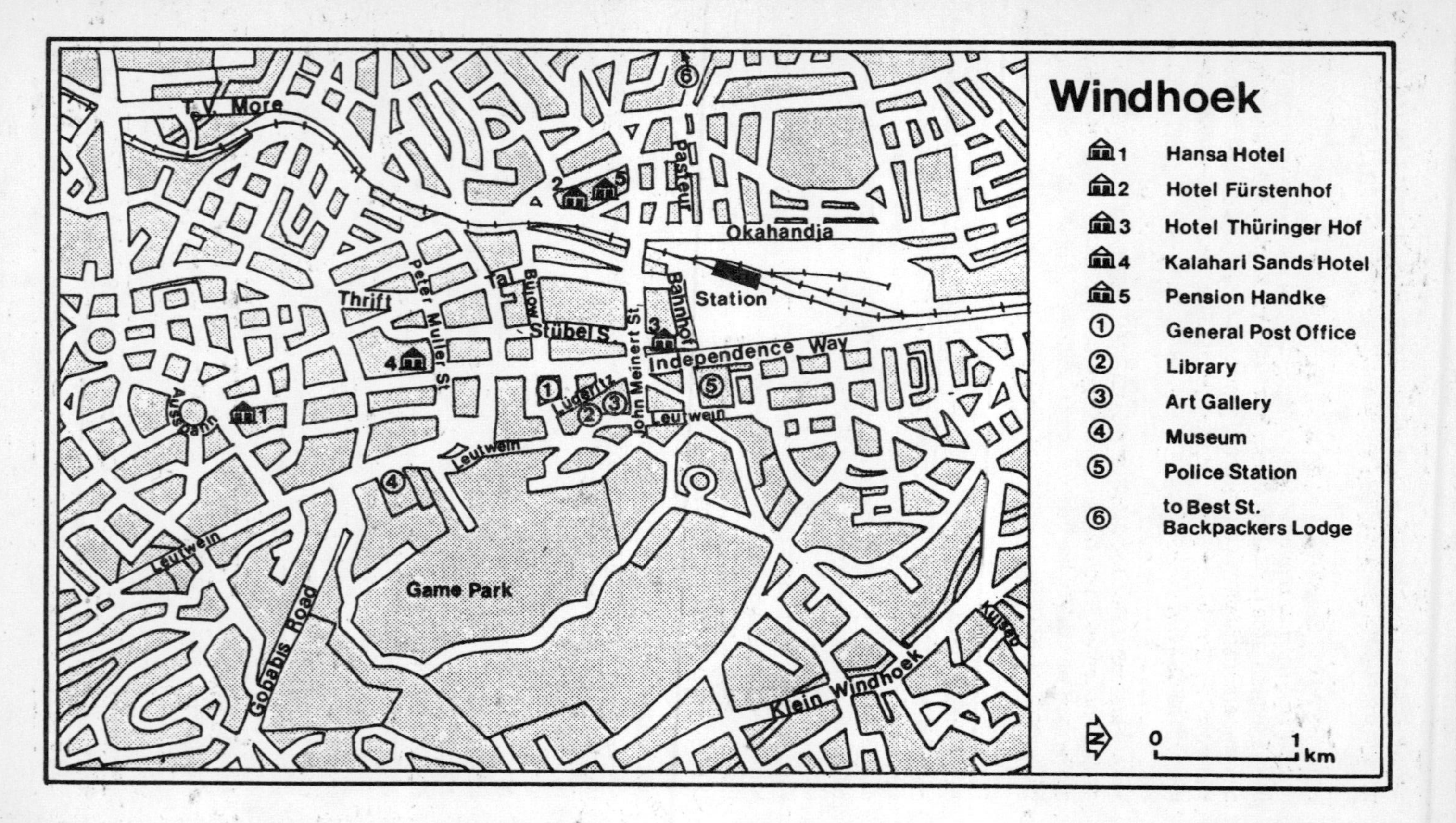

Windhoek
1 Hansa Hotel
2 Hotel Fürstenhof
3 Hotel Thüringer Hof
4 Kalahari Sands Hotel
5 Pension Handke
1 General Post Office
2 Library
3 Art Gallery
4 Museum
5 Police Station
6 to Best St. Backpackers Lodge
N
0
1 km
T.V. More
Pasteur
Okahandja
Station
Bahnhof
Tal
Bülow
Thrift
Peter Muller St
Stübel S.
John Meinert St.
Independence Way
Lüderitz
Leutwein
Ausspann
Game Park
Gobabis Road
Klein Windhoek
Kuiseb

central, plush and in character rather like a Sheraton. It's the most expensive hotel in town. Singles R225-R260, doubles R275-R320, including breakfast.

Hotel Safari PO Box 3900. Tel: (061) 38560. About 3km from the centre of town on the road to Rehoboth, the Hotel Safari sprawls over several acres and includes a large pool set in lawns. Singles R170, doubles R230, including an excellent breakfast. If you've no transport, there's a regular free minibus into and out of town which starts opposite the Kalahari Sands on Independence Way.

Hotel Fürstenhof PO Box 316. Tel: (061) 37380. Less than 1km west of the centre, Fürstenhof is perched in a quiet spot on Romberg St. It's small, very stylish, and we thought the best value of the expensive hotels. Singles R128-R132, doubles R178-R184, including breakfast.

Category B
Hotel Thüringer Hof PO Box 112. Tel: (061) 26031. Towards the northern end of Independence Way, near Bahnhof St, one of the city's two Namib Sun hotels. Its rooms are well furnished but it lacked atmosphere and seemed over-priced. Singles R120, doubles R165, including breakfast. The lively beer garden serves snacks for R6-R12.

Continental Hotel PO Box 977. Tel: (061) 37293 Very centrally placed, tucked away opposite the MODEL store on Independence Way, it's recently been refurbished. Singles R85-R165, doubles around R190, extra beds R25 and breakfast R10. The first floor cafe is OK as a meeting point.

Hansa Hotel PO Box 5374. Tel: (061) 223249. At the southern end of Independence Way, it's fairly uninspiring. Singles R67-R87, doubles R96-R120, including breakfast. The large public bar gets very busy, so get a room far from it!

Aris Hotel Tel: (161) 36006. 25km south of the city, this unusual hotel has only six rooms and yet a large restaurant and bar. The food is reputed to be excellent, with all the normal main courses below R20 (excluding seafood!), and the menu looks mouthwatering. Singles R42.50-R46, doubles R35-R40, breakfast R10. Book in advance.

Category C
Hotel-Pension Handke PO Box 20831. Tel: (061) 34904. Just out of the centre on Rossini St, this is run by an older, German-speaking woman and it's the cheapest hotel not out of town. Singles R71.50, doubles R99, including a German breakfast of cold meats, cheeses and coffee. Good value, if you get along well with the owner!

South West Star Hotel PO Box 10319, Khomasdal. Tel: (061) 224689. About 4km out of the centre in Khomasdal, it's run down and not at all plush! Has the dubious advantage of being next to the country's top night club, Namibia Nite (see below). Singles R30-R32, doubles R60-R64. Don't expect food here.

Hotel Kapps Farm 20km east of the city on the Gobabis Rd, this didn't impress us at all. Singles R59 — 71.50, doubles R66 — 93, breakfast R8.50.

Backpacker's Lodge Mr H.L. Sachse, PO Box 8541, Brachbrecht, Windhoek 9000. In a residential area some 2km north of the city centre is 25 Best St. Here for R15 per person per night there's a dorm bed (normally 10 beds available but will take more), an excellent shower, a small kitchen with fridge, and even use of the pool. The owners prefer you to vacate the flat between 10am and 4.30pm, but they can be flexible about it. To book in advance, drop a note to the above address to let him know when you're arriving.

Campsite Situated just behind the Safari Hotel on the road to Rehoboth, this is Windhoek's only campsite at the moment. It has a reasonable ablution block and costs around R12 per person per night, though check with the hotel first to see if any of the permanent caravans are free as their rent can be quite cheap. Hitching into and out of the city is not difficult as plenty of the site's residents work there. This is one of the best places to arrange long-distance lifts, just ask around!

Where to eat

With about two dozen restaurants to choose from, you shouldn't have problems finding somewhere to eat! Most serve fairly 'international' fare, often with a German bias, though there are a few Asian specialists and even one serving Japanese food! Small cafe's — especially in the townships — serve good local food.

During the day in town, the two cafes in the Trip arcade, **Schneider** and the **Central**, are always busy and good places to meet other travellers — from there you can watch the world go by as the paper sellers hassle people in the arcade. For the evening, the more memorable restaurants in (alphabetical) order are:

The Front Page Go up a flight of outside stairs on the east side of Stübel, south of Bülow. Mainly inexpensive Italian dishes, burgers and steaks. Pizza R14, Pasta R11, for large portions. It's the liveliest place in town with a young cliental and a separate bar — so you don't have to eat. Highly recommended.

Hotel Fürstenhof West of the centre on Romberg St., an excellent, dress-for-dinner type of place with an award winning chef, a selective cellar, and superb food (French/German bias) — you can even choose your own crayfish from the tank! Starters R5-R15, mains R5(!)-R30, sweets R6-R12.

Kaiserkrone Set back in a trendy little arcade about 100m west of the central First National Bank, off Independence Way. By day it's a smart cafe/bar, by night a very good restaurant — and includes dishes of kudu, zebra, springbok and oryx! It's expensive though with soups R6, main courses R18-R35, sweets R7.

Sam's About 2.5km from the centre, Sam's is on the left of Gobabis Rd about 100m past Klein Windhoek. Relaxed air with starters R4-R7, vegetarian meals R11, pasta R10-R12, steaks R24, sweets R4. This is *the* place to be on Saturday afternoons when there's a band in the courtyard.

Seoul House Restaurant A sparsely furnished Korean restaurant towards the south end of Independence Way opposite Aisspann St. Could be good for a trendy late-night rendezvous before continuing in the club behind.

Spurs Situated above street level on Independence Way near Bülow. American burgers, steaks, a host of side orders and the city's best help-yourself salad bar. Atmosphere a little more subdued than Front Page, prices similar — rather like a Hard Rock Cafe! Recommended.

Tokyo Tei Just south of the centre on Leutwein, this restaurant isn't cheap, but it is unusual. The food is served raw, with a range of sauces and a small grill on which you cook individual morsels. Great fun! Set meal for two costs R55.

Yang Tse A large and efficient restaurant with the best Chinese food in town, found on the corner of Gobabis and Klein Windhoek. More a spot for important business dinners than cheap snacks!

Finally, if you've transport, then consider a trip to the **Aris Hotel** to eat. It's 50km round trip but if you feel like a drive...see above under *Where to stay*.

Getting around

In and around the city it's usually best to walk as everything is close together. There are small vans which ply between Katutura, Khomasdal, and town — usually starting from behind the model supermarket on Stübel St — but little else in the way of local transport except a few taxi companies, which are quite expensive. Try Tel: 37070 or 223020 if you need one late at night.

What to see and do

Behind the Library, near Lüderitz St, is the city's small **museum**. It's free and has some interesting displays on desert types, ethnic groups, karakuls and an unusual 'touch room' open only on Mondays.

The **Art Gallery**, on the corner of Leutwein and John Meinert St, is even smaller than the museum — and has only a single exhibition room! Check the press for what's on.

Nightlife

Windhoek really isn't the place to keep up with the latest films, but you could try the **Kine 300** on Klein Windhoek close to Kuiseb Rd and the post office. There's also a **drive-in cinema** near the stadium on the road to Rehoboth, and during the early evening the hills and the sunset make a marvellous backdrop to the screen. A magical place to watch a movie!

Namibia Nite Next to the South West Star Hotel in the centre of Khomasdal township. Step into here and you'll find one of the most mixed and cosmopolitan clubs in Southern Africa — a great place to while away those early morning hours! There's one dance floor, split-level bars, a video screen, and excellent live bands. Don't come earlier than about 11pm and expect to leave at around 4.30am. It's a must! Cover charge of R12 on Friday and Saturday. Taxis back to the centre of town are possible, but infrequent.

Club Thriller Katutura township. Smaller than Namibia Nite, consciously more trendy, and further from the centre of town, this is for the dedicated only — we've heard good reports of it!

Seoul House Night Club On Independence Way behind the restaurant of the same name. This was closed when we last visited, but is your main option if you haven't got transport out of the city.

Getting organised and shopping

Most of Namibia's consumer goods and a sizable portion of its food are produced in, and imported from, South Africa — with the exception of high-tech goods which are usually European or Japanese in origin. Generally you can expect to find food, clothes and basics cheaper than in Europe, whilst watches, cassettes and luxuries will be a little more expensive.

Windhoek's best buys are probably rocks and gems. You will find very few 'African curios', although there are some Bushmen crafts on sale, including ostrich eggshell jewellery. If you're passing through Ghanzi, in Botswana, wait and buy Bushmen crafts there instead.

To buy **rocks and minerals** you have a choice of two sources. There is a rather eyecatching shop on Independence Way, but here many of the agates are imported from Brazil and rather expensive. Alternatively, seek out the 'House of Gems' which is tucked away at 131 Stübel St, near John Meinert St. Run by Sid Peters, this is a real collector's place stuffed full of original bits and pieces and even if you're not buying it's still worth a visit as the stones from Sid's two Tourmaline mines (including the world's best Blue Tourmaline) are sorted, cut, faceted and polished here.

For **food** the best supermarket is probably the MODEL 7-day store on Independence Way, opposite the Continental Hotel. This has an excellent fresh section, and a good range of **packaged foods for campers**. If you're worried about weight, then try the 'toppers' range of dried soya bean meals — they're the best we've found in Africa. For **alcohol** of any sort, and **ice** for packing cool boxes, Keurwyn has the widest choice at 123 Tal St near the railway station.

If you need **camping kit** or spares then remember that South African equipment makes up the majority of what's available, and often you will not be able to find any European or American equivalent. The best places are the Safari Den, on Messum Rd, off Krupp St, which has some useful spares and smaller bits and pieces or, failing that, try upstairs at Cymot on Tal St, which is also the best cycling shop in town. As a last resort, Gorelick's Motors — opposite the open parking on Independence Way — may have what you are looking for.

Information and useful addresses

AMEX Woker Travel Services are the local American Express Agent and can be found at 6 Peter Müller St. They're an excellent travel agent and, if you have either an American Express card or AMEX travellers cheques, they can be used as an efficient mailing address. Mail should be addressed: c/o American Express, Woker Travel Services, P.O. Box 11, Windhoek 9000.

Automobile Association For advice about road conditions, contact the AA at 15 Cark List House, Independence Way, Box 61. Tel: (061) 224201.

Banks The centre of town has several efficient major banks — First National (ex-Barclays!), Bank of Windhoek, Nedbank and Trust.

Gav's Camping Hire 11 Sydney Atkinson St, Olympia. Tel: (061) 51526. Here there's a good range of equipment, so this is the place to hire all that's necessary for an expedition into the bush. Typical daily costs are: small cool box R1.00, pan R0.50, jerry can (for fuel) R1, camping stools R0.60, folding bed R3.00, tents R5-R15.

Car Hire

For a detailed discussion of where to hire from and the costs, see *In Namibia*, chapter 7. However, the firms in Windhoek are:

Kessler Car Hire for 4WDs, on the corner of Peter Müller and Tal St. This is the only company to allow vehicles to be taken into Botswana, South Africa and Zimbabwe — we used them and found them excellent. (See advert on page 287.)

Avis can be found next to the entrance to the Safari Hotel, just off the Rehoboth road, and as the region's biggest car-hire company they are ideal for one-way rentals throughout Namibia, Botswana and South Africa.

Budget rent-a-car are at 71, Tal St, with a range similar to Avis's though not as extensive.

Imperial car rental have a small network throughout Namibia and RSA, can be found at 43 Stübel St.

Post Office On Independence Way, the GPO has an efficient Post Restante and it's cheap and easy to send packages overseas. At the counter to the right of the main hall, a registered package of under 1kg costs R4.65 to send by sea mail — complete with dripping sealing wax — but you'll need your own string to tie it up, and it will take about two months to reach the UK.

Excursions from Windhoek

Daan Viljoen Game Park

2WD. Entrance fees: R5 per person, R5 per car.

A small game park some 20km east of the city, well provided for in terms of facilities and a popular weekend retreat for the locals.

Getting there Take Curt von Francois east onto Khomas Hochland, and then follow the signs on the C28 – it's an easy hitch!

Where to stay Bungalows R40 for two people, camping R25 per site. All should be booked at the DNC in the city, although if you're only coming for the day then just ring Tel: (061)226806 to let them know.

Amenities There's a restaurant, a kiosk, and even a swimming pool, all on the shores of a veritable oasis named the Augeigas Dam. The game in the park excludes potentially dangerous elephant, buffalo or large predators – so you can safely walk alone on the game trails or follow one of two of the prescribed routes.

Gobabis

This busy town, standing at the centre of an important cattle farming region on the western edges of the Kalahari, forms Namibia's gateway into Botswana via the Buitepos border post. It's an ideal place to use the banks, fill up with fuel or get supplies before heading east towards Ghanzi, where most goods aren't so easily available.

Where to stay and eat

Category C

There are two hotels in town, the **Central** (PO Box 233. Tel: (0681)2094) and the **Gobabis** (PO Box 474. Tel: (0681)2041). Both charge R40-R50 for a single and R60-R70 a double. The Central, which we marginally preferred, includes morning coffee in the price, while breakfast in either is around R12.

For snacks during the day there is a great little cafe, complete with menu in German, at the back of the general store – just to the right of the Municipal Offices on the main street.

Crossing the border into Botswana

Car Bear in mind that while the Namibian road to Buitepos is in reasonable condition, the road on the other side of the border is exceedingly sandy and rutted. It will usually require at least a high-clearance vehicle and preferably a 4WD – so do not attempt to cross into Botswana this way in a normal saloon car without getting reliable advice first.

Hitching This is the best town and route into Botswana, with many trucks passing through. Try to get a lift at least as far as the border post – and ignore vehicles which aren't 4WD as they won't be going much past it. Don't forget to carry plenty of food and water!

OKAHANDJA

Historically the administrative centre for the Herero people and situated about 71km north of Windhoek, this small town has banks, fuel and is the turn-off point for Gross-Barmen Hot Springs and the Von Bach Recreational Resort.

Where to stay and eat

Okahandja Hotel PO Box 770. Tel: (06221)3024. (*Category C*). This is the only place in town and it offers fairly simple singles for R35-R60, doubles R70-R100. Its restaurant is rather like a cafe and serves toasties for R2, burgers R7, and steaks R18.

Gross-Barmen Hot Springs

2WD. Entrance fees: R5 per person and R5 for a car.

A popular resort for locals with its well appointed facilities and hot thermal springs, this is built around a dam some 25km south-west of Okahandja.

Where to stay A 2-bed bungalow is R40, and a camping is R25 per site. Booking is done through the DNC in Windhoek, and day visitors must phone Tel: (06221)2091 in advance, to arrange their visits.

Von Bach Recreational Resort

2WD. Entrance fees: R5 per person and R5 for a car.

This dam supplies the majority of the capital's water, and has a nature reserve around it. Unfortunately there aren't many animals around to spot, but it is a quiet place to stay for a night as there isn't the usual development here — only campsites and communal ablution blocks.

KARIBIB

For nearly 90 years, this small town has been known for the very hard, high quality marble quarried nearby. Now it could be set to expand rapidly as gold has been found on a nearby farm.

Where to stay and eat

Category C

Hotel Erongoblick PO Box 17. Tel: (062252)9. This is currently being refurbished and radically expanded — so it could be a real bargain, or an overpriced executive stop-over! Singles were R30, doubles R55, including breakfast, and it has a small terrace restaurant.

Hotel Stroblhof On the east side of town, this comfortable hotel has air conditioning in all rooms and singles for R45, doubles R75, including breakfast.

What to see and do

On the main street there's a Namib information centre which doubles as a curio shop, with a large selection of carvings and gems. Also for rocks and minerals try the shop just outside town on the road to Swakopmund, it's certainly worth a visit.

USAKOS

This small town used to be the centre of the country's railway industry, though now its little more than a stop on the line, with banks and fuel to tempt those who might pass right through. If you linger here then the old station is worth a brief look, and the Namib Information office is useful if you're planning on doing much exploration of the local area.

Where to stay and eat

The Usakos Hotel PO Box 129. Tel: (062242). (*Category C*). The only place in town, with singles for R48-R60, doubles R80-R100. It's plain but clean and family run. The food is simple, and a good bar lunch costs around R8.

If you've no transport then you can arrange trips from here with the owner to **Spitzkoppe** (see Chapter 13, page 172) which can be visited in a day, or even further afield — they often suggest overnight stops at the expensive Desert Lodge (a guest farm).

Ameib rock paintings

This is another guest farm with excellent rock paintings, many in Phillip's Cave which was made famous by Abbé Breuil's book of the same name (see *Bibliography*). There are also unusual rock formations, the most noted being the Bull's Party — a group of large rounded boulders which look like a collection of bulls talking together. As with most guest farms, Ameib offers excellent accommodation, though at a pricy R120 per person including breakfast.

OMARURU

This green and picturesque town is set astride the river of the same name, and surrounded by an area full of sculptured rocks and bushman paintings. The main problem for the visitor is that most, if not all, of the more interesting sites are located on guest farms around the town — and thus are open only to their (paying) guests.

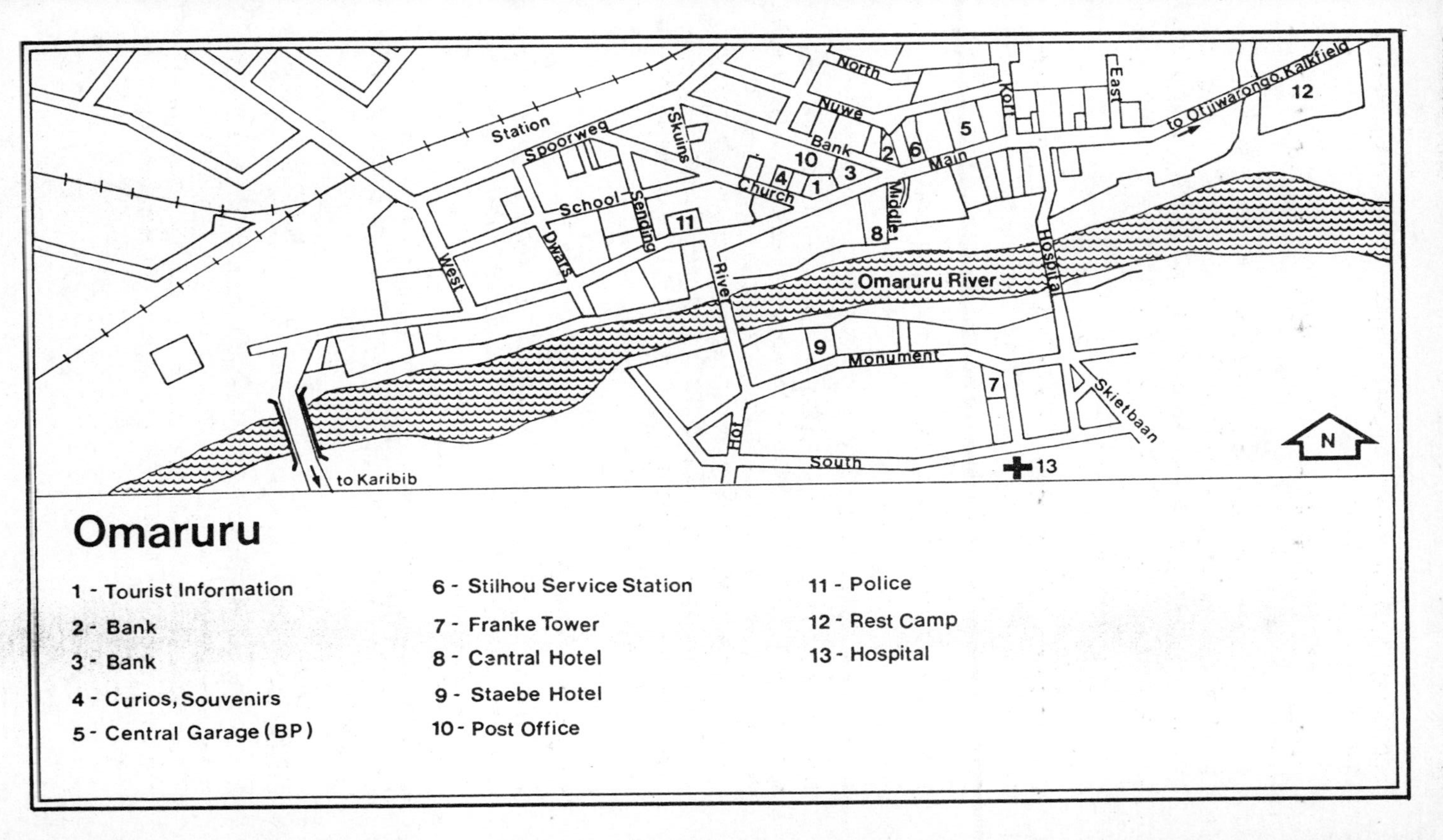
North
Nuwe
Kort
East
to Otjiwarongo, Kalkfield
12
Station
Spoorweg
Skuins
Bank
10
3
2
6
5
Main
4
1
Church
Middle
School
Sending
11
8
Dwars
West
River
Hospital
Omaruru River
9
Monument
7
Skietbaan
Hof
South
13
N
to Karibib
Omaruru
1 - Tourist Information
2 - Bank
3 - Bank
4 - Curios, Souvenirs
5 - Central Garage (BP)
6 - Stilhou Service Station
7 - Franke Tower
8 - Central Hotel
9 - Staebe Hotel
10 - Post Office
11 - Police
12 - Rest Camp
13 - Hospital

Where to stay

Category C

Hotel Steabe PO Box 92. Tel: (062232)35. The hotel, situated on Monument Street to the south of the river, is well furnished and almost cosy, though with a distinct German atmosphere! Singles R65, doubles R95, including breakfast.

The Central Hotel PO Box 29. Tel: (062232)29. Located on the other side of the river on the main street. It's less well furnished, though the new block being built promises to make the competition more equal. Singles R40, doubles R80, some with bath, others without. Breakfast R7.50.

Where to eat

Both hotels have restaurants — the only ones in town — and will do food to order, despite not having menus! Expect to pay around R8 for an omelette, R20 for steak. Better still if you are passing through, there's a good cafe/bakery opposite the shell garage on the main street.

What to see and do

There's a reasonable Namib information office opposite the Central Hotel on Main St, and the mediocre curio shop next to the post office may be worth a visit. Otherwise the town's only attraction is **Franke Tower**. This is a monument to Captain Victor Franke who is said to have heroically relieved the garrison here, after they were besieged by the Herero in 1904. The achievement earned him Germany's highest military honour and this monument — built by the grateful German settlers in 1908. It's normally locked, but to climb up it just ask at either hotel for a set of keys.

Anibib rock paintings

One of the largest collections of rock paintings in the country, and some interesting artifacts, is situated on the guest farm Anibib, which is some 50km west of Omaruru, (almost in Damaraland) just off the D2315. They do guided tours for day visitors which make a good introduction to bushman art. Phone them on Tel: (062232) 1711 to make arrangements for a visit.

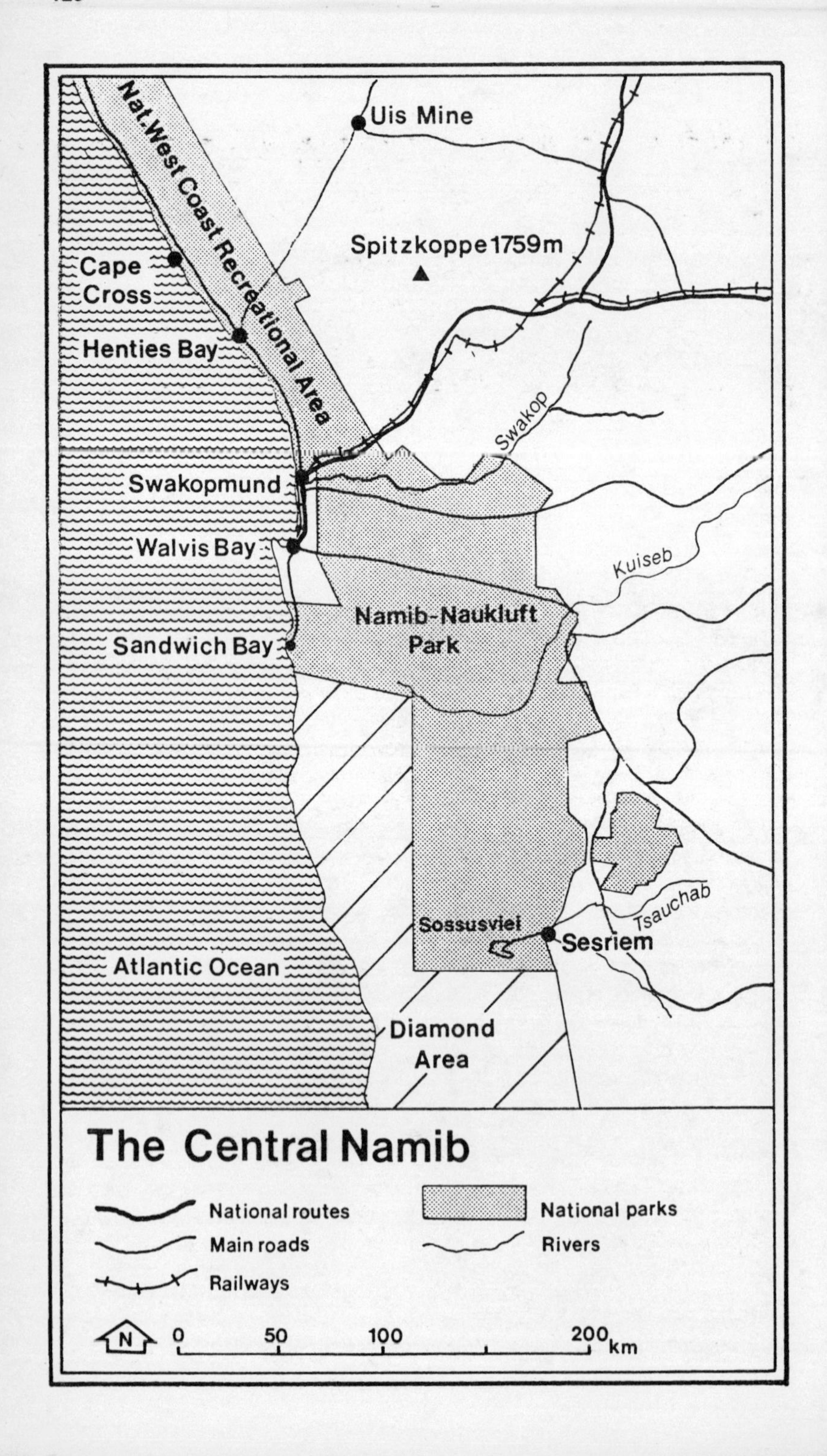
Uis Mine
Nat.West Coast Recreational Area
Spitzkoppe 1759m
Cape Cross
Henties Bay
Swakop
Swakopmund
Walvis Bay
Kuiseb
Namib-Naukluft Park
Sandwich Bay
Tsauchab
Sossusvlei
Sesriem
Atlantic Ocean
Diamond Area
The Central Namib
National routes
Main roads
Railways
National parks
Rivers
N
0
50
100
200 km

Chapter 10

The Central Namib

This region encompasses the heart of the Namib Desert, the Namib-Naukluft Desert Park, and the two main coastal towns, Swakopmund and Walvis Bay. To visit the desert you need to be fairly self-sufficient, at least in terms of transport, while Swakopmund — as a major centre for local tourism — is easy to reach by bus or rail and is well prepared for visitors.

The Namib Desert stretches in a narrow band, seldom more than about 200km wide, along the whole coast of Namibia and into both South Africa and Angola. Its western border is the Atlantic and its eastern border, though not so clearly defined, is usually taken at the line of 100mm rainfall — which generally occurs at around 1,000m on the escarpment. Much of it is effectively protected, either within one of the diamond concession areas, one of the parks, or simply by being inaccessible for all practical purposes.

The Namib-Naukluft Park is one of the largest protected areas in Africa and gives us, as visitors, our best chance actually to spend time in the desert, camp, and get to know a little about it — without facing the difficulties of a long and potentially hazardous trip into one of its more remote corners. Here, where the band of desert is at its widest, there is the opportunity to explore many different desert environments and their associated ecosystems, occurring within short distances of each other.

The two towns in this area, Swakopmund and Walvis Bay, are close together and form a busy nucleus for this largely unpopulated section of the country. Outside these, there are no hotel facilities at all — so if you wish to explore, you must be able to take advantage of the excellent camping facilities provided throughout the region.

Getting around the region

Both Swakopmund and Walvis Bay are linked into the air, rail and coach networks, with three bus and three train services to and from Windhoek every

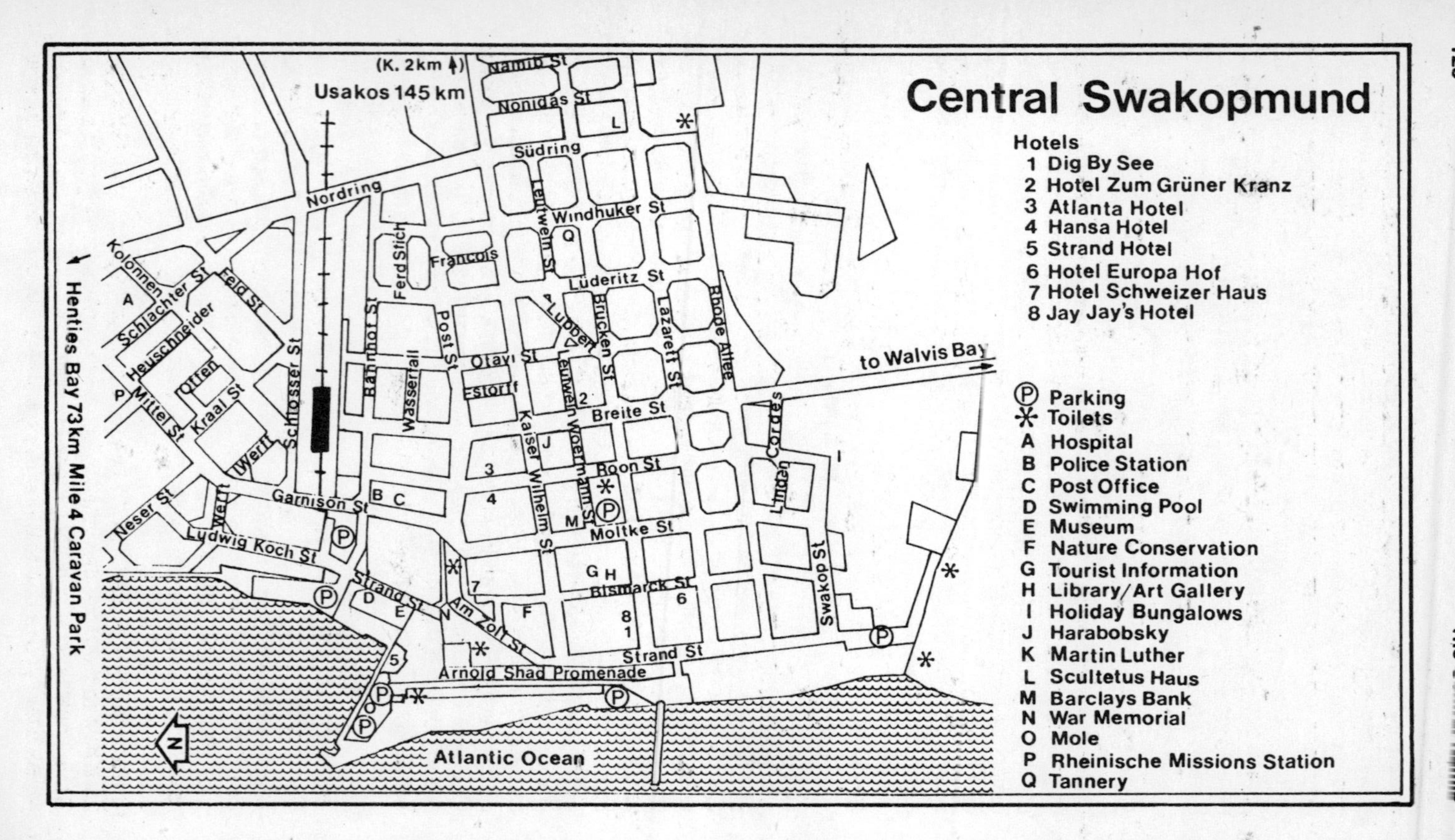
Central Swakopmund
Hotels
1 Dig By See
2 Hotel Zum Grüner Kranz
3 Atlanta Hotel
4 Hansa Hotel
5 Strand Hotel
6 Hotel Europa Hof
7 Hotel Schweizer Haus
8 Jay Jay's Hotel
P Parking
* Toilets
A Hospital
B Police Station
C Post Office
D Swimming Pool
E Museum
F Nature Conservation
G Tourist Information
H Library/Art Gallery
I Holiday Bungalows
J Harabobsky
K Martin Luther
L Scultetus Haus
M Barclays Bank
N War Memorial
O Mole
P Rheinische Missions Station
Q Tannery
to Walvis Bay
(K. 2km)
Usakos 145 km
Henties Bay 73km Mile 4 Caravan Park
Atlantic Ocean
N
Namib St
Nonidas St
Südring
Nordring
Leutwein St
Windhuker St
Francois
Ferd Stich
Lüderitz St
Lazarett St
Rhode Allee
Brucken St
Lubbert
Post St
Bahnhof St
Wasserfall
Olavi St
Estorff
Breite St
Kaiser Wilhelm St
Woermann St
Roon St
Linden
Cordes
Moltke St
Bismarck St
Swakop St
Strand St
Arnold Shad Promenade
Am Zoll St
Garnison St
Ludwig Koch St
Werft
Neser St
Schlosser St
Kolonnen
Schlachter St
Feld St
Heuschneider
Otten
Kraal St
Mittel St

week (see *In Namibia*, Chapter 7, page 80).

Hitching is quite easy between the main centres, and even to some of the less obvious places provided that you go fully self-sufficient with the necessities of life. Often you'll get really helpful lifts visiting the very places that you aimed at, but sometimes you'll sit by a road junction for days and you must be prepared for this. There are very few shops in this area — and none in the national park — so don't expect to buy food along the way, take it with you.

SWAKOPMUND

Often considered to be Namibia's only real 'holiday resort', this old German town stands by the mouth of the usually dry Swakop River, and spreads out from the shore onto the flat desert plain which surrounds it. Climatically more temperate than the interior, the palm-lined streets, immaculate old buildings and well-kept gardens give it a feel all of its own, making a pleasant oasis in which to spend a few days, and a good base from which to explore the surrounding desert.

Unlike much of Namibia, Swakopmund is used to visitors and has a good choice of places to stay, eat, and even tours into the desert itself.

History

In 1884, the whole of present-day Namibia was declared a protectorate of Germany, whilst the region's only large natural harbour, Walvis Bay, remained under British control. Thus, in order to develop their interests in the area, the German authorities decided to make their own harbour on the northern banks of the Swakop River, and in 1892 two beacons were planted — where the Mole is today — to mark the spot (see page 00).

Following this, there were several largely unsuccessful attempts to develop landing facilities. A quay was built, although it subsequently silted up, followed by a wooden, and later an iron, jetty. Finally in 1915, German control of the country was surrendered to South Africa and all ocean trading returned to Walvis Bay. During the South African administration of Namibia before Independence, Swakopmund remained undeveloped as an alternative port to Walvis Bay, which is still part of South Africa.

Where to stay

Category A

Hansa Hotel PO Box 44. Tel: (0641)311. Centrally positioned on Roon St, beautifully furnished and somewhat colonial in atmosphere, this is the town's top hotel. Singles R98-R120, doubles R118-R166, including breakfast. Its restaurant is of similar calibre with fresh oysters at R8 for half a dozen!

Strand Hotel PO Box 20. Tel: (0641)315. With an excellent sea-front location, right next to the Mole, this hotel can be quite expensive. Singles are about R115, doubles R139, including breakfast. Some have a balcony, some don't — ask when you're checking in. The restaurant has fish dishes for around

R17 and steaks for R20, though there's a popular coffee shop overlooking the beach which is a ideal for writing postcards or just relaxing in the sea breeze.

Hotel Europa Hof PO Box 1333. Tel: (0641)5061. Situated to the south of Bismark St, and by far the most modern of the hotels. Singles for R55, doubles for R85-R204, including breakfast. Its posh restaurant has a good selection of seafood, with a good meal of prawns for R32.

Category B

Hotel-Pension Prinzessin-Rupprecht-Heim PO Box 124. Tel: (0641)2231. This old hospital on Lazarett St, just west of Bismark St, has recently been refurbished and can be strongly recommended for its spacious and well-furnished rooms. Singles are around R50, doubles R80, including breakfast. It has no menu as yet, but snacks can be arranged.

Hotel-Pension Schweizer Haus , Box 445. Tel: (0641)2419. A comfortable hotel, overlooking the sea, to the north of Bismark St, this has a distinctly German feel to it and an exceedingly trendy cafe below known as Cafe Anton. Singles are R60-R80, doubles R100-R120, including breakfast.

Hotel Grüner Kranz PO Box 546. Tel: (0641)5016. On the north side of Breite St, this could be the place for you if you're missing the bright lights! Each room has a television and there are three videos shown nightly, as well as a lively music bar on the first floor. The rooms are reasonable value with singles at R49 and doubles for R69, including breakfast. The restaurant is fairly plain with steaks for R16-R20.

Hotel Burg Nonidas PO Box 171. Tel: (0641)4544. This unusual hotel, built in the style of a fort some 10km out of the town on the Windhoek road, is set around the ruins of an old German customs post dating back to the turn of the century. Its bar, which includes sections of the old building, is full of photographs taken before the restoration as well as many other items of historical interest, while its restaurant overlooks the desert plain. Singles are R55, doubles R85, including breakfast.

Category C

Hotel Jay Jay's PO Box 835. Tel: (0641)2909. Found at the western end of Brücken St, Namibian hotels don't come any cheaper than this. It's basic but very good value — singles R11.50-18, doubles R25-33, without breakfast. The informal restaurant here serves a memorable curry for R7.50 and steaks for R14, while the bar is often the liveliest place in town.

Hotel-Pension Dig By See PO Box 1530. Tel: (0641)4130. Next to Jay Jay's, this small family-run hotel has singles for R40 and doubles for R70, including breakfast.

Chalets At the far, southern end of Roon St stands a conspicuous complex of holiday bungalows which belong to the municipality. While lacking a bit in individuality, they are excellent value and have useful laundry facilities nearby, though bear in mind that they're often booked up over the weekends and holiday periods.

All have at least a basic stove, a fridge, shower/toilet, and a sink. A two-bed bungalow costs R18.70; four-beds (bunk beds) cost R22; a six-bed split-level A-frame chalet is R44; a luxury flat for six is R66; and a VIP bungalow for six (complete with cutlery, crockery and even a barbecue) is R99.

Camping With fairly cheap accommodation in town, we wouldn't recommend camping here because of the awkward and exposed location of the sites. However, if you must, then there are plenty of sites available.

The least inconvenient is probably **Langstrand** PO Box 86. Tel: (0642)5981. It is situated within South Africa(!), on the coast road, about half way between Swakopmund and Walvis Bay. Here sites are R10 and there are some tidal pools to swim in. The restaurant is well known throughout the area for its steaks, and hitching to and from the towns is especially easy.

Failing that, there are camp/caravan sites at four and 14 miles north of town as you go towards Henties Bay, as well as some much further into the National West Coast Recreational Area. These are mainly used by fishing groups and consist of little more than pegged out areas of the sand next to the shore. The charge is R10 per site, though water is extra at 10c for a litre (if you haven't brought your own), and hot showers cost R1.00 each.

Where to eat

There is no shortage of choice, but ask around to find out where the current 'in' places are; you'll probably find a very lively crowd. Here are some perennial favourites:

Garfields on the corner of Brücken and Roon St, is always busy with its pizzas and pastas at around R13.

Atlanta Hotel restaurant opposite the Hansa on Roon St, is excellent value for money: their steaks start from R10.

Kücki's Pub with its spit-and-sawdust atmosphere, is not only a popular watering hole but also a reasonable place to eat with steaks for R14-R20 and crayfish for R45 if you really want to splash out.

For more special occasions try the subterranean delights of the cosy **Sea Food Haven**, also opposite the Hansa, or the reputedly excellent **Erich's** on Post Street. Then of course there's always the hotels.

What to see and do

A friend of mine, new in town, went along to the tourist information office a few years ago to ask what there was to do in Swakopmund. The reply from the woman behind the counter was succinct: 'There's nothing to do in Swakopmund.'

Should you not want to believe this, try some of the following:

The Museum next to the Strand, is open from 10am to 12.30pm and 3pm until 5.30. It costs R3 (R1 for children) to enter, and has an extensive display of rocks and minerals and some fascinating equipment used in the not-so-distant past by doctors and dentists.

Swimming Opposite the museum there's an olympic-size swimming pool, entry R2. There are also saunas for which a day pass costs R7.50. Masochists shouldn't miss the opportunity to use these and then run straight into the cold surf!

The Mole With a little time to spare, it's worth wandering down to the 'Mole'. This was to be a harbour wall when first built, but the ocean currents continually shifted the sandbanks and effectively blocked the harbour before it was even completed. A similar 'longshore drift' effect can be seen all along the coast — especially at inlets like Sandwich Harbour. Partially because of this sandbank's protection, the beach by the Mole is pleasant and safe to swim in, if a little busy at times.

ENOC centre Near the corner of Mittel and Nordring St, this small business centre houses a souvenir gem shop, a small art gallery and a carpet weaving co-operative selling some excellent value rugs — don't miss it.

Hansa Brewery A look around this is fairly easy to arrange by phoning them on (0641)5021, with as much advance notice as possible. The beer is brewed, we're told, according to the most rigorous German standards — but it's distressing to find out just how many of its ingredients are imported.

Historical Buildings As you might expect, this town is full of amazing old German architecture in perfect condition. If you want a guide to the individual buildings then get in touch with Frau Flamm at Historical Sightseeing Tours, on (0461) 61647. Alternatively, the handout from the municipality itself, or the short book entitled *Swakopmund — A Chronicle of the Town's People, Places and Progress*, available at the museum, both give descriptions and brief histories for some of the buildings.

Nightlife

The Grüner Kranz's first floor bar and Jay Jay's bar with its pool table are usually among the best places during the week, however there's sometimes a 'public' party on the beach on Saturday nights — just bring your own drink and food to the *braii* (barbecue). If that's not on then check to see if the local football club is holding one of its weekend discos, which we're told can be very entertaining.

Getting organised

There are three main operators here, all offering a variety of short trips into the local area, jaunts to Sesriem and Naukluft, and longer expeditions into Damaraland and Kaokoland. These longer trips are usually done using combinations of light aircraft and 4WD vehicles, costing in the region of R250 per person per day including food and accommodation. They generally require organising well in advance with a group of least four people.

The local day trips don't require any notice, they set off regardless of numbers and we felt they were well worth doing as an introduction to the various aspects of the desert.

Charly's Desert Tours PO Box 1400. Tel: (0641)4341. From the office on Kaiser Wilhelm St, they offer the widest range of daily tours, typically costing R60 for half a day and R80 for full-day trips, which venture as far as Sandwich Harbour, Cape Cross and even Spitzkoppe.

Desert Adventure Safaris, found next to the passage by the Hansa hotel. PO Box 339. Tel: (0641)4072/2027. Usually slightly cheaper than Charly's, DAS charge R55 for a half day and R75 for full-day trips. They are probably the best people to go into Damaraland with as they have a home base at Palmwag lodge.

DAS do very occasionally run trips into Damaraland and Kaokoland in conjunction with The Endangered Wildlife Trust, guided by Garth Owen-Smith. He's a local conservationist, highly respected internationally, involved in projects working with the indigenous peoples of these areas. If you have a chance to go on one of these, don't miss it at any cost!

See Africa Tours PO Box 127. Tel: (0641)5243. Based, not surprisingly, at the See Africa Safari Shop which is also just by the Hansa hotel. They do daily tours into the nearby desert, but seem to specialise in more costly trips further afield to virtually anywhere in the country.

Excursions

Camel Farm You might think there would be more of these in Namibia, but this does seem to be the only one. It's found on the D1901 about 12km out of town, and the usual 15 minute camel ride, starting at 3pm, costs R12.50. There's even the chance to dress 'Arabian' if you like! With a small party you could organise longer, overnight, rides into the desert — though they don't do these very often. To book, talk to Desert Gems opposite the Hansa Hotel.

If camels are a little too adventurous (or uncomfortable) for you then how about **horse riding** in the desert? It can sometimes be arranged through Frau Doris Herholdt at Blatt Shoe Store, across from Charly's.

Fishing trips Heinz Göthje will hire out his boat, 'Bronzy', and himself as skipper, for about R400 per day. The boat will take up to eight people. Contact him on (0641)2357 or at PO Box 153, Swakopmund.

Alternatively, try Sunrise Fishing Trips on Kurze St, run by H.D. Herzig who can be reached by phoning (0641)4923.

Information and useful addresses

Namibia Tourist Information Office. This is by the corner of Bismark and

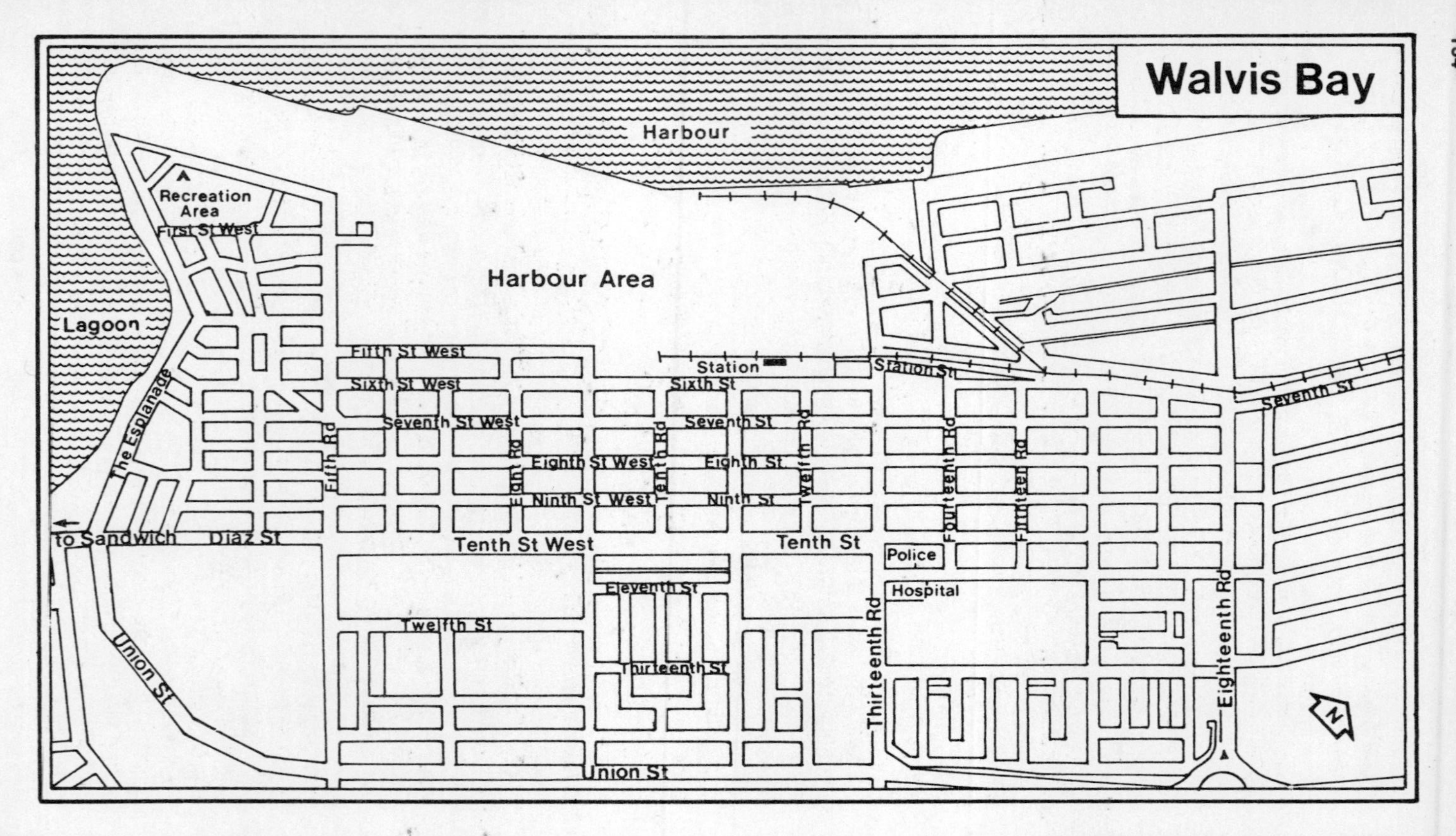

Walvis Bay
Harbour
Recreation Area
First St West
Harbour Area
Lagoon
The Esplanade
to Sandwich
Diaz St
Union St
Fifth St West
Sixth St West
Seventh St West
Eighth St West
Ninth St West
Tenth St West
Fifth Rd
Eighth Rd
Tenth Rd
Twelfth Rd
Station
Sixth St
Seventh St
Eighth St
Ninth St
Tenth St
Eleventh St
Twelfth St
Thirteenth St
Station St
Thirteenth Rd
Fourteenth Rd
Fifteenth Rd
Police
Hospital
Seventh St
Eighteenth Rd
N

Kaiser Wilhelm St. and the staff are quite helpful. The book *Swakopmund – A Chronicle of the Town's People, Places and Progress* produced by the municipality is well worth getting as an additional source of information.

DNC. For the permits to pass through the Namib-Naukluft Park, or to go north of the Ugab River (but not to stop overnight there), see the DNC on the corner of Kaiser Wilhelm and Bismark St. When closed try Charly's, the Hans Kriess Service Station, or the fuel stations in Walvis Bay.

The best **bottle stall** (or *drankwinkel*) is probably 'Harabobsky' on Kaiser Wilhelm near Breite St, though there are lots of others about.

WALVIS BAY (SOUTH AFRICA)

Walvis Bay, and the enclave which surrounds it, is not part of Namibia but part of South Africa. Whilst it's possible that the territory will eventually come under Namibian control, as enshrined in the new constitution, this looks unlikely in the near future. Its present remains as bound by regional strategic considerations as its past was shaped by global ones (see Chapter 1, page 7).

What this means in practice is that getting to Walvis Bay entails all the same formalities as crossing Namibia's southern border to South Africa. While the local officials have been quite relaxed in the recent past, stamping separate pieces of paper for some travellers instead of their passports, there's no reason to assume that they'll continue to be so. Hence if you're worried about South African stamps in your passport — approach with care.

Where to stay

Category B

Casa Mia Hotel PO Box 1786. Tel: (0642)5975. Found on 7th street, between roads 17 and 18, this seemed expensive to us with singles costing R78-R120 and doubles R99-R130, including breakfast. That said, the bars and restaurant lived up to expectations.

Atlantic Hotel PO Box 46. Tel: (0642)2811. On 7th street again, but between roads 10 and 12, this is comfortable and good value with singles at R56-R86 and doubles R89-R120, including breakfast.

Flamingo Hotel PO Box 30. Tel: (0642)3011 A reasonable hotel on the corner of 7th street and 10th road, though its restaurant is more like a cafe.

Category C

The **Golden Fish** PO Box 577. Tel: (0642)2775. This is on 7th street a block south-west of the Casa Mia and is a guest house rather than a hotel, but it does have singles from R20 and doubles from R30, though some have shared facilities. If there are four of you then there's a flat with a bathroom, a kitchen and a dining room available for only R60 per day. Breakfast here costs R8 extra.

Chalets. Located by the road running along the lagoon, the municipality has 27 very well-furnished bungalows. One to sleep five costs R75, while one sleeping seven is R115 per night — making it a good option for larger groups.

Camping. Opposite the yacht club, to the west of the harbour area, is the camping park. The ground is hard and the sites are small, if thankfully well sheltered, costing R11 per site. There's a small kiosk for cool drinks and a swimming pool nearby.

Where to eat

Probst Bakery and Cafe, a German style coffee shop by the corner of 9th St and 12th Rd, is good for a mid-morning snack.

Georgio's Steakhouse, on 7th St, and **Bacher's Braai**, at 122 9th St, both serve steaks for around R15 as well as lighter meals.

Lalainya's, on 7th St between roads 11 and 12, is very good and decidedly up-market, yet not too expensive. Their seafood platter for two, at R65, has been recommended.

La Perla, in the Nictus Arcade on 8th St, and **La Tratoria**, again on 8th, both serve less expensive fare. La Perla's an informal spot for Spanish dishes, notably seafood, while the Italian La Tratoria concentrates more on pastas and pizzas.

What to see and do

The city is very much built for the harbour, with the numbered streets and roads forming an unexciting, if easily navigable, grid around it. There isn't Swakopmund's beautiful architecture or its holiday air and hence Walvis seemed to us to have little of interest during the day, although there are a few possible evening attractions.

There is, however, some excellent **birdlife**. Just take a walk on the southwest side of town, around the lagoon. The flock of feeding flamingos and pelicans which we found there allowed us to get much closer than any others which we came across in the area. Bird watchers might also look into the **bird sanctuary** at the end of 13 St, as well as stopping by at one of the guano platforms in the sea between Walvis and Swakopmund.

The **Namib Park Sports Club**, opposite the Flamingo Hotel on 7th St, allows visitors to use the squash courts and snooker tables for a weekly membership of R5, while there are tennis courts available at the camping site.

Nightlife

The bar at the **Casa Mia** is popular, while at the weekends, **La Plaza** offers not only a cinema but also a bar with a lively dance floor. For the more adventurous, try **Le Palace** — a lively disco by the Desert Inn in the nearby township of Narraville, which is comparable to Windhoek's Namibia Nite club.

Getting organised

Generally it seemed easier to arrange excursions within Namibia from Swakopmund, though **Gloriosa Safaris**, based at the Golden Fish Guest House, deserves a mention here. They offer similar long camping trips to those available in Swakopmund, though the day trips available are more limited.

THE NAMIB-NAUKLUFT PARK

2WD/4WD (see under relevant section). Entrance fees: R5 per person and R5 per vehicle (one-off charge).

People have different reactions when encountering a desert for the first time. A few find it threatening, too arid and empty, so they rush from city to city to avoid spending any time here at all. Some try hard to like it for those same reasons, but ultimately find little here which holds their attention, so they too come and go with scarcely a pause. Finally there are those who stop and give the place their time, delighting in the stillness, the strange beauty and the sheer uniqueness of the environment. To them the desert's ever-changing patterns and subtly adapted life forms are a constant fascination which will draw them back time after time.

Because of the park's size, we have split it into five sections which are ordered as follows: Sesriem and Sossusvlei; Naukluft; the northern section between the Kuiseb and Swakop Rivers; Welwitschia Drive; and Sandwich Harbour.

Getting organised

Permits to enter the park — which is the fourth largest national park in the world — are obtainable at any DNC office, as well as from Charly's Desert Tours or Hans Kreiss Service Station in Swakopmund, and from Troost Transport, Namib Ford or CWB service stations in Walvis Bay.

Camping fees for the sites in the northern section are R10 per site and also available at these garages. However, the sites at Sesriem and Naukluft cost R25 per site and must be booked in advance at the Windhoek DNC office.

Sesriem and Sossusvlei

2WD/4WD.

Sesriem and Sossusvlei lie on the Tsauchab River — one of two large rivers (the other being the Tsondab, further north) which flow westward into the great dunefield of the central Namib but never reach the ocean. Both rivers end by forming flat white pans dotted with green trees, surrounded by spectacular dunes — islands of life within a sea of sand.

The National Park's camp at Sesriem, where the Tsauchab enters the great dunefield, makes an excellent base from which to see this area, and the only place to start on the 65km drive through the desert to Sossusvlei — the pan into which the river disappears. The classic desert scenery between Sesriem and Sossusvlei really is the stuff that postcards are made of — enormous apricot dunes with gracefully curving ridges, invariably pictured in the sharp light of dawn with a photogenic gemsbok or feathery acacia close by!

Getting there

Car — Sesriem presents no problems to drive to even in a 2WD, though getting there by hitching is a little more tricky. If you do manage to hitch to Sesriem then getting a lift for the trip along the valley should not be difficult — if you ask the warden when you arrive, he will probably help you to arrange one.

Driving from Sesriem to Sossusvlei itself does require a 4WD, but you can get right along the river valley, to within a kilometre or so of the pan, with a normal 2WD and then walk the rest. There's a petrol station and basic shop at Solitaire — and not a lot more at Maltahöhe — with nothing else for miles, so take a week's food and a couple of days' water with you.

Hitching — Route 36 to the west of Maltahöhe is the closest place to hitch from, but route C24 which turns west off the B1 just south of Rehoboth is probably better. In either case, expect to spend several days getting there — and plan your reservations accordingly.

Where to stay

Sesriem campsite Of all Namibia's camp grounds, the one at Sesriem — with only ten sites — can be the most difficult in which to reserve space. It's always necessary to book ahead through Windhoek DNC, so do so as far in advance as possible, and try to allow yourself at least two nights here. The sites themselves are each surrounded by a low circular wall, which has a shady tree in the centre — with a tap positioned conveniently by its trunk. The ablution blocks only have electricity until 10pm. After that, take a torch.

Fuel, wood and even cold drinks are usually available from the warden, who will open the gates to Sossusvlei about an hour before sunrise. It's worth the effort to brave the cold (it can go below freezing here at night!) and get up well before sunrise so as to leave for Sossusvlei as soon as the warden opens the gates. That way, with luck, you should be there as the sun rises, preferably sitting high up on a dune.

Nara Bushes

Nara bushes (*Acanthosicyos horrida*) are perhaps the most striking of Namibia's endemic plants, occurring in the driest of areas and forming large tangles of green spiked stems - perhaps several metres across and a metre tall — but without a single leaf in sight. Not truly desert plants, their roots go down for many meters to reach underground reserves of water, without which they cannot survive. Thus their presence verifies the existence of water at Sossusvlei, while their demise warns us of a lowering of the water table in the Kuiseb river.

What to see and do: Sesriem

It is tempting to regard Sesriem as just the DNC's campsite and office on the way to Sossusvlei, but it does have several attractions of its own nearby. Only about 4km from the camp is the narrow **Sesriem canyon**, so called because the early settlers drew water from it by knotting together six lengths of hide rope called *riems*. There's usually some blissfully cool water in here, especially following good rains, and after descending via the steps which have been cut into the rock you can take a swim if it's deep enough.

Nearly 5km from camp (in the opposite direction) is **Elim dune**. This is the nearest of the dunes and if you arrive towards dusk then, like us, you'll probably mistake it for a mountain. There's a parking spot at its base and it can be climbed, though it takes longer than you'd expect — allow at least an hour to get to the top. The views from there — over plains to distant mountains on the one side and dune crests on the other — are remarkable, especially at sunset, and well worth the long climb.

If you visit the area in the winter then it's difficult to imagine that the gravel plains surrounding the campsite will turn green with the summer showers, and carpets of small yellow flowers appear from nowhere.

The road from Sesriem to Sossusvlei

Beyond Sesriem, the road westwards is confined by huge dunes on either side to a narrow corridor, a few kilometres wide at most. This parting of the sand sea has probably been maintained by the seasonal action of the river and the wind over the millennia. About 24km after leaving Sesriem the present course of the Tsauchab River is crossed, and although it is seldom seen to flow note the green *Acacia erioloba* (camel thorn) which thrives here — a clear indication of underground water reserves.

Continuing westwards and parallel with the road, the present course of the river is easy to spot, but look around for the number of dead acacias which mark old courses of the river, now dried up. Some of these dead trees have been dated at over 500 years old. After a further 36km this road terminates in a shady parking area, with low sand dunes finally forming a barrier to the further progress of either the river or the road.

What to see and do: Sossusvlei

No more than 4km beyond the parking area, over a fairly low ridge of sand, lies the series of spectacular white clay pans — surrounded on all sides by apricot dunes and dotted with green camel thorns and *nara* bushes. You can either walk here from your car, or plough your way through the sand if you have a high-clearance 4WD. Either way, it's definitely worth the effort. Ideally, its best to be sitting high on one of the dunes overlooking the *vlei* for sunset or (better) sunrise, as then you'll catch the light at its best — casting sharp shadows on the ridges and bringing the dunes to life. Come with plenty of film as there's nowhere else quite like it — it is exceedingly photogenic.

On very rare occasions, during years when the rainfall on the eastern plateau has been exceptional, the Tsauchab will flow along the full length of its course and breach this sand barrier. When this happens Sossusvlei undergoes a complete transformation, with the pans becoming lakes and attracting water birds to the desert scene.

Naukluft

2WD

This area was created as a separate reserve in 1964, with the aim of preserving the unique ecosystem and saving the rare Hartmann's mountain zebra. More recently, it has been expanded by a narrow neck of land which now links it to the main Namib park, allowing a vital corridor for the migration of some of the park's larger herbivores.

The uniqueness of the area stems from its geology as well as its geographical position. Separated from the rest of the highlands by steep, spectacular cliffs, the Naukluft Mountains form a plateau — consisting mainly of limestone and dolomite. This is deeply incised with steep ravines — cut over the millennia as rainwater has dissolved the rock — and it covers a network of mainly subterranean water-courses and natural reservoirs. Where these waters surface, in the deeper valleys, there are crystal clear springs and pools — ideal for cooling dips — and they are often decorated by impressive displays of tufa (limestone which has been redeposited by the water as it has gone over a waterfall).

Scenically it is comparable in some ways to the Matopos Hills of Zimbabwe, though smaller and much less visited, with its mosaic of exposed rock areas, barren slopes and thickly vegetated ravines. The birdwatching here is excellent as Naukluft lies at the northern extreme of typical Namaqualand species, while also being just within the range of many species characteristic of northern Namibia. Where else will you hear the water-loving hamerkop one moment and see rockrunners the next?

Getting there

Car — Driving here, the entrance is on the D854 about 10km south-west of its junction with the C14 which links Solitaire and Maltahöhe. Alternatively, if you are coming from Sesriem, turn left after leaving the camp, right at the next junction onto route 36, and then after about 27km take a left onto the D854. The gate is about 66km along this very quiet road.

Hitching — Not advised! We have waited from morning until nightfall by the side of busier roads than these without being passed by a single vehicle.

Where to stay

There are four campsites here, but all are within a small area, and numbers at each are restricted to eight people — so book early through Windhoek DNC. Despite the water, firewood and basic ablutions that are available, these small sites still give the feeling of camping alone in the wilderness, miles from anywhere or anyone.

What to see and do

This is one of those increasingly rare corners of Africa where you can walk alone through a landscape that man has hardly affected, amongst game that is still not used to people — and so is often sensed, though rarely seen — without meeting another soul for days. Perhaps this is mostly due to the lack of roads through the area, for in this landscape you have no choice but to walk.

There are currently three trails mapped out, two of which are for day visitors, while one is for serious hikers only. The Olive trail takes about four and a half hours, while the Waterkloof trail (*kloof* means a steep valley or ravine, from the Afrikaans) is an hour or so longer. Ask for route plans as you book at the DNC in Windhoek.

A wilderness trail has recently been introduced here and is designed to last eight days — though it is possible to stop after the fourth. This trail, only available in the winter, from March 1 to October 31, can be started on the first and third Sundays and Wednesdays of the month. It needs to be booked through the DNC at Windhoek, and costs R25 per person — with a minimum group size of three, and a maximum of 12. For such an extended hike you must carry all your food, as well as sleeping bags and mats. Your efforts will be rewarded as it is definitely the best way to really get a feel for any wild area such as this.

Because the area is mainly used for walking (which invariably involves an amount of scrambling) and is also fairly remote, the DNC have become concerned about the risks to visitors here, especially foreign tourists, and thus they now advise people to come as groups of at least three. Though this is only insisted upon if you plan to do the longest trail, it is good advice if you are new to the area and it is easy to find people in Windhoek who will share costs on a trip here.

The northern section between the Kuiseb and Swakop Rivers

2WD/4WD

The desert between these two important river-beds is largely one of rock and stone. Though the area has few classic desert scenes of shifting dunes etc., the landscapes are perhaps all the more unusual and certainly no less memorable. They range from the deeply incised canyons of the Swakop River valley to the open plains around Ganab, flat and featureless but for the occasional isolated *inselburgs* — islands of granite which jut up through the desert floor like giant worm casts on a well-kept lawn.

When to visit

The best time to visit this part of the park is just towards the end of the rains when the vegetation is at its best and, if you are lucky, there's the added attraction of herds of gemsbok, springbok or zebra. During this time the best sites to go to are the more open ones, like Ganab, on the plains. If, however, you visit during the dry season then perhaps it's better to visit Homeb or one of the *inselburgs*, as the flora and fauna there remain a little more constant than that on the plains — not shrivelling up so much in the dryness of winter.

Getting organised

Whenever you visit, you really need to spend at least a couple of nights camping here in order to do the area justice — though this requires you to be fully independent in terms of fuel, food and water. The permit to camp confers the freedom to use any of the sites in the area and as the map shows, most of the roads are navigable by 2WD, while only a few around Gemsbokwater and Groot Tinkas are classed as 4WD. Even these are probably negotiable with a high-clearance 2WD and a skilled driver, though you'd be waiting a very long time indeed for anyone to pass by if you became stuck.

What to see and do

Whist not famous for its game, the park is home to over 30 species of mammal including gemsbok, kudu, springbok, hartmann's mountain zebra, klipspringer, baboon, black-backed jackal, leopard, aardwolf, bat-eared fox, spotted hyena and even the rare brown hyena. One real delight that is not so difficult to spot is the sight of a group of meerkats foraging under the guard of a couple of 'sentries', members of the group that have been posted to stand watch — by balancing on their hind legs while their keen eyes scan the area around.

Key to map

Main road - no permit required
Tourist road - permit required
Four-wheel drive vehicles only
Official overnight camping sites
Prohibited area
Watering places for game
① Vegetation-lined lagoon with Pelicans, Flamingoes, Ducks
② Salt-works at lagoon with Pelicans, Flamingoes, Waders
③ Sewage disposal ponds with reeds & aquatic birds
④ Guano platform - Cormorants, Pelicans
⑤ Salt-works & guano platform with Cormorants, Flamingoes
⑥ Old riverine farm in bed of Swakop River
⑦ Moon Landscape - age old erosion
⑧ Plain with fossil plants
⑨ Desert Ecological Research Institute (NO VISITORS)
⑩ View of Kuiseb Canyon

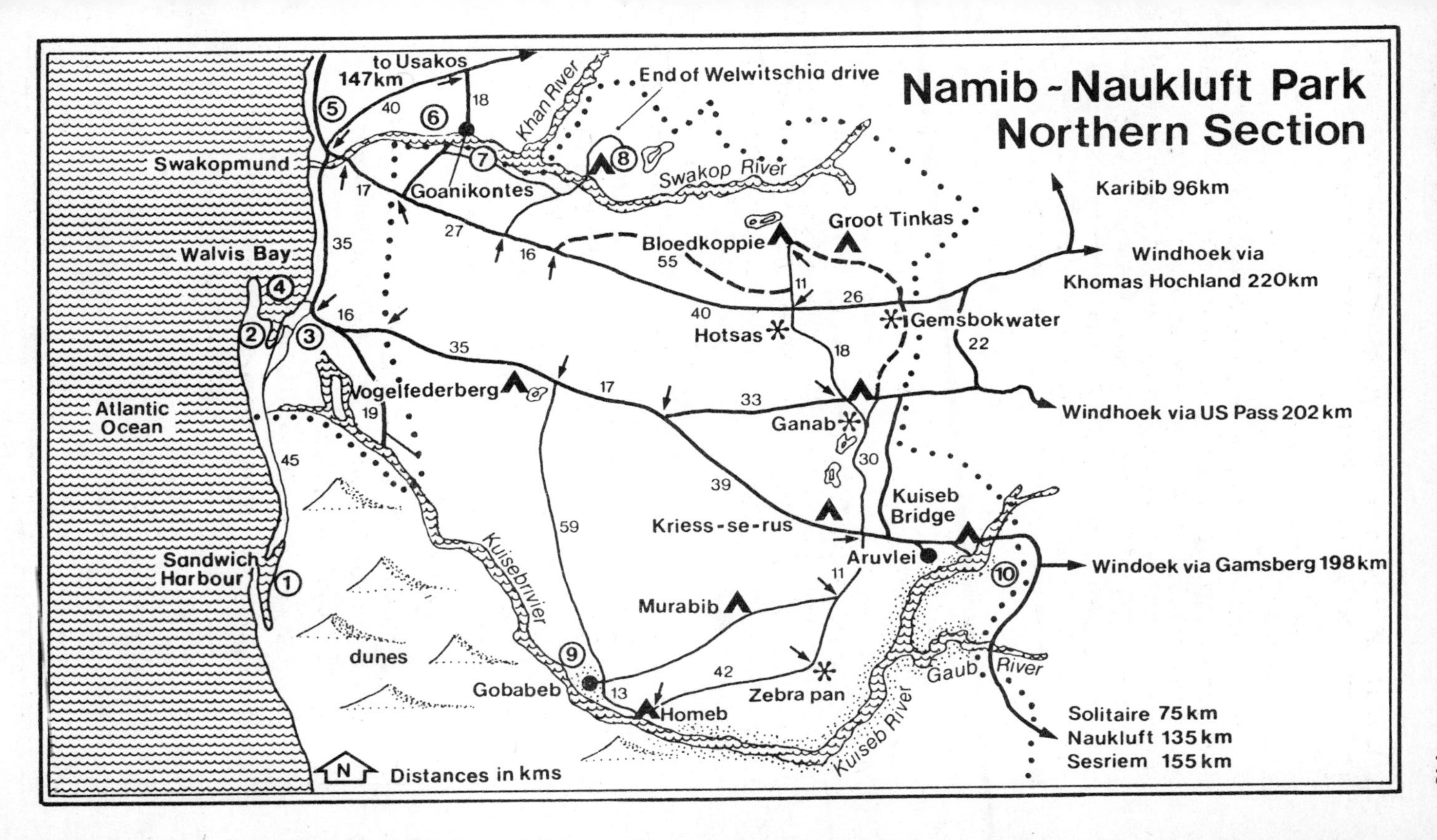
Namib - Naukluft Park
Northern Section
to Usakos
147km
End of Welwitschia drive
Khan River
Swakop River
Swakopmund
Goanikontes
Karibib 96km
Groot Tinkas
Bloedkoppie
Windhoek via
Khomas Hochland 220km
Walvis Bay
Hotsas
Gemsbokwater
Vogelfederberg
Windhoek via US Pass 202 km
Atlantic
Ocean
Ganab
Kuiseb
Bridge
Kriess-se-rus
Aruvlei
Windoek via Gamsberg 198 km
Sandwich
Harbour
Murabib
Kuisebrivier
dunes
Gobabeb
Homeb
Zebra pan
Gaub
River
Kuiseb River
Solitaire 75 km
Naukluft 135 km
Sesriem 155 km
N
Distances in kms

Where to stay — the campsites

Bloedkoppie. This large granite *inselburg* rises out of the Tinkas Flats and can provide some challenging scrambles if the heat's not drained your energies too much. *Be careful* not to approach any birds' nests, as some of the raptors in the park are very sensitive to disturbances. They may even abandon them if you go too close.

Ganab. Immediately next to a dry watercourse, which winds like a thin green snake through the middle of a large gravel plain, this open site has a wind-powered water pump nearby. Around March, if the rains have been good, then it can be an excellent spot for herds of springbok and gemsbok — and you can see for miles!

Groot Tinkas. Hidden away in a valley amidst an area of *kopjes* (small rocky hills), there's a small dam with sheer walls of rock here and some fairly rocky driving too!

Homeb. This excellent site is in the Kuiseb River valley which, with its perennial vegetation, forms the northern boundary of the great southern dune field. Its well placed location leaves you with the opportunity to cross the river-bed and climb amongst the dunes, as well as to explore the valley itself.

Kriess-se-Rus. Again found in a dry river-bed, Kriess-se-rus lies just below a bank of exposed schist — with the layers of rock clearly seen, providing an interesting contrast to the flat calcrete plains nearby.

Kuiseb bridge. Just off the main C14 route, west of the Gamsberg pass, the river is said to have less underground water stored here than further down its course, though it is more prone to flash floods. It can be very bare during the dry season, but is really pleasant after the rains.

Mirabib. Yet another great grey *inselburg*, but one that is even quieter than the others. It has great views from the top.

Swakop River. Being also beacon number 10 on the Welwitschia drive (see next page) means that this beautiful dry river-bed can get rather busy at times.

Vogelfederberg. This rounded granite outcrop is the closest of the sites to the ocean, and as such it gets more moisture from the fog than the others. Its gentle shape helps form a number of fascinating temporary pools which contain a remarkable amount of life — including species of brine shrimp whose drought-resistant eggs can survive dry periods lasting many years, only to hatch within hours of the first rain. Polaroid glasses will help you to see past the reflections and into these pools, so if you've a pair, take them!

Welwitschia Drive

2WD

The Welwitschia Drive is situated in the most northerly part of the Namib-Naukluft park, a short drive from Swakopmund along the B2 towards Windhoek.

It's a route through the desert along which the DNC have set 13 numbered stone beacons at points of particular interest. It takes about four hours to drive, stopping at each place to get out and explore, and culminates at one of the country's largest, and hence oldest, Welwitschia plants.

An excellent, detailed little booklet — well worth getting — is available from the DNC to cover this route. However as it is often difficult to obtain here's a brief outline of the different points of interest at the beacons:

1. A lichen field Look carefully at the ground to see these small 'plants', which are in fact the result of a symbiotic relationship (ie a mutually beneficial relationship between two organisms — each depending on the other for its survival) between an alga, producing food by photosynthesis, and a fungus, providing a physical structure. If you look closely, you'll see many different types of lichen. Some of these are thought to be hundreds of years old, and all are exceedingly fragile and vulnerable.

2. Drought-resistant bushes Two types of bush found all over the Namib are the Dollar Bush, so called because its leaves are the size of a dollar coin, and the Ink Bush. Both can survive without rain for years.

3. Tracks of oxwagons made decades ago are still visible here, showing clearly the damage that can so easily be done to the lichen fields by driving over them.

4. This is the unusual and spectacular **moonscape** view, over a landscape formed by the valleys of the Swakop river.

5. More lichen fields These remarkable plants can extract all their moisture requirements from the air. To simulate the dramatic effect that a morning fog can have, simply sprinkle a little water on one and watch carefully for a few minutes.

6. Here's another impressive view of the endless 'moonscape'.

7. This beacon marks the site of an old **South African camp**, occupied for only a few days during the First World War.

8. Now you must turn left to visit the next few beacons:

9. Here the road goes across a **dolerite dyke**. These dark strips of rock, which are a common feature of this part of the Namib, were formed when molten lava welled up through cracks in the existing grey granite. After cooling it formed dark, hard bands of rock which resisted erosion more than the granite — and thus has formed the spine of many ridges in the area.

10. The Swakop River valley Picnicking in the river-bed, with a profusion of tall trees around, you might find it difficult to believe that you're really in a desert. It could be said that you're not — after all, this rich vegetation is not made up of desert adapted species. It includes *Tamarix usurious* (wild tamarisk) and *Acacia albida* (anaboom), better known for its occurrence in the humid Zambezi valley almost 1000 miles to the east. They are only sustained by the supply of underground water which percolates through the sand far beneath your feet.

11. Welwitschia Flats This open, supremely barren expanse of gravel and sand is home to the Namib's most celebrated endemic plant, *Welwitschia mirabilis*. These plants are only found in the Namib and even then only at a few locations which suit their highly adapted biology.

12. This beacon marks the end of the trail, and one of the largest *Welwitschia mirabilis* known — its age is estimated to be over 1,500 years old!

On the way back, continue straight past beacon 8, without turning right, and where the road joins route C28 to Swakopmund there's one of the

Welwitschia Mirabilis

Welwitschia, perhaps Namibia's most famous species of plant, are usually found growing in groups on the harshest gravel plains of the central Namib desert. Each plant has only two long, shredded leaves and is separated from the other *welwitschia* plants by some distance. They appear as a tangle of foliage — some of which is green though most is a desiccated grey — which emerges from a stubby 'wooden' base.

They were first described in the west by Friedrich Welwitsch, an Austrian botanist who came across the plants as recently as 1859. Ever since then scientists have been fascinated by *welwitschia*, earning the plant the specific name *mirabilis* — Latin for marvellous!

Research suggests that *welwitschia* can live to over one thousand years of age, and are in fact members of the conifer family (though some sources class them with the succulents). Though their leaves can spread for several meters across, and their roots over a meter down, it is still a mystery exactly how moisture is obtained by the plants. One theory suggests that dew condenses on the leaves only to drip down where it is absorbed by the fine roots near the surface of the ground.

Another puzzle was how they reproduce. It's now thought that some of the specialist insects which live on the plants act as pollinators, the wind then distributing the seeds far and wide. Young *welwitschia* are rare indeed, only germinating when the conditions are right in years of exceptional rain. I was shown one on the skeleton coast that was known to be eight years old. It was minute, consisting of just two seedling leaves and no more than an inch tall.

Their ability to thrive in such a harsh environment is amazing, and their adaptations are still being studied. There has even been a recent suggestion that the older plants change the chemical composition of the soil around them, making it harder for young plants to germinate next to them and compete for space.

desert's many old mine workings — marked by the final beacon, number 13. In the 1950s iron ore was mined by hand here, but now it's yet another reminder of the park's chequered past.

Sandwich Harbour

High-clearance 4WD only

This small area about 40km south of Walvis, contains a large saltwater lagoon, extensive tidal mudflats, and a band of reed-lined pools fed by freshwater springs — which together form one of the most important refuges for birdlife in southern Africa. It offers food and shelter to countless thousands of migrants every year, and some of the most spectacular scenery in the country for those visitors lucky enough to reach it. Where else can you walk alone along a pelican-covered beach while nearby pink flamingos glide photogenically above apricot-coloured sand dunes?

Getting there

Take the road by the lagoon south-west out of Walvis Bay and after about 4km ignore the sign to Paaltjies (where the road divides) and keep to your left. The tracks then split as you make your way across the **Kuiseb Delta**, but converge again near the shore about 16km later. Here there's a checkpoint at a gate in the fence which marks the boundary between South Africa and the Namib-Naukluft Park (Namibia), and you'll be turned away if you don't have a permit.

From this checkpoint it's about 20km of sandy terrain to Sandwich Harbour. You can drive all the way on the beach if you wish, following in the footsteps of the fishermen, although the going is exceedingly rough. It's better to take an immediate left after passing the control post, and follow these tracks. After some 200m, they turn parallel to the sea and are considerably firmer than the ones on the beach. Note that leaving this set of tracks and trying to go across the apparently dry pans, where there are no tracks, is asking for trouble!

What to see and do

Once you reach the entry to the bird sanctuary of Sandwich, vehicles must be left though you can proceed on foot. The northern part consists of a number of almost enclosed reed-lined pools at the top of the beach, which back directly onto the huge desert dunes. These are fed partly by the sea via narrow channels which fill at high tide, and partly with freshwater which seeps from a subterranean watercourse under the dunes and enables reeds (albeit salt-tolerant ones) to grow. These in turn provide food and nesting sites for a number of the resident water birds to be found here.

On my last visit here I managed to spot dabchicks, moorhens, shelducks, common and marsh sandpipers, several species of tern (caspian, swift, white-winged and whiskered all visit) and even avocets and African spoonbills — as well as the pelicans and flamingos.

Continuing along the beach, the 'harbour' itself comes into view. During the early 18th Century it was used by whalers for its deep, sheltered anchorage and ready supply of fresh water, and subsequently a small station was established there to trade in seal pelts, fish and guano. Later, in the early part of this century, it was used as a major source of guano, but after difficulties with the mouth of the harbour silting up, this operation finally ground to a halt in 1947, leaving only a few bits of rusting machinery to be seen to this day.

It's worth making the effort to climb at least a little way up one of the enormous dunes. From such a vantage point you can see clearly the deep lagoon, protected from the ocean's pounding by a sand spit, and then to the south the extensive mudflats — which are covered from time to time by the high tide.

This is definitely a trip to make a whole day of, so when you start walking from your vehicle, bring some windproof clothes and a little to eat and drink, as well as your binoculars, camera and several spare films. Even if you're not an avid ornithologist, the scenery is so spectacular that you're bound to take endless photos!

Quoted in *The Okavango River* by C J Andersson:

'There's an island that lies on West Africa's shore,
Where the penguins have lived since the flood or before,
And raised up a hill there, a mile high or more.
This hill is all guano, and lately 'tis shown,
That finer potatoes and turnips are grown,
By means of this compost, than ever were known;
And the peach and the nectarine, the apple, the pear,
Attain such a size that the gardeners stare,
And cry, 'Well! I never saw fruit like that 'ere!'
One cabbage thus reared, as a paper maintains,
Weighed twenty-one stone, thirteen pounds and six grains,
So no wonder Guano celebrity gains.'

Flamingos

Of the world's half-dozen or so species of flamingo, two are found within southern Africa: the Greater, *phoenicopterus ruber*, and the Lesser, *phoenicopterus minor*. Both species have wide distributions — from southern Africa north into East Africa and the Red Sea — and are highly nomadic in their habits.

Flamingos are usually found wading in large areas of shallow saline water where they filter feed by holding their specially adapted beaks upside down in the water. The Lesser Flamingo will walk or swim whilst swinging its head from side to side, mainly taking blue-green algae from the surface of the water. The larger Greater Flamingo will hold its head submerged while filtering out small organisms (detritus and algae), even stirring the mud with its feet to help the process. Both species are very gregarious and flocks can have millions of birds, though a few hundred is more common.

Only occasionally do flamingos breed in southern Africa, choosing Etosha pan, the Makgadikgadi pans or even Lake Ngami. When the conditions are right (usually March to June, following the rains) both species build low mud cones in the water and lay one (or rarely two) eggs in a small hollow on the top. These are then incubated by both parents for about a month until they hatch, and after a further week the young birds flock together and start to forage with their parents. Some ten weeks later the young can fly and fend for themselves.

During this time the young are very susceptible to the shallow water in the pans drying out. In 1969, a rescue operation was mounted when the main pan at Etosha dried out, necessitating the moving of thousands of chicks to nearby Fisher's pan which was still covered in water!

The best way to tell the two species apart is by their beaks: that of the Greater Flamingo is almost white with a black tip, whilst the Lesser Flamingo has a uniformly dark beak. If you are further away then the body of the Greater will appear white, whilst that of the Lesser looks smaller and more pink.

The best place to see them is probably around Walvis Bay or Sandwich Harbour — unless you hear specific news that they are breeding on one of the great pans.

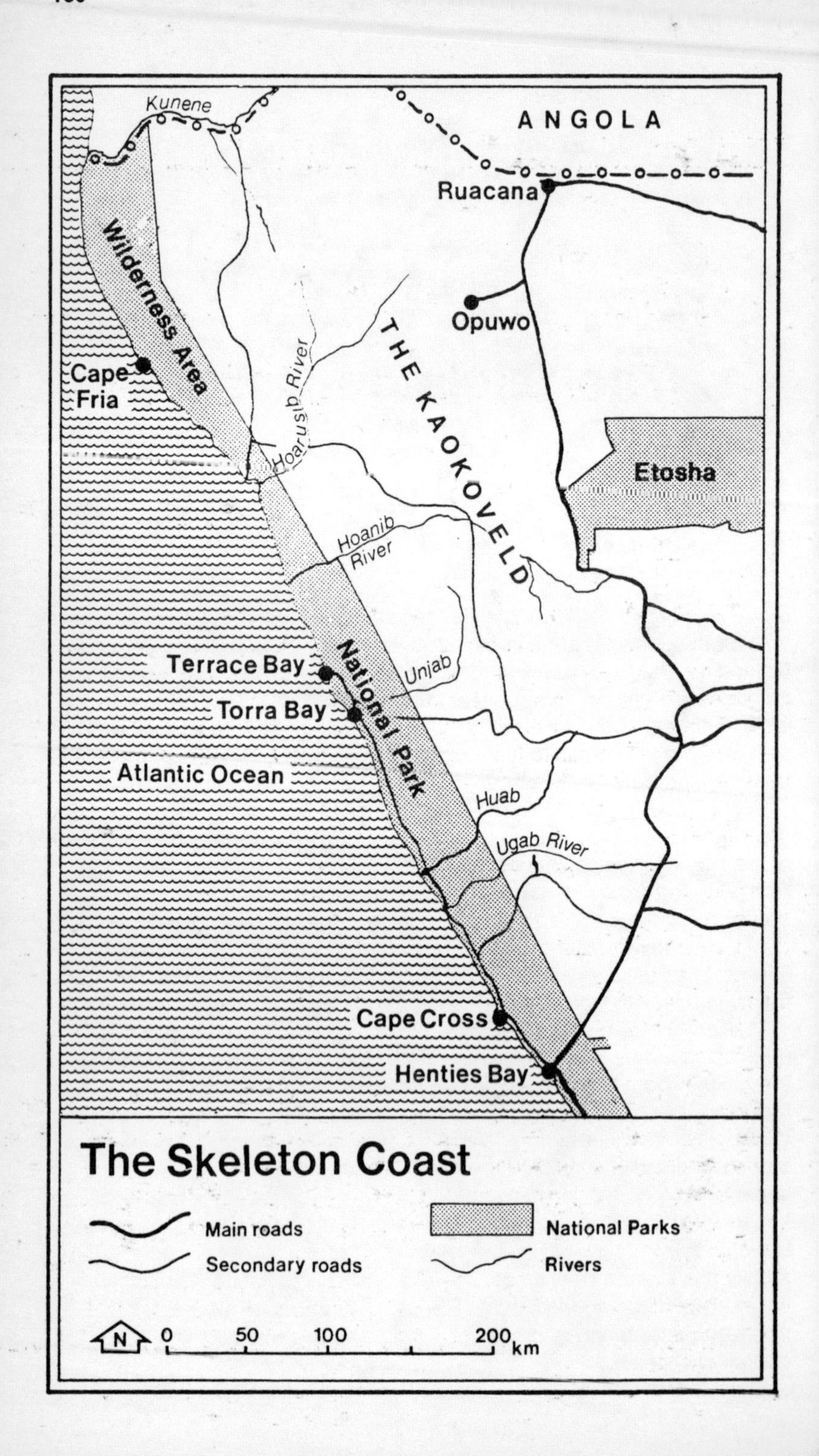

The Skeleton Coast

Chapter 11

The Skeleton Coast

By the end of the 17th Century, the long stretch of coast north of Walvis Bay and Swakopmund had attracted the attention of the Dutch East India Company. They sent several exploratory missions, but after finding only barren desert shores, impenetrable fogs and dangerous seas, their journeys were curtailed. Later, in the 19th Century, English and American whalers operated out of Lüderitz to the south, but they gave the northern Kaokoveld coast a wide berth — it was gaining a formidable reputation.

Today, driving north from Swakopmund along the coast, you pass shipwreck after shipwreck stranded on the sand-banks by the shore. It's easy to see how this stretch of coast earned its names — 'The Coast of Skulls' and 'The Skeleton Coast'. Once a ship had fallen prey to the treacherous fogs and currents, the surviving sailors' problems had only just begun — the coast is but a thin barren line between the pounding ocean and the stark desert interior. Their only hope was to find one of the few 'linear oases', formed by the rivers that wind through the desert to reach the ocean.

These ribbons of green are few and far between, but each supports a surprising amount of life. Starting in the highlands of the Kaokoveld plateau, the water seldom flows above ground but instead filters through the sands of these apparently dry river-beds, allowing shrubs and trees to thrive, and creating narrow bands of vegetation. Occasionally, these rivers rise to the surface and trickle overland for a few hundred metres, perhaps avoiding an impervious rock barrier beneath, only to vanish into the sand again as suddenly as they appeared. Such watering places are few and far between, but of vital importance to all the inhabitants of the area. This scarce water supply has allowed isolated groups of the Himba people to stay in the area, whilst also sustaining the famous 'desert' populations of elephant and black rhino, and extending the ranges of giraffe, zebra, gemsbok, springbok, lion and even cheetah.

Outside the river valleys the scenery changes, with an astounding variety of colours and forms, from gravel plains to huge sand dunes — whilst farther inland, toward the Kaokoveld, jagged mountains rise up through the smooth sand to form strange, unearthly landscapes. Even here there is life. The gravel plains are covered by ancient lichens, whilst specially adapted bushes grow within the areas of sand — some species even forming their own small dunes as an aid to survival — and everywhere, if you search, you'll find small *tenebrionid* beetles.

North of the Hoarusib river, sandwiched between the dunefields and the wide sandy beaches, there are occasional reed-fringed pools of *fresh* water. These are well worth seeking out; we found one pool with a resident pair of moorhen, visiting plovers and avocets, and even fish!

The coast is divided into three separate regions: the **National West Coast Recreational Area**, the **Skeleton Coast National Park** and the **Skeleton Coast Wilderness Area**. For the Recreational Area no permits are needed (you just pay your entrance fees at the gate), while access to the national park is controlled and a permit is required from the DNC (see below under *Skeleton Coast National Park*, page 154). The northern section of the Skeleton Coast — the wilderness area — is only accessible to tourists and visitors if you join an exclusive fly-in safari (see below under *The Wilderness Area*, page 157).

NATIONAL WEST COAST RECREATIONAL PARK

This stretch of coastline between Swakopmund and the Ugab River is mainly used for fishing. Driving north along the road you'll undoubtedly pass a succession of Toyota 4WD's parked on the sand every few kilometres. Nearby, three or four anglers will be casting their long lines out to sea, with a coolbox of cold beers close to hand. (The fishing is reputedly excellent and attracts anglers from all over the subcontinent.)

The scenery is barren in the extreme, with the flat beach becoming indistinguishable at times from the sand-and-gravel plains of the interior. The only real attraction is Cape Cross (the site where the first European set foot in Namibia in 1485), which is currently home to a large breeding colony of Cape fur seals. For those in search of total desolation, try driving along the C35 from just north of Henties Bay to Uis Mine — it's quite an experience.

Getting there

Car A normal 2WD car is fine for all of the main road along the coast, though 4WDs do come in useful for turning onto the beach. In either case, great care should be taken not to drive over the gravel plains on account of the permanent damage that tracks do to the flora and fauna (however lifeless the areas may appear — they'll be a lot more lifeless if you drive over them).

Hitching should be good (if you can put up with the strong sun and icy winds by the roadside), as there's only one coast road and lots of 4WD pick-ups cruising up and down with space in the back. Hitching is much better on the weekends and school holidays.

Where to stay

The small town of Henties Bay has a small hotel and a rest camp (see next page). Otherwise there are numerous campsites along the coast, although all are rather bare in appearance and have only the most basic facilities. The ones at Mile 14, Mile 72, Mile 108 and Jakkalsputz are all run by the DNC and a site costs R10. Mile 72 and Mile 108 have filling stations, whilst all have hot showers for R1 per turn and drinking water is for sale at 10c per litre.

If you want to fish, but haven't the gear, then your best bet would probably be to stay at a specialist lodge like **Sanpedi** (PO Box 1089. Tel: Edenvale 1610) where full board and all fishing trips will cost around R200 per person per night.

The sea ponds

About 7km north of Swakopmund lie a number of large shallow ponds. Some are used for salt production — by filling them with seawater and leaving it to evaporate — while others are used for rearing young oysters. Sometimes you'll find one coloured bright red by algae, or pink with a flock of feeding flamingos!

Henties Bay

76km from Swakopmund, this windblown town is set astride the river Omaruru and immediately above the shore. There's little to do here (apart from fishing), though exploring the lower parts of the Omaruru on foot could provide a pleasant walk for a few hours. The town has a couple of garages, several shops, and a paint and hardware store that will rent out camping equipment.

Hotel De Duin This is the town's only hotel, and its busy bar and restaurant stands overlooking the sea. Singles are R35-R39 and doubles R53-R58, with breakfast for R9. If you're just passing through and want a break then breakfast is served from 8am to 10am, lunch from 12.30pm to 2pm, and dinner from 7pm until 9pm.

The **Swaou-oord rest camp** has well-equipped bungalows for R35-R50, with R5 for each extra bed.

Cape Cross

2WD. Entrance fees: R5 per person and R5 for a car.

Situated about 128km north of Swakopmund, Cape Cross was probably the site of the first landing by a European on the Namibian coast. Here, in 1485, the Portuguese captain, Diego Cão, landed and erected a stone cross on the headland to mark his visit. This remained in place until, in the 1890s, it was taken to Germany and replaced by the one that still stands there today. More recently, a replica of Diego's original cross — fashioned from local stone — has been erected on its original spot and the whole area has been carefully terraced with translations of the inscriptions on the terraces.

The animals here have been exploited by man for centuries. Firstly the seal colony was used by the early mariners as a supply of fresh meat, skins and oil; then later the offshore bird colonies were decimated by traders for the rich deposits of guano found there. Nowadays the area is a reserve where Cape fur seals congregate in their thousands to breed. The amazing sight of the ocean full of bobbing heads is matched only by the strong stench which strikes you as you approach the colony.

In October, the bulls come ashore to stake out their territories and compete for females, then about November/December the pups are born. Many of the pups die young, however, accidentally squashed by the huge bulls or preyed upon by the scavenging jackals — the mortality rate is high. After only a few months, the surviving pups are off into the surf on their own to feed in the ocean.

Park opening times From December 16 to the end of February — every day from 8am until 5pm.

From March 1 to June 30 — open for the same hours, but only on Saturdays, Sundays, public holidays and during the Easter school holidays.

From July 1 to December 15 — open only on Tuesdays and Wednesdays from 12pm until 4pm.

SKELETON COAST NATIONAL PARK

2WD. Entrance fees: R8 per person and R10 per vehicle. An entry permit is required from the DNC.

From the Ugab to the Kunene River, the border with Angola, the Skeleton Coast national park and wilderness area cover roughly one-third of Namibia's coastline and encompass the transition zone from the higher Kaokoveld interior to the foggy ocean shore. The landscapes become more interesting as you travel north, and the number of people that you see certainly become less.

The national park itself lies between the Ugab and Hoanib rivers and entry is carefully controlled. Visitors need a day permit to drive through the park, which is available from the DNC offices in Windhoek, Swakopmund, or Okaukuejo. This does not allow you to visit Torra or Terrace Bays though, the only camps in the area (see below). The description below imagines a route from south to north along the coast.

Note the entry gates — on the Ugab or inland at Springbokwasser — must be passed by 3pm.

Ugab River valley

The Ugab is one of the longest rivers to cross the Namib, its waters coming from as far east as Outjo and Otjiwarongo, and its valley forms an important corridor for animal movement between the interior and the coast. The dense vegetation found here is mostly wild tobacco (*Nicotiana glauca*) — a foreign import which has run riot — though various indigenous plants are also present. Some of the larger mammals do come right down to the sea, and

I've often heard the tale of a lion seen lounging around by the park's skull-and-crossbones gate!

Hiking trail One of the best ways to learn about the river valley is to go on the three-day hiking trail, which has been set up by the DNC. It can be tough going in the harsh climate, but should leave you with a good appreciation of the complex ecosystem present in this specialised environment – and you may even spot an oryx or two.

For the trail, which is accompanied by a game ranger, you need to bring all your own equipment and supplies. As with the Fish River Canyon, the hike must be booked well in advance through the Windhoek DNC office. It costs R75 per person, and groups should be six to eight people — all with medical certificates of fitness issued within the previous 40 days.

Huab River valley

About 38km north of the Ugab River, the coast road crosses the Huab River, and there's a small loop road off to the east which explores the valley further inland. It's worth getting out and wandering around on foot, among the **dollar bushes** (*Zygophyllum stapffii*) with their thick, fleshy leaves about the size of a US dollar coin. Notice how they collect a mound of sand on their leeward side, appearing to grow out of their own small dune. The dollar bush is a classic example of a plant which seems to alter its environment to suit itself. As sand collects in its lee, so does windblown detritus and on this feed a variety of beetles which live in the mounds and hence fertilise the bushes with their faeces. For moisture, the plants must survive on the morning fog, and the occasional shower, but it's noticeable that the higher mounds collect more dew than the lower ones – giving the older bushes (with larger mounds) yet another advantage in the survival stakes.

To the north of the river-bed, inland, are a few crescent-shaped *barchan* dunes (see Chapter 3, page 31), emerging from the river's sands and 'marching' northwards. Further north still, the wreck of the *Atlantic Pride* lies just off the shore.

Koigab River valley

This is one of the smaller rivers, and yet it still supports perennial vegetation and even flows occasionally. It's a good place to look for what are possibly the world's only **white beetles** — and the focus of much scientific study since their discovery. The unique coloration of these beetles, from the genus *Onymacris*, is thought to be an adaptation to reduce their absorption of heat, and hence allow them to forage above the sand's surface during the middle of the day. However, if this is the case then it remains to be explained why they only occur in the northern Namib, and why the vast majority of other desert beetles are black.

Torra Bay campsite

Open December 1 to January 31.

This seasonal camp-site, between the Koigab and the Uniab rivers, lies just south of the first dunes in the Namib's great northern dunefield. Here the first low *barchan* dunes start migrating north, eventually forming a sand sea stretching as far as the Curoca river in Angola.

You might notice that some of the dunes have purple tinges to their crests, contrasting with the lighter coloured sand below. This is caused by a high proportion of purple-brown garnet crystals in the sand — they collect on the surface, being less dense than the quartz sand grains. If you've a magnifying glass then look closely at a handful of the sand — you'll find a whole kaleidoscope of colours sparkling like jewels in your palm.

The camping site here is open only during the high season, December 1 to January 31, and it has a basic shop, a filling station and toilets. It costs R10 per site, and must be booked in Windhoek or you won't be let past the gates.

Uniab River valley

Though fairly short, this is one of the most important rivers to cross the Namib as far as wildlife is concerned. Its headwaters come from around Palmwag, an area of relatively abundant game, and its lower reaches have formed an impressive, well vegetated delta. In between, there is a wide valley supporting rich flora and fauna, surrounded for some of its course by dunes on either side. The area by the road is a fascinating one to explore on foot for a few hours, so park the car and bring along your binoculars and a flask of water.

It seems that in the past the Uniab's mouth formed a large delta. This has subsequently been raised up above sea level, only to be cut into again by the river to form a series of five alternative routes to the sea. Only one of these has water flowing through it at present (and then only after good rains), though most have freshwater pools fed by underground seepage — forming small verdant oases dotted around the watercourses. These are a home for resident water birds and an important stop-over for migrants, including the delicate black and white avocets.

Currently, it is the second course from the north which hosts the flow, and if you walk upstream there is often an overground trickle through the canyon, which has been carved smooth by the water. Move quietly and you may see some of the springbok or gemsbok which often graze down here — or even catch a glimpse of the rare brown hyena, a harmless scavenger that's mainly nocturnal and known to inhabit the area.

Terrace Bay camp and chalets

Open all year

The camp This is the most northerly public camp on the coast, with luxury chalets which are open throughout the year and must be booked in advance at Windhoek. It costs R120 for a single, R200 for a double, but includes a full three meals per day — and even space in the freezer! Fuel is available, and there is also a shop and a couple of bars — this camp is aimed primarily at anglers.

Dunes and beetles Around Terrace Bay the dune belt widens to stretch down to the ocean. The crests of these dunes are good places to search for some of the highly unusual beetles which perform 'headstands' or dig trenches in order to drink, but you'll have to be up by sunrise to catch them at it.

The 'headstanding' beetles can be seen high on the dunes — with their backs to the wind and their heads down — 'fog basking' a little before sunrise. Water condenses out of the moist fog and onto their bodies, dripping down to hang in droplets below their mouths. By drinking this they obtain all the water that they need to survive.

The large round beetles of the *lepidochora* genus illustrate another way of collecting moisture from the fog. These dig small trenches (a couple of centimetres deep) near the dune crests, perpendicular to the prevailing wind and then collect the moisture which tends to condense on the trench walls!

SKELETON COAST WILDERNESS AREA

Covered by a patchwork of dunefields, and separated from the country's main populated areas by the arid regions of western Kaokoland, this most inaccessible area has remained largely unaffected by events further inland. In the distant past, perhaps when rains were better, bushmen moved here from the interior — leaving behind them only round stone circles as remnants of their shelters. More recently, earlier in this century, there was an attempt to mine amethysts at Sarusas — but that too proved impractical, and left only ruins remain.

Visitors approaching from the ocean fared little better. The countless wrecks, dating from as early as the American whalers of the 18th Century, earned the coast its name and formidable reputation. Driving along the shoreline you'll see endless piles of driftwood and scraps of metal which have been washed up from the wrecks. Old drums, winches, ropes — all lie exactly where they came ashore.

Perhaps it was this 'untouched' aspect of the northern coast which, together with the northern Namib's unique desert ecosystem, persuaded the government to proclaim it a 'wilderness area'. This important status allows for no permanent developments to take place at all — and forbids anything which would change the unspoilt character of the region. Consequently, entry to the area is prohibited unless you are booked on a professionally organised tour.

Getting there with 'Skeleton Coast Fly-in Safaris'

Louw Schoeman — who was instrumental in persuading the government to protect the Skeleton Coast — conducts the area's only tours: Skeleton Coast Fly-in Safaris, PO Box 2195, Windhoek. Tel:(061)224248. Fax:(061)225713).

The tours are expensive, but operating in such a remote area is costly, and has many logistical problems — including the bringing of all the supplies almost 1000km from Windhoek, and the removal of all rubbish. The safaris are typically between five and 10 days long, and at present there are five 'permanent camps' in the park, with visitors usually based at one for several days while they explore the surrounding area in 4WD vehicles.

Accommodation is in substantial two-person tents (complete with beds, lights, and a chemical toilet) which are about as comfortable as it's possible to be while not altering the area by erecting permanent buildings. The price, at around R500 per person per day, includes everything (flights, 4WD excursions, all meals and drinks).

What to see and do

After visiting the area on an excellent five-day fly-in safari, the impression which I'm left with is of a number of incredibly beautiful landscapes — each with its own fragile ecosystem — existing side by side within a fairly small area. While out on safari, which took most of the day, we would frequently stop to study more closely the plants and animals, or try and capture the landscapes on film, and back at camp we relaxed by talking to the guides with a drink over dinner.

Some of the Fly-in safaris include a trip to an isolated settlement of Himba people — a fascinating and humbling experience — in which the cost of the trip includes an amount for the Himba whom you visit (see section on *Conservation and Development*, page 37).

There were also a number of specific 'sights' to see, but these seemed almost incidental when compared with simply experiencing the strange solitude and singular beauty in the area:

Sand temples of the Hoarusib Canyon Here the sides of the Hoarusib's steep canyon are lined with tall structures which the wind has carved — implausibly — out of soft sand to resemble some of the ancient Egyptian temples. Watch out for the patch of quicksand on the river near here!

The beaches Driving through the mist along these desolate beaches, fiddler crabs scuttle amongst the flotsam and jetsam of the centuries, while rare damara terns fly overhead. There is always something of interest here to take a closer look at or to photograph.

Cape Frio Here there is a large colony of cape fur seals, and with care you can approach close enough to get a good portrait photograph.

Roaring dunes Perhaps the strangest experience here, these large sand dunes make an amazing and unexpected loud 'roar' (reverberating all through the dune) if you slide down one of the steep lee sides. A truly weird sensation that really has to be felt to be believed! One current theory links the 'roar' with electrostatic discharges between the individual grains of sand when they are caused to rub against each other. Why some dunes 'roar' and others don't remains a mystery.

Rocky point This rocky pinnacle, jutting out from a long, open stretch of sand, was an important landmark on the coast for passing ships in times gone by.

Bushmen rock circles These occur further inland and are thought to be the remains of their shelters.

Lichen fields and Welwitschia plants are widespread throughout the gravel plains further inland. One Welwitschia plant, no more than a few centimetres high, is known by Louw and his guides to have germinated in 1982 — demonstrating just how slowly these plants do actually grow.

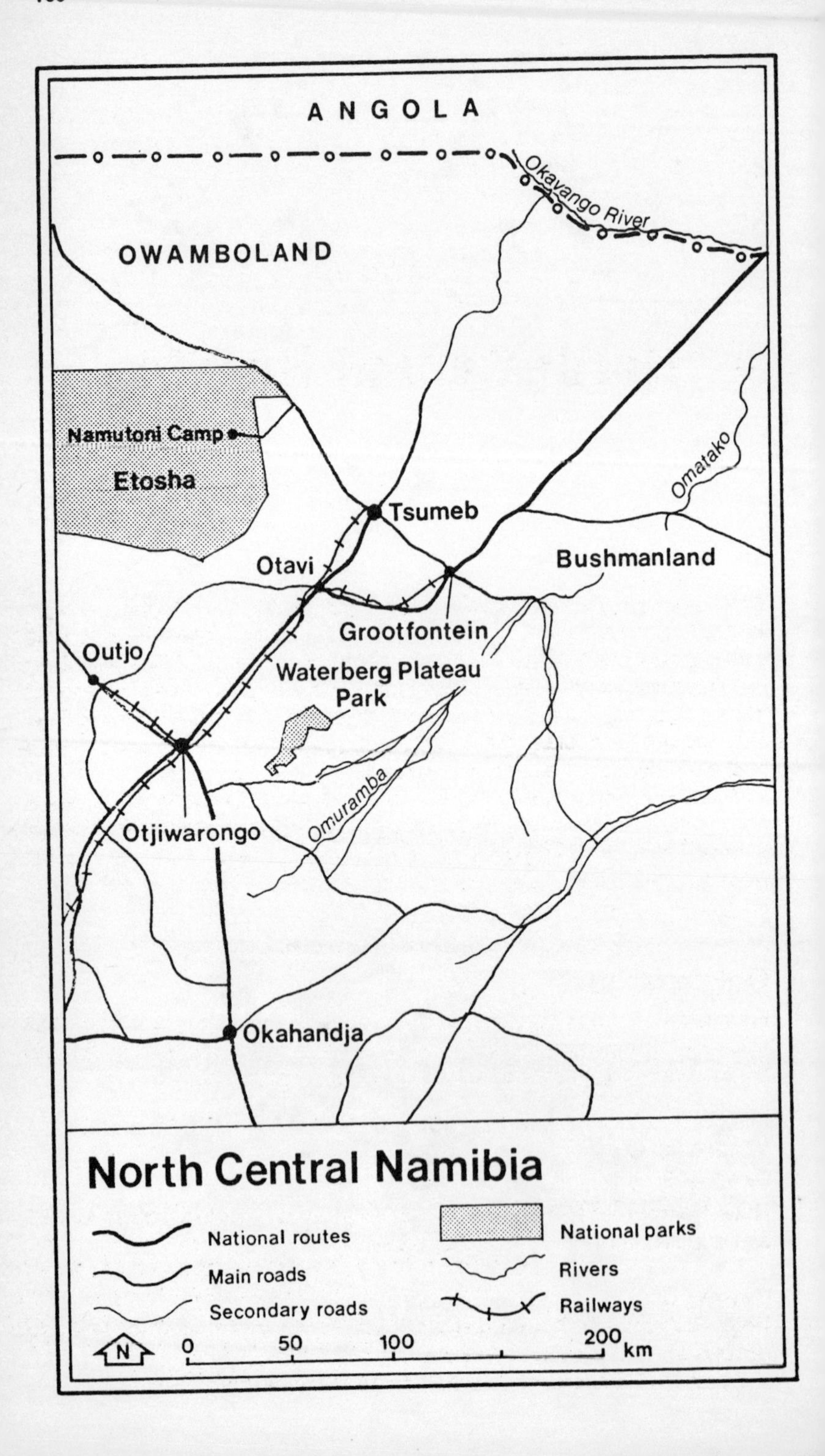
ANGOLA
Okavango River
OWAMBOLAND
Namutoni Camp
Etosha
Omatako
Tsumeb
Otavi
Bushmanland
Grootfontein
Outjo
Waterberg Plateau Park
Omuramba
Otjiwarongo
Okahandja
North Central Namibia
National routes
Main roads
Secondary roads
National parks
Rivers
Railways
N
0
50
100
200 km

Chapter 12

North Central Namibia

While Etosha is the main attraction in the north of the country, this region to its south and east often tends to be overlooked by those who just dash through, oblivious that there are other places of interest here. The Waterberg Plateau is well worth a visit, especially if you're a hiker or interested in trying a 'walking safari', while geologists will find the area around Grootfontein, Otavi and Tsumeb particularly fascinating, with several interesting underground caverns as well as the famous Tsumeb mine.

On the western side, Hereroland and Bushmanland extend from the central agricultural plains into the Kalahari desert, adjacent to Botswana. Though these are fairly sparsely populated and inaccessible areas, they can offer the well-prepared with a fascinating 'desert experience', distinctly different in landscape and people from the Namib.

Otjiwarongo

Formed as a staging post on the railway from Tsumeb to Swakopmund, this small town is conveniently situated at a crossroads for both the railway and the road network, in an area used mainly for cattle ranching.

Where to stay

Category B

Hotel Hamburger Hof PO Box 8. Tel: (0651)2520. This has singles for R97 and doubles from R150, including breakfast.

Category C

Hotel Brumme PO Box 63. Tel: (0651)2420. This has singles for R50 and doubles for R70, excluding breakfast.

Whilst the Hamburger is plusher, the Brumme seemed better value.

Campsite There is a reasonable site next to the Crocodile Farm (which opens 9.00am to 6.00pm daily) — it costs R8 per site plus R2 per person.

Dinosaur footprints

About 25m of footprints, made almost 200 million years ago, have been preserved here in sandstone, on the Otjihaenamaparero farm. To get there take the C33 south for about 66km then turn left onto the D2414. The farm — with the unforgettable name — is 30km along this road.

WATERBERG PLATEAU PARK

2WD. Entrance fees: R5 per person and R5 for a car.

This game park, proclaimed in 1972, is a well signposted 97km drive east of Otjiwarongo — follow the B1, the C22 and finally the D2512. Historically important during the war between the German colonial forces and the Herero people, the plateau was first envisaged as a reserve for eland, the largest of the antelope family, though has since become a sanctuary for several rare animals. While you can't drive around in the park itself, there are guided tours and a network of hides and viewing platforms for more peaceful viewing — in addition to some excellent organised walking safaris. The park is therefore a good option for those without a vehicle who want to do a bit of game viewing.

The park is centred around a plateau some 250m high composed of compacted *etjo* sandstone, formed about 200-180 million years ago, which is the remnant of a much larger plateau that once covered the area. The sandstone is highly permeable (surface water flows through it like a sieve), but the mudstones below are impermeable, resulting in the emergence of several springs at the base of the southern cliffs.

For a fairly small park, there are a large number of different environments. The top of the plateau forms a patchwork of wooded areas and open grasslands, while the foothills and flats at the base of the escarpment are dominated by acacia bush, but dotted with evergreen trees and lush undergrowth where the springs well up on the southern side. It is this diversity of vegetation which gives the park its ability to support a large variety of animals.

Recently, Waterberg has become an integral part of a number of conservation projects, seeing the relocation of several endangered species — including white rhino, roan and sable antelope, and tsessebe — in an attempt to start viable breeding herds. These have added to the game already found here which ranges from giraffe and kudu to leopard, brown hyena, cheetah, and wild dogs.

The birdlife is no less impressive, with more than 200 species on record. Most memorable are the spectacular black eagles, and Namibia's only breeding colony of Cape vultures — a species whose numbers have sharply declined in recent years due to the changing environment and the increasing use of farm poisons (in the form of fertilisers and pesticides etc.). A recent innovation is to encourage the vultures to stay by maintaining a 'vulture restaurant', where carcases are prepared and left out for them!

Where to stay

The park was made for the animals really, not the visitors, and it is only since June 1989 that the **Bernabé de la Bat rest camp** has been operating. Situated on the woody slopes of the escarpment, this extensive camp has a restaurant, kiosk, pool and a range of accommodation. Camping costs R25 per site, and bungalows are R120 for five people or R70 for three people. Alternatively, there are *tourisettes* for R108 per person which include three meals per day. Accommodation can be booked in advance through the Windhoek DNC, or at the park office between 8am and sunset, except lunch from 1pm to 2pm.

Getting around

This park is unusual in that you can't drive yourself around in it. Instead you've either got to hire your own 4WD jeep with driver (R220 per day), or take the 'scheduled' service up to the plateau — where it's possible to drop off at one of the hides or platforms to sit and watch.

Hiking

From April to November, during the dry season, there is a three-day trail on the second, third, and fourth weekends of every month. It starts at 4pm on the Thursday and continues until Sunday afternoon, taking between six and eight people for R75 per person. You must book it well in advance at Windhoek and bring your own sleeping bag and food, but all other equipment is supplied and the walk is accompanied by an armed guide. With no designated route, you'll wander through the wilderness area and camp out under the stars — there's no better way to experience a game park.

Outjo

Situated 65km north-west of Otjiwarongo, this small ranching town of about 5,000 people lies in a grassland area of cattle and sheep farms, 115km directly south of Etosha's Okaukuejo camp.

Where to stay

Category B/C

Hotel Onduri PO Box 14. Tel: (06542)14. Singles from R75 and doubles from R100, with breakfast at R12.

Hotel Etosha PO Box 31. Tel: (06542)26. Costs R65 for a single or R110 for a double excluding breakfast.

Municipal camp and campsite A four-person bungalow is only R45, complete with a fridge, a hot plate and bedding. You can also camp here for R8 per site plus R1 for each person.

OTAVI AREA

Situated in a fertile farming area, near one of the country's biggest irrigation schemes, this small town has a 24-hour Total service station, a reasonable Sentra store for groceries and also a few take-aways. Nearby there are several cave systems of particular interest, though a visit to see them needs to be carefully organised — preferably in advance.

Where to stay

Category C

Otavi Hotel PO Box 11. Tel: (06742)5. It's pleasant, though not luxurious, and currently costs R35-R50 for a single, R55-R85 a double. This includes breakfast, and a fan in each room, though all may change as it is undergoing considerable renovation. A restaurant and pool are planned.

Municipal camp and campsite This has half a dozen well-equipped, but not plush, bungalows for R16.50 each plus R1.10 per person. Thus a full bungalow with four people costs a bargain R20.90. Alternatively, you can camp here for R5.50 per site plus R1.10 per person.

Khorab memorial

This marks the spot where the German colonial troops surrendered to the South African forces on 9th July 1915 — it's only a few kilometres out of town and exceedingly well signposted.

Gaub caves

Here on the Gaub farm, 35km north-east of Otavi, are some caves famous for their stalactites and Bushman paintings. Permits to visit must be obtained from the Windhoek DNC.

Aigamas caves

Some 33km north-west of Otavi, on a tectonic fault line, this cave system is some 5km long. It has aroused particular interest recently as the home of *clarius cavernieola*, a species of fish which appears to be endemic to this cave system (ie it occurs nowhere else in the world). These fish, members of the catfish family, are a translucent light pink in colour and totally blind — having evolved for life in the lightless caves. Interestingly, their breeding habits are still unknown and no young fish have ever been found.

To visit the cave, you must make arrangements with Mr Boye at the municipal offices, just to the right of the rest camp, or phone him at home. Tel: (06742) 222. He has known the caves for years and, with a day or two of notice, will guide you to them.

Uiseb caves

More extensive than Gaub, these caves are described as 'unspoilt' and as having 'several chambers and passages and some pretty impressive stalactites and stalagmites'. Again, talk to the municipal offices for details of how to get to them.

TSUMEB

This very attractive town, its streets lined by bougainvillaea and jacaranda trees, has grown up on the rich mineral wealth of the area. The Tsumeb corporation mines a rich ore pipe producing large amounts of copper, zinc, lead, silver, germanium, cadmium and a large variety of unusual crystals (for which it is world famous). It has so far produced about 217 different minerals and gemstones, 40 of which have been found nowhere else on earth.

Where to stay and eat

Category B

Hotel Eckleben PO Box 27. Tel: (0671)3051. The hotel is a member of the Namib Sun group and is in the centre of town (see map) with singles from R71.50-R82.50, while doubles are R121, including breakfast. The restaurant has a reasonable menu, but is rather expensive with a steak costing R21-R24. It has reputedly good discos on Saturdays, which are very lively in this young mining town.

Category C

Minen Hotel PO Box 244. Tel: (0671)3071. Just off Hospital St. and opposite the park, the Minen is cheaper than the Eckleben with singles for R50 and doubles for R70 — but it's somewhat run-down and unhelpful.

The rest camp and campsite is situated half way between the town and the main road intersection — about 1km from each — with a site costing R10 plus R2 per person. The ablutions are good, though the camp does feel a long way from the centre of things.

Museum

This small museum, facing the park on Main St, has good sections of minerals from the mine and a *Khorab room* displaying some old German weaponry recovered from Lake Otjikoto. It had been dumped in the lake by the retreating German forces in 1915, to prevent the rapidly advancing Union troops from capturing it, and pieces have been recovered periodically since then — one of the latest being the Sandfontein cannon on display in the museum.

Lake Otjikoto

About 22km from Tsumeb, just west off the B1 to Namutoni, this lake was probably formed when the roof of a huge subterranean cave collapsed in on itself, leaving an enormous sink hole with very steep sides. Together with Lake Guinas, the lake has several endemic species of fish — including some

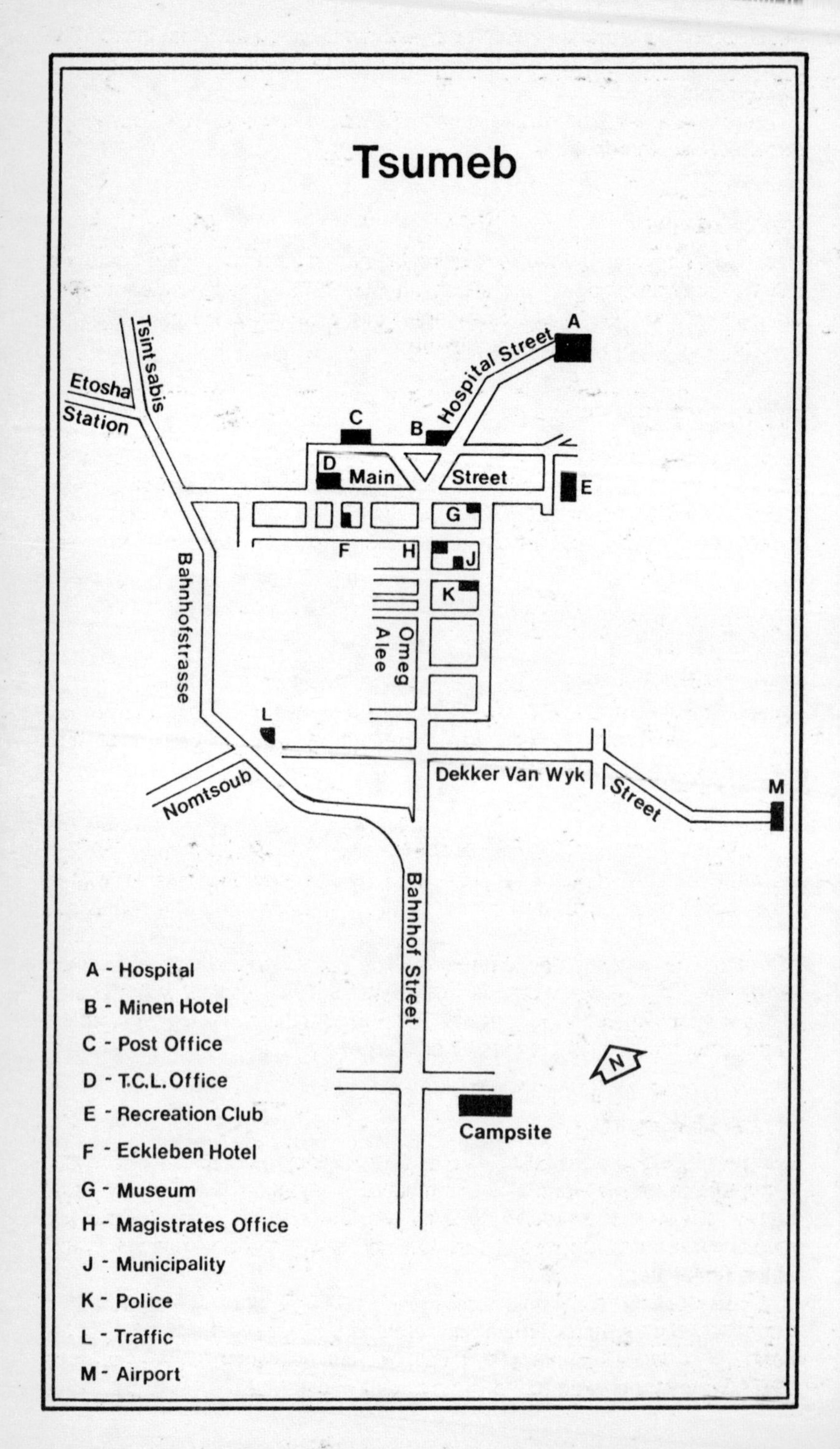
Tsumeb
A
Hospital Street
Tsintsabis
Etosha
Station
C
B
D
Main
Street
E
G
F
H
J
K
Bahnhofstrasse
Omeg
Alee
L
Dekker Van Wyk
Street
M
Nomtsoub
Bahnhof Street
N
Campsite
A - Hospital
B - Minen Hotel
C - Post Office
D - T.C.L. Office
E - Recreation Club
F - Eckleben Hotel
G - Museum
H - Magistrates Office
J - Municipality
K - Police
L - Traffic
M - Airport

mouth-brooding cichlids — which have attracted much scientific interest for changes in their colour and behaviour as a result of this restricted environment.

There is a kiosk here selling drinks and wood carvings from dawn until dusk, but no other facilities.

Lake Guinas

Reached 32km after Tsumeb by turning left off the B1 (to Namutoni) onto the D3043, and then left again after 19km onto the D3031. The lake is about 5km along, near the road. It is both deeper and more attractive than Otjikoto, though there are no facilities at all here.

GROOTFONTEIN

Another colourful, pleasant town built on the mineral wealth and cheap black labour of the area, Grootfontein is the gateway to both Bushmanland and Caprivi. If you're heading to either then resting here for a night can make sense, allowing you to tackle the long drive ahead in the cool of the morning.

Where to stay and eat

Category B/C

Meteor Hotel PO Box 346. Tel: (06731)2078. Situated on the main road. The Meteor has singles for R60, doubles for R100, but it's often fully booked up. The large bar, complete with four pool tables, usually stays open until midnight — so ask for a room far away from it.

Nord Hotel PO Box 168. Tel: (06731)2049. Set back off the main road. The Nord is smaller than the Meteor and its rooms aren't as pleasant — though it's a much better venue for a quiet drink, having a more pleasant bar (and an excellent wine list). Single rooms are R50 per person, including breakfast.

Municipal rest camp and campsite There are a couple of four-person bungalows for R60 per night, as well as the usual campsites which charge R10 per vehicle plus R2 per person. The ablutions here are excellent but the mosquitos can be bad in the rainy season.

Hoba Meteorite

Lying a well-signposted 20km west of Grootfontein, on the farm 'Hoba', this is thought to be the world's largest metallic meteorite — weighing about 50 tonnes. It was discovered in 1920 by the farm's owner and analysis has revealed that it is composed of over 80% iron, with nickel accounting for most of the remainder.

It was declared a national monument in 1955 and recently received the protection of a permanent tourist officer because it was suffering badly at the hands of souvenir hunters. (The locals became particularly irate when even UNTAG personnel were found to be chipping bits off!)

Dragon's Breath Cave and lake

This cave is claimed to contain the world's largest known underground lake. It's situated about 46km from Grootfontein, just off the Tsumeb road — on the farm Hariseb, owned by Mr Pretorius — and identified by a roadside board with the head of a cow on it.

The lake has crystal clear, drinkable water with a surface area of almost two hectares, and lies beneath a dome-shaped roof of solid rock. The water is about 60m below ground level and to get to it at present requires the use of ropes and caving equipment, with a final vertical abseil descent of 25m from the roof down to the surface of the water! This perhaps explains why it is not, as yet, open to visitors — though it is quite likely to be developed in the near future, when an easier approach can be made to it.

BUSHMANLAND

To the east of Grootfontein lies the area known as Bushmanland, an almost rectangular region bordering on Botswana, stretching 90km from north to south and about 200km from east to west. The land itself is flat and dry, with a sparse mixture of low bush and grassland growing on sandy soil befitting an area on the edge of the Kalahari Desert. It is very poor agricultural land, but is nevertheless home to a large number of Bushmen settlements.

To the east of the region, especially south of Tsumkwe, there is a network of seasonal pans dotted around, whilst straddling the border itself are the Aha Hills (see page 278).

One attraction here is the game, which sometimes gathers in herds around the area of the pans. The best time to see animals probably corresponds to the end of the dry season — around August to October — as then the game will congregate around any remaining water and travelling along the tracks will not be too difficult. During and after the rains — from January to March — beware: this region sometimes becomes a completely impassable floodplain! Whenever you come, don't expect to see vast herds comparable to Etosha's or you'll be disappointed.

Getting organised

To visit this area you must, as with Kaokoland, be totally self-sufficient and part of a two-vehicle party. The region's centre, Tsumkwe, has basic supplies and usually fuel — though if it's empty the nearest fuel stop will be Grootfontein or Mukwe (just before Bagani as you enter Caprivi). It's essential to have supplies for your complete trip, with the exception of water which can usually be found (and purified if necessary) along the way.

Before embarking on such a trip it would certainly be wise to obtain maps or aerial photos from Windhoek, with a view to keeping a fairly close watch on the navigation, as travel in this sandy terrain is slow. We didn't leave second gear for miles on some occasions — and retracing tracks is a time-consuming business.

Bushmen soldiers on the move again

Four thousand dispossessed Bushmen of southern Africa have once more been 'moved on' caught up in the politics of the region, and unable to find a secure place to settle.

Many young Namibian Bushmen, deprived of their lands and no longer able to be hunters, found escape from the semi-slavery of work as farm labourers or the dead-end of life on government handouts by enroling in the South African army. The army was eager to recruit them, valuing their (partly mythical) skills as trackers, and trading on the age-long distrust between them and the other black peoples of Namibia.

In early March 1990, 4,000 Bushmen — former soldiers of the Bushmen battalions of the South African army, and their families — were airlifted from their camp near Windhoek in Namibia to Schmidtsdrift in South Africa. It was felt they were in danger from Namibia's independence forces following independence later that month.

Local farmers are objecting to the resettlement in Schmidtsdrift, saying they were "kept in the dark" about it. One farmer said, "the land simply won't support 4,000 people."

This piece is an edited extract from the Survival International newsletter no. 27, 1990.

In Namibia, Survival has supported the Ju-Wa Bushmen in their fight to regain economic independence by helping fund their cattle-herding projects. Once independent hunter-gatherers, the Ju-Wa have been reduced to working as labourers for little or no wages.

Survival International is a worldwide movement to support tribal peoples. It stands for their right to decide their own future and helps them protect their lands, environment and way of life. If you would like to join Survival and take part in their campaigns for tribal people in Africa and worldwide, you can contact them at: Survival International, 310 Edgware Rd, London W2 1DY. Tel: 071-723 5535.

Getting there

The C44 road through to Tsumkwe is the main access route into the area and is navigable by 2WD. For any of the other roads you will need a 4WD. One good way to visit the area is by combining it with a trip through Kaudom game reserve (see page 191), thus making a round journey between Grootfontein and the Caprivi Strip. Alternatively, approaching the region from the south via Summerdown, Otjinene, and Hereroland looks interesting but I've never met anyone who's been that way, and I'd expect the going to get quite difficult.

Where to stay

Camping is possible anywhere, with no permits necessary, though obviously you must take great care not to offend local people by your behaviour or choice of campsite. Wherever possible, it is usually best to camp away from areas of settlement, and also to ensure that you're not in a place that might block a game trail or keep any animals from a waterhole.

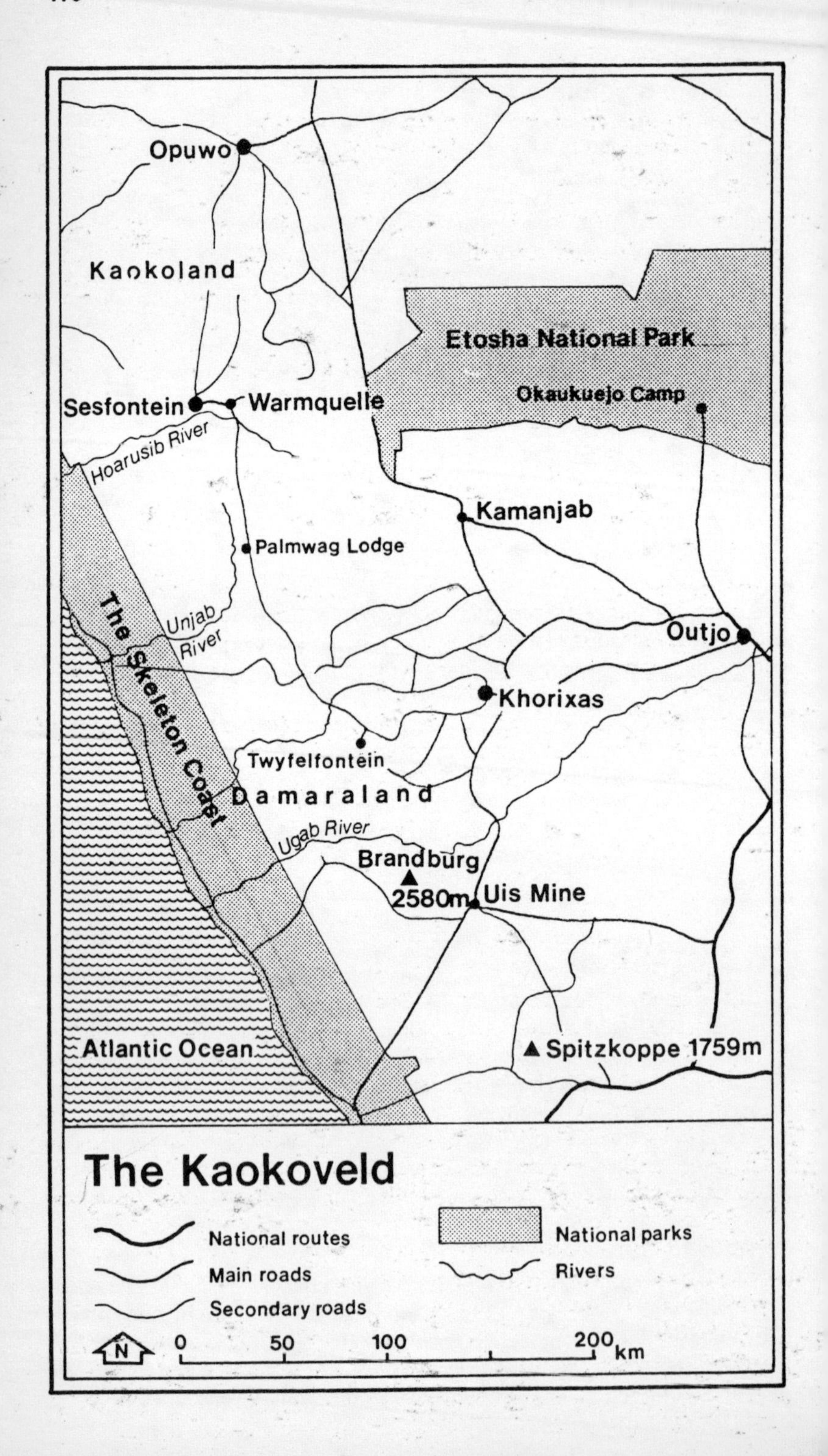
Opuwo
Kaokoland
Etosha National Park
Okaukuejo Camp
Sesfontein
Warmquelle
Hoarusib River
Kamanjab
Palmwag Lodge
Unjab River
The Skeleton Coast
Outjo
Khorixas
Twyfelfontein
Damaraland
Ugab River
Brandburg
2580m
Uis Mine
Atlantic Ocean
Spitzkoppe 1759m
The Kaokoveld
National routes
Main roads
Secondary roads
National parks
Rivers
N
0
50
100
200
km

Chapter 13

The Kaokoveld

Stretching back from the coastal desert plain, the Kaokoveld rises into a wild and rugged landscape where slow-growing trees cling to the rocky mountains and hidden springs water the game, far beyond the boundaries of any reserve.

For the visitor, the obvious points of interest in Damaraland, the southern part of the Kaokoveld, can be reached by 2WD (though 4WD is easier). To visit Kaokoland, the northern part of the Kaokoveld, you should be thinking in terms of a minimum of two well-equipped 4WD vehicles if the services of one of the local operators are not going to be used.

The various sights and towns described below, are ordered in general from south to north.

DAMARALAND

Most of sites described here, such as Spitzkoppe, Brandberg, Twyfelfontein and the Burnt Mountain are cared for by the DNC and as yet have few regulations attached to them. However, the rest of Damaraland (with the exception of the farms in the east) is split into a number of concession areas — each of which is managed by a local operator who, in theory, is responsible for maintaining the area and issuing permits for those who wish to enter it. So, before coming here, it's perhaps wise to ask the advice of Windhoek's DNC about the current permit requirements, as there are fines if you're found in a concession area without the necessary permit.

Because of the unpopulated nature of the region, it's unwise to travel here without at least warm bedding and supplies of food and water. It is altogether better to be fully equipped to camp and fend for yourself, as then you can still use the facilities at the camps in Khorixas and Palmwag, but without depending on them. There's usually no problem camping out by the roadside if you get stuck — but make sure you're not offending anyone by inadvertently camping on their land.

If you see people hitching, bear in mind that there's no public transport here. In somewhere so rural, Namibians will invariably stop to help if there's even a chance of cramming a further person into their vehicle. Seeing foreign tourists drive by with empty cars leaves behind very negative feelings!

Spitzkoppe

At the far southern end of the Kaokoveld lies a small cluster of mountains which rise from the desert floor and include Spitzkoppe, Klein Spitzkoppe and Pondok Mountain. Of these the highest, Spitzkoppe, towers 600m above the surrounding plains and is a demanding technical climb. Its resemblance to the famous Swiss mountain earned it the name of 'The Matterhorn of Africa', while the extreme conditions found on its faces ensured that it remained unclimbed until 1946.

Getting there

Spitzkoppe is reached on the D3716. Approaching from **Henties Bay** take the D1918 westwards for 103km, then turn left onto the D3716. Coming from **Usakos**, take the Henties Bay turn-off after 23km on the B2 and follow it for about 18km before a right turn onto the D3716. From **Uis Mine**, leave on the C36 to Omaruru, but turn right onto the D1930 after only 1km. From there it's about 75km to the right turn onto the D3716

What to see and do

Currently there are no facilities here, though for the self-sufficient it's yet another spectacular place to camp — and its lower slopes provide some difficult scrambles. At the extreme eastern end of this group of hills is a verdant valley known as Bushman's Paradise, which you can reach with the help of a fixed steel cable. Sadly the rock paintings under the overhang have been vandalised (even here!) and little is left of them, but the valley is still worth a visit. If you have an hour to spare then an alternative descent is to continue to follow the gully out of the valley — though this route is not an easy option.

Because of their height and proximity to the ocean, these mountains do tend to receive more fog and precipitation than most, and with smooth granite sides much of it runs off to form small pools near the base. These are ideal places to search for the shrimps and invertebrates which have adapted to the environment's extremes by laying drought-resistant eggs.

Uis Mine

As its name suggests, this small town is essentially just an extension of the tin mine which dominates it. The fuel station opens from 7am to 7pm every day apart from Sunday, when it opens at 10.30am and closes at 4.30pm. There is also a small supermarket which opens from 8.30am to 2pm and 5pm to 7.30pm, from Monday to Saturday. On Sundays it opens from 11am to

2pm, and from 5pm to 7.30pm. If you're desperate, then you can camp at the Sports Club.

Brandberg

Measuring about 30km by 23km at its base, and 2573m at its highest point, this ravine-split massif of granite totally dominates the desert plains which surround it.

Getting there

Though you can't miss seeing it when driving anywhere in the vicinity, getting to Brandberg without driving over the fragile plains around needs thought. Its eastern side, around the Tsisab Ravine, is easily reached using a 2WD car via the D2359, which turns west off the C35 about 14km after Uis Mine on the way to Khorixas. It is signposted to the White Lady (*Witvrou* in Afrikaans), a famous rock painting.

Those with 4WD vehicles can also use the extensive network of rougher tracks which turn towards the massif from the north, west and south, off the D2342, starting some 14km south-west of Uis Mine on the Henties Bay road.

What to see and what to do

Two attractions are drawing increasing numbers of visitors here:

Climbing With the highest point in Namibia and some good technical routes in a very demanding environment, the massif attracts serious mountaineers as well as those in search of a few days' interesting scrambling. It's very important to remember to take adequate safety precautions though, as the temperatures can be extreme and the place very isolated. Unless you're fully used to such conditions, it's perhaps best to stick to short trips in the early morning or late afternoon, leaving time for a long siesta in the scorching midday heat. Serious climbers should seek advice from the Mountain Club of Namibia, in Windhoek, well before they arrive.

Paintings This area has been occupied by Bushmen for several thousand years and still holds a wealth of their artifacts and rock paintings, of which only a fraction have been studied in detail, and some are undoubtedly still to be found. The richest section for art has so far been the Tsisab Ravine, on the north-eastern side of the massif. Here one painting in particular has been the subject of much scientific debate, ever since its discovery by the outside world in 1918: the famous *White Lady of Brandberg*.

The figure of the *white lady* stands about 40cm tall, and is central to a large frieze which apparently depicts some sort of procession — in which one or two of the figures have animal features. In her right hand is a flower, or perhaps an ostrich egg cup, whilst in her left she holds a bow and some arrows. Unlike the other figures, she has been painted white from below the chest.

The coloration and form of the figure is very reminiscent of some early

Mediterranean styles and, together with points gleaned from a more detailed analysis of the pictures, this led early scholars to credit the painters as having links with Europe. Among the site's first visitors was the Abbé Henri Breuil, a world authority on rock art who studied these paintings and others nearby in the late 1940s, and subsequently published four classic volumes entitled *The Rock Paintings of Southern Africa*. He concluded that the *lady* had elements of Egyptian, Cretean and Grecian origin.

More recent scholars seem to think that the people represented are indigenous, with no European links, and they regard the *lady* as being a boy, covered in white clay whilst undergoing an initiation ceremony. Whichever school of thought you prefer, the *white lady* is well signposted and worth the scramble needed to reach it.

Further up the Tsisab Ravine there are many other sites, including the friezes within the *Girls' School*, *Pyramid*, and *Ostrich* shelters. If you wish to get the most out of a visit to the rock art here, then Breuil's books cannot be recommended too highly — though difficult to find, and very expensive to buy. They are certainly worth seeking out at your local library before you arrive in Namibia.

Twyfelfontein rock paintings

Twyfelfontein means 'doubtful spring', a reference to the perennial spring of water which wells up near the base of the valley. In the past such a spring — being on the margins of a very arid area — would have attracted huge herds of game from the sparse plains around, and thus an uninviting valley could have made an excellent base for the early hunters in the area. This perhaps explains why this boulder-strewn valley, amid the flat-topped mountains which are so typical of Damaraland, conceals one of the greatest concentrations of rock art on the sub-continent. Though not obvious when you first arrive, the boulders which litter the slopes are dotted with both engravings and the more familiar rock paintings. Thousands have already been catalogued in this one valley,

Getting there

To reach the valley, which is well signposted, take the C39 for 73km west from **Khorixas**, then left onto the D3254 for 15km, then right for about 11km (ignoring a left fork after 6km) to the base of the valley. There are several small buildings here — some with doors and even walls made out of empty tin cans! From there, climb directly up the slope to reach a terrace. A well worn path winds among the boulders and up to some of the bigger friezes. You really need several hours just to start to discover what's here, and many of the paintings you'll have to locate for yourself — so begin early and beware of the midday heat!

Organ Pipes

Retracing your tracks from Twyfelfontein, turn right onto the left fork which you ignored earlier (see directions above), then after about 3km there's a gorge to your left, followed by a flat area used for parking. Leave your vehicle and take one of the paths down into the gorge where you'll find hundreds of tall angular columns of dolerite in a most unusual formation.

Burnt Mountain

Continuing about 2km on the road past the Organ Pipes, you'll reach what's locally known as the 'Burnt Mountain'. Seen by the midday sun this can be a real disappointment, but when the red-brown shales catch the early morning or late afternoon light, the mountain side glows with a startling rainbow of colours — as if on fire.

Khorixas

Placed fairly centrally, this is a useful town for supplies but is otherwise unremarkable. It does have quite a large rest camp, signposted as **ruskamp**, which includes a swimming pool and a small restaurant. Camping is R11 per site, plus R3.85 per person, while bungalows range from R25 per person. Fuel is available, as are basic supplies — and if you're heading towards Palmwag then this could be your last chance.

Petrified Forest

Clearly signposted off the C39, west of Khorixas, lie a number of petrified trees on a bed of sandstone. Some are partially buried, while others lie completely exposed — the sandstone surrounding them having been eroded away. It is thought that they were originally carried here as logs by a river, some 250 million years ago, when they became stranded on a sandbank. Subsequently sand was deposited around them, creating ideal conditions for the cells of the wood to be replaced by silica and thus become petrified.

Kamanjab

Just to the east of Damaraland, this pleasant town comes as a welcome relief to those driving south from Kaokoland, with its sealed roads and well-stocked fuel station. However, there are no obvious attractions here, and nowhere to stay, so people usually just pass right through after refuelling with petrol and cold drinks.

About 80km north of Kamanjab, on the road past Etosha's western fence, is the entrance to **Hobatere private game park** — one of Damaraland's concession areas. Here there are luxurious facilities and professional guides to accompany you, though at correspondingly high prices.

Palmwag Lodge

This is the base for visiting the Palmwag concession area, the centre of operations for Desert Adventure Safaris (PO Box 339, Swakopmund. Tel: (0641) 4459), and is the farthest point north in the region that you should try going with a 2WD!

Getting there

To reach it, take the C39 about 117km westwards from Khorixas before branching northwards onto the D2620. 40km later take a left onto the D3706 towards Sesfontein. This leads through a veterinary fence after 6km and the lodge is soon signposted on your left. Alternatively...you can always fly in!

Where to stay and eat

Pleasant reed bungalows here are R85 per person full board (with no reductions for less food), whilst camping costs R7.50 per person per night, plus a one-off charge of R10 for the site. If camping you can still eat in the restaurant, where a good evening meal costs around R20, or sample the draught Hansa beers in the bar. There's also a poorly stocked shop here and fuel is available from 8am to 12.30pm, and 2.30pm to 6pm on Monday to Saturday; 8am until 12.30pm on Sundays. Outside these hours there's an extra R2 charge from the reluctant attendant.

What to see and do

The Palmwag concession area, stretching west to the Skeleton Coast and north to the Hoanib River, has been set aside for game and from the lodge you can explore it by hiring one of DAS's 4WD vehicles with a guide, at R50 per hour. There may not be huge herds of wildlife here, but neither are there convoys of tourists, and the area has surprises — like the herd of giraffe which seemed so incongruous to us in the landscape of low trees. DAS's vehicles take a maximum of four persons and their guides know the area well, picking out the more obscure tracks and going to areas frequented by game. It's also possible to organise longer safaris of several days' duration from here, but better to do so in advance with the DAS offices in either Swakopmund or Windhoek.

If you want to drive your own 4WD around then for a few Rand they'll very reluctantly issue you with a permit to enter their concession. This reluctance is justified as the area is very remote and potentially quite dangerous. There are no maps available here at all, so if you want to go onto the smaller tracks then get hold of aerial photos of the area from the surveyor general's office (by the post office in Windhoek) before you come — otherwise you'll simply get lost. Ideally a two-vehicle party would also be a good idea as the nearest (only!) help in case of emergency would be Palmwag.

Warmquelle

About 87km north of Palmwag Lodge, on the way to Sesfontein lies Warmquelle, a small settlement situated on the site of a spring. In the early years of this century, the spring was used in an irrigation project, for which an aqueduct was even constructed. Now only a few parts of the old aqueduct remain, though there is a small Damara settlement and quite a large school.

What to see and do

The nearby **Ongongo waterfall** is definitely worth a visit, for under it lies a deep, clear pool. To get there, turn right at the sign to *Warmquelle Skool*, and then left past the school. After about 3.1km, the track splits, and you take the left branch – crossing a dry river bed 200m later and then bending to the right for a further 1.2km as you follow the bank upstream. There's an area to park and you can descend into the river-bed before going a farther few hundred metres upstream to where the pool lies hidden beneath the waterfall.

Few resist the temptation to strip off and swim in here, which given the temperatures isn't surprising. After your dip, go back downstream a little to see the river just disappearing into the sandy bed again. It will reappear again as another linear oasis miles later.

Sesfontein

This village in the Hoanib valley marks the northern edge of Damaraland, beyond which you need a minimum of two fully equipped 4WD vehicles in order to continue safely. Named after the 'six springs' which surface nearby, there is still the remains of an old German fort which was an important control post in the earlier part of this century.

Most of the local people in the area live by farming goats, with the occasional field of maize as well, and this is their main centre – with a school and several shops. It's usually fairly busy (at least when compared with anywhere else within a 100km or so) so don't miss the chance to stop and watch village life go by. There's no better way than sitting with a cold drink on the steps of one of the shops.

KAOKOLAND

This vast tract of land is Namibia at its most enticing – and yet most inhospitable. Kaokoland appeals to the adventurer and explorer in us, keeping quiet about the dangers involved. On the eastern side, hilly tracks become mudslides as they get washed away by the rains, while the baking desert on the west affords no comfort for those who get stranded. Even dry river-beds can hide soft traps of deep sand, whilst the few which seem damp and hard may turn to quicksand within metres. Having struggled to free a land rover with just one wheel stuck in quicksand, I find it easy to believe the tales that I've heard about vehicles vanishing completely within an hour or so!

One road on the eastern side was particularly memorable, starting favourably as a good gravel track. After 20km or so, it gradually deteriorated into a series of rocky ruts, shaking us to our bones and forcing a speed below 10kph. About an hour of this, when we'd come too far to think of returning, the track descended into a sandy river-bed – strewn with boulders and enclosed on both sides by walls of rock. The only way to progress at all was for all but the driver to get out and walk ahead, guiding the vehicle through – taking the boulders one at a time, and watching nervously as the tyres lurched from one rock to the next. Several hours later we emerged from the bed onto another difficult track – happy to make a speed of 10kph for a while – only to be completely halted by one of a series of rivers in flood. We slept dry in our tents, thankful that the floods hadn't reach the rocky river-bed whilst we were there.

To spend time in Kaokoland at all, you need a two-vehicle 4WD party, all your supplies, and a good navigator equipped with detailed maps — and even then you'll probably get lost a few times! It's not a trip to undertake lightly because if anything does go wrong you'll be hundreds of kilometres from the nearest garage or hospital.

If you can get a party together to visit, then in contrast to Damaraland's concession areas, Kaokoland has yet to adopt any system — so you are free to travel where you can. Having said that, the drier areas are part of a very fragile ecosystem and even by driving a vehicle off the existing tracks and 'across country', you'll do permanent damage by killing plants and animals, and leaving an unsightly trail behind you. Vehicle trails made 40 years ago can still be seen — the crushed plants and lichens haven't recovered yet. Here, more than anywhere, there's a need to treat the environment with care. *Don't drive off the tracks.*

Where to stay

There's no alternative to camping here, but remember that however tempting the river valleys are — never camp in one. Firstly, if it rains in the mountains then you could be in for a flash flood: described by someone who had been caught by one as 'a wall of water thundering towards them'. Secondly, the river courses are important thoroughfares for the increasingly scarce animals, as they go to and from the region's scattered waterholes. If you camp near one of these, then the animals simply stop using them — taking long detours to look for water, as they tend to be more wary of people than most of their cousins in the game parks.

Opuwo

This rough-and-ready frontier town is the hub of Kaokoland, with a bakery, shops, a large school, several garages, and even a short stretch of tarred road! In the middle of town its buildings are functional rather than attractive, whilst on the outskirts there are small shantytowns.

Take a stroll round town — there's a fascinating mix of people, varying from the proud Himba, with their traditional goatskin dress and red-stained skins, to the smart local businessmen in their three-piece suits, not to mention the variety of eccentric characters who seem to emerge from the bush to replenish their supplies, only to vanish again as quickly as they appeared.

Whilst we were here there was no petrol (except from a few private 'entrepreneurs' who sold it from drums for twice the normal price) but it is normally available, we are told. The bakery next to the BP garage is very welcome for its fresh bread and rolls, whilst for general supplies go to the **Groothandel Wholesale**. Here there is an excellent selection of tins and staples as well as large blocks of ice for cool-boxes. If you need to change money, they will normally cash travellers cheques, but won't exchange foreign notes.

Chapter 14

Etosha National Park

2WD. Entrance fees: R8 per person and R10 for a car, one-off charge on entry.

Translated as the 'Place of Mirages', 'Land of Dry Water' or the 'Great White Place', Etosha is an apparently endless pan of silvery-white sand, upon which dust devils play and mirages blur the horizon. As a *game park* it excels during the dry season when huge herds of animals can be seen amidst some of the most startling and photogenic scenery on the continent. The roads are all navigable in a 2WD car, its rest camps have excellent facilities, and it is never very busy in comparison with the crowded parks in the rest of Africa.

BACKGROUND INFORMATION

History

Etosha first became known to Europeans in the early 1850s when it was visited by Francis Galton and Charles Andersson. They recorded their first impressions:

> "...we traversed an immense hollow, called Etosha, covered with saline encrustations, and having wooded and well-defined borders. Such places are in Africa designate 'salt pans'... In some rainy seasons, the Ovambo informed us, the locality was flooded and had all the appearance of a lake; but now it was quite dry, and the soil strongly impregnated with salt. Indeed, close in shore, the commodity was to be had of a very pure quality."

Geography, landscape and flora

It is thought that the present pan is the remnant of a large inland lake which

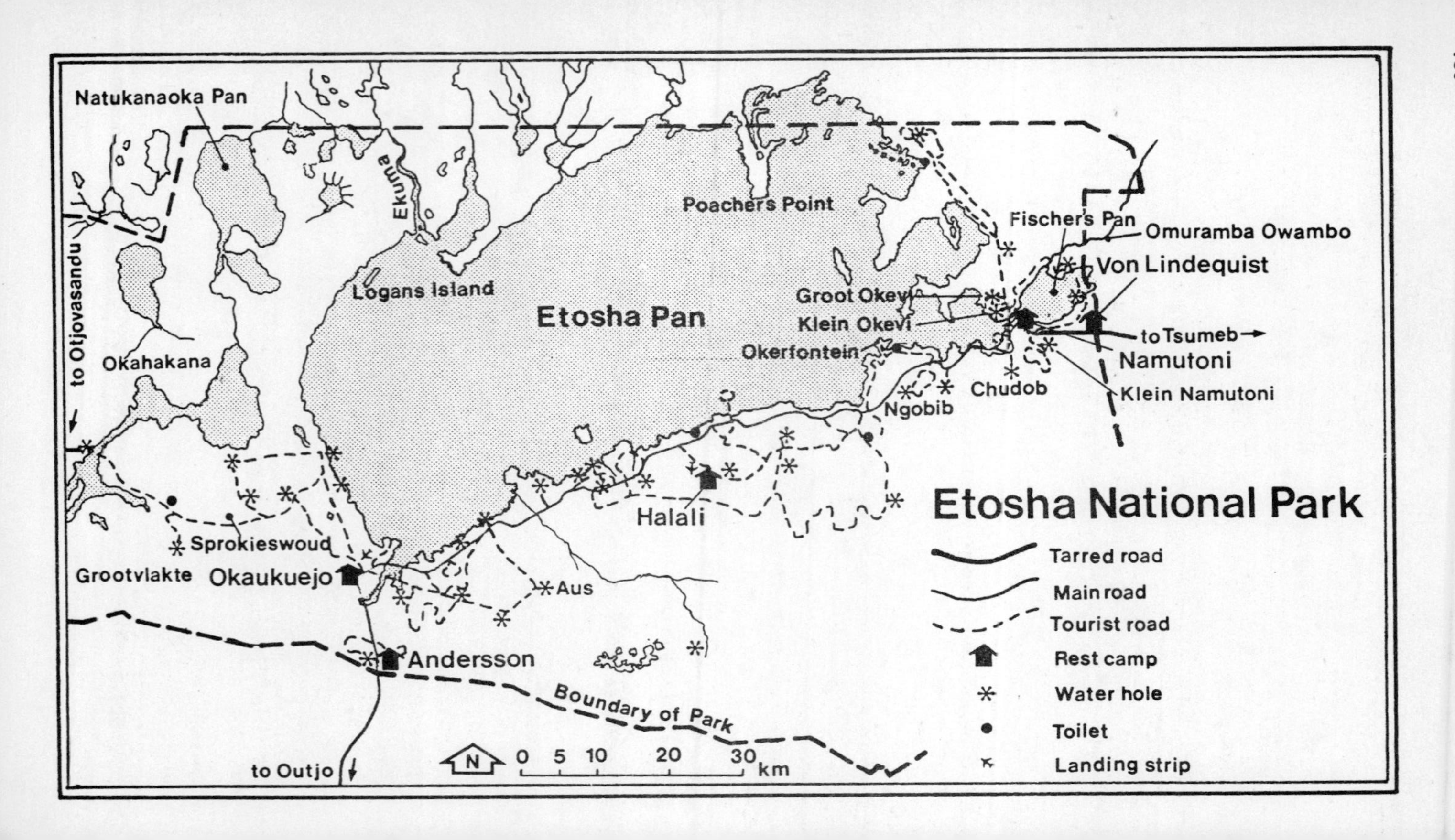
Natukanaoka Pan
Ekuma
Poachers Point
Fischer's Pan
Omuramba Owambo
Von Lindequist
Logans Island
Groot Okevi
Klein Okevi
Etosha Pan
to Tsumeb
Okerfontein
Namutoni
to Otjovasandu
Okahakana
Chudob
Klein Namutoni
Ngobib
Etosha National Park
Halali
Sprokieswoud
Grootvlakte
Okaukuejo
Aus
Tarred road
Main road
Tourist road
Andersson
Rest camp
Water hole
Boundary of Park
Toilet
N
0 5 10 20 30 km
to Outjo
Landing strip

was once fed by rivers flowing into it from the north and east. However, some 12 million years ago, continental uplift changed the course of its major tributaries, including the Kunene (which now flows west from the Ruacana Falls and into the Atlantic, rather than south-east, as it used to), and thus deprived, it slowly vanished in the scorching sun to leave behind only a salty residue. Few plants will grow upon this and so erosion by the wind was easy, allowing the pan to be gradually hollowed out to its present depth.

Since then the pan has probably changed very little in appearance. It is roughly 129km from east to west and 72km from north to south, covering an area of some 6,133 square kilometres with flat, barren sand and shimmering heat. If the rains to the north and east have been good, then the pan will often hold some water for a few months at the start of the year — thanks mainly to the Ekuma River and Omuramba Owambo — but only very rarely does it fill completely.

In the rest of the park, beyond the pan's borders, the terrain is generally flat with a variety of habitats ranging from *mopane* woodland to wide open, virtually treeless, plains. In the west of the park, around Namutoni, the attractive Makalani palms (*Hyphaene ventricosa*) are found — often in picturesque groups around waterholes. The small, round fruit of these palms, a favourite food of elephants, is sometimes called 'vegetable ivory' for its hard white kernel. In the east, one of the more unusual areas is the **Haunted Forest** — *Sprokieswoud* in Afrikaans — where a large number of strange Moringa trees (*Moringa ovalifolia*) lend their contorted forms to a make very weird woodland scene.

What makes Etosha special above all is the great concentration of water holes which occur around the southern edges of the pan and increasingly draw the game as the dry season progresses. In fact, the best way of game viewing here is often just to sit in your vehicle by a waterhole and wait. There are three types of spring creating these waterholes, and they differ in both appearance and geology.

Contact springs These occur in situations where two adjacent layers of rock have very different permeabilities. There are many to be seen just on the edge of the pan. Here the water-bearing calcrete comes to an end and the water flows out onto the surface because the underlying layers of clay are impermeable. Okerfontein is the best example of this type of spring, a type which is generally weak in terms of water supply.

Water-level springs Found in hollows where the surface of the ground actually cuts below the level of the water table, often in large depressions in the limestone formations. These are inevitably dependant on the level of the water table, and hence vary greatly from year to year. Typical of this type are Ngobib, Groot Okevi and Klein Okevi.

Artesian springs Formed when pressure from overlying rocks forces water up to the surface from deeper lying aquifers. In this park, they normally occur on limestone hillocks, forming deep pools which will often have clumps of reeds in their centre. These springs are usually very reliable and include Namutoni, Klein Namutoni, Chudob and Aus.

Mammals

The game and birds found here are typical of the savannah plains of Southern Africa, but include several species endemic to this western side of the continent, adjacent to the Namib desert.

The more common herbivores include elephant, giraffe, eland, blue wildebeest, kudu, gemsbok, springbok, impala, steenbok, and zebra. The most numerous of these are the **springbok** which can often be seen in herds numbering thousands, spread out over the most barren of plains. These finely marked antelope have a marvellous habit of 'pronking', either (it appears) for fun or to avoid predators. It has also been suggested that the 'pronking' is intended to put predators off *in the first place* by showing the animal's strength and stamina — the weakest 'pronkers' are the ones predators are seen to go for! Andersson described these elegant leaps:

> "This animal bounds without an effort to a height of 10 or 12 feet at one spring, clearing from 12 to 14 feet of ground. It appears to soar, to be suspended for a moment in the air, then, touching the ground, to make another dart, or another flight, aloft, without the aid of wings, by the elastic springiness of its legs."

Elephant are common (though big tuskers are rare) and often seen in quite large family groups when they troop down to waterholes to drink, wallow and bathe. The park's population has recently come under scientific scrutiny for the noises which they make in the infrasonic region, below the range of human hearing. It's thought that groups can communicate with each other over long distances in this way.

Among the rarer species, **black rhino** continue to thrive here — the floodlit waterhole at Okaukuejo camp providing one of the continent's best chances to observe this aggressive and secretive species. On one visit here, we watched as a herd of 20 or so elephants, silently drinking in the cool of the night, were frightened away from the water — and kept at bay — by the arrival of a single black rhino. It returned several times in the space of an hour or so, each time causing the much larger elephants to flee before it settled down to enjoy a leisurely drink from the pool on its own.

Both **Hartmann's mountain zebra** and the **black-faced impala** are restricted to areas of Namibia and Southern Angola, though within that range the Hartmann's zebra is by far the more numerous — occurring in good numbers here, as well as in Naukluft and in the Kaokoveld. The black-faced impala is more threatened, with only a few isolated populations numbering under a thousand or so. The **Damara dik-dik** is the park's smallest antelope and is also endemic to Namibia, but it's locally quite common in areas of dense bush.

Roan antelope and **red hartebeest** do occur all over the subcontinent — though they are common nowhere — and this is definitely one of the better parks in which to look for them.

All of the **larger carnivores** are found here, with good numbers of lion, leopard, cheetah and wild dog. The lion tend to prey mainly upon zebra and wildebeest, whilst the cheetah rely largely upon springbok — and the seldom-seen leopard take a more varied diet including antelope, small mammals and even jackals.

Also found in the park are both spotted and brown **hyenas**, together with silver, red and the more common black-backed **jackal** — many of which can be seen every evening, skulking around the camps in search of titbits.

Birds

For the ornithologists, over 300 species of birds have been recorded including many uncommon members of the hawk and vulture families. The **black vulture**, largest of the vulture species, is often seen here — though elsewhere (like many vultures) its numbers are declining as farming increases.

The number of **large birds** stalking around the plains struck us as quite unusual, as invariably during the day we would see several groups of ostriches and pairs of secretary birds. It was easy to drive within metres of many kori bustards and black korhaans which just sat by the roadside and watched us.

When to visit

To decide when to visit, it's worth thinking about the weather, the number of other visitors around and the best wildlife viewing.

Weather At the beginning of the year, in **January**, it's hot and fairly damp with average temperatures around 27°C and cloud cover for some of the time. This gradually disperses until the rains cease, around **April**. The plants are bright and green during this time — but we felt that the park had lost some of its stark beauty and wasn't nearly as striking to photograph.

From **May to July** the land cools down a little and dries out, with some of the winter nights becoming quite cool. There is a tremendous range of temperatures between the cloudless days and nights. After **August** (which is hot in itself), the plants shrivel as the heat builds up steadily towards the coming of the rains in **November** — when again the skies cloud over.

Other visitors Etosha could never be called a crowded park at any time of year — compared to the tourist hordes that fill the game parks of East Africa, Etosha is relatively deserted. However, it does get more busy around Easter time and in August, especially during the South African school holidays. At these times, advanced booking through Windhoek DNC is advised.

Game viewing Etosha's dry season is the time to see game. Then, as the small bush pools dry up and the green shrivels to brown, the animals move closer to the springs on the edge of the pan. Before the fences were erected (which now surround the park completely) they would have migrated between Etosha and the Kaokoveld, but now most are forced to stay within the park. Only bull elephants commonly break out of their confines to cause problems for the surrounding farmers.

Hence the months between August and late October are ideal for game — though the prospect of sitting in a car by a waterhole as the thermometer approaches 40°C can deter even the most enthusiastic. During and after the rains, you'll not see very much game, partly because the plants hide the animals and partly because most of them will have moved away from the water holes and gone deeper into the bush.

Bird watching The start of the rainy season witnesses the arrival of many summer migrants and — if the rains have been good — the aquatic species which come for the water in the pan itself. If the rains are particularly good thousands of flamingos may come to the pan to breed — an amazing spectacle, not to be missed (see box on flamingos, page 149). However, bear in mind that the ordinary residents can be seen more easily when there is less vegetation around — in the dry season.

PRACTICAL INFORMATION

Getting there

You can enter the park via either the gate near Namutoni, which is 106km from Tsumeb, or Okaukuejo, 121km from Outjo. Entry to the park can be paid at either of these two gates and is R8 per person and R10 for a car, regardless of how long you stay for. The gates open around sunrise and close about 20 minutes before sunset, as driving through the park in the dark is not allowed. There is a gate on the eastern border of the park but until a planned fourth camp opens up nearby it is kept locked.

Hitching is not allowed in the park — you'll certainly not get any lifts from the wardens! None of the roads require 4WD, though it's useful to be that much higher off the ground when you're trying to spot game through the bushes.

Where to stay

There are currently three National Parks camps, all of which are good value and exceedingly well appointed. They each offer a full range of accommodation including a campsite and have a swimming pool, a shop, fuel and a restaurant. The shops sell tins, cold drinks, bread, meat, cheese — as well as curios, wildlife books and the ubiquitous postcards.

Accommodation prices vary slightly between camps, though a **campsite** is always R25 — for up to eight people and two vehicles. This makes camping very cheap for large parties — but for two or three people it's often better to go for a chalet.

Booking accommodation in advance at the Windhoek DNC is advised — but of course you need to be very organised and stick to your itinerary. The alternative is to hope for spaces or get cancellations by going to the camp office just before it closes at sunset — this is usually successful out of the main holiday times, but you'll need a tent in case it's not.

In either case, if you're visiting in the dry season then aim to spend a minimum of two nights at any camp you visit — don't miss out on Okaukuejo camp with its floodlit waterhole. In an ideal world, we'd suggest spending two nights at Namutoni camp, two at Halali and three at Okaukuejo!

Namutoni camp Situated on the eastern edge of the pan, Namutoni is based around a beautiful old fort in an area dotted with graceful Makalani palm trees. It originally dates back to a German police post, built here before the turn of the century, and was later used as an army base and for English prisoners in the First World War, before being restored to its present state in 1957. Perhaps as a reminder of its military past, each sunrise and sunset are observed by a bugler calling from the top of the watch tower, in the fort's north-eastern corner — onto which you too can climb for a better view of the surrounding country in the setting sun.

The rooms within the fort itself are not air-conditioned and cost from R30 for two beds whilst the newer ones, in rectangular blocks, have all mod-cons and cost half as much again. Four-bed tents — of a traditional canvas design — are available for R25.

Halali camp The newest of the camps, Halali is in between the others — 75km from Namutoni and 70km from Okaukuejo — and just to the northwest of the landmark *Tweekoppies*. It normally closes from November 1 to March 15, though if plans to install air conditioning materialise, then it will be open all year round. It tends to be the quietest of the three camps.

Rooms currently start at R30 for two, though the bungalows are worth the extra at R40 for two beds with a kitchen and bathroom. Again four-bed tents are available for R25.

Okaukuejo camp This was the first camp to open to tourists and it currently functions as the administrative hub of the park, and the centre of the Etosha Ecological Institute. It is situated at the western end of the pan, and about 120km north of Outjo.

The unique attraction of this camp is that it overlooks a permanent waterhole which is floodlit at night, giving you a chance to see some of the shy, nocturnal wildlife. The animals that come appear totally oblivious of the camp — not noticing the bright lights or the people sitting on benches just behind the low stone wall. The light doesn't penetrate into the surrounding bush at all, instead it creates something of a stage — with the water at its centre — focusing everybody's attention on the animals that come to drink.

During the dry season, you'll be very unlucky if you don't see something of interest by just sitting here for a few hours in the evening — so bring a couple of drinks, binoculars, and some warm clothes to settle down and watch. Among the regulars are elephants and jackals, while lion and black rhino often visit in the dry season.

The bungalows start at R50 for two beds and are wonderfully luxurious. Alternatively, there are four-bed tents for R25.

Mokuti Lodge Situated just on the park's boundaries, on the left before Namutoni's gate, this is a plush Namib Sun hotel with all the facilities you'd expect, and even hiking trails on its own game ranch. At R135 for a single or R190 for a double it is rather expensive, however, and so strictly for those who can't live without room service.

Where to eat

Cooking your own food is cheaper than the camp restaurant, though check the opening times of the shop as you may want food before leaving in the afternoon. If you're planning on a drink in the bar afterwards, remember that it will shut remarkably early and be warned that the shops won't sell any alcohol on a Sunday.

Game drives

The best times to go on game drives are in the early morning and late afternoon, when the animals are at their most active. So, if you have the energy, try to leave camp as the gates open at sunrise for a few hours drive before breakfast. We preferred to use the middle of the day for either travelling between camps or just sitting in the car, parked by one of the more remote waterholes — though this can get very hot if you're not in the shade.

Check the time that the camp's gates close for the night and spend the last few hours before sunset at one of the nearby springs, leaving just in time to get back into camp.

Organised trips

Several operators do organise all-inclusive trips into the park, including the specialists 'Etosha Fly-in Safaris'. Most operate from a base in Windhoek, though several are from Johannesburg, and all are expensive when compared with hiring your own car and using National Park's accommodation.

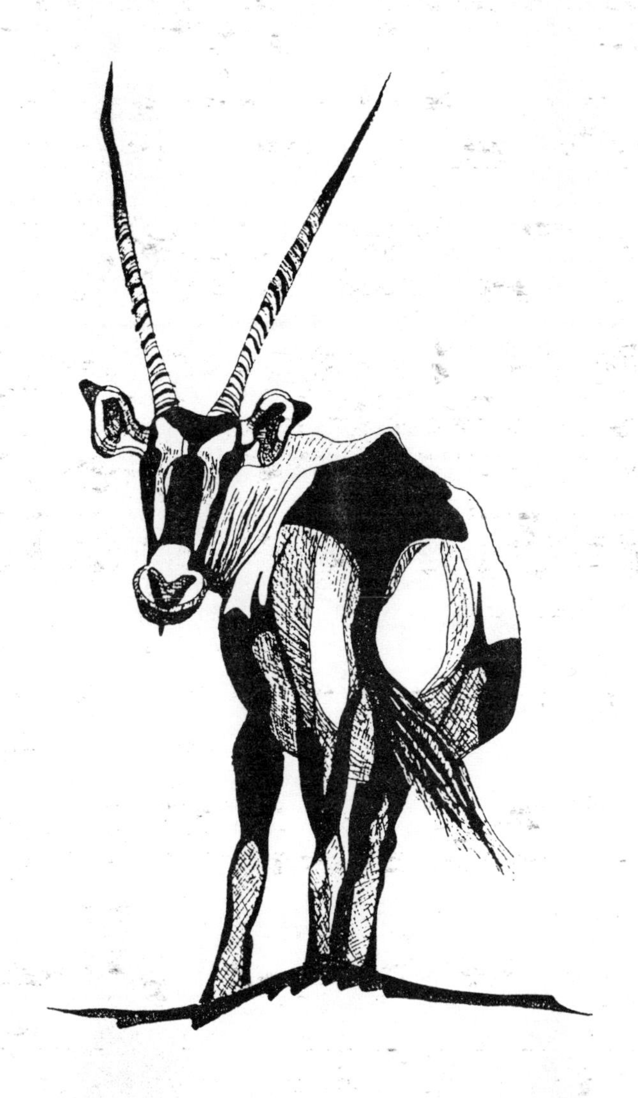

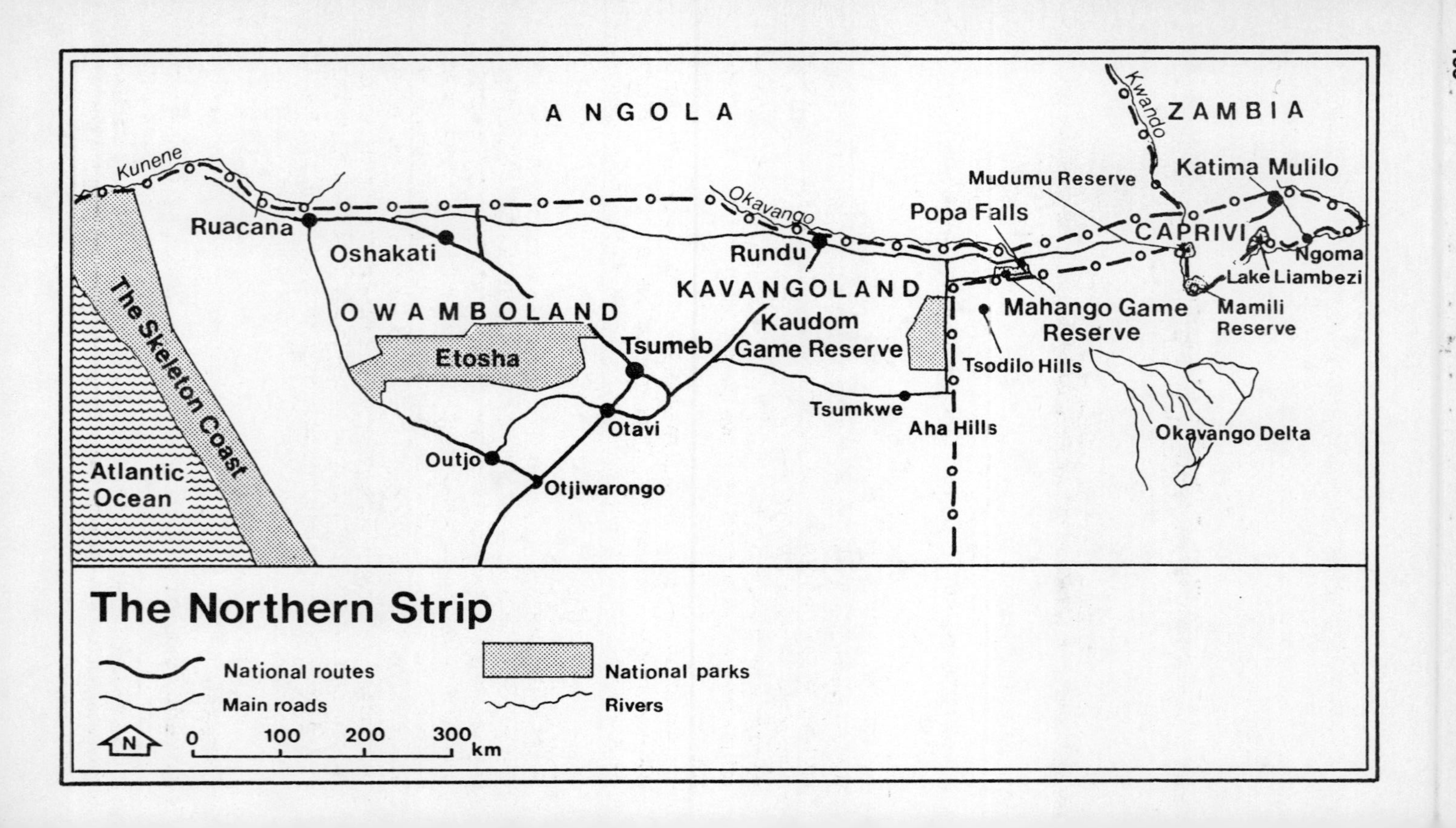
ANGOLA
ZAMBIA
Kwando
Kunene
Katima Mulilo
Mudumu Reserve
Okavango
Popa Falls
CAPRIVI
Ruacana
Oshakati
Rundu
Ngoma
Lake Liambezi
KAVANGOLAND
Mamili Reserve
OWAMBOLAND
Kaudom Game Reserve
Mahango Game Reserve
Tsumeb
Etosha
Tsodilo Hills
The Skeleton Coast
Otavi
Tsumkwe
Aha Hills
Okavango Delta
Outjo
Atlantic Ocean
Otjiwarongo
The Northern Strip
National routes
Main roads
National parks
Rivers
N
0
100
200
300
km

Chapter 15

The Northern Strip

Home to over half of the country's population, this verdant strip of land stretches eastward from the flat plains south of the Kunene River to the 'panhandle' of land between Angola, Zambia and Botswana. During the summer, it appears quite unlike the rest of Namibia, receiving over 500mm of rain and supporting a thick cover of vegetation and extensive arable farming.

From west to east, the region consists of the three provinces of Owamboland, Kavangoland and Caprivi, which are described below in this order.

OWAMBOLAND

To the north of Etosha lies the province of Owamboland, a highly populated region adjacent to Angola where the people rely mainly upon subsistence farming of maize, sorghum and millet. Home of the Owambo ethnic group, this was the heartland of SWAPO's support during the struggle for independence, and has consequently suffered much during the last few decades (see *Owambo*, Chapter 2, page 20). Hopefully the situation will now change for the better, and though very few tourists visit the area as yet, it should prove to be an interesting excursion if you're not looking for specific 'sights' to see.

Oshakati

Along with Ondangwa, this is one of the two largest towns in Owamboland.

Where to stay One of the few hotels in the region is the **International Guest House** PO Box 542. Tel: (06752)75. Singles cost R50, doubles R75, and breakfast is R6 extra.

Ruacana

A small town in the far north of the country right on the border with Angola. It's important for the large hydroelectric station built on the Kunene River, which is fed by a reservoir in Angola and supplies over half of the country's electric power. Be careful when taking photographs — the area is still politically/militarily sensitive.

KAVANGOLAND AND CAPRIVI

North-east of Grootfontein lie the provinces of Kavangoland and Caprivi, which between them offer not only a short cut from Namibia into Zimbabwe or Zambia, but also some excellent places to stop and explore. Kaudom National Park provides a Kalahari wilderness, nearby Mahango is similar to the lusher parks in the east of the continent, whilst the area around the Linyanti is reminiscent of the Okavango Delta. Very recently two new National Parks have been created here, Mamili and Mudumu, both of which are partially floodplain and should prove fascinating to explore. In short, a tremendous variety of habitats — all in this out-of-the-way section of the country.

Perhaps because of its position in the far north, well away from Windhoek or the routes to South Africa, the facilities here are generally not well developed. Travel information is hard to come by and the roads can often be poor. The main gravel road east to Kongola (and Katima Mulilo) is certainly navigable by normal 2WD cars — but its poor condition is the cause of many accidents — though a high-clearance vehicle (preferably 4WD) is a necessity for most of the secondary roads, especially after the rains.

It's worth remembering that a high-clearance 4WD is in at least as much danger of overturning after hitting a pothole as a 2WD car is. One 4WD firm told me that they have several vehicles written off each month on the road from Rundu to Kongola, as drivers tend to emerge from the slow sandy roads of Chobe or Kaudom and regard the gravel along here as 'easy, fast driving' in comparison.

Looking ahead, with the tarred road being extended from Rundu towards Katima Mulilo, these problems may soon end and the region is likely to become a strategically important and prosperous corridor for trade across the continent — of which there is little at the present time. Equally, the rivers in the area are so picturesque that I'd be surprised if more rest camps don't open up on their banks, to benefit from an increase in tourism in the region.

The people who live here, the Kavango and the Caprivians, have close links with peoples just north of the border in Angola (See *Kavango and Caprivians*, page 19). As you drive around, look out for the stalls by the side of the road, piled with neat pyramids of tomatoes or exotic fruits — evidence of the great agricultural potential in the rich alluvial soils and heavy rainfall. Here at last you can get some fresh vegetables without cellophane wrappers. There are also many excellent wooden carvings — amongst the best souvenirs available in the country.

Rundu

Situated 250km north-east of Grootfontein, and 500km west of Katima Mulilo, this town sits just above the beautiful Okavango floodplain — and comes as a pleasant relief after the long, hot journey to reach it. There is a good supermarket with plenty of supplies, a couple of garages, an excellent bottle stall, and several places to stay. It can feel like a bit of an outpost, with few attractions in itself, but it's a pleasant enough place to stay for the night.

Where to stay and eat

Kavango Motel PO Box 203. Tel: (067372)320. Situated on the northern side of town, this pleasant motel has single rooms for R50 and doubles for R70, with breakfast at R12.50 extra. The restaurant and bar can be used even if you're not staying here and both are quite pleasant — the bar has a good choice of lagers, including Hansa draught.

Mayana camp This camp which has recently opened on the banks of the Okavango has a good bar and restaurant, though its huts are very basic — perhaps a reflection on its previous use as a *Koevoet* base! To get there, take the gravel road for about 20km east of Rundu, before turning left onto a signposted track, then follow the signs and tyre tracks for several kilometres farther, heading towards the river. A four-person rondavel, with outside facilities, costs R25.

Municipal Rest camp Situated immediately to the right of the Motel, this camp never seems busy but is always open and the very helpful attendant will find you later if he's not around when you arrive. The ablution blocks are clean and camping costs about R7 per person, so don't be deterred by the roughness of the track that leads a few hundred yards from the main road — it's a very convenient spot to camp.

Kaudom Game Reserve

Two or more 4WDs. Entrance fees: R5 per person and R5 per vehicle.

Situated next to Botswana and immediately north of Bushmanland, Kaudom is a wild, seldom-visited area of dry woodland savannah growing on old stabilised Kalahari sand dunes. These are interspersed with flat, clay pans and the whole area laced with a life-giving network of *omurambas*.

Omuramba is a Herero word meaning 'vague river bed', used to describe a drainage line that rarely, if ever, actually flows above ground, but usually gives rise to a number of waterholes along its course. In Kaudom, the *omurambas* generally lie along east-west axes and link into the Okavango river system, flowing underground into the Delta when the rains come. However, during the dry season the flood in the Delta helps to raise the level of the water-table in these *omurambas* — ensuring that the waterholes don't dry up, and thus attracting game into Kaudom.

The vegetation here can be quite thick in comparison with Namibia's other parks. Rhodesian teak and false *mopane* dominate the dunes — while acacias and leadwoods are found in the clay pans. The wildlife is definitely best

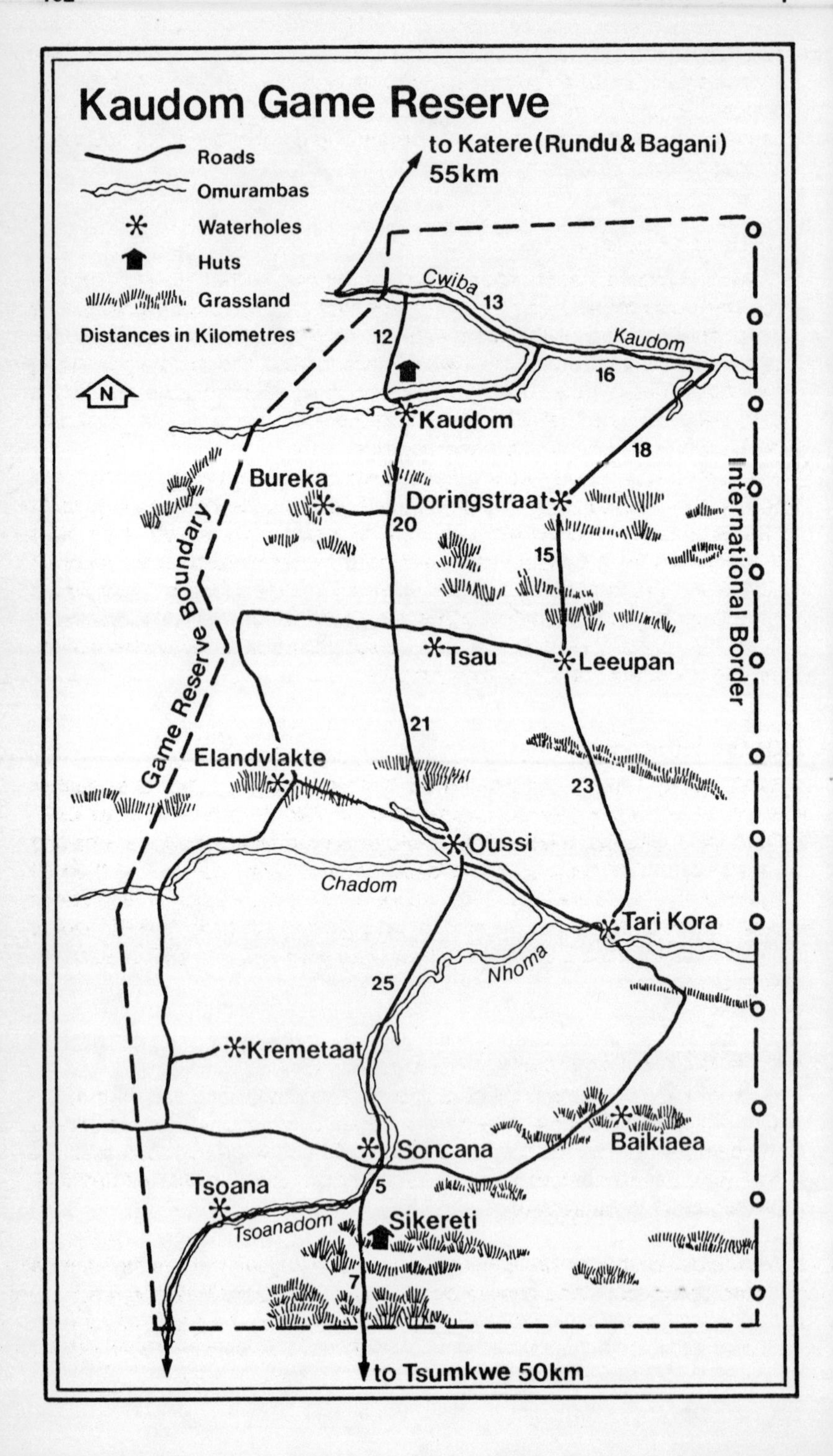
Kaudom Game Reserve
Roads
Omurambas
Waterholes
Huts
Grassland
Distances in Kilometres
N
to Katere (Rundu & Bagani) 55km
Cwiba
13
12
Kaudom
16
Kaudom
18
Bureka
Doringstraat
20
15
Game Reserve Boundary
International Border
Tsau
Leeupan
21
Elandvlakte
23
Oussi
Chadom
Tari Kora
Nhoma
25
Kremetaat
Soncana
Baikiaea
Tsoana
5
Sikereti
Tsoanadom
7
to Tsumkwe 50km

observed in the dry season, and though seldom occurring in numbers to rival Etosha's vast herds, there's much wilder feel about the place. Notable are populations of the uncommon tsessebe and roan antelope, as well as the usual big game species (interestingly excluding rhino and buffalo) and many smaller animals typical of the Kalahari.

Getting organised

Within the reserve, tracks either follow *omurambas*, or they link the dozen or so waterholes together, and even the distinct tracks are slow going, so a good detailed map of the area — or a set of aerial photos — would be invaluable. Try the Surveyor General's office in Windhoek before you arrive, if you can. Map number 1820 MUKWE is only a 1:250,000 scale, but it's the best available and definitely worth having — especially when used in conjunction with one on the previous page.

Water is available but nothing else — so come fully self-contained with fuel and supplies. Because of the reserve's remote nature, **entry is limited to parties with two or more 4WD vehicles** and each will need about 120 litres of fuel simply to get through the park from Tsumkwe to the fuel station at Mukwe, on the Rundu-Bagani road. This doesn't include any driving whilst there. Bear in mind also that you'll need to use 4WD almost constantly, even in the dry season (and in the wet, wheel chains might even be useful), making travel slow and very heavy on fuel.

Getting there

Approaching from the north, turn off the main road about 115km east of Rundu at Katere, then Kaudom camp is about 75km of slow, soft sand away. From the south, the park is reached via Tsumkwe and Klein Döbe. Entering Tsumkwe, turn left at the crossroads just beyond the schoolhouse — then left again to go around the back of the school. Branch right just before the track bends back to rejoin the main road, and head north towards Klein Döbe. Sikereti camp is about 60km away from Tsumkwe and some 77km south of Kaudom camp.

Where to stay

Kaudom has two camps: **Sikereti camp** in the south and **Kaudom** in the north. Each has a couple of basic wooden huts with outside facilities and a few camp sites. The four-bed huts cost R25 each while the campsites are only R20. Even here you must make advanced reservations at Windhoek DNC in order to be admitted.

Remember neither camp is fenced — so leave nothing outside that can be picked up or eaten, and beware of things that go bump in the night!

Mahango Game Reserve

2WD/4WD. R5 per person and R5 per vehicle.

This small reserve is tucked away in a corner of the Caprivi Strip, bounded by the upper Okavango River to its east and the Botswanan border to its south, and bisected by one of the main roads between Namibia and Botswana — from which several game drives explore the area. Perhaps what makes Mahango stand out amongst Namibian parks is the presence of the mighty Okavango River, which spreads out and widens here, giving rise to extensive reedbeds at its edge, and lush vegetation all round. This brings water-loving species like the rare red lechwe and sitatunga into the park, and encourages good numbers of reedbuck, bushbuck, waterbuck and buffalo.

When to go

The game varies greatly with the season, and while in the dry season it's sometimes inundated with elephants, it can be disappointing during the rains. We once visited in early March when the highlights of the day's trip turned out to be a distant kudu spotted through dense vegetation, and snatched glimpses of a few fleeing sable.

Getting organised

Entry here is R5 per person and R5 for the vehicle, though if you're just going straight through on the main road into Botswana then there's no charge.

There are no facilities or accommodation, so you must stay elsewhere and come in for day trips. **Popa Falls rest camp** or **Suclabo lodge** (see following page) are the obvious choices.

What to see and do

Game drives There are two game drives to explore, both starting about 800m south of the main gate. The left road, which has a good gravel surface, soon overlooks the floodplain and passes a picnic spot before returning to the main road farther south. The right course, suitable for high-clearance 4WD's only, follows an *omuramba* going away from the river, before splitting after about 10.7km. The right fork continues along the *omuramba*, terminating at a waterhole, while the left joins the main road again some 19km later.

Bush walking One real bonus is that walking in the park is officially encouraged. However **beware** — the summer's lush growth is far too thick to walk safely in, so better to visit when the plants and shrubs have died down during the winter, and you are able to see for a good distance around you. Then you can get out of the car and go for it — but watch for the elephants, buffalo and occasional lion! (For comments on how to walk safely in the bush, see Chapter 6, page 71.)

Popa Falls

2WD. R5 per person and R5 per vehicle.

The Popa Falls are really a set of rapids where the Okavango River drops a height of about 2.5m over a rocky section, before beginning its journey into the sands of the Kalahari desert and the Okavango Delta.

Getting there

The rest camp and falls are conveniently placed right on the western bank of the Okavango, about 5km south-east of the Bagani bridge. Take the turn-off to Botswana just west of the bridge.

Where to stay

Popa falls rest camp Accommodation is either camping at R20 per site, or four-bed bungalows for R60. The bungalows are well built of local wild teak and come with their own bedding and gas lamps, though kitchens and ablutions are communal.

Suclabo Lodge This private lodge is just a few kilometres down the river from the Popa Falls and has a swimming pool, a restaurant, a bar, and rather plusher bungalows than Popa's — but for R60 per person, including breakfast. They'll organise river trips, fishing tackle hire and safaris into Mahango and Kaudom for you — though if you just want to camp here it might take a little persuasion. There were rumours that this camp was about to be catapulted into the expensive world of fly-in safaris, but no concrete details as yet.

What to see and do

The camp area is thickly vegetated with tall riverine trees and lush green shrubs, encouraging waterbirds typically found in the Okavango Delta and a variety of small reptiles. Small wooden footbridges have been built between some of the islands, and it's worth spending a morning island-hopping between the rushing channels, or walking upstream a little where there's a good view of the river before it plunges over the rapids. Just in a few hours, we spotted a leguvaan (water monitor), several snakes, and many different frogs — as well as a cormorant whose underwater fishing technique was captivating.

This camp makes an excellent base from which to explore Mahango Game Reserve by day, while the bar at the nearby Suclabo Lodge is an obvious excursion for the evenings. The gates are usually locked between sunset and sunrise though, so borrow a key from the manager's house (on the right as you enter) if you're likely to come back late. If you arrive late then Suclabo Lodge may well have its own spare key to the gates.

Border crossing: Mohembo to Shakawe

4WD advised. Open from 8am to 6pm (check times if possible).

At the southern end of Mahango Game Reserve lies the Namibian border post, followed shortly by a well-camouflaged Botswana Defence Force (BDF) post. To complete immigration formalities and enter Botswana, you must take a left turn some 13km further south of this (just after an incongruous 'fasten your seat belt' road sign), and seek out Shakawe's police station by the riverside. The road on the Botswanan side is for high-clearance 4WDs only in the wet season, though a good high-clearance 2WD would probably get through during the dry season.

Katima Mulilo

The regional capital of the eastern Caprivi, Katima Mulilo is rather cut off from the rest of the country. It's quite a large town, beautifully placed on the banks of the Zambezi River, and has good facilities, including a supermarket, bottle stall, garage, bank and an open central square dotted with trees.

Getting there: the Caprivi Game Park

This large chunk of the Caprivi Strip is said to be home to much wildlife, though there are no facilities and you are not allowed off the main road. The main road (B8), connecting Katima Mulilo with the rest of Namibia, cuts straight through the middle of the park, so watch out for animals on the road.

For many years a permit was needed to travel through this sensitive military area and, although this is no longer the case, there are still control posts at each end of the strip as well as settlements within it. It seems likely that its boundaries will soon be changed — with a view to either reducing its size or developing it properly as an attraction for visitors.

Where to stay and eat

The Zambezi Lodge is an excellent hotel with a swimming pool, restaurant and — connected to the bank by a wooden jetty — a memorable bar floating on the Zambezi. Single rooms here are R88 and doubles R99, while **camping** costs R5 per person plus R5 for the vehicle.

If you want to **hire a vehicle**, the lodge is the Avis depot — though prices are amongst the highest in the country. (Latest reports indicate that this may have closed — check with Avis before arriving).

What to see and do

If you do have any time here, then it makes a good base from which to explore the whole region. The stretch of the Zambezi that borders onto Caprivi has numerous channels and islands — there is even a DNC hut on **Kalembeza Island**, some 25km downstream from Katima. Local enquiries would probably result in the loan of a boat; failing that you can always hire one — with its owner as chauffeur — from one of the riverside villages. To reach the Kwando River, the best starting point is the village of Liansulu.

Border crossing: Ngoma to Kasane

2WD. Open from 8am to 4pm.

This is the only road link between Namibia and Botswana which is good gravel and suitable for all vehicles. With Namibia's post almost overlooking the Chobe river, and the few Botswana soldiers on the opposite bank—you'll probably have your passport checked and be told to report to Kasane police station for the completion of immigration formalities. Don't delay doing this.

Lake Liambezi, Mamili and Madumu Reserves

Researched by Robin and Jannice Heath

The southern border of eastern Caprivi, with Botswana, is defined rather indistinctly along the line of the Kwando, the Linyanti and the Chobe Rivers. These are basically the same river in different stages, as it comes south from Angola and makes a sharp turn north-east, forming a swampy region of reedbeds and waterways north of the Kalahari. Finally it flows on to join the Zambezi and discharge into the Indian Ocean.

These Linyanti swamps make a fascinating area to explore in a couple of 4WDs. Like the Okavango Delta, the seasonal flood of the Kwando River is highly variable from one year to the next, making tracks very unreliable and maps usually useless. The best way to explore would be to come towards the end of the dry season, bringing a map and compass and seek local advice for the best routes to take.

As Robin Heath writes, 'For those to whom the wilderness has appeal, this is the place for a safari'.

Lake Liambezi

This large, shallow lake which covers some 10,000 hectares when full, is located between the Linyanti and Chobe — about 60km south of Katima Mulilo on the D3507. It has been dry since 1985, though it is known to be cyclical in nature, with previous dry phases, and is expected to flood again — when the seasonal floods of the Zambezi are high enough to overflow into the Bukalo Channel, which feeds it.

Mamili Reserve

This unfenced swampland reserve of about 35,000 acres was created soon after Independence and consists largely of marshland, veined by a network of reeded channels. It includes two large islands: Nkasa and Lupala. Together with Mudumu Reserve, it has over 90% of Namibia's population of sitatunga and red lechwe antelope — and a handful of the rare, and rather shy, Puku.

It is located in the south-west corner of the region, where the Kwando sharply changes direction to become the Linyanti, and as yet there are apparently no facilities for visitors and few passable roads — even in a 4WD! The DNC will issue camping permits if you want to visit and it's also worth checking with them for the latest information on the area. There are bound to be basic facilities developed in the near future.

Mudumu Reserve

The more northerly of the region's two new reserves, Mudumu (also created after Independence) is about 45km from Kongola on the D3511. Bordered by the Kwando River on the west, the reserve has, amongst other game, a large number of elephants and may be explored on foot or by 4WD — though don't expect an extensive network of game drives! There is a basic, unfenced camp here — which is likely to be expanded soon — and little else in the way of facilities. Ideal!

Part 3
Botswana

Botswana Regions

- **A** Eastern Corridor - Chapter 17
- **B** Chobe & The Great Salt Pans of The North-East - Chapter 18
- **C** Maun & The Okvango Delta - Chapter 19
- **D** Central Kalahari - Chapter 20
- **E** The Western Fringes - Chapter 21

National Parks & Forest Reserves

1. Kasane F.R.
2. Maikaelelo F.R.
3. Chobe F.R.
4. Chobe
5. Kazuma F.R.
6. Sibuyu F.R.
7. Moremi
8. Nxai Pan
9. Makgadikgadi Pans
10. Central Kalahari
11. Kutse
12. Gemsbok
13. Mabuasehube
14. Kalahari Gemsbok

Chapter 16

In Botswana

TOURISM IN BOTSWANA

'Low-density, high cost' tourism is the defined government policy. Whilst there has been a good deal of development of luxury lodges and exclusive safari operations in Botswana, the lower end of the market is barely catered for. Some may argue that from the government's point of view, and from the point of view of environmental conservation, this represents the best compromise — few people, maximum money. Alternatively, you can argue that it's not possible (or ultimately beneficial) to try to slow development in this way, and that a realistic and carefully planned budget tourist policy will be better than one that just chaotically springs up to the increasing demand.

Whatever view you take, it's undeniable that Botswana is one of the few countries in the world where the mark of the tourist is barely felt. A visitor to Botswana can look forward to uncrowded parks and reserves and a pristine landscape. Even the Okavango, which is probably the most visited part of the country, still offers an unspoilt water wilderness experience.

COST OF LIVING/TRAVELLING

Botswana is in many ways similar to Namibia but the absence of any budget accommodation or comprehensive public transport system does conspire to make Botswana difficult for budget travellers. This is then compounded by the very expensive national park and reserve entrance fees and the fact that much of Botswana's food and supplies are imported and therefore also expensive. However, it is possible to travel round Botswana at a reasonable cost, by, for example, sharing a hired 4WD vehicle, camping and cooking your own food. There are still some fascinating places to visit that don't require you to pay park fees and there are few reasons to spend much time in the (expensive) large towns anyway. Alternatively, hitching to main tourist destinations, such as the Okavango, is easy and there are a number of budget options available for those who look.

Estimating your daily expenditure depends so much on how you choose to travel. A careful read of *Planning and Preparations*, Chapter 4, together with the specific information in this chapter, should enable you to come up with a figure.

Currency

The unit of currency is the Pula (P), which is sub-divided into 100 Thebe. *Pula* means 'rain' in Setswana — water being one of Botswana's most precious commodities. The Pula only came into existence in 1976, displacing South Africa's Rand as the national currency. Even so, the financial and trading links between Botswana and South Africa remain very strong, and the Pula's strength varies with the Rand's. This means that the Pula is a 'hard' currency, and since it's freely convertible, there's no black market.

All people leaving Botswana are allowed to carry with them a maximum of P500 in cash, and the equivalent of P1,000 in foreign currency.

Exchange rates At the time of writing (June 1991) the exchange rates are £1=P3.30; and US$1=P2.00.

Banks

Currency can be exchanged at the commercial banks, hotels and at Gaborone International Airport. Normal banking hours are 0815-1245 weekdays and 0815-1045 Saturdays in the larger towns. Many smaller towns and settlements may have shorter hours or have an agent open for banking a few days a week. Having money sent in from abroad is not a problem in Gaborone, Francistown or Maun — and you can always use a credit card for a cash advance. Always make sure you have plenty of cash on hand — the main towns and banks are few and far between! Travellers cheques can be cashed at smaller places, and are the next best thing to straight cash.

Entrance fees to the national parks and game reserves

In July 1989, the Botswanan government increased ten-fold the national park and game reserve fees for visitors as part of its low-density, high cost tourist policy. Part of the policy was undoubtedly to milk something from the relatively large number of self-sufficient South African tourists driving their own vehicles into Botswana's parks, bringing their own supplies, and spending next to nothing in Botswana itself during their stay. The difference in rates between organising your own trip privately and being on an official tour or at one of the lodges, reflects this.

The prices quoted are for visitors to Botswana — residents and citizens pay very much less, as do children.

South African fees apply to Gemsbok National Park (as it is in practice, if not in theory, a South African park).

Don't forget that apart from the Moremi Wildlife Reserve, the great majority of the Okavango Delta has no entrance or camping fees and there are still huge tracts of the country that are wild, full of game, and outside the protected areas.

	Privately organised	**Official tour/lodge**
Park/reserve entry (per person, per day)	P50	P30
Camping fee (per person, per night)	P20	P10
Vehicle entrance (per day)		
Botswana registered	P2	P2
Foreign registered	P10	P10

TRANSPORT

The little Shell road map is deceptively small and simple. Distances in Botswana are huge — as is the time it can take to get from one place to another away from the few tarred roads. If time is short, it does make sense to consider flying. Buses are much slower than driving and often even slower than hitching. Taking the train is more for the romantic than the pragmatist, but you don't need to be a train buff to appreciate the steam trains which occasionally run along the eastern corridor.

Air

International flights Scheduled Air Botswana flights link Sir Seretse Khama International Airport (15km NW of Gaborone) to Harare, Victoria Falls, Bulawayo, Windhoek, Lusaka, Luanda, Maputo, Manzini, Maseru, and Johannesburg. In addition, there are direct flights run by foreign carriers to Lilongwe (Air Malawi), Dar-es-Salaam (Air Tanzania), Nairobi (Kenya Airways), Paris (UTA) and London (British Airways).

Internal flights There are frequent internal flights between Gaborone, Francistown, Selebi-Phikwe, Maun and Ghanzi. There's no public transport between the airport and Gaborone — you have to take a taxi, or convince a hotel 'courtesy' minibus to give you a lift. Bookings and reservations can be made at any of the Air Botswana offices in the main towns. The foreign airline offices are almost all in the main Mall, Gaborone.

Rail

The railway line that defines Botswana's Eastern Corridor is part of the route from Mafikeng (South Africa) to Bulawayo (Zimbabwe). The route used to be run by National Railways of Zimbabwe, but has now been taken over by Botswana Railways.

The trains are slow but comfortable and quite stylish in first or second class. They include private sleeper accommodation for the overnight services. Booking ahead of departure is recommended, particularly at month-end (government pay day), weekends and public holidays.

Passenger train timetable (effective from January 1991, except for day services effective from July 1991 — see notes below)

South-bound trains	*Daily*	*Daily*	*Thurs*	*Daily*
Bulawayo	-	-	1030	1340
Plumtree	-	-	1335	1735
Francistown	0610	1410	1520	1955
Serule	0732	1531	1710	2150
Palapye	0839	1638	1830	2345
Mahalapye	1005	1805	2012	0145
Gaborone	1300a	2100a	0025	0720
Lobatse	-	-	0208	0910a
Mafeking	-	-	0430	-
Johannesburg	-	-	1035a	-

North-bound trains	*Tues*	*Daily*	*Daily*	*Daily*
Johannesburg	1300	-	-	-
Mafikeng	2100	-	-	-
Lobatse	2255	-	-	1710
Gaborone	0035	0610	1410	1900
Mahalapye	0440	0905	1705	0001
Palapye	0556	1027	1827	0133
Serule	0733	1133	1933	0318
Francistown	0930	1255a	2055a	0535
Plumtree	1150	-	-	0830
Bulawayo	1420a	-	-	1150a

Notes

1. The day services between Gaborone and Francistown are new, and operative from July 1991.
2. All times are departure times unless indicated with an *a* for arrival time.
3. This timetable is not comprehensive — there are numerous small sidings and settlements at which the train may stop to pick up or put down — except for the overnight service between Lobatse and Bulawayo which stops at principal stations only and is faster.

Buses and minibuses

Buses do run fairly frequently between the main towns and it's possible to travel by 'express' bus as far as Johannesburg, Harare or Lusaka. Although guidelines to routes and times have been given under each of the main town headings in the regional chapters, it's always best to ask locally about the stopping places and times of the services. Fares are low. Minibuses — or *combis* as they're called locally — run over smaller distances, mainly around the capital, Gaborone.

Taxis

Taxis operate in the main towns and even some of the larger villages. Licensed vehicles have blue and white number plates. Metres are not used — bargain for a long journey or one outside normal routes.

Ferry

A ferry carries trucks and private cars across the Zambezi River at Kazungula, near Kasane — the border between Botswana and Zambia.

Driving

Only a small fraction of Botswana's roads are tarred and suitable for an ordinary vehicle. Whilst some of the dirt or gravel roads are passable in a high-clearance and tough 2WD, if you're exploring any of the national parks or game reserves you're bound to need — and know how to use — a 4WD vehicle. Full details on hiring a car, preparations and driving are in chapters 4 and 6.

Petrol costs are reasonable, but increase with remoteness. Supplies in many of the smaller villages are liable to run out, so away from the main centres it is always advisable to carry extra petrol.

Your can use an **international driving permit** for up to six months, after which you need to apply for a Botswanan licence. These cost £3 in Britain and are available from any AA office — take along your driving license, proof of identity and a couple of passport photographs.

Speed limits and safety belts On main roads, the upper speed limit is 110 km/h, whilst in towns and villages it is 60 km/h. National parks and game reserves have their own speed limits which are indicated at the entrance gates. Wearing safety belts (in all vehicles in which they are fitted!) is compulsory.

Hitchhiking

If you don't have your own vehicle, hitching is probably the best way to travel. Although traffic can be very light, you're more than likely to get a lift from any vehicle that does pass. As there is so little public transport, people know why you're hitching, and regard it as a perfectly normal and acceptable thing to do. Apart from lifts from other travellers and expats, you should expect to pay for your transport — hitching is not so much a cheaper way to travel compared to the scanty public transport, but a more convenient way.

As with hitching anywhere in the world, a tidy appearance and easily identifiable 'image' (eg traveller with backpack) helps your prospects. Talking to drivers at fuel stations or other stops is better than just standing on the road, but if you are opting for the latter, make sure you walk sufficiently out of town so that it's obvious where you are going.

Hitching off the main roads and heading west is for the intrepid only — ensure you have water for a few days with you.

Hiking and cycling

The obvious problem with cycling or hiking in Botswana is the severe lack of water. Apart from the Okavango, there is very little surface water of any kind and wherever there are boreholes there are settlements or cattleposts. However, hiking or cycling from village to village can be a very interesting and challenging experience, and you're sure to be away from any other travellers! Cycling is perhaps the more rewarding, since with a strong bike you can carry water for several days and can reach places where no 4WD vehicle can go. The relatively large number of villages and the hilly landscape in parts of the Eastern Corridor and especially the Tuli area are recommended. Phil Deutschle (see below) is currently cycling through Botswana and Namibia. He has survived so far!

Travelling and exploring well off the beaten track

The most obviously spectacular and remote spots in Botswana are almost certainly all well known and documented. Even so, the number of visitors to Botswana is very small, considering its size, and the out-of-the-way places written about in the following chapters will not be overrun with people. There are large, remote areas of the country that are never visited, and extremely rewarding to explore on your own. Phil Deutschle — who has spent the last few years teaching in Botswana, and exploring in his time off — wrote with the following comments:

'In my wanderings, I have discovered many new, magnificent places. But it was the act of discovery itself that made these places extraordinary. After a day's or a week's journey through harsh terrain, a simple shady glen becomes a wonderment. To follow a route description robs one of the "thrill of discovery", and the same shady glen becomes a few scraggy trees, a disappointment. The beauty of Botswana is the chance to explore — the immensity of the landscape gives you the feeling of being the first person on earth...so rather than give directions to any specific destinations, here are a few regions where no one goes, but which are well worth exploring.

'The whole area east of Chobe National Park — the Kasane, Maikaelelo, Kazuma, and Sibuyu forest reserves, and all the land between.

'The region east of Lake Ngami, including the Khwebe Hills and surroundings.

'The whole of the Makgadikgadi Pans area.'

If sensible precautions are taken, there is no reason why Botswana should not be a very safe place to explore.

Maps

See page 52.

ACCOMMODATION

There is little budget accommodation in Botswana, few official campsites, and no youth hostels. 'Bush' camping, however, is easy, exciting, and free.

Hotels

Essentially Botswana's hotels cater for business people — those with expense accounts — and not for the medium to low budget visitor or tourist. They are mostly plush and upmarket, though rarely distinctive or particularly interesting. Prices drop as you move away from the main centres and can range from about P30 to P150 for a single room, and P40 to P200 for a double. An exception is Francistown which does have a couple of cheap hotels. Where appropriate, we've bracketed the hotels into three categories — A, B and C (see page 85 for an explanation of these categories). Even the cheapest are mostly clean and pleasant with no horror stories!

Tourist lodges and camps

Each lodge or camp — unlike most of Botswana's hotels — is distinctive and individual; many of the smaller ones are run by individuals or couples who impart their own hospitality on the place (they probably set it up in the first place). The vast majority are in the Chobe-Okavango region, with a few in the private game reserves of the Tuli Block.

Although the prices may seem very high — especially those camps in the Okavango or in Chobe National Park — they do often include sumptuous meals, and the full range of camp activities, including game drives and *mokoro*/canoe trips.

Camping

Combining camping with a 4WD vehicle is really the only way to see many of Botswana's most spectacular places. Though there are few official campsites — and these are frequently quite basic or run down — Botswana must be a camper's paradise. Most land is not privately owned (the main exception being the Tuli Block), and once away from the Eastern Corridor and main towns, people are very scarce. If you're well prepared with your own supplies and water, you can camp almost anywhere.

FOOD AND DRINK

Local food

The main staples in Botswana are sorghum and maize flour (mealie meal). These are both used to make a stiff savoury 'porridge', which is then eaten with a sauce or 'relish' made from meat and whatever vegetables are available. The mealie meal version is called *shadza*, and is a staple food throughout sub-Saharan Africa — albeit with a large variety of different names. Some travellers can't cope with the general stodginess of it all, but it's tasty, clean, nutritious and very cheap. You'll find local women selling *shadza* and stew for next to nothing in all the main population centres, usually around bus stations or markets.

Western food

Apart from the staples and beef, Botswana imports almost all its food — much of it from South Africa — and consequently prices are quite high by comparison with Zimbabwe, Zambia and East Africa. However, by Western standards, food is good value with a take-away costing P3-P5 and an excellent restaurant meal in Gaborone costing only P20.

The supermarkets are well stocked in the main towns, and you can easily find all the camping/travelling supplies you might need for your trip at reasonable prices. Vegetables are rare and expensive — make the most of the few markets in Gaborone and Francistown. Even the smallest settlements usually have a general store, with a small selection of essential supplies, and the occasional luxuries. Don't expect these dealers to be able to offer you the low prices of the cities.

Vegetarians

The local cuisine is not exactly oriented toward the vegetarian — which is not entirely surprising in a country for which beef is the second largest export after diamonds! Equally, much of the Western food for sale in restaurants and take-aways is also meat biased. However, good vegetarian meals out can be found in Gaborone and Francistown, and there's bound to be something to eat in most of the take-aways, even if it's only an omelette or chip butty! If you're camping you'll be cooking your own food, and there are plenty of suitable camping supplies available in the main towns.

Alcohol

Drinking must be the dominant national pastime. Bottle stores (off-licences) are spread throughout the country in even the smallest settlements — you'd be amazed where you can pick up a cold beer! The range is usually limited to a small selection of bottled beers, and a few soft drinks. Legally, alcohol is not sold before 10am, and bottle stores close at 7pm and on Sundays. The bars of the larger hotels usually have an excellent selection of wines and spirits imported from around the world. For a treat, try a single malt whilst pondering life and the sunset, looking out over the Okavango!

Water

All piped and borehole water is on the whole safe to drink. Water from the Okavango or one of the few perennial rivers should be boiled or purified, though many do drink unpurified water from the Okavango and live to tell the tale!

Tipping

Tipping is not demanded in restaurants or hotels — many restaurants add a service charge. If you feel it is appropriate to tip, 10% is the usual practice.

HANDICRAFTS AND WHAT TO BUY

Botswana's crafts industry can be neatly divided into three regions. Most dominant and famous is the **basket weaving** of the Okavango Delta and areas to the north. The baskets are woven from a palm that grows in the swamps and come in an amazing variety of shapes, sizes and patterns. Each individual pattern is based on a number of basic design motifs that represent the many different practical and spiritual aspects of local life. The best range of baskets is in Maun, though as you travel around the Okavango you're sure to be offered them direct by the weavers. When poling in the Delta, we were on more than one occasion unexpectedly taken into a small parting in the reeds, where a woman basket weaver nervously displayed her creations.

Bushmen crafts — centred almost entirely around Ghanzi — are genuinely authentic and very unusual. If you're one of those people who shrinks at the sight of gifts and curios made specially for tourists around the world, then you might be surprised at these. The ostrich eggshell jewellery, and leather pouches, are exactly as the Bushmen have always made them — the mark of individual craftsmanship very evident.

A few small towns and villages in the Eastern Corridor have quite recently developed a new craft in Botswana, using imported **textiles** from Zimbabwe and South Africa. All sorts of very original wall-hangings and tapestries are being made by small community-based co-operatives, using new designs based on rural village life. The villages of Odi and Mochudi near Gaborone stand out.

For **general purchases**, the shops in the main towns are very well stocked with almost all basics and consumer items. Most goods are imported from South Africa and therefore cost more than in their country of origin.

ORGANISING AND BOOKING

Opening hours

Office hours are 8am to 1pm, and 2pm to 5pm weekdays only. Shop hours are roughly the same, though they are also open on Saturday morning. A few general stores stay open till the early evening for basic essentials.

Public holidays

January 1, 2
Good Friday, Saturday, Easter Sunday and Monday
Ascension Day (40 days after Easter Sunday)
President's Day (third Monday in July)
Day after President's Day
September 30 — Botswana Day
Day after Botswana Day (or if on a weekend, the following Monday)
Christmas Day & Boxing Day

The Botswana telephone directory

This relatively thin volume is an excellent source of all sorts of information and essential to locating a particular service you might want. Track it down in post offices, hotels and government departments. The single book which covers the whole of the country (oh such simplicity!) contains information and lists on the following: telephone, fax and telex numbers; international codes, and dialling direct from Botswana; PO box numbers and private bag numbers; lists of all government departments, region by region; comprehensive 'yellow pages' for all major services and businesses; street maps of Gaborone and Francistown, including the industrial areas; easy to find list of doctors, dentists and hospitals.

Tourism office

P. Bag 0047, Gaborone. Tel: 353024. (Located on the first floor of the BBS Building in Broadhurst Mall — it looks like an office block!) Good for a useful range of brochures etc. There's also an information office in town, in the main mall.

Visas

The Chief Immigration Officer, PO Box 942, Gaborone. Tel: 374545.

COMMUNICATIONS

Post

Incoming Post will be held for you by the central Gaborone Post Office — labelled 'Post Restante'. If you have an American Express card or travellers cheques, you can use the 'AMEX Customer's Mail Service' at the AMEX agent: Manica Travel Services, Botsalano House, The Mall, PO Box 1188, Gaborone. Tel: 352021.

International air mail is fast and reliable if sent from a main town — mail posted in Gaborone is by far the fastest. Internal mail to post office box numbers and private bags is reliable, but can be rather slow to the remoter areas. There is an express letter delivery service and a registered letter service. There's no door-to-door mail delivery in Botswana.

Telephone, fax and telex

Botswana has a good direct dialling system including international direct dialling to anywhere in the world. There are public phones in Gaborone and Francistown, and by the post office of many of the smaller towns. In Gaborone, international calls can be made at Standard House from where telegrams can also be sent. Major hotels offer telex and increasingly fax facilities. Where there are no phones, there is usually some sort of radio contact in case of an emergency.

There are no area codes in Botswana — to phone you just dial the number.

MISCELLANEOUS

Electricity

A 'European' 220/230V supply at 50Hz is standard and available in all the main towns and settlements

Embassies and High Commissions in Botswana

British High Commission, Queen's Road, P. Bag 0023, Gaborone. Tel: 352841.
Danish Consulate, 142 Mengwe Close, PO Box 367, Gaborone. Tel: 353770.
French Consulate, 761 Robinson Road, PO Box 1424, Gaborone. Tel: 353683.
German Embassy, 2nd Floor, IGI House, PO Box 315, Gaborone. Tel: 353143.
Netherlands Consulate, Tel: 356376.
Nigerian High Commission, The Mall, PO Box 274, Gaborone. Tel: 313561.
Norwegian Consulate, Development House, The Mall, PO Box 879, Gaborone. Tel: 351501.
Swedish Embassy, Development House, The Mall, P. Bag 0017, Gaborone. Tel: 353912.
USA Embassy, Badiredi House, The Mall, PO Box 90, Gaborone. Tel: 353982.
USSR Embassy, 4711 Tawana Close, PO Box 81, Gaborone. Tel: 353389.
Zambian High Commission, The Mall, PO Box 362, Gaborone. Tel: 351951.
Zimbabwean High Commission, 1st Floor, IGI House, PO Box 1232, Gaborone. Tel: 314495.

Hospitals, dentists and pharmacies

Although scantily distributed, Botswana's medical facilities are of a high standard and comparable to anything you'll find in the West. The main danger is the remoteness of much of the country — it is essential to carry full first aid equipment if you intend spending much time exploring away from the main towns. There are doctors and generally pharmacies in Francistown, Gaborone, Kanye, Lobatse, Mahalapye, Maun, Mochudi, Molepolole, Palapye and Selebi-Phikwe (full details in the Botswana telephone directory). The main hospital and the most comprehensive facilities are at Gaborone. Dentists only in Gaborone, Francistown and Lobatse.

Imports and exports

There are strict restrictions on taking into the country many agricultural products, plants, skins and hides, and other animal products. If you do have any of these, declare them to customs. Equally, if you must buy 'trophies', game skins or ivory, and wish to take them out of the country, make sure that you have the necessary documentation.

That said, remember that the recent CITES ban makes it an offence to import or export ivory from any participating country (these include UK and USA). While there is a legitimate case in favour of controlled ivory exports from Botswana — based on the necessity of culling elephants to prevent over population of the game parks — it's unlikely that you will be able to import ivory into your own country. Our advice is, don't buy it.

Botswana is a member of the Southern African Customs Union (SACU), along with South Africa, Namibia, Lesotho and Swaziland. This means that there are no customs restrictions between any of these countries, except for the specifically restricted items. Otherwise, if you are permanently importing any new items into the country from outside the SACU, be warned that duties are very high!

Newspapers, radio and TV

Whilst Botswana has a free press and no restrictions on broadcasting, it nevertheless seems very conservative compared to Western media. The government Department of Information and Broadcasting controls and runs Radio Botswana which broadcasts daily in English and Setswana. It also publishes the *Botswana Daily News* newspaper, which is printed Monday to Friday. Arguably one of the best newspapers, however, is the new and independent weekly *Newslink Africa*, published in English.

South African newspapers and journals are readily available in Gaborone and Francistown, and South African radio and TV can be received in most of the Eastern Corridor's main towns.

Theft

On the whole, Botswana is an extremely safe place to travel in. Violent crime is very rare, though don't tempt fate by walking through unlit and deserted parts of Gaborone at night. Petty theft from unattended vehicles and pick-pockets in busy shopping areas and bus stations are as common as any other city and should be guarded against.

Herd of springbok in the shade of the only tree for miles (Etosha)

Waterhole scene, Etosha

The Fish River Canyon from the main viewing point

Acacias mark the course of the Tsauchab river between Sesriem and Sossusvlei

Putting your feet up in the Okavango

Local boys get around — surprisingly fast — in a mokoro

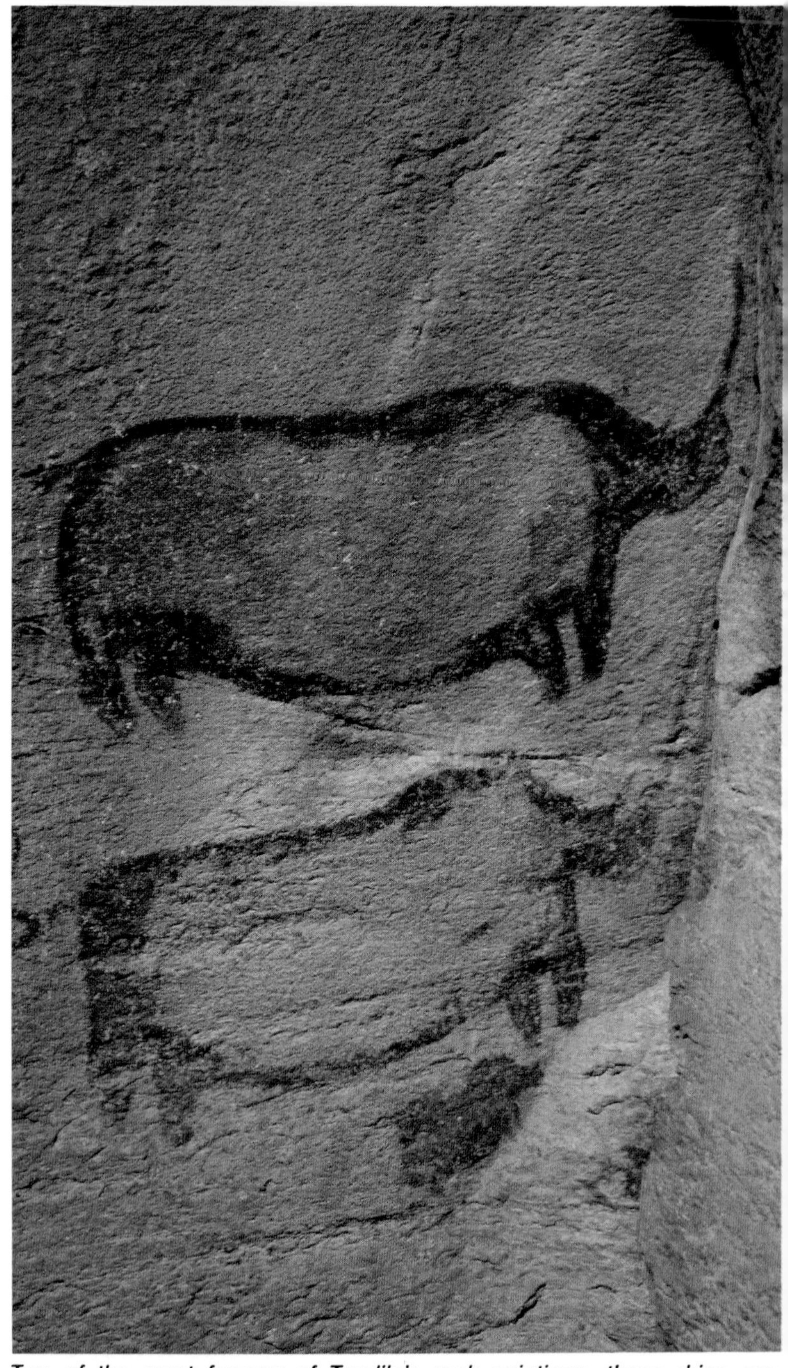

Two of the most famous of Tsodilo's rock paintings, these rhino are probably over 1,000 years old

Botswana's Baskets

Basket weaving has been a tradition in Botswana for centuries. Although most of the baskets are being made in the Okavango Delta area of north-western Botswana, basket weaving is still carried on in many other areas of Botswana, each with its own particular style.

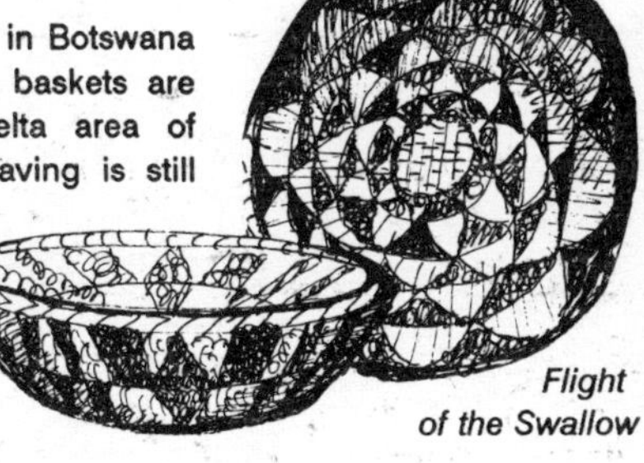

Palm Leaf *Flight of the Swallow*

Construction The coil foundation of the basket is either made of bundled grass, split palm leaves or a single vine rod. The coils are then wrapped with a split palm leaf from the mokolane palm (*hyphoene ventricosa*). By drying and boiling the mokolane palm with the root of the mothakola tree (*euclea sp.*), the palm is dyed various shades of brown. This brown and natural coloured palm is then used to weave designs into the baskets.

Forehead of the Zebra *Forehead of the Kudu*

Traditional designs Designs on baskets have traditionally been used to commemorate an important aspect of the weaver's lives. For example, 'the flight of swallows' design is shown to mark the occasion of the first rain, whilst the 'urine trail of the bull' design symbolises the importance of cattle. Weavers often incorporate more than one design into their baskets as well as creating new designs with traditional meaning.

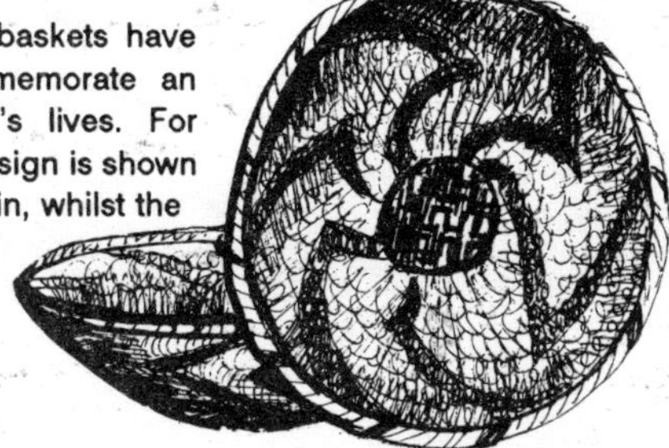

Urine trail of the bull

Usage Each basket is made for a particular purpose. Round container-baskets, when made with a rod foundation, are used for storing grain — but if made with bundled grass or split palm leaves, the basket will hold liquids (such as traditional beer) due to the swelling of the weaving material. Open bowl shapes are commonly used for winnowing or for transport and storage of grains, vegetables or ground sorghum.

Knees of the Tortoise

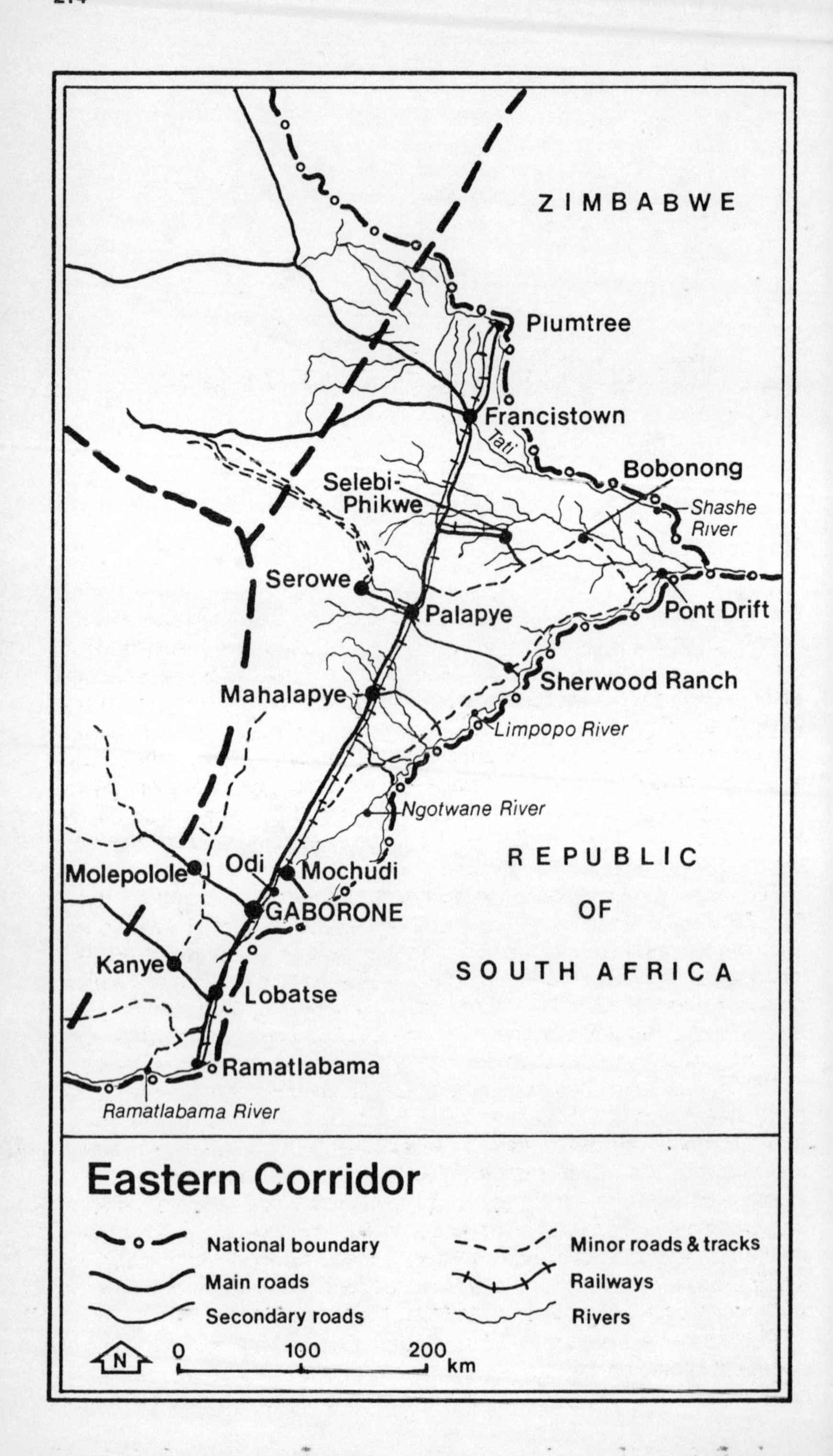
ZIMBABWE
Plumtree
Francistown
Tati
Bobonong
Selebi-
Phikwe
Shashe
River
Serowe
Palapye
Pont Drift
Sherwood Ranch
Mahalapye
Limpopo River
Ngotwane River
REPUBLIC
OF
SOUTH AFRICA
Molepolole
Odi
Mochudi
GABORONE
Kanye
Lobatse
Ramatlabama
Ramatlabama River
Eastern Corridor
National boundary
Main roads
Secondary roads
Minor roads & tracks
Railways
Rivers
N
0
100
200
km

Chapter 17

The Eastern Corridor

The eastern edge of Botswana is an area that lies outside the sands of the Kalahari Desert, and looks and feels more like neighbouring Zimbabwe than parts of the rest of the country. There are rivers and readily available ground water, giving a fertile environment which can support fair numbers of people. When Rhodes' British South Africa Company was looking for ways to get the rich mineral resources of the northern territories out to the sea, the railway was built through eastern Bechuanaland as Botswana was then called, connecting Zimbabwe with the Cape. Along this route, many small settlements sprung up, feeding off the meagre amount of wealth that was imparted by the rich railway corridor.

The region today contains the country's two main towns — the capital, Gaborone, and Francistown — and most of the population and infrastructure. The railway, good tarred roads linking Zimbabwe to South Africa, and the international airport at Gaborone, make the Eastern Corridor one of the main gateways into this part of the continent. In Gaborone or Francistown, you'll be able to pick up any supplies or spare parts that you might need for your trip, get yourself organised and prepare yourself for exploring the interior.

The capital Gaborone has a rather soulless feel about it, characteristic of many new towns. It's also very expensive, with little in the way of cheap accommodation. However, there are several interesting day trips to be made, and Khutse Game Reserve is within long-weekend striking distance.

Francistown, by comparison, is more compact and with an excellent campsite and cheap hotels an affordable place to mellow out and resupply. At the gateway for travel north to Maun, the Okavango, Chobe and the spectacular salt pans of Nxai and Makgadikgadi, Francistown has become a main stopover for travellers and overlanders.

Most travellers see no more of the Eastern Corridor than endless vistas of bush and tarmac as they travel north or south. But for those with a 4WD or even without a car, the region offers the chance to explore many off-the-track places with relative ease, including the private game reserves of the Tuli Block. Tucked away in the east between the South African and Zimbabwean borders, the Tuli Block offers some of the most remarkable scenery in the country and excellent private game country. Here you'll be able to view game and trek through the bush for a fraction of the cost of the main national parks and reserves and a car isn't essential.

GABORONE

Gaborone, was chosen as the site of the new capital in 1962 (in preparation for formal independence in 1966), because of its proximity to the railway line and the availability of water from the Ngotwane River. Prior to this it was just a small, traditional village named after chief Gaborone of the Batlokwa tribe. The initial projection of the city's population was a maximum of 20,000. However, the discovery of diamonds shortly after independence, led to a massive growth in the economy and now Gaborone is one of the fastest growing cities in the world, with a population of about 130,000. (Botswana as a whole has the fastest growing economy in black Africa.) This, needless to say, made much of the city's careful planning somewhat redundant and there is an acute shortage of housing, schools and other social amenities. Constant construction work is characteristic of the sprawling industrial areas.

The city is still looking for a heart, and most people find it frustrating in its anonymity. Gaborone is not so much a place to visit, as the place you may well fly into, or use to get things organised.

Cheap accommodation is a major problem — indeed during the week any accommodation can be a problem — and there is no campsite. However, if you're in town, enjoy the chance to treat yourself to a good meal (vegetarians, this is your only chance!), and take some time to wander about the interesting museum and art gallery. Gaborone is Botswana's only attempt at being cosmopolitan — there are several nightclubs, discos and a cinema.

Getting there

Air There are regular internal air services from Francistown, Maun, Ghanzi, and Selebi Phikwe — and international flights to and from all neighbouring countries (see page 203).

Train Daily services link Gaborone with Lobatse in the south and Bulawayo in Zimbabwe, with one service a week continuing on to Johannesburg. See the train timetable on page 203.

Bus Buses and minibuses leave at least once a day for Francistown in the morning, and more frequently for Lobatse and closer towns. There is also a bus link with Harare via Bulawayo which leaves from the African Mall on Tuesdays and Saturdays at 6.00am.

Where to stay

There is really no satisfactory budget accommodation in Gaborone. If you don't want to stay at one of the hotels listed below — or if they are all full — you should consider staying in Molepolole 50km away. There's a small cheap hotel there run by the Brigades and it's easy to get a lift or bus to Gaborone. Another possibility is to ask a taxi driver for 'private accommodation'. He's bound to know a friend of a friend who can give a traveller a place to sleep. Another possibility again, for those with a car, is just to head out of town and camp.

Category A
The **Sheraton** (Molepohole Road) is the most expensive at P220 (single) whilst the **Cresta Lodge** (135 Independence Ave) is the cheapest at P99. The **Gaborone Sun**, **Oasis**, and **President Hotel** are an intermediate price.

Category B
Cheaper hotels are generally all out of town. The **Morning Star Motel** is the closest, 5km east of Gaborone on the Zeerust road. This has single rooms for P55 and doubles for P75 with bathrooms en suite. Tel: 352301.

The **Mogotel** at Mogotishane on the road to Molepolole is more run down and cheaper. Tel: 372228.

There is one fairly central hotel — the new **Gaborone Hotel**. Tel: 375200 — just over the footbridge from the train station. Singles P70 and doubles P90.

There is also a **guest house** near the university (2km from the Mall along Notwane Road), run by R.K. Accountants, PO Box 2288. Tel: 372466. This has rooms for P55 each. They're often full, but it's worth ringing to check vacancies and to get directions.

Category C
The only relatively cheap place to stay is the **YWCA**, which has dormitory beds for women only for P20, though it's often booked out by university students. It's situated just opposite the Princes' Marina Hospital on Notwane Road.

Where to eat

Unlike its accommodation, Gaborone does have a good selection of places to eat that should suit most budgets. There are take-away chicken-and-chips and burger joints everywhere and street food (maize, peanuts and fruits) is cheap and clean. The cheapest hot meal must be the ubiquitous *shadza* and meat from the stalls around the bus station. The bars and restaurants of the central hotels are good for whiling away a few hours during the day — the **Pergola**, part of the President Hotel in the Mall, is a favourite meeting place for afternoon coffee, tea and cakes.

Other than the hotel restaurants which all serve the usual upmarket Botswanan fare of steaks and hamburgers, the best places to eat out are all located in the African Mall, a few minutes walk from the town centre. Here you'll find a choice of good Indian, Italian, French and Chinese food.

Park Restaurant and Pizzeria African Mall. The Park is very popular with visitors and residents alike and was voted best restaurant in town by a local newspaper. The food is good and the prices reasonable (not cheap). Although it's often very busy — you may have a problem getting a seat — it has an excellent, relaxed atmosphere. It serves a good selection of pizzas, seafood, salads and crepes in addition to the more usual burgers and grills. The vegetarian selection is excellent. Expect to pay around P6 for a starter or salad, and P8-P12 for a main course — the seafood is not surprisingly more expensive.

Taj Restaurant Norman Centre, African Mall. Similarly priced and less crowded than the Park, The Taj serves good curries and Indian food.

Mandarin Restaurant African Mall. A new, very popular Chinese restaurant, with main courses from P7 to P15.

The Bourgainville African Mall. An excellent, but pricey, French restaurant.
Outside the African Mall, there are a number of places worth mentioning.

The Bull and Bush is modelled on an English pub, and serves steaks, salads and fish and chips for P8-15. On Old Francistown Road, opposite Red Square flats, **Mama's Kitchen** does pasta and pizzas for P9.50-P15 in the New Broadhurst Mall some way north of the town centre, and was recently awarded a five star ('excellent — don't miss out') rating by the new *Newslink* newspaper. If you're waiting for a train or bus, the **Crazy Bull** near the station has good burgers and chips for P5.

Getting around

Finding your way around Gaborone is straightforward even if the distances are more that you're used to in a Botswanan town. The railway station, bus station and market all cluster together at the far end of Khama Crescent, about 15 minutes walk from the Mall and the centre of town. The Mall is a modern pedestrianised precinct with a good selection of shops, most of the embassies, and hundreds of offices. At the western end of this are the government offices, ministries and the national assembly — whilst at the eastern end is the library, museum and art gallery. One of the most interesting areas is the African Mall, five minutes from the conspicuous President Hotel in the main Mall, with a good variety of shops and restaurants.

Since the city is quite spread out, there's an efficient system of minibuses that operate up and down the main roads, and are useful to get to one of the suburbs or an out-of-town hotel. Though cheap, these are frequently crammed with people, and difficult if you're carrying a large backpack. Taxis can always be found outside the railway station and in the Mall. There's no public transport to the airport — take one of the hotel minibuses or a taxi.

What to see and do

The National Museum and Art Gallery Open from 9am-6pm Tuesdays to Fridays and 9am-5pm on weekends and public holidays. Admission free. The

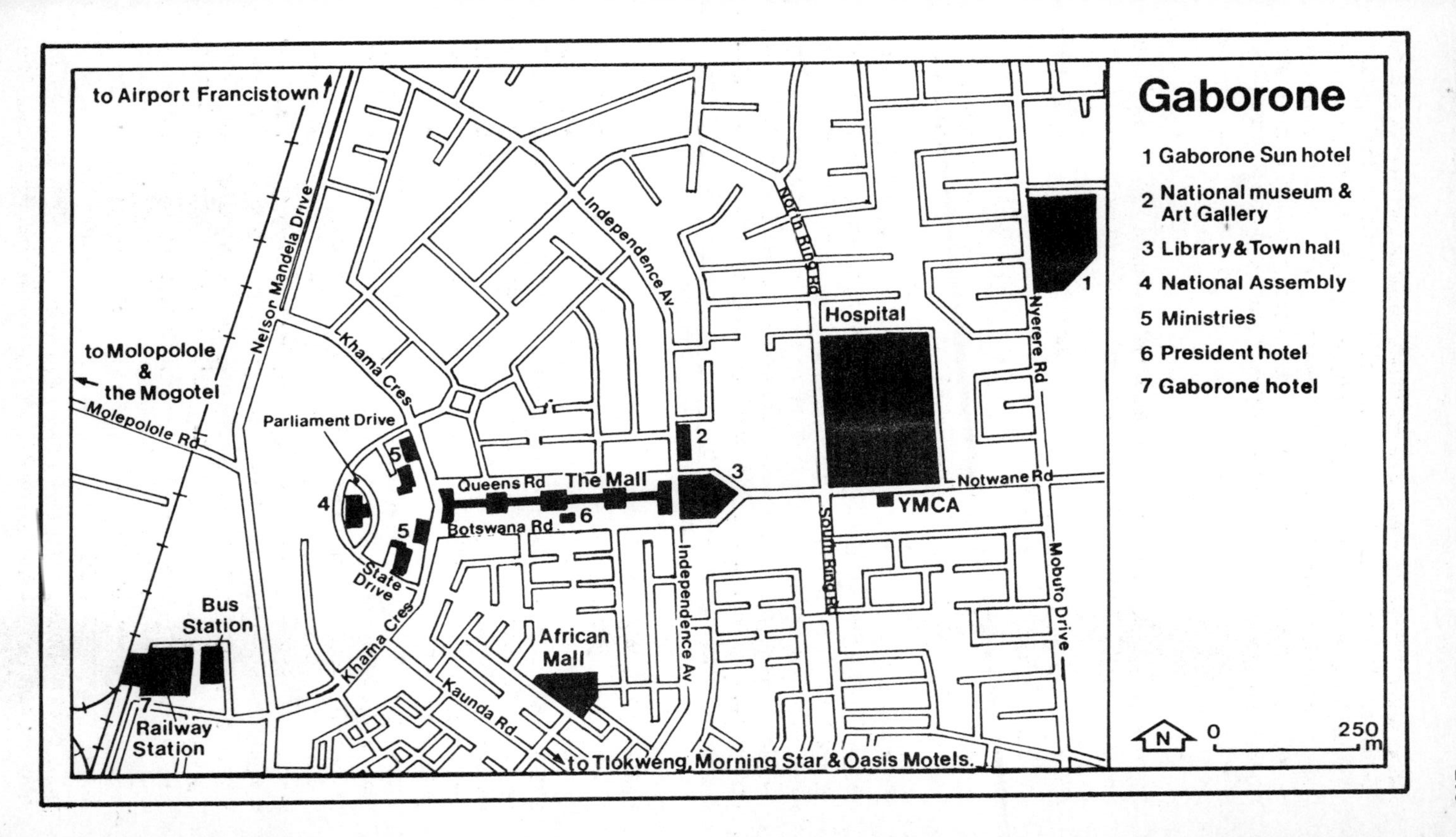
to Airport Francistown
Gaborone
1 Gaborone Sun hotel
2 National museum & Art Gallery
3 Library & Town hall
4 National Assembly
5 Ministries
6 President hotel
7 Gaborone hotel
Nelson Mandela Drive
Independence Av
North Ring Rd
Hospital
Nyerere Rd
to Molopolole & the Mogotel
Molepolole Rd
Khama Cres
Parliament Drive
Queens Rd
The Mall
Notwane Rd
YMCA
Botswana Rd
South Ring Rd
State Drive
Independence Av
Mobuto Drive
Bus Station
Khama Cres
African Mall
Kaunda Rd
Railway Station
to Tlokweng, Morning Star & Oasis Motels.
N
0
250 m

museum has excellent exhibits on the history, geography and peoples of the country, with good displays of craftwork. This is complemented by the small but rich art gallery, with collections of paintings, crafts and sculptures from all of sub-Saharan Africa, as well as Batswanan artists.

Nightlife

The Gaborone Sun hotel has probably the most lively of the hotel bars, with dancing to African and contemporary western sounds. The Oasis disco is reputedly also worth checking out. There are a number of nightclubs and the occasional live performances, but as these are constantly changing it's best to ask around, or check for advertisements in the local press and on roadside banners and posters. Weekends, particularly at month-end (pay day!) are the best times, with performances by visiting artists from neighbouring states. The Capitol Cinema is right in the centre of town on the Mall, with the latest Hollywood releases.

Getting organised and shopping

All the airline offices, travel agents, the post office, main branches of the banks, and shops selling imported goods are situated around the central Mall. The Botswana Book Centre here has an excellent selection. For general food supplies, try the supermarkets in the Mall, or near the station.

Souvenirs The African Mall has shops selling more traditional goods in addition to people selling carvings from Zimbabwe and Zambia in the Mall centre. There's one craft shop — Botswanacraft — in the central Mall, which has a good selection of crafts from around the country. However, prices are greater, and the selection poorer than the craft shops in Maun (baskets) or Ghanzi (Bushmen crafts and ostrich egg jewellery).

Kalahari Conservation Society On the fifth floor of Botsalano House in the Mall. The Society has endless information on the interior, gives occasional lectures, and sells some excellent T-shirts. PO Box 859, Gaborone. Tel: 314259.

Excursions from Gaborone

Near town

Gaborone dam is just outside town and is a good place to relax and watch birds. The two traditional villages of **Odi** and **Mochudi** are 25km and 40km from Gaborone respectively, on the main road to Francistown. Both make worthwhile day trips from the capital, or are worth a slight detour if you're on your way driving north. At Odi, the **Lentswe-la-Odi weavers** co-operative makes distinctive tapestries based on mythological designs and rural scenes. Mochudi is another pretty village, and the capital of the Bakgatla tribe. On a hill above the village, in the buildings of an old school, is the **Phuthadikobo Museum** with an interesting historical and photographic collection on the settlement. There are some amazing textiles and wall-hangings for sale here, made by a local silkscreen workshop.

Further afield

Khutse game reserve is readily accessible from Gaborone with a 4WD, and is popular with city residents over the long-weekends. For full details of this reserve, see the *Central Kalahari* chapter, page 264.

Jwaneng and Orapa diamond mines can be visited, but you have to arrange this in advance with Debswana (De Beers Botswana Mining Company), Botsalano House, The Mall, Gaborone, PO Box 329. Tel: 351131. Mine tours are organised regularly.

FRANCISTOWN

Botswana's second largest town is one of the oldest settlements in the country. Traditionally it had close cultural and trading links with Bulawayo in Zimbabwe before the artificial international boundaries were drawn up. Today, a good tarred road and a railway line links Francistown and Bulawayo which are only three hours away by car. Francistown has a bit of a Zimbabwean feel to it, except for the very well-stocked shops and stores. It's a popular shopping destination for Zimbabweans looking for hard-to-get imported luxuries and spare parts — if they can get their hands on some foreign currency. Francistown's initial prosperity derived from acting as a service town to the gold, copper and nickel mining industry — now overshadowed by the diamond mine at Orapa and the soda ash plant being constructed on Sowa Pan.

Other main roads radiating from Francistown link it with Kasane and Maun in the north and the capital Gaborone in the south, making the town a pleasant and convenient stop-over and a good place to restock and resupply. It's also an excellent place for getting hold of vehicle spares.

Getting there

The town itself is very compact with the railway station at the northern end and the bus station at the southern end — both just a few minutes' walk from the centre. The airport is a few kilometres away, and you'll need to get a taxi — there's no public transport.

Air Air Botswana has recently expanded and there are regular services to and from Gaborone, Maun, Harare, and Windhoek. The Air Botswana office is in the Thapama Lodge on Blue Jacket Street in the centre of town. Tel: 212393.

Train These run daily between Lobatse and Gaborone in the south of the country and Bulawayo in Zimbabwe. (See the national rail timetable in the *In Botswana* chapter, page 203.)

Bus Most run in the morning and when they're full enough! It's best to get to the bus station by 9.00am or try and check the latest times, the day before departure.

Francistown to Gaborone: at least one each day. Francistown to Kasane: Mondays, Wednesdays and Fridays. Francistown to Maun: one each day.

There are also less regular services to Bulawayo and Harare.

Hitching By Botswanan standards, Francistown is easy to hitch to and from. There are always numerous trucks coming in and out of town which may offer you a lift, though you should expect to pay. There are also a significant number of 'aid' workers with vehicles, always a good bet for a fast, free long-distance hitch! If you're hitching on the road to Nata and Maun, it's best to walk out past the airport turn-off to a tree under which locals wait for the buses and trucks.

Where to stay

Francistown has a good range of accommodation, with a choice of two budget hotels, an upmarket hotel, and the delightful Marang Motel just out of town. The campsite at the Marang is a major traveller/overlander stop-over and meeting point, and highly recommended for its pleasant grounds and situation. Alternatively, as in any of the larger towns, asking a taxi driver for 'private accommodation' should find you a cheap and hospitable roof over your head. And if you have a car. you can drive a few kilometres out of town and camp in the bush.

Category B

Marang Motel Situated 4km from the centre of town — head south from the town centre to the main roundabout and take a left turn, the motel is 4km further along past the golf course, on the right. Other than the campsite, the Marang has a number of attractive thatched chalets in amongst the acacia trees and mown lawns which offer good value for money if your budget can stretch to it. These cost from P150, and if you've a group of four you can get a chalet for a total of P170. The *á la carte* restaurant has kept its prices almost the same for three years, serving good food with generous portions. Breakfast is highly recommended at P8. PO Box 807, Francistown. Tel: 213991/2/3.

Marang Motel Campsite The 'in place' for most travellers, it's not hard to see why at only P10 per person, inclusive of use of the swimming pool. The campsite has a beautiful setting near the banks of the Tati river and has a very clean shower/toilet block with hot water. This is a good place to meet other travellers and also look for lifts.

Thapame Lodge Centrally located, near the southern end of town by the roundabout, Thapama Lodge is an unmemorable business hotel, complete with air conditioning and TV's in the rooms. Expect to pay around P110 for a single and P120 for a double, inclusive of breakfast. The 'Sizzlers' cafe bar does reasonable budget burgers. Private Bag 31, Francistown. Tel: 213872.

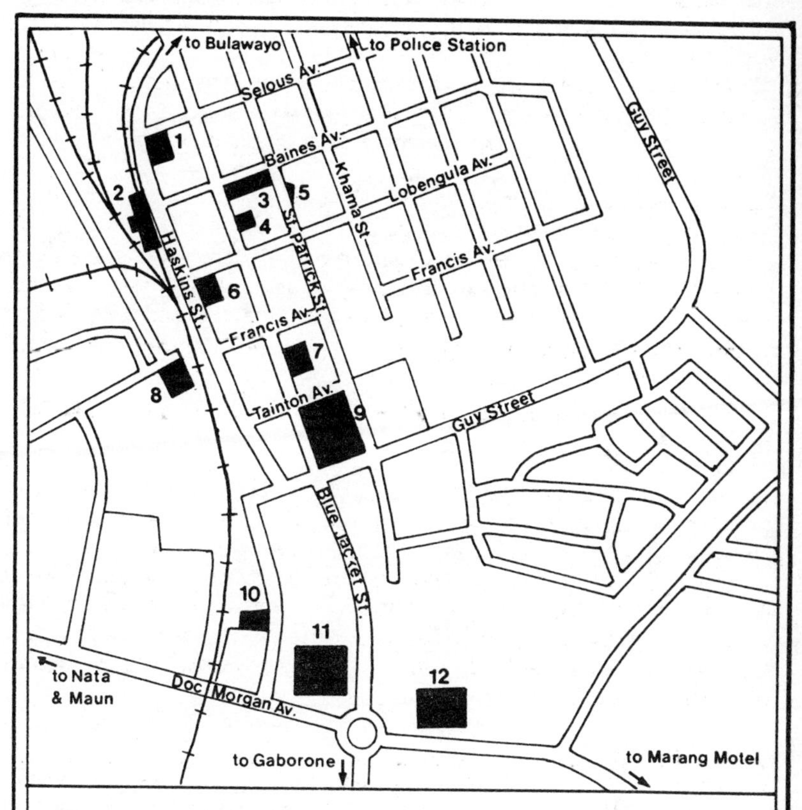

Francistown

1 Grand hotel
2 Railway station
3 Fruit & vegetable market
4 Post office
5 Swimming pool
6 Tati hotel
7 Fairways supermarket
8 BGI Craft shop
9 Mall shopping centre
10 Bus station
11 Thapame Lodge hotel
12 Hospital

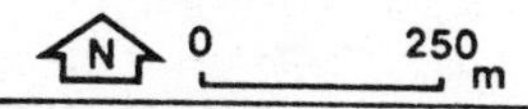

Category C

Grand Hotel In the town centre, opposite the railway station, the Grand is much the same as its competitor, the Tati. It all depends on which rooms happen to be available — some can be a bit dark and run down, whilst others are perfectly reasonable. Singles from P44, doubles P55 with shower. There's a bar with set menu dining room which will serve a simple breakfast for P5. PO Box 30, Francistown. Tel: 212300.

Tati Hotel Like the Grand, this is right in the town centre, on Haskins St. and Lobengula Ave. The Tati Hotel is similarly priced to the Grand and offers roughly the same standard of room. Camping is sometimes permitted in the back garden. PO Box 15, Francistown. Tel: 212321

Where to Eat

There are a number of take-aways in the shopping mall and around the bus station which are reasonable and fairly cheap. Alternatively, there are always women selling *shadza* (maize porridge) and meat, and cooked maize cobs around the vegetable market during the day. If you want to sit down there are a couple of small restaurants:

Ma Kim's A block east of the Grand Hotel on Selous Drive. Ma Kim's serves Chinese and Korean dishes from P7 to P12 for a main course. Quiet and recommended.

Silver Spur Steak House Near the shopping mall on Blue Jacket St. Main courses from P5 to P10

Nightlife

Nighttime activity centres around the hotel bars and the one cinema in town — Cine 2000 — on Blue Jacket Street.

Getting organised and shopping

Fairway's Supermarket in the centre of town carries a good range of most general foods, whilst more specialist camping and dried foods can be obtained in the Mall Shopping Centre. There's also a fruit and vegetable market on Baines Avenue up from the railway station.

Crafts There's one craft shop with a fair selection of goods across the railway line from the Tati Hotel. If you're planning on visiting Maun or Ghanzi, save your money for the excellent craft markets there instead.

Selebi-Phikwe

This is Botswana's third largest town after Gaborone and Francistown — it was built after independence, to support one of the country's main mining centres. Other than being on one of the main routes into the private game reserves of the Tuli Block, there is little to attract the visitor here.

Where to stay

Category A

The one hotel here is the **Bosele** on the outskirts of town — plush and expensive at P110 for a single and P130 for a double. PO Box 177, Selebi-Phikwe. Tel: 810675

Serowe

Serowe is the largest of Botswana's traditional 'villages settlements' (as against purpose-built urban centres) with a population of over 80,000. Serowe has two main claims to fame: it was the birth place of the late Sir Seretse Khama, Botswana's first president; Bessie Head, Botswana's most prominent internationally known writer, made her home here and immortalised the village in her writings. The 'village' is an attractive place to visit for no particular reason other than to experience a traditional Botswanan town.

Where to stay

Category C

A basic and clean place to stay is the **Coop Hotel** run by the Brigades (a local cooperative organisation). It also serves reasonable meals.

TULI BLOCK & MASHATU GAME RESERVE

The Tuli Block and surrounding region in the far east of Botswana, adjacent to the Zimbabwean and South African borders, must be the most underrated part of the country. The landscape is quite different from elsewhere in Botswana, away from the sands of the Kalahari Desert and dominated by large rocky outcrops, hills and valleys. It's exciting game country — the hills and outcrops help viewing and make a change from Botswana's usual flat bush and plains — and is also good for walks and treks.

The Tuli Block itself is mostly white-owned land — a combination of game farms and private game reserves — which forms a long narrow strip next to the South African border. This was once land owned by Rhodes' British South Africa Company and was intended to be used for the building of the railway line. When the plans were changed, the land was sold off to white settlers instead. Outside this strip, there are a relatively large number of interesting and attractive traditional villages. These are worth exploring in their own right if you have your own vehicle or are thinking of some off-the-trail hiking and camping. Basic supplies are available in many of the villages, and the people are very friendly.

Despite being privately owned, some of the reserves have opened up for tourists, and offer the potential of good game viewing for a fraction of the cost of the government national parks and game reserves. Having a car is undoubtedly useful (4WD isn't necessary), but it's possible to explore much

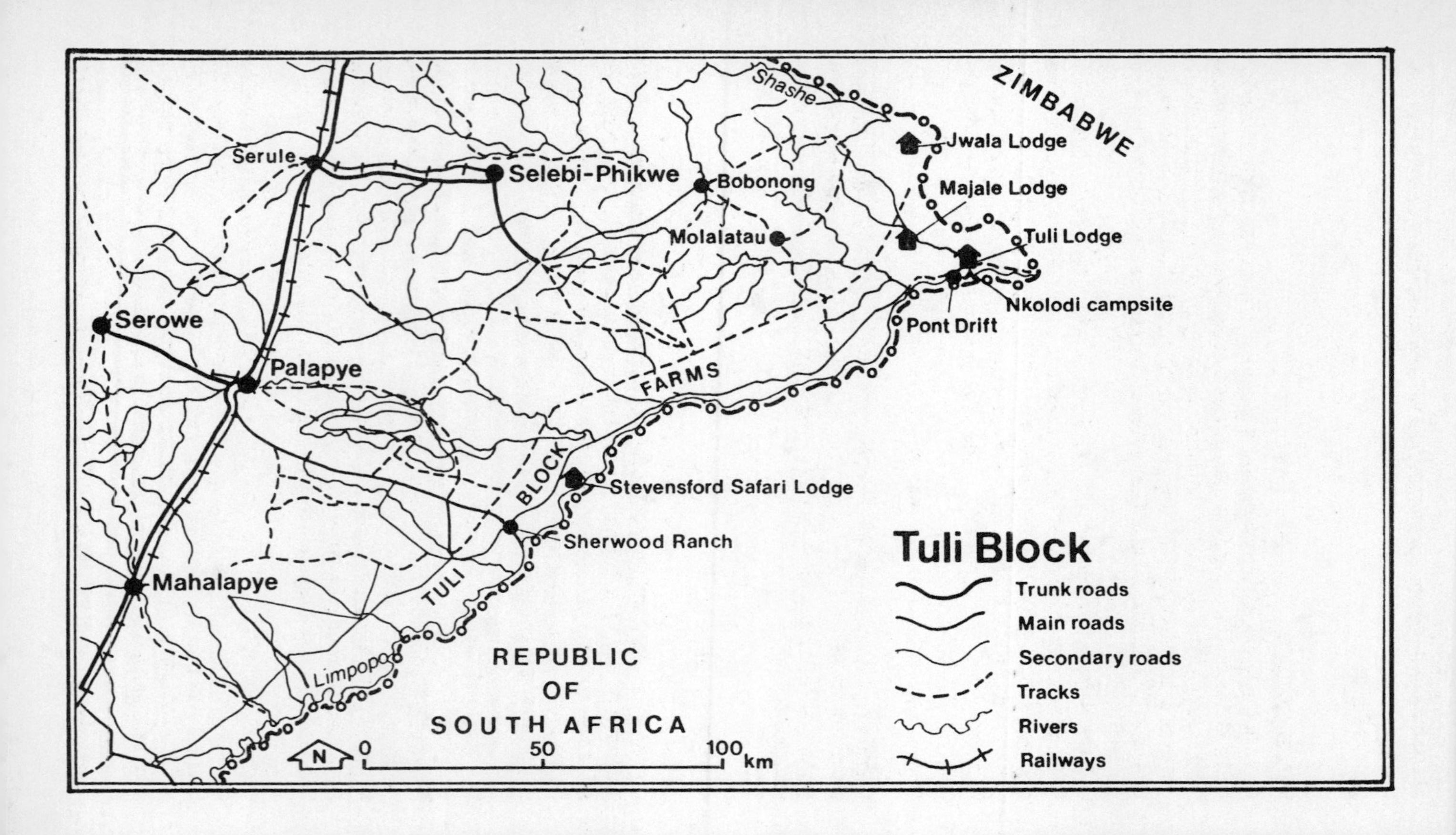
ZIMBABWE
Shashe
Jwala Lodge
Majale Lodge
Tuli Lodge
Nkolodi campsite
Pont Drift
Serule
Selebi-Phikwe
Bobonong
Molalatau
Serowe
Palapye
FARMS
BLOCK
TULI
Stevensford Safari Lodge
Sherwood Ranch
Mahalapye
Limpopo
REPUBLIC
OF
SOUTH AFRICA
N
0
50
100 km
Tuli Block
Trunk roads
Main roads
Secondary roads
Tracks
Rivers
Railways

of the area and visit the game reserves without a vehicle. Most of the private reserves include game drives in their entrance fee, and some also include guided walks.

Getting there

Car In many ways, the reserves and lodges of the Tuli Block are designed more for South African visitors than those from Botswana. Road connections from South Africa are easier than from Botswana and the roads are tarred once across the border in South Africa. Many of the white residents do business and go shopping in South Africa — Johannesburg is only six hours away.

From Botswana, the main route to the Tuli Block follows the Gaborone — Francistown road, turning east on a smaller dirt road just before the town of Palapye, heading toward the border post at Martins Drift. 89km down this you'll reach the crossroads at Sherwood Ranch, at which you should turn left and head north — following the signs to Baines Drift. This will take you past Stevensford Safari Lodge, before eventually leading you to the border crossing at Pont Drift, and the Mashatu Game Reserve area.

Hitching The roads have very little traffic, though there is slightly more on weekends. Hitching is possible, but you might consider going via Selebi-Phikwe and Bobonong. Pont Drift itself is just a border post, there are no facilities.

Where to stay

Of the four lodges in the area, only two — Jwala and Stevensford — could be described as easily affordable for the budget traveller, whilst Majale and Tuli lodges are very much more up-market and expensive. Undoubtedly it's advisable to try to book ahead. The cheapest place to stay is at the newly developed Nokolodi campsite, near Pont Drift. Unofficial camping in any of the private land or reserves in the Tuli Block is not allowed.

Stevensford Game Reserve Stevensford is the easiest of the game reserves to get to, being situated only about 20km north-east of the Sherwood Ranch turn-off on the road to Pont Drift. Here, on the banks of the Limpopo river, accommodation is in thatched self-catering chalets which go for about P50 per person per day. The price includes game drives, horse-riding and use of the bicycles. There are no predators or dangerous game in this reserve — the horse-riding and cycling is quite safe!

Jwala Game Lodge Similar in cost to Stevensford, Jwala has self-catering chalets, and game drives and walks included in the price. The main difference is that Jwala has no boundary fences with the large Mashatu Game Reserve and you're bound to see plenty of big game in the area. The game lodge is some distance north of Pont Drift on the Zimbabwean border.

Majale Lodge and the **Mashatu Game Reserve** This is the largest private 'conservation' area in southern Africa, with a great variety of landscapes and wildlife. It's especially known for its large elephant population. There is no access to the reserve unless you are staying at the lodge or on an organised trek, such as the **Ivory Trail**. This is a five-day organised trek through the Mashatu Game Reserve, strolling from one tented camp to the next. It's organised by Educational Wildlife Expeditions and costs over 500 Rand. Their address is: EWE, PO Box 645, Bedford View, R.S.A. 2008.

The only accommodation in the reserve is the very expensive Majale Lodge, complete with a thatched observation bar overlooking a floodlit waterhole! Access to the reserve and lodge is from Pont Drift.

Tuli Lodge Adjacent to the Mashatu Game Reserve, only 7km west of the border at Pont Drift and near the Limpopo river. Tuli is another plush lodge like Majale, with very impressive gardens and grounds. Even if you can't afford to stay here, it's worth making the slight detour to check out its wonderful bar and swimming pool.

Nokolodi Campsite This is a new development and the only cheap place to stay in the area. The campsite is situated in a beautiful setting on the banks of the Limpopo river, close to Pont Drift, and costs P15 per person per night. Ask for directions at the border post, or at Tuli Lodge.

Mmilili's Day

by Phil Deutschle

Mmilili wakes at 5.30am as his sister, Opha, shouts, 'Mmilili, *muka!* get up!' He shares two blankets on the mud floor with his brother, Knowledge. He pulls on an old shirt and shorts. Then, shivering, he walks out of the compound into the surrounding bush that serves as the family toilet.

Back in the kitchen, he sits by the fire and waits for the water to heat up for washing himself. He carries the basin back to the children's hut and washes his hands and face. He empties the basin into the hedge and trades it in at the kitchen for a cold piece of yesterday's steam bread. Finally, he gets dressed in his blue and grey school uniform and starts off on his three-mile jaunt to school. Before long, he stops to wrench a branch from a thorn-bush. Students are required to bring a stick of firewood to school each day. The bell is rung at seven o'clock. First the classrooms have to be cleaned. Mmilili starts moving the desks to the back, so that the girls can sweep. he knows that he can't get into trouble with the teachers if he's moving desks. At assembly, after a song and a prayer, all the students not wearing full school uniform are told to remain behind. The offenders are going to be beaten.

His class's first subject is Setswana, the national language. Mmilili *hates* Setswana. The teacher calls them names if they can't answer her questions. And no matter how hard you work on an assignment it always comes back with a bad mark on it. Next comes Agriculture, his favourite subject. The teacher, who is from Swaziland, never beats them and they sometimes have a lot of fun in the garden.

Break is over before it really begins. Coming all the way from the garden, they are among the last in line to get their bowl of sweetened milk tea and one thick slice of bread. The last four periods are not so busy. The class still has no Social Studies teacher, whilst in English they are told to go away and 'study hard.' The maths teacher unexpectedly collects the assignment, which Mmilili luckily did during the time they were supposed to have had Social Studies.

Lunch is the highpoint. Tuesday's fare is *samp* (boiled maize kernels) and soup. Mmilili eats with his fingers, washes his bowl and then puts it away in the locker that he shares with Simisani.

He's sitting and rocking on the edge of the open locker door, when the teacher comes in and shouts, 'Is that a chair?' Mmilili jumps up scared, not knowing what to do. The teacher looks down at Mmilili. 'Do you have a chair at home?'

'Yes,' answers Mmilili in a whisper.

'You have a *chair*?'

'No,' stutters Mmilili, too flustered to think. Everyone is looking at him and he just wants to cry. The teacher shakes his head and walks away.

Throughout afternoon studies, Mmilili tries to do his homework, but he is still upset. The schoolwork is hard enough as it is, being all in English or Setswana. He has never seen a single book in his own language, Kalanga.

Sports-time is spent kicking a ball around with the other boys who are not on the soccer team. Supper is a bowl of soft porridge. Evening studies gives him a chance to finally do his work, but he is already dreading the long, dark walk home. The lights of the school are nice, even magic. The school also has water, right in the tap, and bread every day, toilets, and you have your own chair. Not like home.

At 7.30pm the final bell is rung. Mmilili, Jabulani, Filbert, Moses and Simisani start the trek to their homes. They talk loudly to chase away the fear of the dark. The last section, Mmilili has to walk alone.

Opha has saved some *shadza* (maize porridge) for him. Then he crawls under the blankets with Knowledge and quickly shivers himself to sleep.

Chobe & The Great Salt Pans

National Parks & Forest Reserves

1 Kasane F.R.
2 Maikaelelo F.R.
3 Chobe F.R.
4 Chobe
5 Kazuma F.R.
6 Sibuyu F.R.
7 Nxai Pan
8 Makgadikgadi Pans

National border
Trunk roads
Main roads
Secondary roads
Tracks
Rivers

N

0 100 200 km

Chapter 18

Chobe and the Great Salt Pans of the North-East

East of the Okavango Delta and to the north of the central Kalahari, the topography becomes dominated by great flat plains and huge shallow depressions or pans — remnants of ancient lakes which once covered the region. Most of the area is wild and uninhabited, but in contrast to the central Kalahari it does hold some permanent water even in the dry season. At this time of year, huge herds of game migrate to the region from the parched interior of the Kalahari and they only return when the Kalahari's plains are flushed green with the summer's rains. This ancient annual migration rivals the more famous migration between the Serengetti and the Masai Mara in East Africa and despite its decline in recent years, due to the human pressure on the land, it still ensures that you're almost as likely to find game outside the reserves as in them.

To explore most of this area you either need to be self-sufficient with a vehicle, or join an organised safari. Apart from in the northern part of Chobe National Park — which is easily accessible without your own transport — you will need a 4WD to explore the rest of Botswana's premier game park, famed for its huge herds of elephants. To travel through the endless expanse of the Makgadikgadi Pans, you have to be well organised, self-sufficient and experienced in bush driving — though the Makgadikgadi Pans Game Reserve itself is a slightly easier option. Nxai Pan National Park, to the north of Makgadikgadi, is much easier to get to and no less spectacular, being a relatively easy detour from the main Maun-Nata road. Whilst Makgadikgadi holds more game in the dry season, the wildlife at Nxai is most bountiful in the wetter months. Just to the south of Nxai, Kudiakam Pan and Baines' Baobabs offer beautiful camping and scenery outside the national parks, and with no park entrance fees, and easy access from the main road these are well worth a visit.

Apart from Kasane in the far north-east, there is very little settlement and the few villages in the area are almost entirely confined along the lines of the

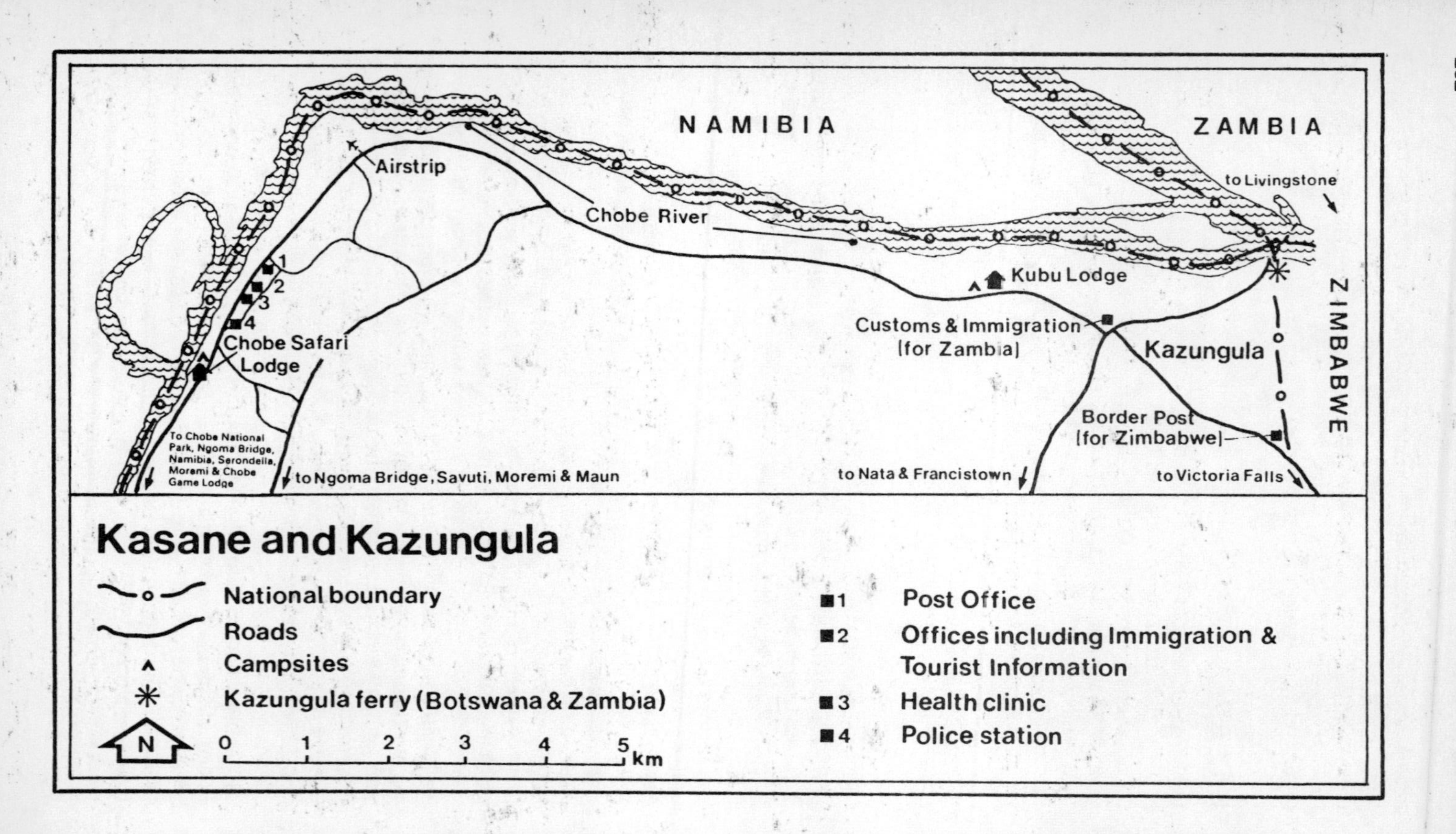
NAMIBIA
ZAMBIA
ZIMBABWE
to Livingstone
Airstrip
Chobe River
Kubu Lodge
Chobe Safari Lodge
Customs & Immigration (for Zambia)
Kazungula
Border Post (for Zimbabwe)
To Chobe National Park, Ngoma Bridge, Namibia, Serondella, Moremi & Chobe Game Lodge
to Ngoma Bridge, Savuti, Moremi & Maun
to Nata & Francistown
to Victoria Falls
Kasane and Kazungula
National boundary
Roads
Campsites
Kazungula ferry (Botswana & Zambia)
N
0 1 2 3 4 5 km
1 Post Office
2 Offices including Immigration & Tourist Information
3 Health clinic
4 Police station

main roads where people rely on passing trade, small scale cattle farming, or subsistence farming from the dry sandy soil. Facilities for visitors are consequently limited — Kasane or Maun are the main base towns for Chobe National Park, whilst a visit to the Nxai-Makgadikgadi Pans area is best organised from Maun again or possibly Francistown to the east.

KASANE

Standing on the Chobe River in the north-east corner of the country, Kasane is a gateway to Namibia's Caprivi Strip, Zimbabwe and Zambia — and a springboard for trips into Chobe National Park. It has several places to stay, garages for vehicle repairs, a few shops for supplies and a most picturesque (if slow and crowded) Barclays bank, operating from a thatched rondavel. Kasane is the probably the best place to stay if you're looking for a hitch into Chobe, or a budget mini-safari.

The tourist information office here is well stocked with brochures and some excellent maps of Chobe, Nxai and the Okavango — it's probably the best place outside of Gaborone for national parks information.

Getting there

From Francistown, Kasane is about 495km of variable tarred road away. Nata, the only fuel stop on the route, is 195km from Francistown and at the junction for the gravel road to Maun. Hitching along here in either direction is easy by Botswanan standards, and with an early start from Francistown you can expect to reach Kasane by nightfall.

From Zimbabwe, there's an excellent tarred road linking Kasane with Victoria Falls, Zimbabwe's biggest tourist attraction and a major centre for travellers. Hitching the 75kms isn't difficult, neither is hiring a car for a few days (see page 47), though the expensive (P90 each way) UTC minibus which shuttles between the two centres every day is an alternative. This calls at all three of Kasane's lodges and UTC's office in Victoria Falls. On the Botswanan side, go to the UTC desk at Chobe Game Lodge (Tel: 250340) to arrange a seat.

To Zambia there's a ferry over the river at nearby Kazungula, 14kms away, but most travellers end up going via Victoria Falls rather than directly across with the ferry since hitching from here to Livingstone is a lot more difficult than from Vic Falls. However, if you do want to give this a go, there are occasionally lorries going all the way. Try standing where the Zimbabwean and Zambian roads fork (hitching on both of them!).

To Namibia, there's a good gravel road — suitable for all vehicles — which is well signposted to Ngoma Bridge, 65kms away. The road cuts inland through Chobe, before heading north over the Chobe River — the border with Namibia. Just before you reach the bridge, you should report to the Botswanan check-point (a few men from the Botswana Defence Force). From the Namibian post in Ngoma, it's 60km to the riverside town of Katima Mulilo in the Caprivi Strip, where most people stop for their first night.

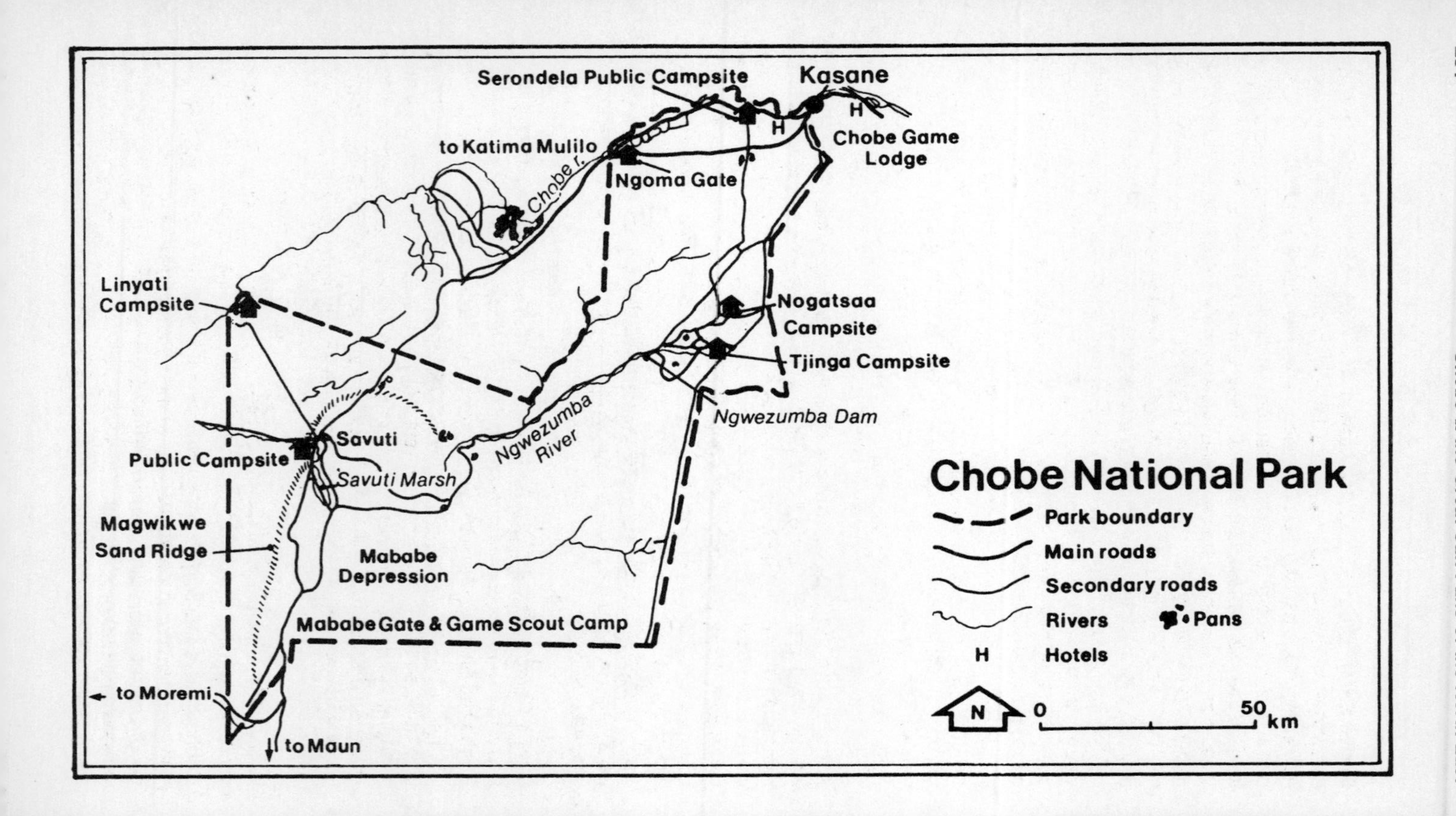
Serondela Public Campsite
Kasane
H
H
Chobe Game Lodge
to Katima Mulilo
Chobe r.
Ngoma Gate
Linyati Campsite
Nogatsaa Campsite
Tjinga Campsite
Ngwezumba Dam
Savuti
Public Campsite
Savuti Marsh
Ngwezumba River
Magwikwe Sand Ridge
Mababe Depression
Mababe Gate & Game Scout Camp
to Moremi
to Maun
Chobe National Park
Park boundary
Main roads
Secondary roads
Rivers
Pans
H
Hotels
N
0
50 km

Where to stay

Chobe Safari Lodge PO Box 10, Kasane. Tel: 250336. Found by the river on the fringes of town as you head for Chobe, this is the original Kasane hotel. Accommodation ranges from camping — with pleasant campsites and fire places along the river at P12 per person per night — to basic chalets (P150 for four people) or private rooms. They serve a range of food and the toasted sandwiches on the bar menu have been recommended whilst the set menu is lousy. Most of the independent backpackers trying to work out a trip into Chobe can be found here, so it's a good place to look for others to form a group if you're planning on hiring a vehicle.

The daily cruises on the river (departing 2.30pm) can give excellent game viewing if you're lucky — especially in the dry season when huge herds of elephant come down to the river to drink — and are lots of fun even if there's no big game around. This costs P20 if you're staying here, P35 otherwise, but you must also pay the park fees for the day of the trip. You're bound to come across hippo and crocs, and the riverside is frequented by one of the region's rarest antelope, the puku — to the uninitiated quite similar to the much more common impala, but lighter in coloration (orange-yellow, paler underneath) and with stouter, more evenly curving horns.

Kubu Lodge PO Box 43, Kasane. Tel: 312 Situated about 10km east of Kasane and just a couple of kilometres from the border crossroads at Kazungula, this is probably the best place to stay if you're planning on an early start to hitch to Nata, Zimbabwe or Zambia. Camping is P5 per person per night on riverside sites that slope steeply in places, and basic A frame chalets are P15 single, P25 double — with outside ablutions. If you don't feel like cooking then there's a great bar, overlooking the river, and a reasonable restaurant. Take a torch as the campsite isn't well lit at night and it's a rough track back from the bar! This is quite a popular stop for overlanders with their own vehicles.

Chobe Game Lodge PO Box 32, Kasane. Tel: 250340. 12km west of Kasane, and within the Park itself is one of Botswana's most famous hotels — Richard Burton and Elizabeth Taylor stayed here during their second honeymoon! The price is high, and you must pay the high park entrance fees for your whole time here, so this is not a place to stay if you care about the cost. It's worth a stop at the bar for a drink, though, or for one of the motorboat trips in late afternoon (P35, depart at 4.30pm) — or perhaps just to marvel at the beautiful lawns and gardens in the middle of the African bush.

CHOBE NATIONAL PARK

4WD, except northern strip by Chobe River, 2WD. Standard entrance fees.

Chobe is fabled as wild country, an expanse of bush and wilderness teeming with game. Whilst the northern part of the park adjoining the Chobe river is becoming increasingly popular with visitors (it is accessible by ordinary vehicles and can gets comparatively crowded during school holidays), the bulk of the park retains its remote mystique and involves some rough 4WD driving between the campsites.

One of the greatest attractions of the park (particularly in the area around the Chobe river itself), are the large herds of elephants. In the afternoons, just before sunset, family groups visit the river banks and afford spectacular viewing and photography. However, do be cautious — the groups mainly consist of mothers with young and they are sensitive to any perceived threat or interference. Stay in your car. Other species include lion, leopard, rhino, hippo, giraffe, eland, zebra, lechwe, puku, tsessebe, waterbuck, Chobe bushbuck, wildebeest, impala, hyena, roan and sable antelope, kudu, warthog, baboons, otter, crocodile, wild dog and many others!

There are four public campsites within the park: Serondela, Tjinga, Savuti and Linyanti. Of these, Serondela can be visited from Kasane with a normal 2WD saloon car, as can the adjacent game viewing drives by the riverside. The other camps require a 4WD vehicle. All require you to be self sufficient in food and fuel, though water is usually available.

Take care Many of the animals local to the camps are very used to humans — and their food and litter! Baboons, elephants, hyenas and even lions can cause major problems for visitors — don't leave anything outside at night and *never* sleep even partially outside a tent. Make sure that your tent is fully zipped up and don't just use mosquito nets for sleeping out under the stars. I tried this at Savuti one night and woke up to find myself face to face with a large hyena. Having scared it off by shouting obscenities at it, I discovered that my mossie net had a number of teeth holes right next to where my head must have been!

Savuti

Savuti, in the heart of Chobe National Park, is one of Botswana's most famous big game areas and has been said to have one of the highest concentrations of game in southern Africa. It is also very beautiful and has an atmosphere all of its own. The key is the mysterious Savuti Channel, which sometimes flows and, inexplicably, sometimes doesn't. The Channel spills out from the Linyanti swamps and, after passing through a gap in the Magwikwe Sand Ridge, spreads out to form the Savuti Marsh, a small area in the Mababe Depression. This grass and bush-covered plain was once the bed of an ancient lake that covered much of northern Botswana and the sand ridge a remnant barrier beach that probably formed the lake's western edge. The Gubatsaa Hills nearby display steep wave-washed cliffs and intriguing rounded pebbles — further evidence of the former lake's existence.

In the early 1850s, when Livingstone arrived here, there was a 'dismal swamp' some 16km long, fed by both the Mababe (now called Khwai) River, which overspilled from the Okavango system, and the 'strongly flowing' Savuti Channel. However, when Selous came in 1879, the swamp and the channel were dry. They remained like this until 1957 when the channel began to flow strongly once again.

This 'water in the desert' seemed permanent and enhanced the area's reputation until, once again, the channel ceased to flow in 1982. Nobody really knows why it stopped, as nobody really understood why it started again after 80 years of dryness. Explanations range from tectonic shifts to changes in the paths used by the Linyanti hippos. Even with the channel dry, Savuti is a classic area with a reputation for lone elephant bulls and lots of lions.

Getting around

To visit Chobe you have a number of options, depending on your budget and whether or not you intend to make the journey all the way through the park to Maun and the Okavango.

Car Undoubtedly, having your own 4WD vehicle is the preferred option and allows you total flexibility to do what you want to do, when you want. On the flip side, Chobe's sandy tracks do require 4WD experience and confidence. The closest places to hire a 4WD are from Kasane, Maun, or Katima Mulilo (Namibia). In Botswana, the charges tend to be high, around P200 per day, whilst in Katima Mulilo the hire isn't on an unlimited mileage basis. For a short one-way rental from Maun, you might consider a chauffeur-driven 4WD from the Island Safari Lodge (see page 251), but you'll pay for the car to return empty — unless you can find people in Kasane and sell the space to them. See chapter 4, *Planning and Preparations*, for details of the cheapest car hire deals.

Organised safari or game drive Without your own vehicle, this is the best option. Short, circular game drives near the riverside leave in the morning and evening from Safari Lodge and Kubu Lodge at around P40. Alternatively, there are quite a few organised safaris which go through the park as part of their overall route. These are mostly along the lines of a short 'overland' type trips — with one or two specially converted vehicles and a fairly rigid itinerary. Typical of these are Afro Ventures, Dragoman, Guerba and Tracks, all of which are large, international and relatively expensive. A more local option would be Okavango Wilderness Safaris which, like the others, is probably best contacted through the agents in either Maun or Victoria Falls. Prices tend to work out at about P100 per day, excluding park fees.

Hitching The only other way to find a vehicle is to hitch on supply trucks or with tourists, but this is strictly for the intrepid. If you're in a position to do a bit of forward planning, it's probably best to approach likely 4WD vehicles in the campsites at Maun or Victoria Falls, offering to share costs for the trip, and giving all parties a chance to get to know each other. On one of our visits, we managed to get a 'hitch' like this from Victoria Falls through Chobe, the Okavango, Nxai, Makgadikgadi and all the way to Francistown!

Where to stay

Serondela The Serondela Campsite is in the very north of the park on the banks of the Chobe River — a few kilometres past the park entrance from Kasane — and has the usual basic ablution facilities. From here, a network of loop roads allows you to explore the surrounding area, from the river floodplains to the *mopane* forest of the interior. This is the area for the huge dry season herds of game which come down to the banks to drink, though don't expect isolation – many of the roads are suitable for 2WD and it can get busy during the holiday periods.

Ngwezumba Pans The Tjinga and Nogatsaa campsites at Ngwezumba Pans lie in an area of small pans surrounded by grassland plains and *mopane* woodlands. These attract herds of elephant and buffalo during and just after the rains, when the animals tend to stay away from the water. Nogatsaa has toilets and showers and is by a dam which has a game viewing hide next to it. Tjinga has no facilities other than a water tank with mechanical pump.

Savuti The public campsite is fairly heavily used, and has toilets, taps and showers. Close by, overlooking the Savuti Channel, there are two luxury bush camps, each costing around P250 per person: Lloyd's Camp, PO Box 37, Maun; and Alan's Camp, bookable through Gametrackers, PO Box 100, Maun. Tel: 260302.

The campsite used to have nightly visits from hyenas which, we discovered, could even carry away a full rucksack at high speed – despite being pursued. Since then the camp has, amazingly, been surrounded by an electrified fence, however at time of writing it had been trampled by elephants, was inoperative, and the hyena were back. *Don't leave anything outside*. Also *don't bring along any citrus fruit* – elephants will find this particularly attractive bounty.

During one visit here we were woken at 5am by people from a neighbouring site driving over to our fire, in search of help and comfort until the morning. They'd been sleeping in the back compartment of their vehicle when, unexpectedly, an elephant had used its tusk as a 'can-opener' to get into the front cab, shattering both the windscreen and their nerves in the process. Foolishly, they'd kept some oranges in there, not knowing of 'Baby Huey' – one of Savuti's bulls – who had developed a liking for citrus fruit. Two days later, the game scouts shot Huey. He had too much of a taste for these forbidden fruits and was becoming a danger – all as a result of being fed by well-meaning tourists.

Linyanti The Linyanti campsite is on the banks of the Linyanti river, looking into Namibia's Caprivi Strip. Like most of the other sites, it has toilet and shower facilities. Since it's off the beaten track, it's not often visited and is ideal for those who want some solitude, though the game concentrations here seldom match up to Savuti's. Linyanti Camp, also run by Gametrackers (address above), offers luxury accommodation and organised game viewing.

Routes through the park

Between Kasane and Savuti, there are two motorable routes through the park. The shortest and most used follows the Chobe River south before crossing the Magwikwe Sand Ridge north of Savuti. Although this route is arguably the more spectacular, it is significantly more difficult and time consuming. To the east, the **Ngwezumba Pans route** provides an alternative route and allows for a stop-over at the Ngwezumba Pans' campsites. The total distance from Kasane to Savuti along this route is 207km and will take from five to six hours.

Nata

Little more than a filling stop for most people, Nata has a garage (complete with handpumps), a basic hotel and the well-stocked 'Sowa Pan Bottle Store' for cool drinks. At the T-junction for the main roads for Kasane, Francistown and Maun, it's a good place to hitch — many vehicles will stop to refuel.

Where to stay

Nata Hotel Basic, but clean and friendly. Prices around P70 a double. If stuck, camping at the hotel is P10.

Nata Lodge Private Bag 10, Francistown. Tel: 611210. About 10km south of Nata, just off the road, lies the Nata Lodge. Here there's a pool, a dining-room, and 3-bed chalets for P150 each — or you can camp for P10 each. For small groups, the manager will organise a trip out to Sowa Pan at about P100 per vehicle. This is the cheapest way to get into one of the Makgadikgadi Pans without your own transport. The lodge is definitely more pleasant than Nata's hotel if you've transport and need somewhere to stay, though it's obviously not such a good hitching spot.

Gweta

Gweta village is a delightful stop on the road between Nata and Maun, and is situated 103km from Nata in a small grove of palm trees. The village is retains a traditional rural atmosphere, whilst at the same time being on a main (tourist) road. It's also excellently situated as a base for exploring the Makgadikgadi and Nxai Pans, with good basic stores and even a vehicle workshop for minor repairs. There is usually fuel available here.

Where to stay

Gweta Rest Camp Budget accommodation in simple thatched rondavels costs around P80 for bed and breakfast. Alternatively, you can camp for P7.50 per person per night. The camp has a reasonable restaurant, and a lively bar. Game drives into the surrounding region can be organised here, if you are travelling without a vehicle.

THE GREAT SALT PANS

The Nxai, Kudiakam and Makgadikgadi Pans are within easy striking distance from the road between Maun and Nata and for those with their own vehicle are one of Botswana's most fascinating areas to explore.

Once submerged beneath warm shallow water, the salt pans are all that's left of one of the world's greatest lakes. It's thought that several million years ago, the whole of the northern Kalahari formed the bed of a huge expanse of fresh water, perhaps stretching as far as the present Okavango delta and the Magwikwe sand ridge. Why it dried out isn't known (though the most popular theory involves the lake's feeder rivers changing course), but as it did the water's mineral salts concentrated in the remaining pools where the lake was deepest. When finally dry, the salts inhibited plants from growing on the clay bottom and so allowed the wind to scour the dusty pans making them still deeper and exposing great expanses of salty grey clay. Adjacent to the pans themselves are large areas of grasslands, in which small depressions have accumulated deposits of wind-blown detritus. These 'islands' of richer soil support trees and other plants and are a fascinating place to sit and just watch the local fauna.

In the dry season from April to October, Makgadikgadi is the best area for game viewing, whilst during the rains from November to March, the animals migrate northwards to the Nxai and Kudiakam Pans area. Other than this the choice of which area to visit will probably depend on the time available — Nxai and Kudiakam are much smaller and more self-contained than Makgadikgadi — and the fact that Nxai Pan has camping facilities. However bear in mind that whereas Nxai has the normal park fees, Makgadikgadi and the Kudiakam Pans area are free.

Makgadikgadi Pans

4WD. No entrance fees.

The Sowa and Ntwetwe Pans that comprise Makgadikgadi cover 12,000 square kilometres to the south of the Nata-Maun road. There are no landmarks for the most part, and so you're left to use the flat, distant horizon as your only line of reference — and even that dissolves into a haze of shimmering mirages in the heat of the afternoon sun. It is only during the rains that the area comes to life, with huge migrating herds of zebra, wildebeest, and occasionally (if the pans fill with water) millions of flamingos. The occasional isolated outcrops of rock in and around the pans add to the sense of mystery, as well as giving an excellent vantage point to view the endless expanse of silver, grey and blue.

If you're exploring the area in a 4WD, you are recommended to have a look at the *Visitor's Guide to Botswana* by Main and Fowkes (see Bibliography), which has excellent detailed sections on the various tracks and routes.

Kubu 'Island' (Sowa Pan).

This is the best known of the isolated rock outcrops in the south-west corner of Sowa Pan. Although the rocks only rise about 10m above the pan floor, the view and general atmosphere is breath-taking — don't miss out on a sunset. The 'island' is also host to a number of ancient and extremely picturesque baobabs, as well as the remains of human settlement. Sometime between 500 and 1600 AD people lived here! Kubu Island is a magic place to visit and highly recommended.

Getting there To get to Kubu Island take the track south from the Nata-Maun road, 16km west of Nata and follow this south for about 100km between Sowa Pan and Ntwetwe Pan. An alternative route is to head north from the Francistown-Orapa road at the turn-off next to Mmatshumo village.

Warning Avoid driving on the deceptive pan surfaces. Although they may look solid and hard, treacherous mud is often lurking just below the surface!

Makgadikgadi Game Reserve

4WD advised, high-clearance 2WD OK away from pans in dry season. Standard entrance fees.

The north-western corner of the Pans, to the east of the Boteti river and south of the road, has been designated as the Makgadikgadi Game Reserve, to give the area some protection from the cattle which now graze most of Sowa Pan. The area has no facilities, no fences and few game scouts — but it does have a network readily distinguishable tracks which, in the dry season, can mostly be negotiated by a high-clearance 2WD vehicle. A good map and compass is recommended for exploring the area and you must be totally self-sufficient in everything, including water and firewood.

Getting there

Since none of the tracks in the reserve are signposted, entry into the area is a bit arbitrary. However a major north-south route through the reserve starts in the north, about 150km from Nata (154km from Maun) on the Nata-Maun road, and ends in the south 105km later, roughly 17km west of Mopipi, near a small group of huts and a cairn of whitewashed stones. The turn off point from the Nata-Maun road is indicated by a fairly new thatched lodge manned by game scouts.

A map of the area is currently being produced and campsites are being marked out, so ask the scouts at the lodge for the latest information regarding camp sites and roads, as well as game movements.

Kudiakam Pan and Baines' Baobabs

4WD only. No entrance fees.

Sandwiched between Nxai Pan and the main road, Kudiakam is the largest of an interesting complex of pans lying in sparse bushland that appears to continue for ever. The game here doesn't usually match Nxai's (see below), the main attraction is an extraordinary group of trees known as 'Baines' Baobabs', which stand at a spectacular site on the eastern edge of the pan. They were immortalised in a painting by Thomas Baines who came here in May 1862 with James Chapman and wrote:

> 'A long circuit brought me, with empty pouch, to the clump of baobabs we had seen yesterday from the wagon; five full-sized trees and two or three younger ones were standing, so that when in leaf their foliage must form one magnificent shade. One gigantic trunk had fallen and lay prostrate but still, losing none of its vitality, sent forth branches and young leaves like the rest...The general colour

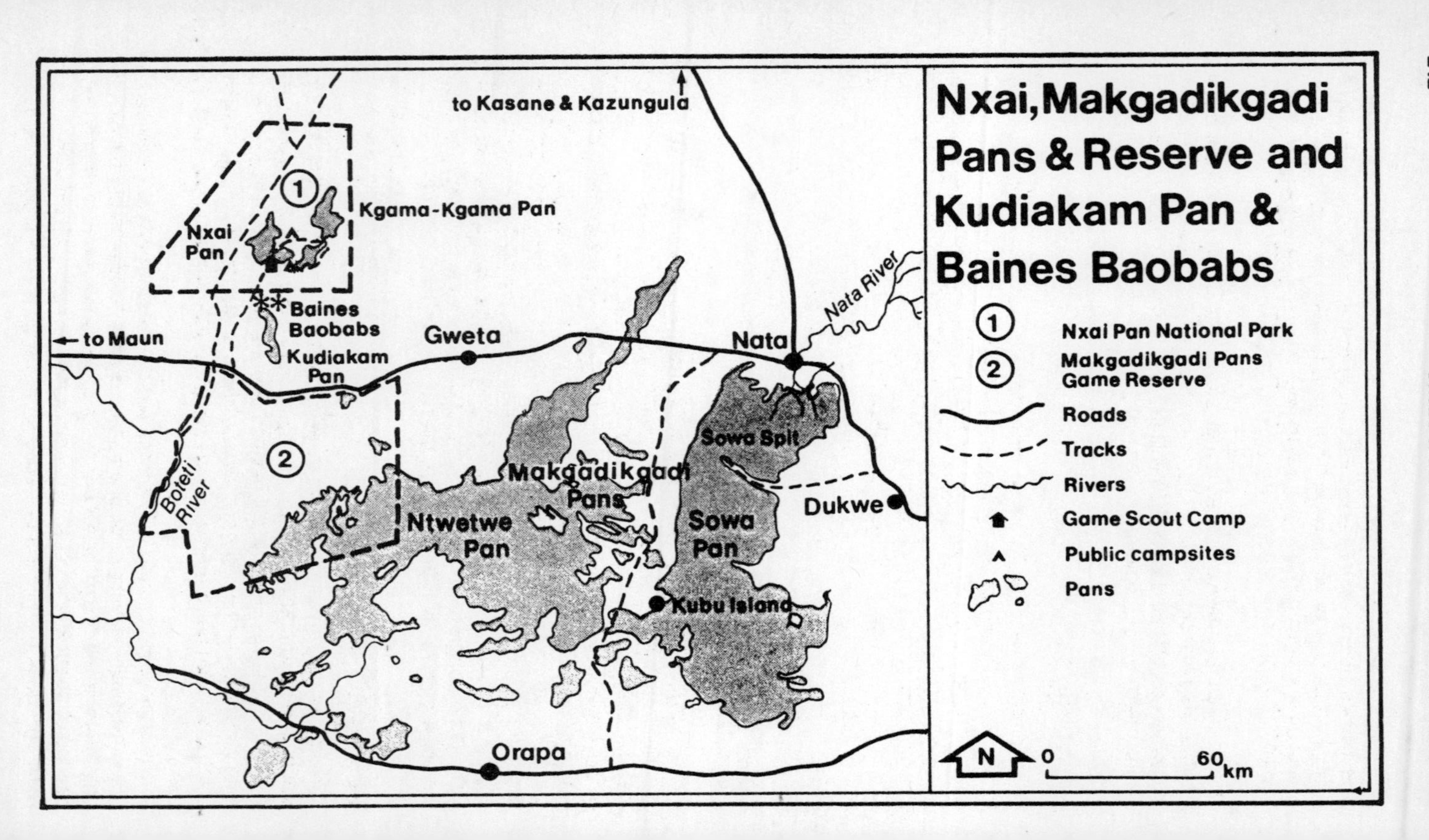

Nxai, Makgadikgadi Pans & Reserve and Kudiakam Pan & Baines Baobabs
1 Nxai Pan National Park
2 Makgadikgadi Pans Game Reserve
Roads
Tracks
Rivers
Game Scout Camp
Public campsites
Pans
N
0
60 km
to Kasane & Kazungula
Kgama-Kgama Pan
Nxai Pan
Baines Baobabs
Kudiakam Pan
to Maun
Boteti River
Gweta
Ntwetwe Pan
Makgadikgadi Pans
Nata
Nata River
Sowa Spit
Sowa Pan
Kubu Island
Dukwe
Orapa

> of the immense stems was grey and rough: but where the old bark had peeled and curled off, the new (of that peculiar metallic coppery-looking red and yellow which Dr Livingstone was wont so strenuously to object in my pictures) shone through over large portions, giving them, according to light or shade, a red or yellow, grey or a deep purple tone."

The baobabs themselves have changed very little since they were painted and that 'magnificent shade' is still marvellous to camp under — if you don't mind the complete absence of facilities. The night sky here is one of the clearest that I've ever seen.

Getting there

To reach them, take the Nxai turn-off on the main road and follow the track for about 17km before turning right at a crossroads. In just under a kilometre the road forks, with the right leading through the pans directly to the trees (about 11km) — though during the early months of the year this is often impassable and shouldn't be attempted. If you take the left fork the route is longer. Skirt around the north of the pans and follow the 'Old Maun Road'. About 13km after the fork, take a right turn and continue for about a further 4km.

Nxai Pan National Park

4WD only. Standard entrance fees.

About 30km north of the Nata-Maun road lies the smallest of Botswana's National Parks, Nxai Pan. The park covers about 2,100 square kilometres of the northern Kalahari wilderness and is based around three pans, two of which usually flood after good rains. We visited it just after the wet season and the game was spectacular with large numbers of giraffe, springbok, gemsbok and zebra. The wide open grasslands, dotted with occasional groups of trees, is said to be ideal for cheetah, though we have never seen any here. From November to April, while the grasslands are still moist and lush, game congregates here, though after that it tends to disappear leaving the place apparently lifeless during the hot, dry months.

Getting there

Turn off the main Nata-Maun road about 171km from Nata (134km from Maun) and head north along the sandy track for about 35km until you reach the park entrance where you'll have to pay the usual entrance fees. From here it's only a few kilometres to either of the two campsites — the one on the south of the pan has a more pleasant situation and hence tends to be slightly busier.

The tracks lead around and across Nxai, Kgama-Kgama and the central (unnamed) pan, leaving most of the park as a wilderness through which the only route is the 'Old Cattle Trek to Pandamatenga' from north-east on a bearing of about 30 degrees, passing around 2km from the western edge of Nxai. This track disappears in places so if you decide to explore, beware.

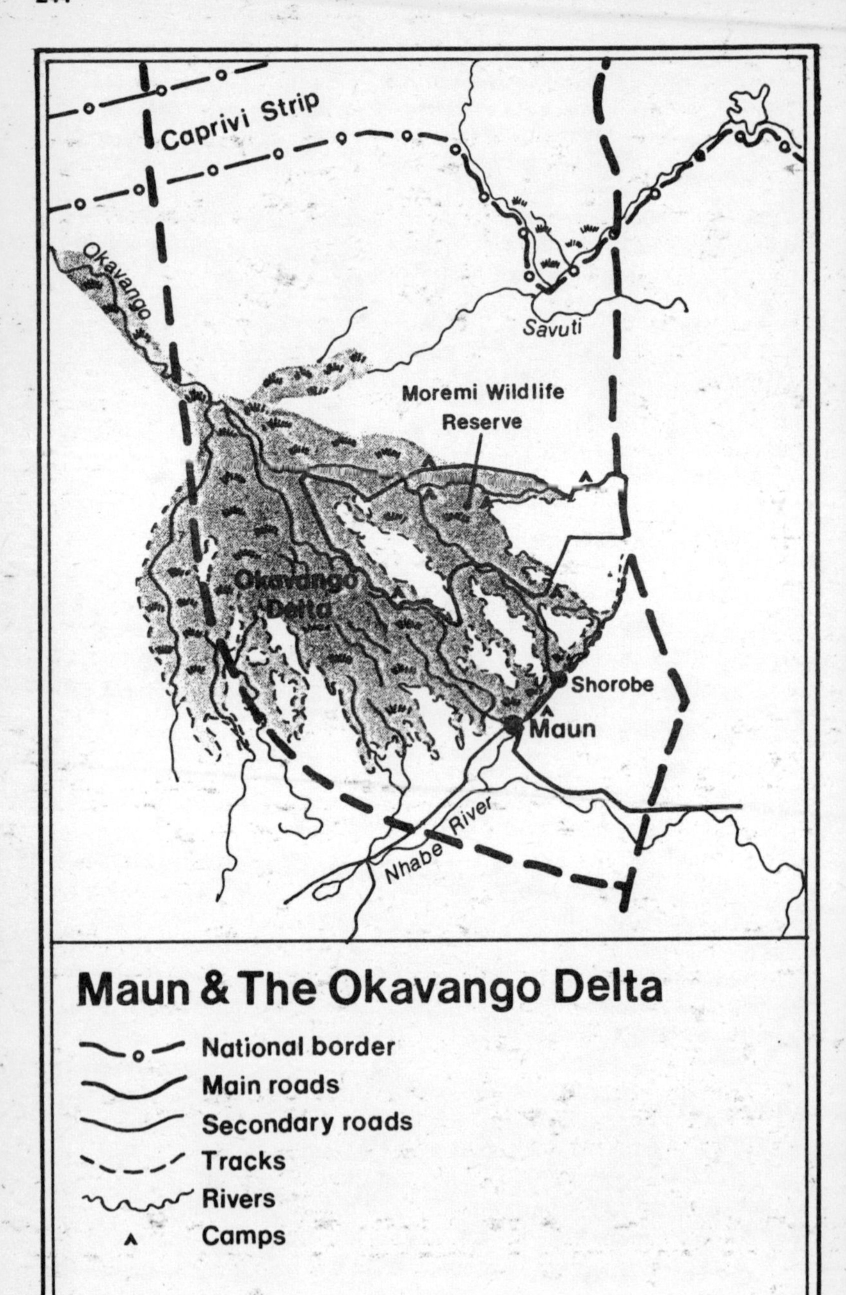
Caprivi Strip
Okavango
Savuti
Moremi Wildlife Reserve
Okavango Delta
Shorobe
Maun
Nhabe River
Maun & The Okavango Delta
National border
Main roads
Secondary roads
Tracks
Rivers
Camps
N
0
50
100
km

Chapter 19

Maun and the Okavango Delta

From its source in the highlands of Angola, the Okavango River flows south-west across Namibia's Caprivi Strip and into the sands of the northern Kalahari. Here it spreads out, forming a unique inland delta — 12,000km² of water wilderness, dotted with islands and laced with a maze of channels.

It's an unusual and highly relaxing environment, where you can glide silently along in a dugout canoe (*mokoro*) through a maze of reeds, watch the wildlife at eye level and soak up the sun. Beneath you, the crystal clear water reveals a myriad of fishes and aquatic animals and plants. It's like floating across a huge fish tank — complete with terrapins and the occasional crocodile or hippo! Some of the larger islands within the Delta are rich with game, so stalking around these with an experienced guide is fascinating. However you'll be disappointed if you come here for a water-based big-game safari. Just take your time, savour the tranquillity, and open yourself up to the white and yellow lilies and the very deep blue sky. The Okavango is a special environment simply to experience.

Centuries ago, the Delta was home to a group of Bushmen, the Banoka, who were displaced by Hambukushu, Bayei and later Batswana tribespeople. At present, the scattered villages are mostly inhabited by Batswana, who keep cattle, though there are still some Hambukushu left. They live deeper within the Delta and rely more on fishing. Many families now seek extra income, by working outside the Delta (some in the mines of South Africa), hunting or even basket weaving.

In response to growing environmental threats, part of the Delta has been included in the Moremi Wildlife Reserve — a fully protected area which joins on to Chobe National Park's south-western boundary. The permits to visit this section of the Delta are, as with Botswana's other parks, expensive. However, the rest of the Delta area is free and the centre is still full of wildlife both inside and outside the park.

Visiting The Delta

The Okavango is by far and away the most popular tourist destination in Botswana and the good range of accommodation and other facilities available at most budgets reflects this. It's possible to spend a fortune here, but equally it's possible to visit the Okavango for a reasonable amount — you don't need a vehicle and you can avoid the park fees by keeping to parts of the Delta which are outside Moremi.

When to go

There isn't one ideal time to visit the Delta. It depends upon which part of it you're going to, what you want to see, and how tolerant you are of the heat.

Because of its immense size, the flood of water coming with the rainy season (November — March) usually takes about six months to get through the delta system — entering the panhandle by Shakawe between February and April, and peaking in the lower delta, near Maun, during the height of the dry season, around September. When the water levels are low, the fishing tends to be better, but higher water does mean less land area and so the game becomes more concentrated and easier to find. The game concentrations are notoriously variable, but from September until the start of December is usually the best time to catch the migrating animals which come to escape the parched lands to the east.

The climate is best around April/May and August/September. June and July can be quite cold, whilst October and November are very hot. December to March brings the rains — some of the camps shut down during January and February, which sometimes makes accommodation difficult to find within the Delta, but less tourists may mean bargain rates at camps which stay open. For the ornithologists, the migrants from the Northern hemisphere visit from October to January, adding extra interest to an already rich birdlife.

Getting Around

The main choice here is whether to use a camp within the Delta as a base for day trips, or go on a long *mokoro* trip with all your food and equipment in the canoe.

Base camp Using a base camp is more expensive, though also more comfortable — with a prepared meal and a bed waiting for you at the end of a long day. You'll transfer to the camp by motorboat or plane (an experience in itself!), and then, depending on the camp, activities might include safaris by 4WD and/or on foot, fishing sorties and *mokoro* trips. Typically everything will be included in the price, and if your time is more limited than your budget then this is the way to go.

Mokoro trip If you're not using a camp then you'll probably aim to spend your days being poled by a guide through the waterways, finding small islands on which to sleep each night. This is cheaper and certainly makes you feel more in touch with nature, but its lack of comfort isn't for everyone.

Making your choice

Arriving in Maun, you'll be faced with a perplexing choice of operators and options for this type of trip, most of whom are based in lodges near Maun on the Thamalakane River — the south-eastern limit of the Delta. Several offer transfers, by vehicle or motorboat, to launch sites deeper within the Delta, though for this you'll normally pay a transfer fee.

Some will offer to pole you by *mokoro* straight from their camps near Maun. This avoids the transport costs, but it can take several days to get through the outer, less interesting reedbeds and reach some of the wilder parts of the Delta beyond the buffalo fence (which stops the cattle from going any further in). You really need at least a week to visit this way.

It's worth basing yourself at one of the lodges in Maun for a few days while you look into all the offers, which seem to change constantly. There are still people who will charge you dearly for a couple of days in the fringes of the swamps — where you'll see little but reeds — so don't be afraid to ask exactly what you get for your money.

Ask about the polers. If you're not conversant in Setswana, are English-speaking polers available? Quite apart from an interest in talking to, and learning from, your guide, people often complain that without a common language they're at the mercy of a poler, with little choice over where, when, or for how long they stop or what they do.

Are wooden dugouts (*mokoros*) or fibreglass canoes used? While *mokoros* are undoubtedly more photogenic and fine for shorter trips, canoes are more stable and have more room — important for storing food and kit on longer trips.

Ask around for the best deals and consider joining up with others to form a group. This can sometimes make transport cheaper and give you more bargaining power. *But* the bottom line is that the Delta's no longer really cheap, so if you're only going to visit it once you might as well do it properly without unduly skimping on the cost.

Draining the Okavango

Edited from an article by Damien Lewis

The Okavango Delta, the last unspoilt wetland in southern Africa, has long been the subject of numerous World Heritage proposals to give it international recognition and protection, but to no avail. Within the Delta there is only one small protected area — the Moremi Game Reserve — which, like much of the Delta, has recently become the subject of 'general management and development plans to raise increased tourist revenue', says Alison Ross, of Greenpeace UK. But the numerous plans to harness the waters of the Delta for industrial and agricultural purposes pose a much more serious threat to the Delta ecosystem. The most recent — the *Southern Okavango Integrated Water Development Project* (SOIWD) — may signal the beginning of the end for the Okavango Delta.

SOIWD was launched in 1985 as part of Botswana's new drive towards food self-sufficiency. It called for the harnessing of the Okavango Delta's waters to irrigate 10,000 square kilometres of land and supply water to the nearby town of Maun, the regional capital and a major tourist centre. This involved raising the outflow of the Delta by dredging 42 kilometres of the Boro River — the main channel through the Delta — and building a series of dams along the its southern fringe. The other main (but understated) aim of SOIWD was to increase the water supply to the Orapa diamond mine — one of the World's richest — 250 kilometres south-east of Maun in the central Kalahari Desert. The Orapa mine — run as a joint venture between the South African mining giant De Beers and the Botswanan government — produces the majority of Botswana's diamonds which account for three-quarters of the country's Gross National Product. By the year 2,000, the Orapa mine is projected to require over twice as much water as it does today for diamond production.

SOIWD has received a mixed reception. Its most enthusiastic exponent — after the Botswanan government — is the Australian-based Snowy Mountain Engineering Corporation (SMEC), the project consultants. But in light of the controversy SOIWD has provoked, even they admit to their limited understanding of the Okavango Delta and their inability fully to predict the effects of draining the Delta. Others — anticipating the storm of protest SOIWD has caused — have divorced themselves from the project. The German aid agency KFW, which funds various water projects in Botswana, have withdrawn funding on environmental, social and developmental grounds.

Although SOIWD would nominally only affect 250 square kilometres directly, or 1% of Okavango's area, critics such as Greenpeace believe it may have much wider effects on the complex Delta ecosystem, which they argue is very vulnerable to outside interference. The 'inherent unpredictability of the Delta...lack of knowledge and shortage of data' are all aspects which the SOIWD scheme fails to take into consideration. Greenpeace have accused SMEC of using inaccurate and insufficient data in their planing of the project. They believe that the SOIWD project threatens the integrity of 'the whole fragile and exceptional delta ecosystem'. As a result of the dredging of the Boro River — the most serious of the proposed works — they predict a general drying of the delta and reduced permanent water levels as the floodplain is disrupted and flooding severely limited.

The proposed benefits of SOIWD have also been questioned by Greenpeace. Local water demand could be met by reservoirs which would not require dredging of the Boro or draining the Delta. Recent studies show that the irrigation potential originally put at 10,000 hectares by SOIWD, is in fact less than 1,300 hectares and will need to be a high-technology, high-input affair. The soils in the region are very poor and require large inputs of fertilisers and pesticides. Mechanised irrigation, using high levels of chemicals in the immediate vicinity of a fragile delta, is an ecologically reckless and impractical way to increase food production, especially when low-tech, sustainable methods have not been considered. Alternative sources of water for the Orapa mine — ground-water or 'dry-processing' — have been identified but are not being considered due to the costs involved.

There is another, contributing factor pushing SOIWD towards completion. Beef represents the second largest export earner after diamonds, and the cattle owners are also a powerful lobby in Botswana. Draining Okavango would release large amounts of land for ranching and boost the profits made by beef exports to the European Community. As inconceivable as an 'Okavango cattle ranch' may seem, other factors — such as the pesticide spraying programme in the Okavango Delta against the tsetse fly (the carrier of sleeping sickness and a major threat to cattle) — reflect the priority already given to cattle over wildlife and the environment in Botswana.

Opposition amongst the local people to SOIWD is strong; most feel it is wrong to interfere with a complex living system that no-one understands. Okavango residents fear that SOIWD will devastate their livelihood — presently based on small-scale agriculture and a world-famous tourist industry. Their concerns are echoed by tour operators, who bring over 30,000 tourists to the Okavango each year to view its unique wildlife and ecology. At a recent meeting with the Minister of Water in Maun, they asked 'What will happen to us if the water dies?' These people have added their voices to the wave of international protest, headed by Greenpeace's threatened campaign — 'Diamonds are for Death'.

All this has won a stay of execution for Okavango. But for how long? Shortly after Greenpeace's February 1990 visit to the region, the Botswanan Government pledged to review SOIWD. Yet, 'rather than being a total review of the project', says Alison Ross, 'this simply means re-consulting the people on the ground, not examining environment-friendly options. Okavango is still not being seen as sacrosanct'. Bearing in mind the efficacy of attacks on the ivory and fur trade, Botswana would have much more to lose from a successful 'Diamonds are for Death' campaign than the Orapa mine would gain by exploiting the Okavango Delta's waters.

The Botswanan government also risks losing one of its greatest potential income earners. Responsible tourist development in the Okavango, coupled with sensitive protection measures, could both preserve Botswana's precious natural heritage and boost foreign exchange earnings. At present, Greenpeace is calling for World Heritage nomination for the Okavango Delta; with the Government's help they could succeed and the Okavango Delta remain the Jewel of The Kalahari for all humankind.

MAUN

This dusty, sprawling town in Botswana's wild west has been the start of expeditions to the north and west since the turn of the century, and it is now the safari capital of the country. It's elongated centre is dotted with modern shops and offices, while its suburbs are mainly traditionally built, thatched rondavels. Everywhere and everything seems geared towards the bonanza that tourism has brought, though some of its rough-and-ready frontier feel has been retained — contemporary cowboys ride into town for their supplies in battered 4WDs, and potholed, dusty roads are everywhere except for 5km of sealed road through the very middle.

This is the place from where to organise your delta trip and buy supplies. There are banks, including a Barclays and Standard Chartered, garages, supermarkets, and several tour agents for the camps in the Delta.

Getting there

Air Maun is well connected by Air Botswana flights: Gaborone and Victoria Falls (Wednesdays, Fridays and Sundays); Johannesburg (Wednesdays and Sundays); Francistown (Wednesdays and Saturdays); Ghanzi (Mondays, Wednesdays and Sundays) and Windhoek (Sundays).

Bus Daily Buses run from Francistown to Maun via Nata in the mornings.

Car Although the Nata to Maun road is (as yet) untarred, it's nevertheless quite fast and suitable for ordinary 2WD vehicles. The road from Ghanzi is a different matter and shouldn't be attempted without a 4WD or, at a pinch, a high-clearance 2WD. The route from Kasane through Chobe National Park is only for those with time and a 4WD.

Hitching Hitching to Maun via Nata from Kasane or Francistown in a day is not difficult and usually a good deal faster than the bus. Hitching to or from Ghanzi is rather more difficult and may require quite a wait. Hitching to or from Kasane through Chobe is only really feasible with a pre-arranged lift.

Where to stay

The only accommodation in the centre of town is **Riley's Hotel** PO Box 1, Maun. Tel: 260204. (The many lodges are all a bit out of town — see below.) This famous old establishment was founded by Harry Riley and is now part of the Cresta chain of up-market hotels. As the only hotel it's expensive, at about P180 for a single, P200 for a double — though the rooms are air conditioned and good.*

Where to eat

Even if you're not staying at Riley's Hotel, the posh restaurant has omelettes for P8 and an 'all you can eat' curry and salad bar for P14 — whilst the bar by the pool is a cool place to escape when the heat gets too much. There are also a few take-aways behind Barclays, or for a strangely English atmosphere the *Duck Inn pub*, just before the airport on the right, is a favourite watering hole for many of the safari guides and residents. It serves drinks, a good basket meal for P8 or hamburger and chips for P7.50. Many of the lodges serve food, though you'll need transport to get there.

Getting organised

Supplies Of the two supermarkets, Maun Fresh Produce, on the south side of the main street, is the better — with most things available, including dairy produce, fresh fruit and vegetables (which can look the worse for wear by the time they reach here). The other, larger supermarket is set back in the shopping mall behind Barclays Bank, to the east of the 'Ice Man' who supplies ice (for cool boxes).

Camping Equipment Also in town, next to Avis by the airport, you'll find Kalahari Kanvas who hire out camping kits (for a minimum of five days) and offer a repair service for overlander's tents. A full kit for one person costs about P14 per day, including a backpack, sleeping bag, tent, cooking pots and cutlery.

Booking agencies There are two main tour agencies here — Bonadventure and OTS by the airport (Okavango Tours and Safaris, PO Box 39, Maun. Tel: 260220) — both of which are very well advertised. In theory, they're both booking agents for any of the camps, though in practice the owner of OTS also runs Delta Camp and Oddballs — and hence OTS will get marginally better deals and encourage you to book with one of these camps.

* *1991 exchange rates: £1=P3.30, US$1-P2.00*

Car hire For renting vehicles, the Avis office is next to Merlin Services, by the airport.

Aircraft charter Hiring a light aircraft could be a cheap way to reach Savuti (see page 238) or the Tsodilo Hills (see page 276), and in the off season — from December to the end of March — you might strike a good bargain. There are several private companies around the airport — the largest is Air Kavango, next to the Duck Inn — who normally charge about P600 per hour (or P2.80 per kilometre), for a five-seater plane.

Maun's Lodges and Camps

These are spread out along the Thamalakane River, individually set back off the road and several kilometres from the centre. To get there, hitching is fairly easy and most will arrange transport in and out of town or the airport (for a price) if you're having trouble — just ask one of the booking agents to ring the camp of your choice.

Island Safari Lodge PO Box 16, Maun. Tel: 260300. The lodge is positioned 14 km north of Maun on the northern bank of the river, 3km in from the main road north of Maun. It's well established, with brick bungalows for P80 single and P95 double, though at P7.50 per person most people prefer to camp on the rambling site by the river. Breakfast is P9, a three course meal P20, and there's a bar and mini-cinema here and also a private cheetah enclosure!

The lodge employs its own polers (none speaks English) and has canoes stationed in the Delta by the buffalo fence, costing P35 per day for a two-seater, and P40 for a three-seater. Return transport to the canoes, by 4WD and/or motorboat, is P75 per person.

Their chauffeur-driven vehicle hire is about as cheap as you can get at P190 per day, excluding fuel but including a driver and 100km free — thereafter it's 75 thebe per kilometre.

Kubu Camp PO Box 482, Maun. Tel: 260307. This is the closest camp to Maun (13km), fairly new with a small camping site (P5 per person) and lots of reed screens for fences. Unfortunately, it's often difficult to find anyone here to help and since it's only a campsite, you'll have to go elsewhere to eat and drink. If the Thamalakane River is dry, then Island Safari Lodge isn't far away, just across the other side. Beware of accidentally climbing over the Lodge's fence into the cheetah enclosure, rather than the restaurant area, as we did!

Crocodile Camp PO Box 46, Maun. Tel: 260265. Perhaps serving the best food in the region, Croc camp is small and well organised with camping for P5 and very pleasant chalets for P65 single, P75 double. A full breakfast costs P10 (continental P8), while for a real treat dinner is P25.

You can hire canoes or *mokoros* from here for P30 per day, though they're stationed at the camp itself which is about two days pole (plus two to return) from the buffalo fence. Don't be tempted to take a canoe from here for just three or four days, as you'll see little but reeds. That said, it is a good base

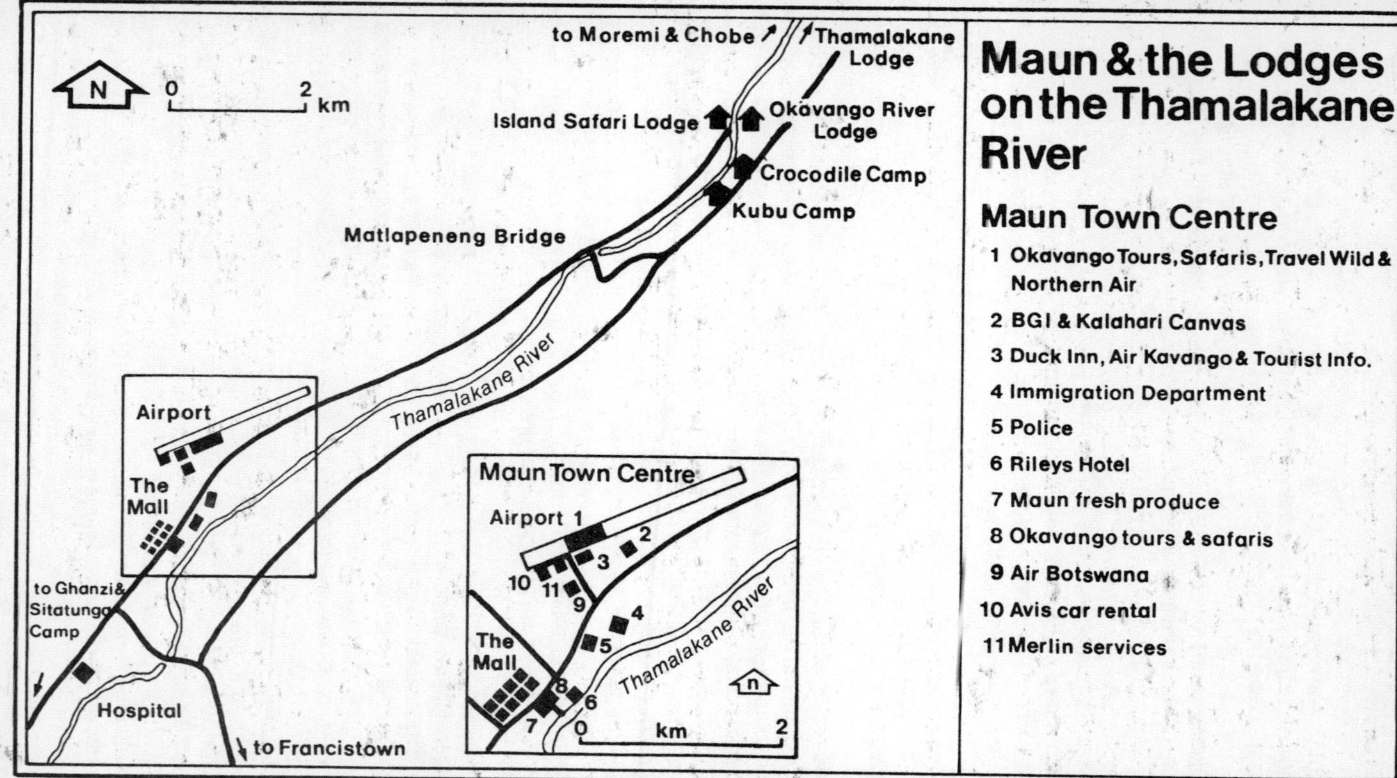
Maun & the Lodges on the Thamalakane River
Maun Town Centre
1 Okavango Tours, Safaris, Travel Wild & Northern Air
2 BGI & Kalahari Canvas
3 Duck Inn, Air Kavango & Tourist Info.
4 Immigration Department
5 Police
6 Rileys Hotel
7 Maun fresh produce
8 Okavango tours & safaris
9 Air Botswana
10 Avis car rental
11 Merlin services
N
0
2 km
to Moremi & Chobe
Thamalakane Lodge
Island Safari Lodge
Okavango River Lodge
Crocodile Camp
Kubu Camp
Matlapeneng Bridge
Thamalakane River
Airport
The Mall
to Ghanzi & Sitatunga Camp
Hospital
to Francistown
Maun Town Centre
Airport 1
2
3
10
11
9
4
5
The Mall
8
6
7
Thamalakane River
n
0
km
2

for a really long expedition and there are some English-speaking guides here if you ask for them well in advance.

To mess about on the river, a self-paddle canoe is P22 per day (or P3 per hour), and its also possible to hire a motorboat — with driver — for P130 per day excluding fuel. If you've no transport, then an airport transfer, or a lift into town, costs P25 during the week and P30 at weekends.

Okavango River Lodge PO Box 32, Maun. Tel: 260298. On the other side of the river, opposite the Island Safari Lodge, this is run personally by the irrepressible Penny Tavares Da Silva. Camping is on a small site by the river and costs P4 per person if you arrive by vehicle, less if you're backpacking. Thatched chalets are P69 single, P72 double, and P22 for each extra bed — with breakfast P8 extra each. The set dinner is P12, and a Sunday *braii* with all-you-can-eat *shadza* and salad is P15. (Beware of eating too much *shadza* if you're not used to it!)

Their *mokoros* are based further into the Delta and they don't operate in Moremi so you're not liable for park fees. They cost P40 per day to hire and a return transfer is P70 per person. Motorboat hire is P140 per day and an airport transfer to town is P20.

Thamalakane Lodge Private Bag 11, Maun. Situated about 20km north of Maun on the old Moremi road, and run by the amiable Chris Blomstrand, this is the furthest of the lodges from town and offers the best of the up-market *mokoro* deals. It's very attractive scenically, on the banks of the lily-covered Thamalakane River, with a delightful bar and a restaurant to rival Croc camp's. The chalets are P75 single and P100 double, a huge breakfast is P7.50 and dinner is good, though expensive, at P30. Camping is P5 per person per night, and a trip to/from town is only P15 (ask OTS to radio the lodge if you need a lift out there).

Unlike the other camps, they canoe up the Santantadibe River (not the Boro) into the Delta, and either Chris or his son accompanies each trip — taking responsibility for all the camp chores, including cooking. Conveniently, between them they speak English, French, German and most of the Scandinavian languages.

Their *mokoros* start from the buffalo fence, two hours drive away, and you've the option to enter Moremi Wildlife Reserve (and pay the park fees) or not. Supplying your own kit, this costs P150 per person per night — including all food and transfers, though for P200 they will supply everything.

Sitatunga Camp PO Box 48, Maun. Tel: 260307. This is 12km south of Maun, right next to the crocodile farm, and caters mainly for campers with vehicles who want a peaceful spot for a few days. There are no bars or restaurants, only a small shop and bottle store which opens from 10am until 8pm. They have two chalets — basic but with hot showers and three beds in each — costing P50, while for P6 per person per night campers have reed-walled toilets and bucket showers from which you can watch the stars.

Medium Priced Camps within the Delta

Choosing to stay in one of the Delta camps is automatically a more expensive option than using a camp near Maun, since you will have to pay a sizable transfer charge for the plane or motorboat to take you there. The camps themselves are also generally more up-market – however you get what you pay for and many offer an unforgettable experience.

Oddballs PO Box 39, Maun. Tel: 260220. Situated in the Delta on the western edge of Chief's Island, Oddballs was originally a cheap alternative to the luxury all-inclusive camps, but it has now become very popular with travellers and its prices have mushroomed. The only way to get there is to fly from Maun (for P180 return), and the minimum stay is five days – of which the first and last nights must be spent at the camp itself, with the rest on a *mokoro*.

The flight baggage allowance is 10kg (enforced in the high season), and budget travellers should think carefully about how to take in the maximum possible amount of food and equipment whilst not exceeding the 10kg limit. Using a mosquito net rather than a tent during the dry season is safe, and keeping your camera equipment with you on the flight, in its own bag, is also a wise move. If you have to buy your supplies at Molly's Pantry when you get there – you pay the premium for doing so. Similarly, if you hire camping equipment there, and you may need to unless your own is ultra-light, prices are, as you'd expect, high. Just a comfy seat for your *mokoro* (you normally sit on the floor) or a knife/fork/spoon set costs P1.50 per day.

Camping here is P15 per person per night, and *mokoros* are P60 per day. Park fees add another P40 per person per day, though you can arrange with the poler not to go into Moremi.

Gunn's Camp Private Bag 33, Maun. Tel: 260351. Run by Mike Gunn, this camp has built up a good reputation since it opened a few years ago. The speciality here is a 14-day 'fitness in the wilderness' course, which aims to get participants fit, teach them the skill of punting a *mokoro*, and instil in them some understanding of the bush. It concludes with a week-long expedition into the Delta by *mokoro*, gathering wild foods as far as possible and exploring areas of the bush with a professional guide.

You can also stay for shorter periods – taking a *mokoro* and poler out for a few days in the normal way. Expect to pay about P40 per day for this, plus park fees if you opt to go into Moremi.

Luxury Camps within the Delta

There are many luxury camps, all charging upwards of P250 per person per night, and offering various standards of decadence. It's worth deciding before you book whether you prefer the conveniences afforded by electricity and carpeted brick rondavels, or like to be closer to nature with thatched, wooden huts where the cries of the wild remain unpolluted by a generator's hum. Make no mistake, all are of a very plush standard. Here are just a few:

Delta Camp PO Box 39, Maun. Tel: 260220 This is the costlier sibling of Oddballs and is also situated at the southern end of Chief's Island. It costs

P250 per person per night, plus P150 for flights, which includes accommodation in thatched, reed-walled chalets, all meals, drinks and excursions by foot and *mokoro* (but not park fees of P30 per person). In the low season, there's a large discount available for residents of Southern Africa (defined as 'south of Malawi') — book through OTS.

Camp Okuti Private Bag 11, Maun. Tel: 260307. One of the independent all-inclusive camps, Okuti is situated in the centre of Moremi on the edge of the Mopane Tongue on Xakanaka Lagoon. It concentrates more on drives than trips by boat and consequently you have better chances of seeing big game. The accommodation is in brick-under-thatch chalets and it costs the standard P250 per person per night.

Gametrackers Camps PO Box 100, Maun. Tel: 260351 If you're booking from overseas with no budget limitations, the most extensive network of private camps belongs to 'Gametrackers'. They have four separate camps in the Delta, two around Savuti and two on the Linyanti/Chobe river Expect to pay about P300 per person per night.

With them you can buy a fully integrated package which flies you to several different camps and includes all food, drinks and flights within the price — allowing you to forget about the organisation of the trip.

MOREMI WILDLIFE RESERVE

4WD. Standard park fees.

Gazetted as a game reserve by the Batawana people (a sub-group of the Batswana 'tribe') in 1962 in order to combat the rapid depletion of the area's game, Moremi is certainly one of the most beautiful and interesting reserves in southern Africa. It includes regions of permanent swamp, floodplain, islands and two large areas of dry land: Chief's Island, the largest island in the Okavango Delta, and the Mopane Tongue, which juts into the Delta and provides Chobe's game with valuable access to water during the dry season.

Chief's Island is usually cut off from the mainland but it's large enough to support its own populations of elephant and buffalo which become concentrated here as the annual floodwaters rise. The Tongue, however, is usually accessible by 4WD from the Maun — Chobe track and hosts some of the continent's best game viewing during the dry season months (April/May to October).

The diverse range of habitats found within this small area, where dry scrub rooted on Kalahari sand gives way to reedbeds and lagoons, results in a wide variety of animals being found. The swamp-loving red lechwe and the shy sitatunga antelope prefer the shallow edges of the water, whilst eland and bat-eared foxes — commonly found in much drier regions — prefer the areas further east.

Getting there

The Reserve can be entered on the water, as part of a *mokoro* trip from Maun, or can be approached directly by vehicle.

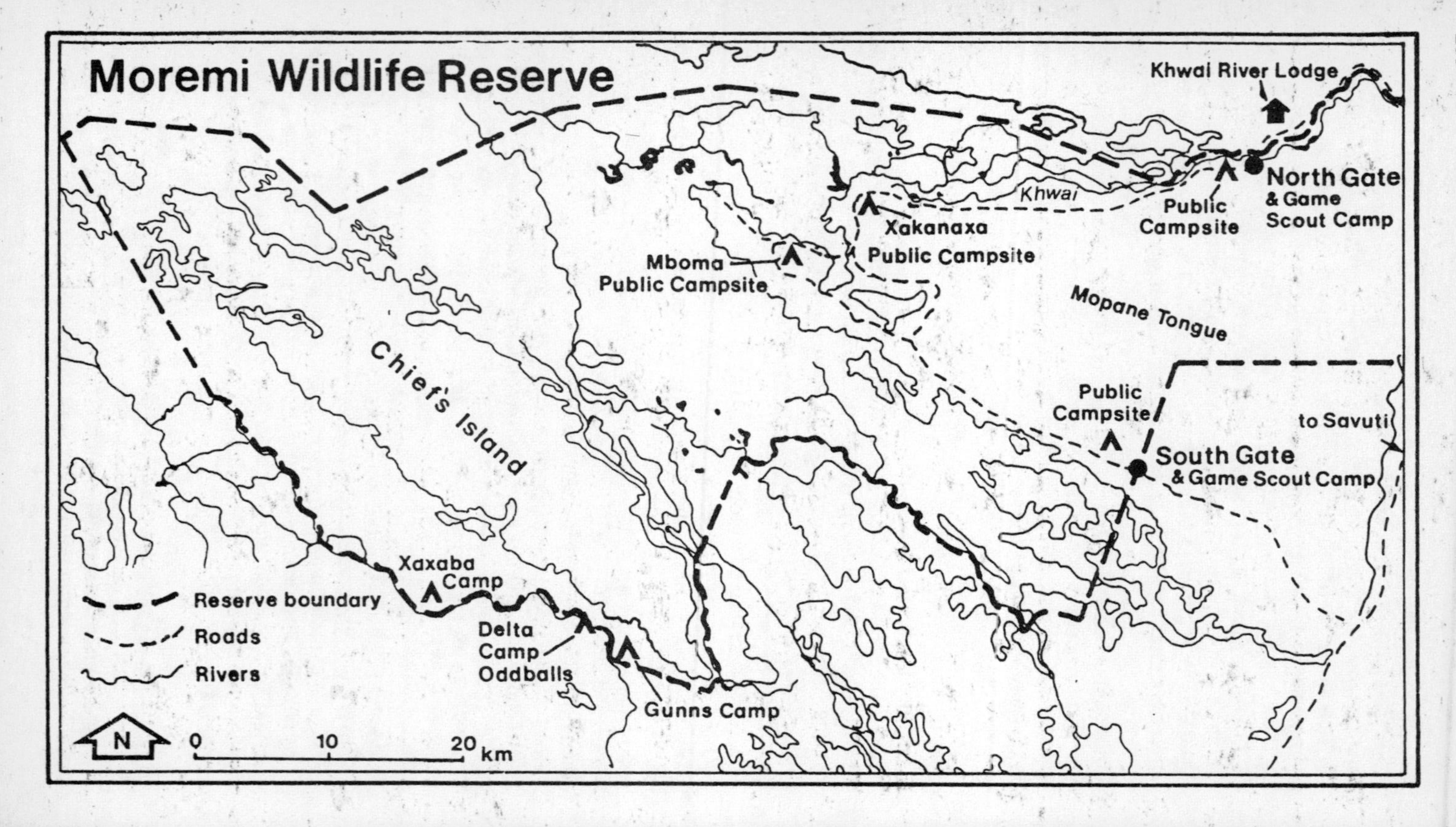
Moremi Wildlife Reserve
Khwai River Lodge
North Gate
& Game
Scout Camp
Public
Campsite
Khwai
Xakanaxa
Public Campsite
Mboma
Public Campsite
Mopane Tongue
Public
Campsite
South Gate
& Game Scout Camp
to Savuti
Chief's Island
Xaxaba
Camp
Delta
Camp
Oddballs
Gunns Camp
Reserve boundary
Roads
Rivers
N
0
10
20
km

From Maun The road is tar all the way to Shorobe, a small village on the Thamalakane where basic supplies and quite good baskets are sold. After that, it's about 27km to the veterinary fence and a further 3km to the signposted left turn for Moremi's South Gate. A left turn about 10km after Shorobe (just beyond the Tsetse Camp), also leads to the south gate, but the road is very difficult to find and not in very good condition.

It's not unknown for 2WD saloon cars to make this trip this far — but it is highly unlikely for them to get any further. If you want to chance your luck, try with a high clearance pick-up and a spade in the back.

From Chobe About 20km from the Reserve's exit at Mababe Gate, is a right turn which crosses the Magwikwe Sand Ridge almost perpendicularly, before reaching Moremi's North Gate some 38km after leaving the main Chobe-Maun track. **Warning**: If you haven't a high clearance 4WD, don't even consider approaching this way across the ridge.

Where to stay

Within the reserve there are four public campsites, one each at the North and South Gates — with a scout camp adjacent — and two near the tip of the Mopane Tongue. The facilities at all of these are basic, with natural river water to drink and basic showers and toilets. The alternatives are exclusive private camps which don't welcome independent visitors, except in dire emergencies — so be self-sufficient in food and fuel when you go.

Of the campsites, **Third Bridge** is perhaps the most attractive and situated some 48km from South Gate (allow five hours for this). The site itself actually consists of about five separate camping areas, each a short distance from the main track to the bridge.

Warning This area has earned a reputation for very aggressive lions and several attacks have recently been reported. Also remember that the wooden bridge is used by animals as well as people — treat it like a game trail and do not camp anywhere near the bridge itself; instead back-track half a kilometre from the site by the bridge, going towards South Gate and take one of the tracks to the right and camp there.

Xakanaka Lagoon (Lediba) is the beautiful site for not only another luxury camp, but also the second of the public campsites on the Mopane Tongue. It is interesting to spend time exploring the numerous tracks at the tip of the Tongue itself. The open water here is a classic spot for hippos which lull campers to sleep with their grunting sessions in the early evening (most campers are unaware that hippos are said to claim more lives than any other animal in Africa!). (See page 73 for advice on animal encounters.)

North Gate, though it doesn't really compare scenically with these, is regularly visited by lion, elephant and hippo — as well as thieving monkeys. We were even lucky enough to see a leopard from our camp fire. Try to find time to take the Khwai River Loop, west from North Gate, and also to follow the river to the east, past the airstrip and the Safari Lodge, which are exceptionally beautiful.

South Gate is the busiest of the camps, being the usual entrance and exit point for visitors. If you want to make an early start into the park, to make the most of your park fees, you might consider camping a few kilometres outside the entrance gate itself. However, we did encounter lion in this area so remember that there is as much game outside the park as in it.

North of the Delta

Between the Okavango and the Chobe/Linyanti river systems lies a very rarely visited, sparsely populated, corner of the country. It's a region where a minimum of two vehicles are needed, and which could provide some really fascinating ground for the well-prepared who want to do a little 'exploration'. The major feature here is the Magwegqana river, which links the Okavango's Selinda Spillway with the Linyanti swamps, and may — unpredictably — form a total barrier at times.

Getting there

In the eastern part of the area, there's a track which runs along the margins of the swamps to Xugana Safari Lodge. It starts by turning west, just to the north of the bridge over the River Khwai and appears to cut across the Spillway, near it's base. From there it reaches Seronga fairly swiftly — though it becomes impassable if there's much water in the spillway and local advice should be sought before it's attempted.

The alternative way into the region is to take the track which starts in Chobe, south of Savuti, and meets the Magwikwe sand ridge squarely before crossing the Magwegqana just south of the Linyanti swamps. This is by far the better, more reliable, track — ask for directions from the game scouts at Savuti.

Seronga

Situated at the panhandle's base, in the centre of 'area five', with an airstrip and, reportedly, a *mokoro* ferry on which you can cross the river — though obviously not with a vehicle. Do not expect to be able to buy fuel. From here the road goes north-west until the border and then, according to some maps, crosses it into the Caprivi Strip. With determination you could cross this border, reaching the Strip's main road, though you'd have to keep police on both sides of the border well informed to avoid getting into a lot of trouble.

On the bus

by Phil Deutschle

We were a mix of twenty men, women, and children in the small combi-bus, heading south to Francistown. A dusty man on the side of the road flagged us down, and we stopped to pick him up.

The man got into the bus and asked how much it would cost to go to his brother's house. "That depends on where your brother;s home is," replied the driver, as he pulled the bus back onto the road. "Where does he live?"

"I will tell you when we get there. He lives just next to my sister."

"But you must pay now. Where do they stay?" asked the driver.

The man shrugged. "I've never taken the bus there before," he said. "I always walk. I go down the track and turn at the tree that hangs out like *this*." And he showed us how the tree hung to one side. As the bus sped along, he looked out of the window and shook his head. "I can't see the tree from here," he said. "It must be further along."

After some minutes and many miles, the driver tried again, asking, "Who else lives near your brother and sister?"

"Which brother and sister? I have many brothers and sisters," was the reply.

"The brother and sister that you are going to see now!" we all cried out.

"Oh! And you want to know who lives near them? On the far side is the man who works in the shop."

"Yes," said the driver, "and who is that?"

"What do you mean — 'who is that?' He's the one who works in the shop, the *Shopkeeper*."

"But what's his *name*?"

"The shopkeeper's name is Monamati. Everyone knows that, but we all call him Shopkeeper."

"Monamati? Monamati's shop is in Butale. That's in the *other* direction. You're going the wrong way!"

The driver slowed the bus and pulled to the side of the road. "Now, when you get out," he explained to the man, "You have to cross the road and try to get a ride going the other way. *That* way."

The man got out, and then, as we drove off, he called out, "But how much do I have to pay?"

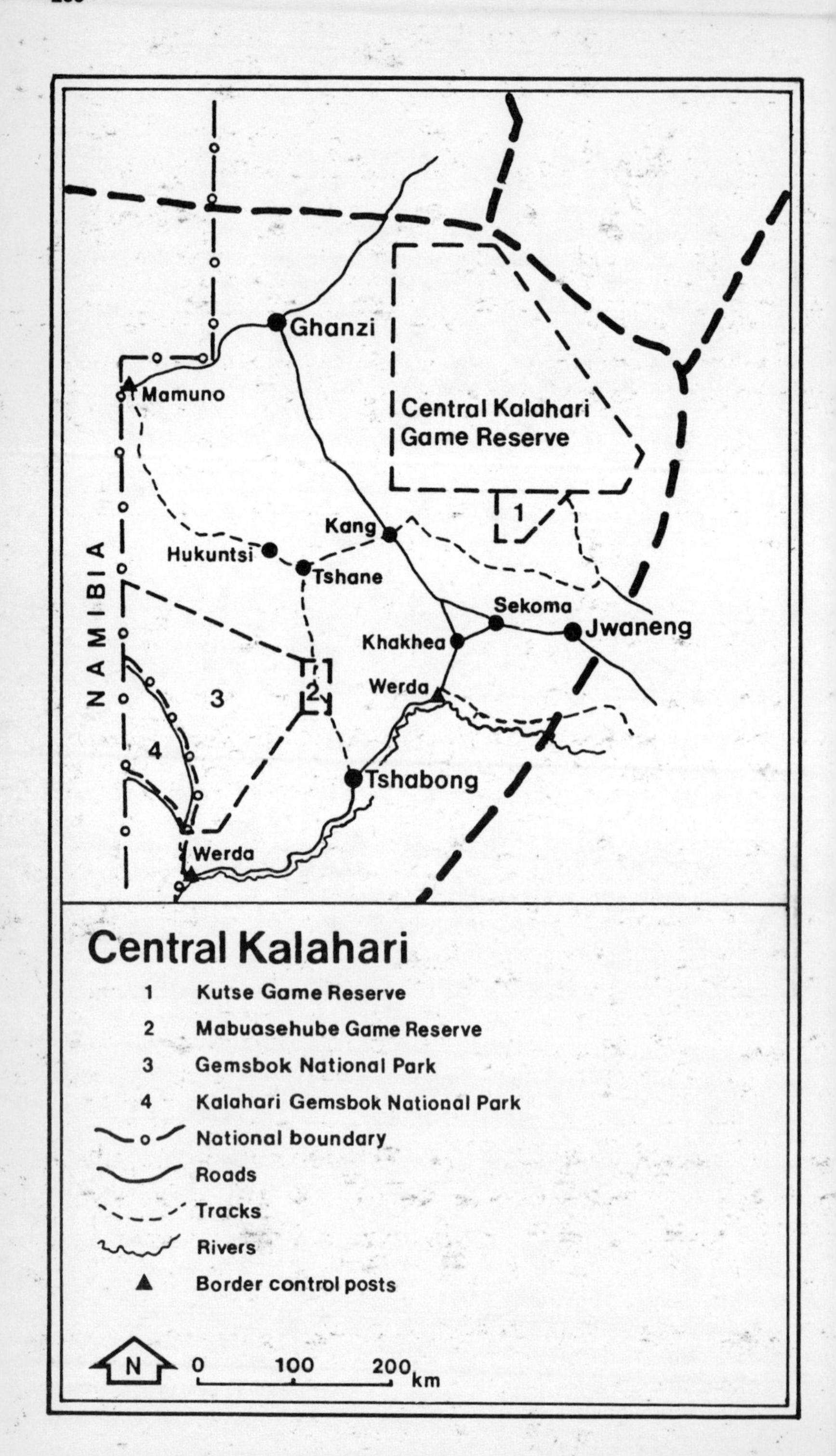

Ghanzi
Mamuno
Central Kalahari
Game Reserve
1
Kang
Hukuntsi
Tshane
NAMIBIA
Sekoma
Jwaneng
Khakhea
Werda
2
3
4
Tshabong
Werda
Central Kalahari
1 Kutse Game Reserve
2 Mabuasehube Game Reserve
3 Gemsbok National Park
4 Kalahari Gemsbok National Park
National boundary
Roads
Tracks
Rivers
Border control posts
N
0
100
200
km

Chapter 20

The Central Kalahari

To many people, the Kalahari Desert is synonymous with Botswana and, indeed, it covers over two-thirds of the surface of the country. Geologically, the Kalahari is a huge sand-filled basin in the centre of southern Africa. Kalahari sands, under the surface of the topsoil, cover an extraordinary 2,500km from the Orange River of South Africa to the equatorial rainforests of Zaire — the largest continuous stretch of sand in the world. The Kalahari Desert today is defined not by sand but according to its very low rainfall. Rain is most scarce in the south (the north-westernmost edge of South Africa) where the Kalahari represents a 'classic' desert environment of extensive sandy plains and ochre-red dunes. As one moves north, rainfall increases, and the Kalahari becomes scrub and bush land through central Botswana, which in turn gradually merges with the woodlands and swamps of the Caprivi Strip region.

The Botswanan central Kalahari is predominantly an area of acacia grasslands and sandy scrub — encompassing most of the area south-west of the Okavango Delta and Makgadikgadi Pans, and north of Botswana's southern border. Only in the extreme south-west of Botswana — around Tshabong and Mabuasehube Game Reserve — does it revert to sand and red dunes.

For the visitor, the wonder of the central Kalahari lies not so much in the large concentrations of game found in the more well-watered areas, but in the unique environment and the fascinating adaptations made to it by its animal, plant and human populations. Some Bushmen (San) still live hunter-gatherer lifestyles in the desert interior — particularly in the Central Kalahari Game Reserve — in ways that haven't changed much for millennia.

Practically, the area is difficult to visit and a 4WD vehicle is more-or-less essential. Ghanzi, the only town in the region, is hundreds of kilometres from anywhere, and generally regarded as the 'capital' of the Kalahari. With San, Tswana, Herero, Afrikaner and English speaking inhabitants, it's a fascinating place to stay for a few days. Without your own vehicle, it is probably the only part of this region that you'll be able to visit being accessible by scheduled air services, or you could try some intrepid hitching.

Khutse Game Reserve is the most accessible part, and easily reached by 4WD from Gaborone. For the well prepared and self-sufficient, Mabuasehube Game Reserve and the fascinating desert settlements around Tshane offer a focus for some adventurous exploration. The Central Kalahari Game Reserve is closed to the public, and requires a special permit for access. Gemsbok National Park is only accessible from South Africa, but has especially beautiful desert sand-dune scenery. Everywhere in the region, there is a great sense of remoteness — and you're unlikely to see many other visitors.

GHANZI — 'CAPITAL OF THE KALAHARI'

Ghanzi must be one of Botswana's most intriguing towns — situated in the middle of nowhere and separated from the rest of the world by hundreds of kilometres of rough dirt track. The town owes its existence to the limestone ridge on which it is situated which supplies it, and the surrounding 200 farms, with a plentiful year-round supply of ground water.

Today it is the centre of a thriving Afrikaner cattle ranching industry, but Ghanzi was once a major centre for several Bushmen hunter-gatherer groups. The town began to grow when at the end of the nineteenth century, Rhodes encouraged bands of Boer trekkers who were already heading north to move to Ghanzi instead, promising excellent ranching land and a wonderful climate. Rhodes's intention was probably to annex this western corner of British Bechuanaland in the name of his own British South Africa Company, so enhancing his own territorial interests in this part of the continent. To do this, Rhodes had to fill the area with (white) people. However, when the Boer trekkers arrived, many found that much of the good land had already been taken by the few previous settlers and that Rhodes's claims were at the most fanciful. Within ten years or so, most of the original trekkers had left. A few remained, and their descendants — and those of the handful of white settlers that arrived shortly after Rhodes under encouragement from the British government — now form the strong Afrikaner and English speaking communities.

Once the road from Ghanzi to Lobatse was completed — allowing relatively easy access to the country's main abattoirs — land prices improved dramatically and Ghanzi established itself firmly on the map. The farming community is now one of the most prosperous in the country.

Getting there and away

Air The quickest way is to fly. There are two flights a week to Ghanzi from Gaborone via Maun. Check details with an Air Botswana office or, if in Ghanzi, at the Kalahari Arms Hotel.

Car Ghanzi lies at the intersection of three main roads through the interior of the country.

Maun to Ghanzi A 4WD is not essential for this route, though as the road can become fairly badly corrugated a high clearance 2WD vehicle really is necessary. The 280km, which should take only about five hours, has no particular points of interest except for the veterinary cordon fence at Kuke. The gate here is manned throughout the day and night, and divides the Okavango region from the Ghanzi farming area.

Ghanzi to Lobatse This epic journey of 644km involves the longest stretch of demanding 4WD in the country and will take at least 12 hours of difficult bone-shaking driving. It is used by the farmers of Ghanzi to take their cattle — driving them on horseback or by truck — to the great slaughterhouses in Lobatse. The boreholes sunk along this route to water the cattle have resulted in a series of tiny settlements on the way which will usually have a small store and bar. Kang, the largest of these, also has petrol usually, though as you would expect it's expensive.

From Lobatse, the tar ends at the diamond mining town of Jwaneng, and turns into a fair gravel road to Sekoma. From here to Ghanzi, the road becomes very poor with very little sign of habitation (the numerous small settlements along the chain of boreholes are often off the road).

Ghanzi to Windhoek (Namibia) via Mamuno The road is in poor condition to the border, but once inside Namibia it improves enormously. The scenery is typical of the Kalahari, consisting of rolling plains and low dunes of bright orange sand. Everything is covered by a sparse undergrowth of grasses and low bushes, above which the occasional tree rises. The sides of the road are sometimes fenced, and often marked by hedge-like mounds of sand where the tracks are lower than the surrounding dunes.

For mile after mile your tyres will try to follow one of the sets of ruts, while you guide the steering wheel and wonder how the undercarriage is avoiding the sand piled between the tracks. A good high-clearance 2WD vehicle should be considered as the bare minimum requirement for this route. The border post at Mamuno (200km from Ghanzi) is just less than half way and will take up to five hours. From here to Windhoek should take another five hours. The road is surfaced from the main town of Gobabis in Namibia.

Hitching

Since all three routes into and out of Ghanzi are frequently used, hitching is a viable — if difficult — proposition. In Ghanzi, it's definitely worth asking around at the Kalahari Arms Hotel for possible lifts from the numerous aid workers, teachers and local cattle farmers who frequently make trips to Maun and Gaborone. Try to avoid getting short lifts and ensure that you'll be dropped off at a settlement of reasonable size.

Where to stay and eat

The spiritual and physical heart of the town is undoubtedly the **Kalahari Arms Hotel** PO Box 29, Ghanzi. Tel: 296311 (*Category B*). This old and well-known establishment is the only place to stay and eat in Ghanzi. Rooms are not cheap at P95 for a single and P110 for a double, but it's possible to camp at the back for P5 with the use of hot showers etc.

The restaurant round the back serves a surprisingly extensive and interesting menu. Contrary to some recommendations, we avoided the 'boot-sole' steaks and instead went for the pizzas (P12) and omelettes (P8). Breakfast is P9, and avoid the coffee. The hotel will also organise laundry — hand in your clothes before 10am and collect after 4pm.

Getting organised

Apart from the hotel, Ghanzi has all the basic necessities, including a hospital, post office, telephone exchange (with somewhat incongruous call boxes outside), a collection of government offices, and a new Barclays bank.. Check out the Oasis bottle store, the Oasis self-service supermarket, the Oasis garage...

Bushmen crafts

Whilst in Ghanzi you must make a point of visiting the **Ghantsicraft shop** between the hotel and the post office. This is one of southern Africa's finest craft centres, with an extensive and authentic collection of Bushmen crafts. It was started in 1983 by several Danish volunteers, with the specific intention of returning as much money as possible from the sale of the crafts back to the Bushmen producers themselves. The prices are considerably lower than you'll find elsewhere and at least 80% goes back to the craftsman or craftswoman. The staff make regular visits to remote Bushmen settlements in the Ghanzi district, including the Central Kalahari Game Reserve, to collect crafts. These are then individually tagged and the name of the maker is recorded.

The ostrich eggshell bracelets and necklaces are particularly attractive — and take weeks of labour to make. The ostrich eggshells are hatched chick shells, collected from within the game reserves and national parks. If you can't see what you want in the shop, ask about it — they keep more stock than is on display. The shop is open from 9.00am-12.00pm Mondays to Fridays.

Khutse Game Reserve

4WD advised. Standard entrance fees.

Khutse is the closest of Botswana's game reserves and parks to the capital Gaborone, and being easily reached in a day from the capital it is a popular long weekend destination for city dwellers. It adjoins the southern boundary of the (restricted) Central Kalahari Game Reserve, and has classic bush, acacia and pan scenery typical of this part of the Kalahari Desert.

Whilst the reserve has small herds of gemsbok, springbok, hartebeest and wildebeest together with the more common predators, the game is limited by the amount of water available and in times of drought may be very scarce — even around the pans. Nevertheless there are many species of fascinating smaller mammals (ground and bush squirrels, hares, foxes, porcupine, pangolin, aardwolf, aardvark, African and black-footed cats) and a huge

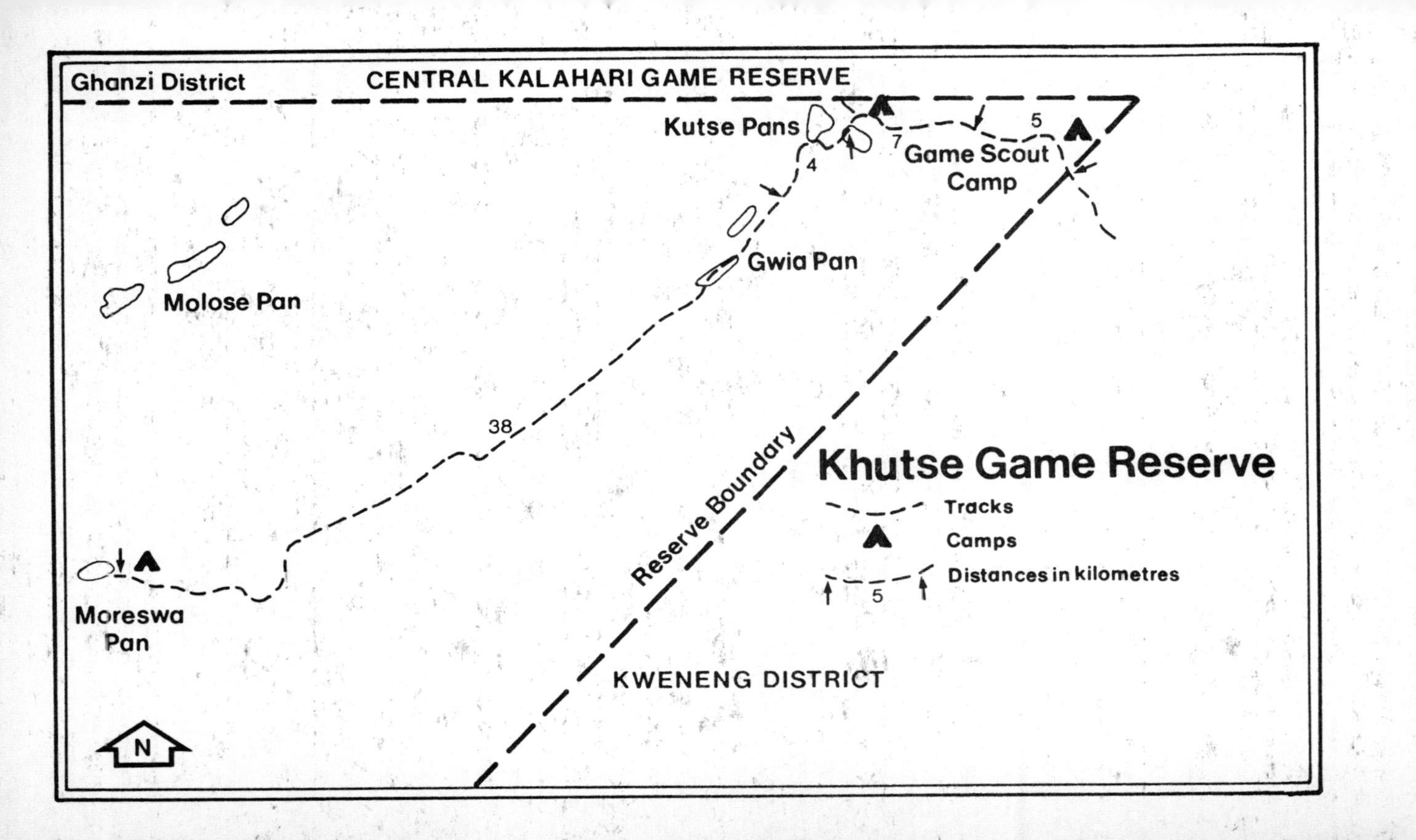
Ghanzi District
CENTRAL KALAHARI GAME RESERVE
Kutse Pans
7
5
Game Scout Camp
4
Gwia Pan
Molose Pan
38
Moreswa Pan
Reserve Boundary
Khutse Game Reserve
Tracks
Camps
Distances in kilometres
5
KWENENG DISTRICT
N

variety of birds, especially around the pan margins. Khutse should be treated as much a Kalahari wilderness experience as an opportunity for game viewing.

Getting there

From Gaborone The 240km journey typically takes around five hours in a 4WD or high-clearance 2WD truck. From Gaborone, head north-west along the tarred road to Letlhakeng via Molepolole (last petrol stop). From Letlhakeng, the road is sandy with poor signposting through the villages of Khudumelapye and Salajwe — if in any doubt stop and ask directions to the Khutse gate.

In the Reserve

At the gate you should pay your entry and camping fees and stock up on water if you need to. Since the water is from a borehole it can be a bit mineralised and salty, so bring your own supplies if possible. You'll also have the option of hiring a guide, though this shouldn't be viewed as essential as there's only one main track through the reserve and it's difficult to get lost. A guide will of course be able to show you the best areas for game viewing, spot hard-to-see animals, as well as help you understand some of the innumerable facets of this unique environment.

From the gate at Galalabodimo Pan, it is a single track to Kutse II Pan 13km away where there is a pleasant campsite, and the track forks. The right fork (more northerly) heads off into the Central Kalahari Game Reserve and should be ignored. The left-hand track heads to Moreswa Pan, 41km further on, into the heart of the Reserve and you will reach a quiet, rarely-used campsite at the edge of the pan by a couple of trees.

The Central Kalahari Game Reserve

No access except with a permit

This massive reserve is reputedly the second largest in the world and dominates the centre of the country. There are no facilities, roads or even water and the reserve is closed to the public unless you have a permit. These are obtainable in principle to groups who can satisfy the authorities of their expedition competence and good intentions. Try the District Commissioner in Ghanzi, or the Department of Wildlife and National Parks in Gaborone.

Other than the dwindling small groups of Bushmen people that still share the land with the animals, the reserve is traversed by exploration geologists for ever in search of minerals and oil.

Mabuasehube Game Reserve

4WD only. Standard entrance fees.

Remote and rarely visited, this is true desert country of the southern Kalahari with dunes, grasslands and plentiful salt and grassy pans. The reserve lies on a huge strip of slightly higher ground, forming a watershed that crosses

The last Bushmen

The situation in 1989

Survival International has issued an 'Urgent Action Bulletin' and written to the President of Botswana protesting at plans to force some of the last Bushmen in southern Africa out of the Central Kalahari Game Reserve. This would evict the very people whose lands the Reserve was set up to safeguard.

Though ostensibly to protect the wildlife from overhunting by the Bushmen, the true reason behind the expulsion of the 1000 or so Bushmen, and of the 300 Bakgalagadi who also live there, may be to create a scapegoat for the real danger to the wild animals — the extensive growth of cattle ranching in the area. The cattle owners — having over-grazed most of their present land — want the government to allow cattle grazing in the Central Kalahari Game Reserve.

The most serious problem for the Bushmen is that alternative lands still do not exist. Previous attempts to re-settle Bushmen in Botswana have been tragic failures. One anthropologist who worked for several years trying to make re-settlement sites work, admits that 'in almost every case' the Bushmen suffer sickness, malnutrition and unemployment — becoming 'dependent, alcoholic and apathetic'.

At the same time as the Bushmen are being obliged to move out, the government is also granting leases to mining companies to prospect in the Reserve. Among the companies involved are De Beers Botswana (a subsidiary of the South African mining giant), Selection Trust/British Petroleum, and Falconbridge Botswana. It is these activities, not the Bushmen and Bakgalagadi who have lived in equilibrium with their environment for millennia, who pose the real threat to the Reserve.

The situation in late 1990

Survival International's campaign met with some success. The Botswanan government assured Survival that it did not intend to move the Bushmen and the Bakgalagadi out of the Reserve by force, and that they were free to continue to live there in peace. Their long-term future however, is far from secure — so long as the government or mining companies covet the Reserve's potential mineral and grazing wealth, the Bushmen's traditional lands will remain under pressure.

Survival International is a worldwide movement to support tribal peoples. It stands for their right to decide their own future and helps them protect their lands, environment and way of life. If you would like to join Survival and take part in their campaigns for tribal people in Africa and worldwide, you can contact them at: Survival International, 310 Edgware Rd, London W2 1DY. Tel: 071-723 5535.

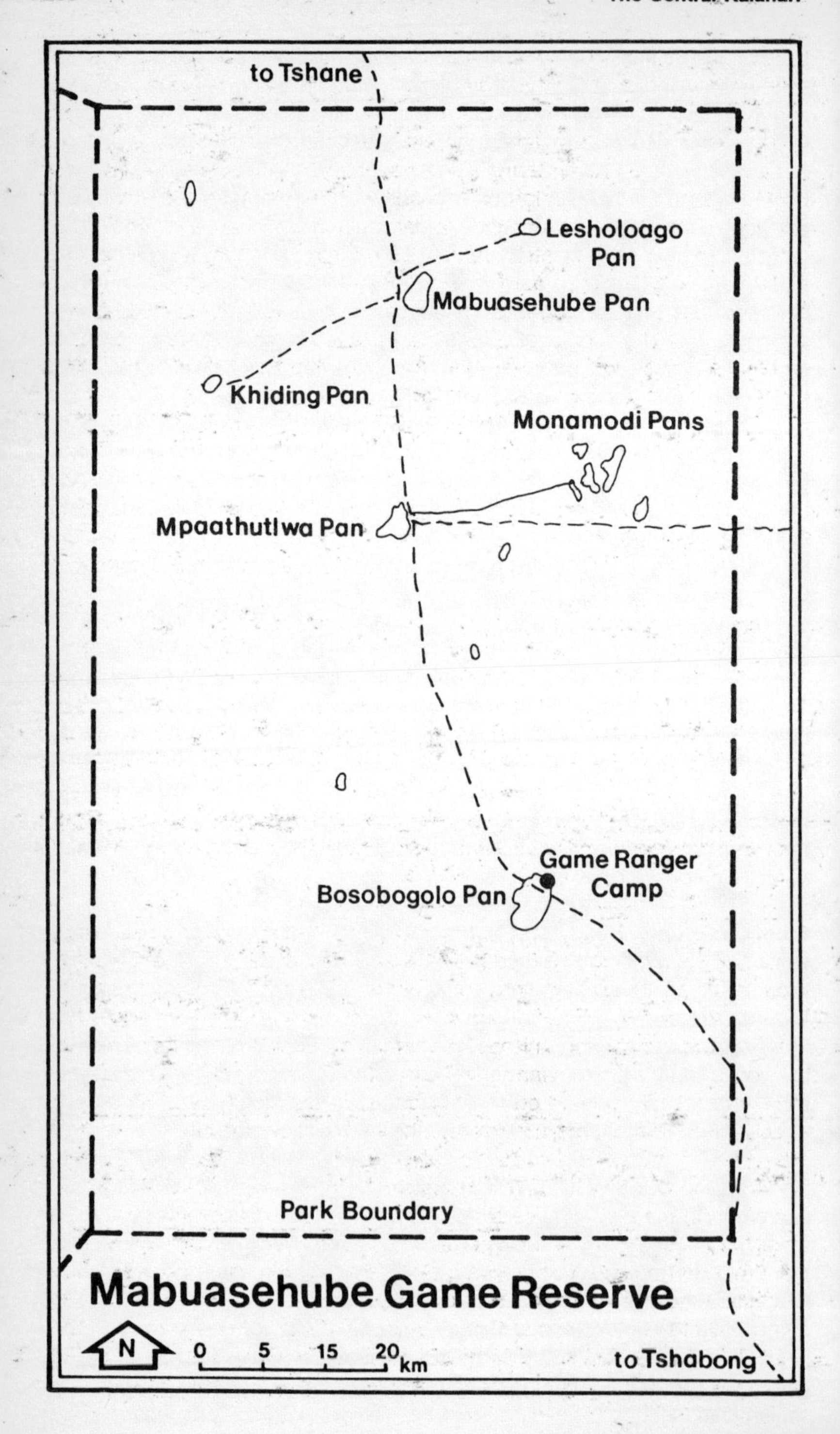
to Tshane
Lesholoago Pan
Mabuasehube Pan
Khiding Pan
Monamodi Pans
Mpaathutlwa Pan
Game Ranger Camp
Bosobogolo Pan
Park Boundary
Mabuasehube Game Reserve
N
0 5 15 20 km
to Tshabong

Botswana from east to west. Some of the pans scattered across this area will even hold water for a few months of each year following the rainy season, and they have played an important role in the understanding of the Kalahari – part of the reason for establishing the reserve in the first place.

The best time of year for game viewing is during the rainy season when the usual Kalahari game (springbok, gemsbok and eland) gather at the six principal pans. Like Khutse, the smaller mammals and birds (including ostrich) can offer endless entertainment even if the larger game is scarce. The small mammals (Cape fox, aardwolf, meerkat and black-footed cat are most common) are best seen around the edges of the pans in the evening (most are nocturnal). The spectacular large dunes to the south of the pans provide an unusual habitat for many of the birds, including Kori bustard, secretary bird and a variety of eagles and vultures.

The reserve has no facilities and you must be fully self-sufficient, with food, water, petrol and spares. In an emergency, you might be able to obtain borehole water from the sporadically resident game ranger at Bosobogolo Pan in the south of the reserve – it's the only pan you actually drive across. Many of the roads are in bad condition, and since you may not see another vehicle for days on end, a visit to the reserve should not be undertaken casually.

Getting there

The main road through the reserve is a poor, very sandy track from Tshabong in the south of the country, to Kang on the main Ghanzi-Gaborone road to the north. This long route (described below) can be incorporated into a larger 4WD circuit of the region, and has the added attraction of passing through the interesting group of villages of Tshane, Hukuntsi, Lokgwabe and Lehututu. The easiest, most direct route to Mabuasehube however, uses a track that enters the reserve from the east joining the main north-south road at Mpaathutlwa Pan.

From Gaborone Head to the end of the tarred road at Jwaneng (last petrol stop) and thence onto Khakhea, taking the left fork at the village of Sekoma. From Khakhea, the road is sandy, and continues like this as you head south towards Werda. The landmark to look out for is the dry river-bed of the Moselebe, about 49km from Khakhea and 20km from Werda. About 1km to the north of the river is an unmarked turn-off to the west, which will take you along a good and almost completely straight track to Mabuasehube. It's about 145km to the junction with the Tshane-Tshabong road.

Through the Reserve from Tshabong to Kang Unlike the route into the reserve from the east, this road can be very difficult, rutted and sandy. To travel the 240km from Tshabong to Tshane in one stretch would take around eight to nine hours. The four villages of Tshane, Hukuntsi, Lokgwabe and Lehututu are all within about 10km of one another, and each is worth a visit if you have the time. Beyond this it's another 104km of sandy road to the junction at Kang where you join the more frequented Ghanzi-Gaborone road – three or four hours driving, which take you through a couple of Bushmen settlements.

Tshane, Hukuntsi, Lokgwabe and Lehututu villages

By about 1750, the Kgalagadi people had begun to settle on the eastern and southern edges of the Kalahari, using the pans to provide seasonal water for themselves and their cattle herds. The village of **Lehututu** was the first to be settled, followed within the next 50 years by other villages nearby. Today, Lehututu is very small and a far cry from the once busy commercial centre it was. **Tshane** has an attractive setting by Tshane Pan and an interesting old police station. **Lokgwabe** is notable for having the Hottentot descendants of Simon Cooper who led an unsuccessful rebellion against the German administration of South West Africa in 1904. In a curious deal between the British and German governments, Cooper and his rebel group were given 'protection' by the British administration in Lokgwabe, whilst being indirectly paid by the Germans to stay at home! **Hukuntsi** village is the administrative headquarters of the area and it's possible to pick up basic supplies here.

Gemsbok National Park

Entry only from South Africa, 2WD, South African entrance fees

This massive area is effectively shared between South Africa and Botswana — the South African portion being called the Kalahari Gemsbok National Park, and separated from the Botswanan Gemsbok National Park by only the dry bed of the Nosop River. The Botswanan side has no roads or facilities, remaining purposefully undeveloped so as to provide a game reservoir and retreat from poachers. The southern Kalahari has always suffered from a poaching problem, which is presently getting worse as the game outside the protected area of Kalahari Gemsbok disappears. The scenery is characteristic of the drier areas of the Kalahari with fossil river-beds and high sand dunes.

The best time of year to visit is probably following the rains from March to May, when you can expect to see large herds of gemsbok, springbok, hartebeest, wildebeest and eland — along with lion, hyena and cheetah.

Getting there

The (dirt) roads on the South African side are good and suitable for ordinary 2WD saloon cars, though if you approach the South African entrance from within Botswana you'll need 4WD. Entry to the park is through Twee Rivieren Camp (South Africa) in the south. Entry also used to be possible at Mata Mata Camp from Namibia in the west. However due to an unprecedented amount of traffic using the park as a fast through-route between Namibia and South Africa — and so causing disturbance — the gate has unfortunately been closed. It would nevertheless be worth checking with the authorities on the current situation.

From Botswana to Twee Rivieren You must first make your way to Bokspits at the extreme southwest corner of the country via the town of Tshabong (see *Getting there* section, *Mabuasehube Game Reserve*, page 269). From Tshabong, there are two possible routes to Bokspits, one staying in Botswana, and the other going through South Africa. The former road follows the (mostly dry) Molopo River, and although used regularly is slow and rough, taking nine or ten hours. Alternatively, you can cross the border post at McCarthy's Rust and travel to Bokspits via Vanzylsrust on good gravel roads. Although about 80km further, it should take you an hour or two less. The park entrance at Twee Rivieren is 55km north of Bokspits.

Where to stay

There are three excellent camps in the Kalahari Gemsbok National Park — Twee Rivieren, Mata Mata and Nosop — all offering chalets, camping sites and basic supplies, including beer and wine! The three main sand roads in the park essentially connect the camps together in a triangle. Do note though that the road from Nosop Camp — north-west along the Nosop River to Unions End, at the Namibian border — is a dead end. You cannot (currently) cross the Namibian border here.

It is advisable to book accommodation in advance during holiday periods from the Chief Director, PO Box 787, Pretoria 1000, South Africa.

Mother of Goats

by Phil Deutschle

In the village of Mapoka, there lived an old woman. She had two goats which she took out each day.

One day, as she was taking her goats out, two young men of the village shouted to her, 'Hello, Mother of Goats!'

The old woman smiled and called back to them, 'Hello, my sons!'

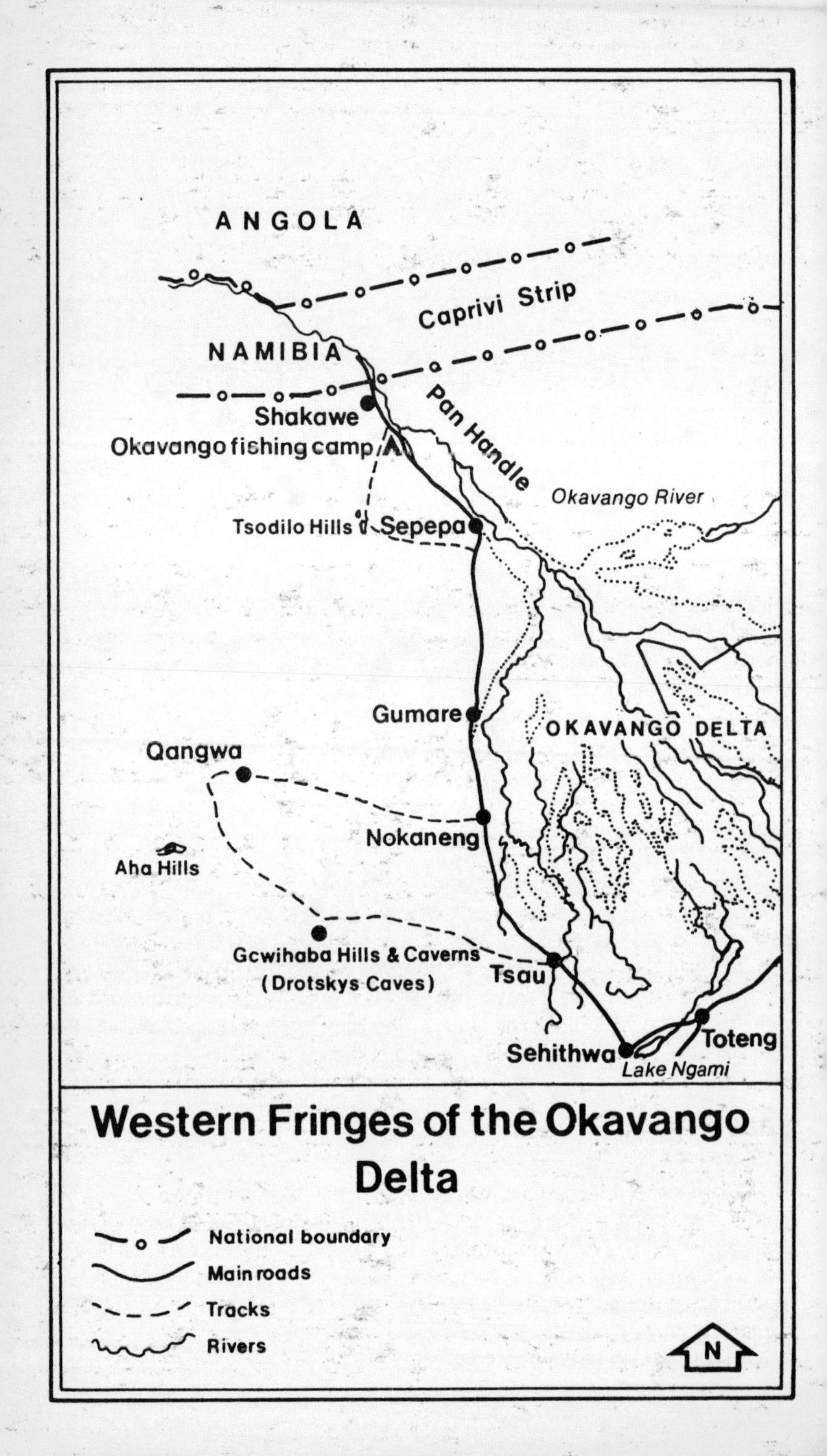

Western Fringes of the Okavango Delta

Chapter 21

The Western Fringes

On the western fringes of the Okavango Delta lie some of Botswana's most mysterious and ancient destinations. The main attraction is undoubtedly the Tsodilo Hills (immortalised by Laurens van der Post in his book *The Lost World of the Kalahari*). Lake Ngami, to the south, is fairly easily accessible, yet untouched and rarely visited. For those with two 4WDs in their group, there's a circular route from Tsao to Nokaneng via Qangwa, allowing access to the Gcwihaba Hills (with Drotsky's Caves) and the ancient Aha Hills. This is a fascinating and remote journey through the Kalahari — though it's not an easy route and takes several days.

Access to the region is made easy by the road from Toteng (68km from Maun on the Maun-Ghanzi route) which skirts the edge of the Delta as it heads up to the Caprivi Strip. At the time of our last visit it had been tarred up to a point 140km north of Sehithwa and work was gradually extending this northwards. Beyond the tarmac, you still need a high-clearance 4WD to cope with the sand and, in the rainy season, the mud. None of these destinations is in national parks or reserves — so no entrance fees.

Lake Ngami

4WD advised

The existence of a great lake within the Kalahari was known to Europeans from early reports of Bekwena and Batawana tribespeople, though it wasn't reached by them until the mid 19th Century. Livingstone arrived in 1849, with Cotton Oswell and Murray, narrowly beating Andersson, who set out specifically to reach it from present-day Namibia. He described it as 'an immense sheet of water bounded only by the Horizon,' and wrote that it was 'the object of my ambition for years, and for which I have abandoned home and friends and risked my life'.

Getting there

These days, getting there isn't quite so difficult, though it still requires tenacity — and preferably a 4WD — as there are no good roads which go near it. One very knowledgeable resident of Maun even suggested that we take a compass bearing from the main road and just head into the bush — walking when we became unable to drive. In the end, we found a way: taking the main road from Toteng, south of the lake, and reaching a track on the right after about 7.7km, opposite a shabby board advertising 'Marothodi Boreholes'.

This sandy track winds its way through sparse bush, past several small cattle-farming compounds, until finally it appears to end at one with a large corral of stock. Here we found a local man who guided us to our right, and after only a few hundred metres we emerged from the bush and onto the tussock grass surrounding the lake's bed.

When to visit

The scene here varies greatly, depending upon whether the Delta's flood — Ngami's main source of water — has been high enough to overflow into the Nhabe river which feeds the lake. Talk to the operators in Maun, and especially the pilots, because if the lake's empty it's better to save yourself a trip — often it's just a wide expanse of clay!

When flooded, Lake Ngami comes alive with birdlife. From October, the ducks, geese, waders and other northern migrants arrive, lining the muddy shores until the weather cools towards the end of April. The flamingos, both greater and lesser, don't choose their times so carefully — being found here in their thousands whenever the conditions are right for the algae on which they feed. They appear from the shore as a pink haze settled on the water's surface.

Where to stay

There's nowhere specific to stay here, but the land's open enough to camp rough — we asked the local villagers, who suggested going a few kilometres away from the lake itself to avoid the mosquitoes. A wise move. You'll need to be self-sufficient, of course, and don't rely upon any drinkable water here — though you'll certainly find enough wood for a campfire.

Shakawe

This large fishing village stands on the northern banks of the panhandle of the Delta, some 279km from Sehithwa and 13km south of the Mohembo border post on the Caprivi Strip. Driving into the village feels like entering a maze of reed walls, with each surrounding a small kraal, as the track split countless ways between the houses.

It's large enough to make finding the police station (where you must complete border formalities if you're crossing to Caprivi) quite a puzzle: you must head through town towards the river and look for several large, white buildings — err more right than left — surrounded by wire fences and probably having 4WDs dotted nearby. The officials were very relaxed when we went through, though you'll be sent back here by the border post if you try to miss out this stop.

If you've the time, take a walk along the river which is immediately behind the police station. Sometimes there's a *mokoro* ferry shuttling local people to and from the eastern side of the river, full with their wares to sell or recent buys to take back home.

Where to stay

Driving further downstream, within the next 30km or so, there are several safari camps on the river which cater mainly for fishing and birdwatching — and are more casual than the expensive ones further into the delta. 12km south of Shakawe is **Drotsky's Cabins** (not to be confused with caves!), further still is the **Fishing Camp** and finally **Nxamaseri**, the most expensive of the lot at about P250 per person per night.

Shakawe Fishing Camp Going south about 17km from Shakawe you come to a crossroads: to the left is the Shakawe Fishing Camp; to the right a sign reading 'Tsodilo Hills' which points, confusingly, to a track that immediately forks into two.

One of the Delta's oldest camps, Shakawe Fishing Camp offers thatched chalets for P50 per person per night and charges P30 for dinner, P20 for lunch, P12.50 for breakfast and P10 per person per night for campers. You can hire a motorboat for P20 per hour (P160 per day) to go fishing, birdwatching, or simply explore the river.

Tsodilo Hills

4WD only

Rising to 400m above the monotony of the Kalahari's thick bush, the smooth steely faces of the hills had an enchanting effect as I approached them one evening in the fading light. Perhaps I had Laurens van der Post's vivid prose in mind, or had been too exhausted by the rough journey, but either way, the balmy quietness all around — so unusual in the bush — added to the watchful presence of the hills on either side of the track, making my arrival at the Tsodilo Hills almost as unsettling as it was fascinating. They undoubtedly have a timeless, spiritual quality: perhaps arising from their isolation in the desert, perhaps their history.

Archaeologists say that the hills have been sporadically inhabited for about 30,000 years — making this one of the world's oldest historical sites. For only about the last millennia has this included Bantu people: previously, for thousands of years, Bushmen (San people) had settled here, hunting, using springs in the hills for water and painting animals (over 2,000 of them) on the rocks. For both Bushmen and Bantu it was a mystical place, 'home of very old and very great spirits' who demanded respect from visitors and as told in *The Lost World of the Kalahari* created so much trouble for some of the first Europeans to visit.

Long ago it must have been, in van der Post's words, '... a great fortress of living bushman culture, a Louvre of the desert filled with treasure'. Though now only a shadow of its former glory, it's well worth a visit if you've the tenacity to reach it and the patience to spend several days there. Some of the individual paintings have been among the most impressive that I've seen on the subcontinent.

Getting there

Air For flights, inquire at Shakawe Fishing Camp, Drotsky's Cabins or at Shakawe's airstrip, or alternatively talk to the air charter firms in Maun — you may be lucky and find a cheap seat. From the air you'll appreciate the hills' uniqueness within the desert, though miss the excitement as they're first sighted over the tree tops.

Car With a 4WD, there are two tracks to the hills, both of which are through dense bush across vegetated dunes (so fold in your wing mirrors). This difficult driving is made all the worse by corrugations in the sand which, when driven over at anything greater than walking pace, cause the whole vehicle to bounce up and down violently with everybody hitting their heads on the ceiling. You physically can't drive at more than 10kph sometimes!

From the north, turn right at Shakawe Fishing Camp and then fork immediately left onto a small track, no wider than a vehicle. (Do not make the mistake of following the clearer, broader track which forks right.) After about 13km of difficult sandy driving you'll reach a dune crest from where you can see the hills. From here it's a further 30km.

From Sehithwa, take the road northwards to Gumare, and continue past the '1st Restaurant' on the left and the Okavango Bottle Stall, before heading by two large steel storage tanks and out of town. Follow this road for about 56km north, before taking an obvious left turn — which may still have a Botswana museum sign, complete with zebra logo, pointing the way. This is a firm track for about 28km until, shortly after two livestock ponds, it deteriorates into sand for the remaining 24km to the hills.

Of the two approaches, we found the southern track from Sehithwa to be slightly faster and easier, even though longer. Either will take two and a half hours at the minimum.

Apart from the car hire firms in Maun or Katima Mulilo (in Namibia), the Shakawe Fishing Camp or Drotsky's Cabins will sometimes organise trips out to the hills — expect to pay about P300 for a five-seater vehicle with a guide for a day trip to the hills.

Hitching You could try to hitch from a base at the Fishing Camp. This could prove a lengthy business, though at least you could conserve valuable food supplies for the hills by eating at the camp.

On foot Some people have walked the 86km into and out of Tsodilo. The journey takes at least two days each way, necessitating carrying in a week's food and water. This isn't a trip to undertake lightly — nor a practical alternative to other forms of transport.

Where to stay

Once there, you can camp anywhere in the bush which surrounds the hills — we found good spots between the two main hills, about a kilometre from the Museum's board — though there are no facilities here at all so you must carry in everything that you need (and take it away when you go).

What to see and do

The hills form a group of four called, from south to north (and in descending order of size), male, female, and child — with the last remaining nameless. The road from the south approaches with the male hill on the right and passes close to the Bantu settlement (where you must stop and sign the visitors book), before going past the Bushman village on the left and splitting: the left fork goes around the female hill, the right between it and the male hill.

To find your way around to any of the paintings, you'll need a guide — Benjamin speaks good English, and will probably find you before you find him. I've heard that several of the Bushmen act as excellent guides, sharing their knowledge of both the bush and the paintings, though as few visitors speak *!Kung*, communication may be difficult. Consider taking both a Bushman guide *and* Benjamin to act as a translator.

For those with images of proud, defiant bushmen stalking game on the open plains, the Bushman village at the hills is a sad place, a poignant reminder of the Western world's extermination of an ancient and wiser culture. The few remaining Bushmen people there rely heavily upon passing tourists, selling bows and arrows, ostrich eggshell necklaces, bracelets, and other curios, for money or food. Before bargaining for goods, consider carefully just how long they have taken to make, and how little they're being sold for.

Gcwihaba (Kwihabe) Hills

4WD only

This isolated range of hills, some 150km west of Tsao, houses a rarely visited and spectacular system or caves known as the Gcwihaba Caverns, or Drotsky's Caves — after Martinus Drotsky, a Ghanzi farmer who was shown the caves by *!Kung* bushmen in 1934.

Getting there

Less than 2km north of Tsao, there's a turning to the west, signposted with one of the Museum's zebra signs and reading 'Drotsky's Cave'. Follow this track over the sandy desert, past a number of pans and through several dry river valleys for about 150km, before taking a signposted left turn onto an even smaller track. This finally reaches the caves after about 26km. You can expect this to take about seven hours of rough, tiring driving — and bringing two 4WDs would be a sensible precaution.

Drotsky's Caves/Gcwihaba Caverns

There are two known entrances to the cave system. The track leads to the main one, with an information board outside it, while the smaller entrance is about 200m from the first, further away from the (dry) river.

Going underground at the main entrance, you'll first enter an outer chamber and then — under a hanging curtain of rock — an inner chamber decorated with huge stalactites, some many metres long. The passage leads on from here through further impressive caverns until it starts to descend more steeply. The route from the other entrance leads through several small caverns to a larger one deep below the surface. Thence a narrow passage does eventually link up with the caves reached from the main entrance. The route is not at all easy as there are many dead-ends.

Warning Because there's no light at all in the caves, and no one to help in an emergency, you must carry with you several torches, spare batteries and bulbs, emergency matches, and some food and water — just in case you encounter problems. A very long ball of string might also come in useful!

It's worth spending a few days here: you probably won't visit a more serene, natural part of the desert. The best plan is perhaps to climb the hills in the cool of morning, and venture underground as it starts to get hotter. Camp anywhere, though there's no water at all (even in the caves) so you must be totally self-sufficient.

Aha Hills

4WD only

Split by the Namibian border and, like the Gcwihaba Hills, composed largely of dolomite and limestone, these isolated hills form a plateau of about 250 square kilometres and afford impressive views of the Kalahari all around. They're largely unexplored and it would be surprising not to find Bushman paintings there and possibly cave systems — though we've found no reports of any, except for two sink holes, both of which are described as vertical and dangerous, so stay well clear of steep chasms in the rock.

Getting there

Take the turn-off to Drotsky's Caves, north of Tsao, and then continue past the left turn, 26km from the Caves. After about 40km, the track passes the village of Xai Xai and then heads straight for the hills — some 15km to the north. Camp anywhere convenient.

There is an alternative route to return to the main road. Continue northwards from Aha, and after about 60km you'll meet a track of deep sand going east-west, following an old *omuramba* (vague river bed). If you go east, then it's a difficult 170km to Nokaneng, while west leads, after 20km or so, to Dobe — the border village where much of the research into Bushman culture was originally done.

Don't expect to average more than 30kph for any of this driving, and remember how heavy it is on fuel — the nearest reliable supplies being at

Maun or in the Caprivi Strip (though Shakawe Fishing Camp, Gumare or Sehithwa are worth checking in an emergency). There is traffic along here, though it's very infrequent, so come in a two vehicle party — and be fully equipped with fuel, food and water for your whole trip, plus some to spare.

Further information

Maps of Drotsky's Caves and information on Aha's sink holes can be found in *Botswana Notes and Records*, volume 6, 1974. It's the journal of the Botswana Society, of which the National Archives, in Gaborone, have a copy.

Cattle, Wildlife and the Veterinary Cordon Fences

Edited from an article by Damien Lewis

Cattle ranching is having as disastrous an effect on Botswana's wildlife as it has had on the Amazon rainforests. Thousands of miles of cattle fences, strung out across the savannah and bushlands of Botswana, have caused the death of countless wild animals and overgrazing has led to the desertification of huge areas of land. Now, a new fencing programme in the north of the country heralds the expansion of cattle ranching into Botswana's last isolated wilderness — the Okavango Delta.

The explosion of ranching (fuelled partly by World Bank livestock loans and by highly subsidised beef prices paid by the EEC) has had catastrophic ecological consequences, according to a recent Greenpeace report, 'causing serious overgrazing, environmental degradation and the decline of wildlife'. Yet the most serious impact of the ranching business has been the *Veterinary Cordon Fencing* (VCF) policy, launched in 1954 by the Botswanan Department of Animal Health.

The fences are designed to keep Botswana's cattle and natural wildlife separate from each other, in the belief that the dreaded *foot-and-mouth disease* is spread from wildlife (especially buffalo) to cattle and that it can be controlled by segregation. Like the beef industry itself, the fencing programme is driven by the EEC, whose disease regulations dictate which animals may be imported to the Community. More than 3,000 kilometres of fencing have been built across huge areas of the country. Yet there is little evidence of the effectiveness of this fencing policy in preventing the spread of disease. The fences criss-cross the country with no relation to regional ecology and block off the wildlife from their traditional migration routes, often with devastating effects. Mark and Delia Owens — zoologists who lived in the Kalahari for seven years between 1974 and 1981, studying the predators — claim that the fences are destroying game populations. They also assert that no one knows for certain that wild animals are a source of infection, or that foot-and-mouth disease can be held in check by the fences.

The most seriously affected area is the central Kalahari — now almost entirely enclosed by the fences. In 1964, at the Kuke fence, 80,000 wildebeest perished, piled up against the wire. Again in 1983, 50,000 wildebeest met their death on the Kuke. Wildlife has died entangled in the wire, or searching for water and grazing in the parched lands left behind them. Bushmen say that elephant, rhino, buffalo, roan, sable and tsessebe, which once regularly roamed the northern Kalahari, are now absent from the area. A recent study funded by the EEC found that the central Kalahari has lost 99% of its wildebeest and 95% of its hartebeest over the last decade. Despite this record of wildlife fatalities, the Government of Botswana has taken few steps to review its fencing policy. Indeed, the new fencing programme in northern Botswana indicates the Government's continuing commitment to the VCFs. The first of the new fences will be 100 kilometres long, stretching across the north of the Okavango Delta. It will extend the 250 kilometre long fence that already runs along Okavango's western and southern flanks and is the first step in a plan to fence in all of northern Ngamiland. The fence — over five feet high and strung with wire and thick steel cable — will be impenetrable to all but the most determined of adult elephants or agile antelope. Zebra and wildebeest are already reported dying along new fences built in 1990, in the Nata region of north-east Ngamiland.

Despite the deadly effects of fences across Botswana and the proximity of the wildlife-rich Okavango Delta, no environmental impact assessment has been carried out for the new fencing scheme. Many animal species migrate to and from the Delta, to take advantage of the availability of grazing and water during the wet and dry seasons. Local people, with in-depth knowledge of the delta and its wildlife, claim the Government has seriously underestimated the size and movements of animal herds, and the impact the fence will have on them. Although Botswana's Department of Wildlife admits that some animals will die on the fences, this is an 'acceptable level of mortality'. Overcrowding of wildlife within the fenced-off areas will be dealt with by 'active management', or culling.

Construction of the fence is well under way. Yet while its justification in terms of disease control is questionable, its effect on wildlife may be disastrous. Greenpeace says 'it heralds the expansion of cattle into northern Botswana...[which] threatens the stability of the region and jeopardises the most ecologically sensitive part of the Okavango Delta, its source'.

While the scientific evidence against the cattle-ranching is very strong, some scientists question the allegations of the anti-fence lobby. The authors felt that the following summary of a paper by Alec Campbell, a Botswanan naturalist, would be of interest.

Wildlife disasters are nothing new. During the early 1930s, after a prolonged drought, wildebeest came out of the central Kalahari only to die in their thousands at Sebele, Mosomane, and around Francistown and Maun. This was before the advent of the new cordon fences and a major cause of death then was the lack of suitable, or any, food during the previous drought years. The contention is that the pressure of expanding human and livestock (especially cattle) populations has progressively squeezed the desert's ecosystem over this last century. The competition for water and food with the cattle has upset the natural game species in the desert and this encroachment has been the major factor in the relatively recent loss of zebra, rhino, giraffe and buffalo from the central Kalahari. However, wildebeest have a population structure which is better suited than most species to recover after herds have been wiped out by famine or drought. Thus, although not truly adapted to the desert, they have come to dominate the central Kalahari this century. Their numbers are naturally subject to large fluctuations, growing bigger and bigger until over-population and drought cause the population to collapse.

During recent years the fences have received much of the blame for these crashes in the wildebeest population, and also the apparent decline in Kalahari species in general. It would appear from the evidence that these changes precede the fences which have really only affected the wildebeest and, even then, not to any permanent extent. So long as the fences are used as a scapegoat, the real problems affecting wildlife in the Kalahari will remain unsolved.

Summary from *A Comment on Kalahari Wildlife and the Khukhe Fence, Botswana Notes and Records* (Volume 13), by Alec Campbell (currently Senior Curator at the National Museum and Art Gallery, Gaborone, Botswana).

BIBLIOGRAPHY

(For natural history guides see page 37)

Reference books

Lake Ngami and *The River Okavango* by Charles John Andersson. Published 1856-61 in London. Fascinating records of one of the region's first white explorers.

Travels and Researches in Southern Africa by David Livingstone. Published 1857 in London. A record of the travels of the continent's most famous missionary and explorer.

Explorations in South-West Africa by Thomas Baines. Published 1864 in London. The travels of the artist who gave his name to the clump of baobab trees south of Nxai National Park, Botswana.

The Rock Paintings of Southern Africa by the Abbé Henri Breuil. Published by Trianon Press Ltd, from 1955-60 in four volumes and distributed through Faber and Faber.

The Skeleton Coast by Amy Schoeman covers the area in detail with stunning photographs. A classic coffee-table book.

The Namib by Dr Mary Seely. Published 1987 in Windhoek, by Shell Oil. A detailed work on the desert's origins, with descriptions of many sites and the animals and plants that live there. This paperback is well worth getting when you arrive in Namibia.

Namib by David Coulson. Published 1991 by Sidgwick and Jackson. Another coffee-table book of breathtaking pictures covering the whole of the desert.

Namibia — Africa's Harsh Paradise by Anthony Bannister and Peter Johnson. Published 1990 by New Holland Ltd, London. Yet another for the coffee-table, this covers the whole country and concentrates on the Bushmen and Himba people.

Namibia — The Facts. Published by IDAF Publications Ltd, London in 1989. Concentrates mainly on the liberation struggle over the last ten years. Highly emotive text and pictures!

History of Resistance in Namibia by Peter H Katjavivi. Co-published by: James Currey, London; OAU in Addis Ababa; Unesco Press, Paris. Rather more 'scholarly' than *Namibia — The Facts*, it's impressive in its detail.

Okavango: Jewel of the Kalahari by Karen Ross. published 1987 by BBC Publications, London. Another one for the coffee-table, with snippets of excellent background information.

Okavango: Sea of Land, Land of Water, P. Johnson and A.Bannister. New Holland. £17.95. A beautiful book of photos.

Botswana: a Brush with the Wild, Paul Augustinus. £43.75. Illustrated by colour paintings, sketches, and photos; records the author's experiences after living in Botswana several years.

Pamphlet entitled *The History of Rehoboth* by Robert Camby is very useful for understanding Rehoboth's history.

Elephant Talk article: National Geographic, Vol 176, No 2, August 1989, pp 264-277. On infrasound communication in elephants, with some interesting comments about desert elephants in the Hoarusib river.

Etosha: Namibia's kingdom of animals article: National Geographic, Vol 163, No.3, March 1983. A general article about managing the park — with discussion of the problems of waterholes, anthrax, and too many lions!

Travelogue

Cry of the Kalahari by Mark and Delia Owens. Published 1985 by William Collins, subsequently in paperback by Fontana (1986-1989). A recent book about the experiences of two American scientists who spent seven years in the wilds of the Central Kalahari Game Reserve studying the wildlife.

The Lost World of the Kalahari by Laurens van der Post. First published in 1958, many subsequent reprints by Penguin. Laurens van der Post's classic account of how he journeyed into the heart of the Kalahari Desert in search of a 'pure' Bushmen group — eventually found at the Tsodilo Hills. His almost mystical description of the Bushmen is fascinating, so long as you can cope with the rather dated turgid prose.

Serowe: Village of the Rain Wind by Bessie Head. Published by Heinemann 1981, last reprinted 1988. By one of Botswana's leading writers, it evokes the history of Serowe through the eyes of some of its inhabitants and contrasts this to the village at present.

The Sheltering Desert by two German geologists (Henno Martin and Hermann Korn) who lived out the war hiding in the Kuiseb canyon promises to be interesting.

Guide books

Rough Guide to Zimbabwe and Botswana by Barbara McCrea and Tony Pinchuck (published 1990). Contains good information on both countries, especially Zimbabwe.

No Frills Guide to Zimbabwe and Botswana by David Else, Bradt Publications. This slim volume gives conveniently brief, up-to-date information if you are travelling into Zimbabwe also.

Visitors Guide to Botswana by Mike Main and John and Sandra Fowkes. Published by Southern Books, Johannesburg (1987). Written primarily for the visitor with a 4WD vehicle, the book has excellent route descriptions on hard-to-get-to places and is recommended for these. Some route descriptions are now very outdated though.

Deserts, Paths and Elephants: Travel Guide to Southwest Africa/ Namibia by Michael Iwanowski, published in West Germany — only English edition; 1986. This rather idiosyncratic guide has some excellent geographical data on Namibia, and is arranged into a series of routes through the country.

For a complete bibliography on Namibia (Botswana is still in preparation) see *Namibia* by Stanley and Elna Shoeman, published by Clio Press, Oxford.

Also due in April 1992 is the *African Travel Resource Guide and Bibliography* by Louis Taussig, published by Hans Zell Associates, Oxford. (Split into two volumes, the *Eastern and Southern Africa* volume will cover this region.)

INDEX